The International Library of Sociology

STATE AND ECONOMICS IN THE MIDDLE EAST

Founded by KARL MANNHEIM

The International Library of Sociology

THE SOCIOLOGY OF DEVELOPMENT
In 18 Volumes

I	Caste and Kinship in Central India	*Mayer*
II	Economics of Development in Village India	*Haswell*
III	Education and Social Change in Ghana	*Foster*
	(The above title is not available through Routledge in North America)	
IV	Growing up in an Egyptian Village	*Ammar*
V	India's Changing Villages	*Dube*
VI	Indian Village	*Dube*
VII	Malay Fishermen	*Firth*
VIII	The Mende of Sierra Leone	*Little*
IX	The Negro Family in British Guiana	*Smith*
X	Peasants in the Pacific	*Mayer*
XI	Population and Society in the Arab East	*Baer*
XII	The Revolution in Anthropology	*Jarvie*
XIII	Settlement Schemes in Tropical Africa	*Chambers*
XIV	Shivapur: A South Indian Village	*Ishwaran*
XV	Social Control in an African Society	*Gulliver*
XVI	State and Economics in the Middle East	*Bonne*
XVII	Tradition and Economy in Village India	*Ishwaran*
XVIII	Transformation Scene	*Hogbin*

STATE AND ECONOMICS IN THE MIDDLE EAST

A Society in Transition

by

ALFRED BONNÉ

LONDON AND NEW YORK

First published in 1948
by Routledge, Trench, Trubner & Co., Ltd

Reprinted in 1998, 2000, 2001
by Routledge
2 Park Square, Milton Park, Abingdon, Oxon, OX14 4RN
711 Third Avenue, New York, NY 10017

Transferred to Digital Printing 2007

Routledge is an imprint of the Taylor & Francis Group, an informa business

First issued in paperback 2013

© 1948 Alfred Bonné

All rights reserved. No part of this book may be reprinted or reproduced or utilized in any form or by any electronic, mechanical, or other means, now known or hereafter invented, including photocopying and recording, or in any information storage or retrieval system, without permission in writing from the publishers.

The publishers have made every effort to contact authors/copyright holders of the works reprinted in *The International Library of Sociology*. This has not been possible in every case, however, and we would welcome correspondence from those individuals/companies we have been unable to trace.

British Library Cataloguing in Publication Data
A CIP catalogue record for this book
is available from the British Library

State and Economics in the Middle East
ISBN13: 978-0-415-17583-8 (hardback)
ISBN13: 978-0-415-86334-6 (paperback)

The Sociology of Development: 18 Volumes
ISBN 0-415-17822-3
The International Library of Sociology: 274 Volumes
ISBN 0-415-17838-X

Publisher's Note
The publisher has gone to great lengths to ensure the quality of this reprint but points out that some imperfections in the original may be apparent

CONTENTS

PART FOUR

PROBLEMS AND ASPECTS OF A CHANGING SOCIETY

MAPS AND CHARTS

AUTHOR'S PREFACE

Since my first contact with the Middle East, more than twenty years ago, I have been under the spell of that momentous phenomenon: the impact of modern civilisation on the social and economic fabric of the East. At the same time it became clear to me that the very scope and complexity of this process must present not a few difficulties in the way of an analysis of the problems and their interrelation. Modern sociology has only just begun to develop instruments and measuring rods for closely observing and registering the social changes brought about by the contact with foreign civilisations. It is only during the last few decades that current and regularly compiled statistics have become available, and even these are incomplete and deficient. Another shortcoming, though of a more technical nature, is the length of time that has elapsed between the completion of this book and its publication. Written during the early war period, the book covers developments only up to that date. But this handicap is probably common to many present-day volumes.

The economic and social problems of this region, rendered acute by the war, induced me, in 1943, to devote a special study to the subject of Middle Eastern reconstruction.* In view of the urgency of the task I confined myself to outlining the economic potentialities of the region, being well aware of the limitations of such an investigation at a time when post-war trends in the economic and political spheres were still uncertain.

Unlike that attempt, which looked towards the future, the present book is retrospective in character. It deals with the problems and changes of the Middle-Eastern scene, beginning with the opening of the present century and leading up to the history of our own days. Each of the four main Parts is sub-divided into two sections, of which the first is an analysis of the static features, while the second dwells upon the signs and problems of transition. A Postscript has been added, which touches upon the latest, that is, the post-war, trends.

The preliminary work for this book dates back a long time. I was fortunate enough to have had opportunities, over a number of

* It appeared in England under the title: *The Economic Development of the Middle East—An Outline of Planned Reconstruction*, in the "International Library of Sociology and Social Reconstruction," London, Kegan Paul, 1945.

years, of visiting the countries of the Middle East and of studying contemporary developments in those areas at close quarters. I also enjoyed the support and co-operation of Government institutions, notably in Egypt, Turkey, the Levant States and Iraq, which provided me with valuable material and information. Numerous conversations with officials and people on the spot helped me to penetrate, and to understand, many important issues, and my thanks are due to all those whose interest and advice have lightened my task.

In particular I wish to express my appreciation to Professor L. A. Mayer, Drs. Goitein, Plessner and Heydt, who have read the whole or part of the book in manuscript, for many helpful suggestions and observations.

I am much obliged to Mr. Stanley Davis for the devotion shown by him in the difficult task of translation. Mrs. B. Maschler has likewise a claim to my gratitude for assisting me with the revision of the English text. To Mr. E. Margalith I am indebted for valuable help with the statistical sections of the book.

ALFRED BONNÉ.

July, 1946.

INTRODUCTION

The transformation of a civilisation manifests itself in far-reaching changes in ways of life and manners of satisfying consumption needs; in social stratification, State organisation, and, by no means least, in new standards and values. Men's minds have always been tempted to try to identify the laws which govern the course of such transformations, and to reduce their various phenomena to a few formulas. This temptation is all the stronger when the process of change is unfolded within a single generation, or a few generations, and takes place in a group of countries which have much in common.

The spatial restriction of our theme, the Middle East in Transition, to the Orient in itself implies that we have to deal with a development that is taking place with a certain degree of inevitability in a specific part of the globe. But this process is not a uniform one; nor are its results always parallel with its motives. The manifold antitheses with which nature and history have equipped this Oriental world go far to exclude any such congruence of its static and dynamic characteristics.

Yet in spite of this there is a remarkable degree of uniformity. Three basic facts justify us in speaking of a good deal of resemblance in those processes of transformation to which the Middle Eastern countries are now being subjected. These facts are, first, the uniform Islamic civilisation which was the dominant spiritual force in the shaping of these countries; second, the Ottoman régime which for centuries held them all in a political unity and many of whose institutions survive in them even today; and, finally, such important natural factors as their arid climate and its effects, e.g., the degree to which regions without rain are dependent on artificial irrigation.

The countries subject to these three basic factors fix the range of our study, which therefore includes contemporary Turkey, Egypt, Palestine, Transjordan, Syria, Lebanon and Iraq. Iran is not dealt with in these pages. She was never a part of the Ottoman Empire, and physically she is clearly separated from the other regions here treated. The great rivers Euphrates and Tigris are common to Turkey, Syria and Iraq. The Lebanon forms an excellent bridge between Asia Minor and Palestine, which is also easy of access from Egypt, both by sea and by land. On the other hand, Iran is isolated from her neighbours, Iraq and Turkey, by high mountain ranges. Some of our conclusions, however, are valid for Iran as well.

The description of the modern transformation process itself, in its various stages and aspects, is a major object of this survey. Here the incompleteness of our observations will not infrequently show itself; they are incomplete because, with the data at our disposal, we are often not in a position to comprehend the social changes precisely, or to draw conclusions from them; also because those processes, which are still in a state of flux and in respect of which we still lack perspective, are not yet ripe for objective appraisal. Nevertheless the attempt should be made, despite the fact that there is no lack of surveys of the new political and economic conditions of the Middle Eastern countries since the First World War. These accounts, however, often do not give adequate consideration to the specific sociological and economic-historical approaches which serve us here. For that reason it follows, on the other hand, that no comprehensive account need be given here of each and every detail of the development; although of necessity certain subjects have had to be touched upon several times, i.e. from various angles, in so far as they belong to various branches of our theme.

The transformation of the Orient, fascinating as certain of its recent results may frequently seem, did not begin in those years which have given the youthful Middle East countries their independent status. Important as were the second and third decades of the present century in this respect, the situation cannot be properly understood without a sketch of the background, namely the State and economic developments of the nineteenth century.

Since we must renounce completeness, our choice of material and its arrangement may not satisfy everyone; but it seemed essential to our subject to include at least a survey of the historical and natural elements of Oriental agrarian society, a sector which still includes by far the greater part of the inhabitants of the Middle East. But apart from this survey, whose purpose is to guide the reader along the main lines of social structure and history, other questions of no less weight arise and likewise demand an answer or an explanation.

What are these questions?

One of the most striking problems in the social history of the Middle East will always be why this area, lying so close to Europe, has not until now participated in the great social and economic development of that continent. The beginnings of modern history in Europe brought with them the first signs of modern forms of enterprise, heralding the approaching technical transformation; vast colonisation projects were initiated, and the rising "capitalist spirit" first became recognisable. During the same period, however, the economic society of the Middle East remained largely unchanged, both in its mode of social life and its methods of production of goods, and it has continued stationary until now at an economic level attained hundreds of years ago.

This difference in development did not spring from any one single cause, such as, say, the shifting of the great East-to-West traffic route which formerly passed through the territories of the Middle East, fructifying all the lands it touched. To be sure, the effect of the shift round the Cape which followed on the discovery of the sea route to the East Indies caused a sensible weakening of the former ties between Europe and Western Asia; but this was no more than one of the manifold causes of the new phase of development in the Orient. We know that even after this shift in the movement of traffic contact between the Levant and Europe was maintained; and that the exchange of people, ideas and goods continued, though with reduced intensity. In European countries many of the territories which lost their economic importance with the change in the trade route have more recently become once again focal points of modern economic development. In the East, on the other hand, many of the old centres never recovered, and up to the very threshold of the present day have remained passive and impoverished witnesses to a great past. Indeed, it is in the light of this stark contrast that the picture of general stagnation became truly impressive: so much so, in fact, that numerous and competent observers had reached a definite negative verdict regarding the regenerative power of these cultural areas, once so important.

In the first quarter of the present century, for the first time for generations, a great change took place. The First World War, which, seen from without, marked the dramatic peak of this change, together with the subsequent years, cleared the ground for a renewal of the Middle East. The latent urge for a renaissance of the State idea among the Oriental peoples came to life, and forces, previously restricted and slumbering, were liberated, clearly marking the beginning of a new epoch of social history.

Moreover, the war and its effects ousted the traditional vital powers previously dominant in the economic sphere, and imbued the Oriental world with new values. A new relation to production was established. In most Middle Eastern countries the war revealed the acuteness of the problem of the settled peasant, the fellah. This problem was not caused by any deterioration in his position as compared with the period before the war, but was implicit in the new recognition of his plight as such, or, to express it in a paradox, it consisted in the potential improvement of his situation. But to make improvement possible meant loosening and breaking down the former foundations of his life, and the creation of a new will to live in those strata in which it had previously been impossible to find anything but lethargy or, at best, an acquiescence in unchangeable circumstances.

But apart from the immediate economic consequences, there was another important result. The opening-up of the countries of the Middle East by new means of transport, the ending of their isolation from one another and from the surrounding world, led to the development of new requirements, which are the prerequisite for any economic and social transformation.

The new political order resulting from the war also gave a strong impulse to the industrialisation of the Orient. Alongside the tendencies towards the improvement of agrarian conditions, we witness a determined industrial policy in Oriental countries, aiming at the production in the country itself of whatever goods of importance could be produced there; in the first place such as might be needed for war purposes. Against the enthusiasm for production, which frequently expressed itself in naive forms, considerations of profitability and the supply of cheap goods—which had been the starting-point of capitalist expansion in the West—became matters of secondary importance. Finally, the political and economic factors involved in the execution of great reforms brought home to the East for the first time the importance of the State and the political means at its disposal for recasting the entire social and economic fabric.

What forces now stand behind these changes? What are the motive powers and movements which are thus serving to renew the shape of this society, here slowly and haltingly, there more rapidly and in a fashion scarcely controllable? What were the brakes on this revival and progress which, in the none too distant past, justified the passing of a verdict of decadence and stagnation on the Oriental world? There can be no doubt that, beside political and economic factors, the religious aspect has also to be taken into account in order to answer these questions. The social system of the Middle East has been largely based on Islam. Changes in the weight of religious tradition and its influence must therefore lead to the development of a new perception of the social world.

All these processes in State, economy and society, initiated or accelerated partly before and partly as a result of the First World War, form the subject of the following pages.

PART ONE

THE MIDDLE EASTERN STATE IN TRANSITION

SECTION I

THE MIDDLE EASTERN STATE UNTIL 1914

CHAPTER I

THE CONCEPTION OF THE STATE IN WEST AND EAST

The Middle East of today offers to politicians and historians alike the dramatic spectacle of new-born national States. Communities or groups which quite recently had still the character of clans and tribal associations are being transformed into nations and States of a modern type. Oriental despotisms which only yesterday were still attempting with success to withstand the drive of the new forces, are now crumbling. Their collapse overwhelms the old régime and, together with the old forms, breaks down the limits of their former areas of domination. A development which in Europe took a thousand years is here being compressed into a few decades, and indicates future political and State-forming potentialities which may transform the entire Middle Eastern world.

It would be wrong, however, to regard the evolution from tribal association into State as an entirely new phenomenon in this area. The growth of States in the Islamic East began in the early Middle Ages and subsequently reached a high level of development. From its very beginnings the Muslim world has evinced State-forming powers of considerable strength, and nothing would be more incorrect than to deny to these political patterns of the past all the criteria of a State form; even though the concept and character of the Islamic State cannot be identified with those of its counterparts in the West.

Meanwhile, however, disintegration has set in. Most of the medieval States have perished, or have succeeded in preserving only the barest vestiges of their one-time development which preceded the War of 1914–1918. Even the great Ottoman Empire was, save in the brief period of its efflorescence, a loose conglomerate of countries the central State power of which rapidly degenerated, to make only a temporary recovery.

A definite renaissance of the State idea in the Middle East came about only at the beginning of the present century. It rode on the wave of national rebirth which passed through all countries, finding its nourishment, here no less than elsewhere, in the rich traditions of the past. Yet the great change for the entire Orient is not to be found merely in the resumption of an old historical tradition during the first decades of the twentieth century. This process did not exhaust itself in its attachment to historical forms and their revival, or in the realisation of an urge towards renewed existence as independent States. Striking changes were also introduced and are now effective in the dominant ideas and the entire internal structure of these States.

The Oriental Islamic State of the old type was based upon a conception fundamentally different from that of the Western State as the latter has developed since the European Middle Ages.

In order to understand this transformation it is necessary first of all briefly to compare the foundations of the modern European State with those of the Islamic Oriental State.

Lord Acton, in his *History of Freedom*, has aptly summarised the achievements of Western State development:

"Looking back over the space of a thousand years, which we call the Middle Ages, to get an estimate of the work they had done, if not towards perfection in their institutions, at least towards attaining the knowledge of political truth, this is what we find: Representative government, which was unknown to the ancients, was almost universal. The methods of election were crude; but the principle that no tax was lawful that was not granted by the class that paid it—that is, that taxation was inseparable from representation—was recognised, not as the privilege of certain countries, but as the right of all. . . . Slavery was almost everywhere extinct; and absolute power was deemed more intolerable and more criminal than slavery. . . . Even the principles of the Habeas Corpus Act, and the method of the Income Tax, were already known. The issue of ancient politics was an absolute state planted on slavery. The political produce of the Middle Ages was a system of states in which authority was restricted by the representation of powerful classes, by privileged associations, and by the acknowledgement of duties superior to those which are imposed by man."[1]

From these foundations, through a protracted and often embittered struggle, emerged the modern democratic constitutional State of the West.

The basic functions of this type of State are the following:

(1) The guarantee of security for the citizen and his property;
(2) Creation of legislation and protection by the Law;
(3) Provision for, and promotion of, the cultural and material

interests and common needs of the citizens (health, elementary education, communications, economic and social policy);

(4) External security for the State's existence.

Its most important means for achieving these objectives are the introduction and maintenance of:

(*a*) Police and military forces;
(*b*) An independent judiciary;
(*c*) A Civil Service loyally attached to the State and, in particular, an honest financial administration;
(*d*) A currency system and a monopoly of the issue of money.

There is general agreement regarding these minimum duties and functions of the State towards its citizens, even though the limitation of its rights and powers in respect of the individual is interpreted very differently in various political philosophies. With all such deviations, however, one fundamental principle is regarded as decisive for the modern idea of the State : that of its sovereignty or supreme authority over all who dwell within its territory. Thus the modern State claims recognition of its authority and its legal and administrative order not only from the individual and all those who are members of the "State Association"—mainly by birth—but also to a very considerable degree in respect of all *actions* which take place in the region under its rule.[2] Hence it not only expects a loyalty of person and of personal opinion, but it also seeks to control all actions affecting the community within the area it governs. It is also generally agreed that the entire population belonging to the State Association has certain duties to fulfil towards it. These are chiefly of a fiscal nature, but may also include other matters such as military service. The Western State, which derives its claims from the concept of sovereignty and has won its position following upon the rupture of old universal extra-State ties, has abrogated the right of groups within its area to realise their separate aims and demands; or has at least opposed and restricted those rights with decided success. At times this struggle has aimed at the removal of even the most personal restrictions, for example, those set up by religious belief. This "great process of expropriation of powers, introduced into and subordinated to the State, by the State itself" which, according to Jellinek, is the particular feature of our own times, characterises the structural process of all modern national

States. The growing political dispossession of separate groups and dominating individual personalities, in brief the strengthening of the modern State, is accompanied by the development of the individual who accepts and affirms this new State; by the protection of him who consciously accepts the State's demands and advances from being a mere town-dweller, ducal subject or feudal serf, to a citizen of the State. His legal position is ever more strictly defined, more firmly established on the basis of written and mutually secured rights. Finally, the constitutional and democratic State of the nineteenth century led to a general and equalitarian shaping of rights and duties, and thence to the transformation of the citizens of the State into a homogeneous body.

At the same time, however, another stratification was developing, in which the extent of property, the actual and potential opportunities for rising, in brief, the new social and economic position decisively influenced the relation between the individual and the State. As stability of income and the chances of advancement grow steadily less, the devotion of the masses to the democratic-capitalist State becomes correspondingly cooler, and a fresh evaluation of the rights offered by that State begins.

In the genuinely Oriental State we stand on entirely different ground. Its life has been controlled and regulated by a fundamentally different structural principle. Instead of the national and often confessional homogeneity of population which the Western State exhibited, or had at least aimed at since the Counter-Reformation, the principle of personality held sway. The State respected the status which the individual had acquired by membership of a given religious or national community, regardless of the frequently far-reaching political or social consequences deriving therefrom. As a result, there was maintained until the present time that remarkable form of plurality of constitution which, whether *de facto* or *de jure*, permitted various national groups and correspondingly varied systems to live a national life of their own within the framework of the State association. Personal status was stronger than the edict of the State. On the basis of the principle of personality there developed from early times in all Oriental territories separate groups of varying national and religious allegiance, the so-called *Millets*, which led a life of their own, separate from that of the dominant Islamic State people, who later were themselves likewise constituted under the form of a *Millet*.

The principle of granting other population groups far-reaching powers of self-administration, a cultural and in part even a political autonomy, derives from pre-Islamic times, and was already current in the Byzantine Empire. The Turks took it over for reasons of apathy, greater convenience in administration and, last but not least, as "a skilful application of the principle *divide et impera*".[3]

Those reasons, however, were no doubt supplemented by the fact that the political and social concepts of the Orient held the segregation of communities within a single territory on the basis of creed to be permissible and even obvious, even if, as a result, the population of that territory came to be separated into several sections divided one from another. Intervention in the internal affairs of these autonomous communities was contrary to the conceptions of Oriental Society.

Here also is to be found the source of the development and expansion of the Capitulations, those special rights which were granted in a number of Oriental lands to the citizens of Western countries. The first of these agreements between the Turkish Empire and a Western power was the Capitulations of 1521, a treaty between Suleiman the Magnificent and the Venetians, by which the privileges already granted to the latter by the Byzantines were confirmed and in some degree expanded. The treaty with Venice was followed by further Capitulation treaties with France, England, Spain and other countries. The right of jurisdiction over subjects of the Ottoman State on the basis of the Capitulations was considerably expanded in the treaty with France, the king of that country arrogating to himself a power of protection over all Roman Catholics of non-Turkish nationality.

Nothing can make the difference of approach more clear than a comparison of this practice with the principle *Cuius regio eius religio*, which was for a long time decisive in determining the State form in post-Reformation Europe. Developments since then have led in Europe, despite enlightenment, liberalism and the consequent weakening of the religious factor, to an increasing uniformity among the people of the State. In the Ottoman Empire, during the same time, there came about an increasing division of the State area into autonomous units, i.e., population groups divided off from one another.[4]

Summing up the distinctive marks of the Islamic Oriental State, in addition to that of the personality principle, which takes first place, we find the following:—

(*b*) A close connection between the religious and the political community, which in early periods found expression in a complete identification of their mutual interests and spheres of influence and led to the development of a legal system common to them both.

(*c*) The absence of a conception or theory of the State in any modern sense. Islam knew nothing of the concept of the State as an independent political institution as it had by then already been developed here and there in Europe. In Islam the State was not a community or an institution, but the totality of those governed (*Umma*), with the *Imam* as their leader.

(*d*) As a result, the Oriental State had no conception of citizens in the modern sense. Such an idea is as alien to Islam as is that of the State itself.[5] Similarly, there is no civic equality as regards taxation. The regular sources of State income were at first only the taxes paid by the protected non-Moslems, called *Dhimmis*, in the form of a poll-tax (*Jizya*) and land tax (*Kharaj*), while the Moslems paid whatever they did pay only as an alms-tax (*Zakat*), placing it in the "Treasury of God" or handing it over directly to the needy. This *Zakat* subsequently developed into one of the main taxes collected from the Believers.

(*e*) For the period of the Ottoman Empire, even more than for that of the preceding Arab Empires, it was true that after the Turkish invasion of Europe its dominion extended predominantly over non-Turkish areas and citizens. The Turkish Sultans ruled over an exceedingly varied group of peoples of diverse languages, races and religions.[6]

(*f*) The development of the Islamic Orient soon led to the replacement of the original warrior community organised as an aristocracy, which had set its stamp on the earlier Islamic States, by the Oriental despotism native to Western Asia. The chief of the State was raised high above his subjects, supplied with the aura of a divine ruler, and separated from ordinary mortals by a protective wall of ceremonial and officialdom. At the same time the continued expropriation of the lower classes and the growing negation of their political rights was made possible by the unparalleled alliance between "Church", State bureaucracy and large landed proprietors.

As contact between the Oriental world and the West grew closer, countries with this flaccid political structure could not withstand the superior power of the expansive European national States. The inner difficulties and contradictions which were increasingly called out by the maintenance of the theological foundations of State life, the "legitimate" intrusion and expansion of foreign, primarily economic interests on the basis of the Capitulations, prepared the ground in the Ottoman Empire of the first half of the nineteenth century for a penetration of the new views of State and society deriving from Europe. By the middle of the nineteenth century the traditional conceptions of the Middle Eastern State had collapsed, and a number of new and weighty principles for the reorganisation of the State structure had already been proclaimed.

CHAPTER II

INTERNAL POLITICAL DEVELOPMENTS IN THE OTTOMAN EMPIRE [7]

The reform era proper, which began in Turkey in the year 1839, had been preceded by measures on the part of certain rulers that created the prerequisite conditions for the proclamation of a new internal organisation of State life. Sultan Selim III, who came to the throne in 1789, was one of the first of European rulers to recognise the newly-established French Republic. He founded new military schools directed by European officers, brought training ships from England for the Turkish fleet, modernised his frontier fortifications, introduced a series of military innovations, particularly in the artillery, and established the famous Topkhane gun-foundry. Selim's reform, like all reforms in Oriental States during that period, extended first and foremost to military and financial affairs.[8]

When Selim appeared to be threatening the existence of the powerful Janissary Corps by his reforms in the army, he fell victim to a revolt, at the head of which the Janissaries placed his cousin Mustapha IV. Mustapha was unable to enjoy his position very long, as Selim's friends, led by the Pasha of Ruschuk, marched against the capital and drove him out. He was replaced by the twenty-four-year-old Mahmud II, who continued Selim's reforms and also introduced a number of measures, quite daring under the conditions then current, affecting the internal administration and particularly the relationship between the provincial and the central authorities. The most important of his reforms was the destruction of the Janissary Corps in 1826. The Janissaries had developed from being the Sultan's bodyguard, once famous for their fighting powers, into an insubordinate Pretorian Guard, an instrument of tyranny feared by ruler and people alike, which had usurped a controlling position in the State.[9] The immediate cause of their destruction was a mutiny on their part against the establishment of a new standing army. This measure, which had its parallel in the slaughter of the Mamelukes by Mohammed Ali at Cairo fifteen years earlier, was accompanied by certain internal political measures that paved the way for the new rights of man proclaimed in 1839. The most important of these were the abolition of the feudal system and the expropriation of feudal property-owners. With the shrinking of the influence of this class and the reduction of their position to that of rentiers entirely dependent upon the Treasury, a further obstacle in the way of the reconstruction of the Empire was removed.

The provincial rulers constituted a further and considerable danger for the Ottoman Empire, at that time gravely threatened from without. Not only the Moslem feudal lords in Greece, Bosnia and Serbia, but also the Arab Pashas in Syria, Palestine and Egypt and the Wahhabis of the Arabian peninsula were in open revolt against their overlord. The unfortunate course of foreign policy threatened the heart of the Empire through the Treaty of Adrianople of 1829, by which the Dardanelles were thrown open. In view of the deadly pressure of external and internal foes, the achievements of Mahmud stand out very brightly. Professor H. Temperley summarises them as follows :

> ". . . What he lost on the outskirts of the empire he gained by asserting his control within it. He found his empire ruled by a set of turbulent feudatories, permanent in the case of derebeys, temporary in the case of the pashas. In each case the rulers of provinces and of tribes had the right of inflicting death, and all those rights of private war, of private justice, of private revenue, which were so dear to medieval barons of the West. Mahmud deprived derebeys and pashas of their independent gibbets, of their independent armies, of their independent incomes. He reasserted the active rule of the Sultan and made a modern unified state for the first time possible in Turkey. He improved the system of government and of taxation, he promoted toleration, he developed commercial intercourse. He built up a new army and a new fleet, he sowed the seeds of many later reforms."[10]

The extraordinary difficulties, however, with which the execution of relatively simple innovations was bound up can be shown by the episode of the striking of coins which were to bear his portrait. This issue hurt the religious feelings of his Moslem subjects, and led to a revolt whose suppression cost 4,000 their lives. Yet finally the coins were withdrawn.

> "That Mahmud and his advisers could carry through such reforms at all in so old a body politic is remarkable: that they carried them through amid the events of his reign is almost miraculous." (Hogarth)

It is therefore the opinion of almost all students that Mahmud, who died in 1839, left his Empire stronger than he found it. Though it was reduced in area, he had at least succeeded in becoming master in his own house. The provinces that were lost meant a strengthening rather than a weakening of the balance of the

Empire. Its non-Turkish population, which always created difficulties for the central administration, would in any case sooner or later have broken away.

It is no accident that the reforms of this period were frequently carried out from above downwards; that the attempts to reform the State began from its highest point and were not at first received with anything like enthusiasm by the lower classes. The State sense had not yet developed in the permanently oppressed masses. The impulse had to come from without and from above.

Besides the Sultan himself, certain prominent representatives of European powers played an important part in this process. First came Sir Stratford Canning, who began his activities in Turkey in 1808 as Secretary to the British Embassy and later, from 1842 till 1858, was to exert a very considerable influence on the Porte as British Ambassador to the Turkish Court. In addition, the summoning of foreign officers as well as of foreign experts in general by Abdul Hamid I towards the end of the eighteenth century, together with the parallel developments in Egypt, contributed in no small degree to the preparation for the reforms.

The Period of the Tanzimat

The death of Sultan Mahmud II, who has been described by modern Turkish historians as the Ottoman Peter the Great, did not mean any interruption in the desire for reform deriving from the Court. His seventeen-year-old son Abdulmajid continued with the work. The birth-certificate of the modern Oriental constitutional State is to be found in the famous letter of the young Sultan Abdulmajid to his Grand Vizier Mustafa Rashid Pasha, dated November 3, 1839, and known as the Hatti Sherif of Guelhane. In this document the youthful Sultan consistently followed the lines already laid down for him by his father Mahmud II. Many decades, to be sure, were to pass before the definite realisation of the modern constitutional State in Turkey; and in addition a sharp struggle regarding the continuation of this policy flared up repeatedly during the subsequent period. Yet this document remains the starting-point of the development of a constitutional State in the Middle East. It marked the beginning of the period of reforms which is recorded by the modern historians of the Ottoman Orient under the name "Tanzimat".[11]

From the purely external viewpoint, it is characteristic that this edict likewise continues to point unequivocally to the basically religious character of the State. The difficulties and mishaps which the Turkish Empire had experienced during the century and a half prior to its issue were a result of the "non-observance of divine and human laws". For that matter, the earlier measures introduced by Mahmud II had also always shown consideration for the feelings and rights of the *Ulema*, by leaving them for all practical purposes unaffected by the reforms. In its objectives, however, the purpose of the letter was, directly, the abolition of the old régime.

The most important of these reform measures, which were announced in 1839 and were afterwards confirmed in the reform decree issued in 1856 following on the Crimean War, set out to satisfy those particular demands which are regarded as the basis of the modern constitutional State:

(1) Guarantees for the security of the life, honour and property of all subjects without exception;
(2) Assurance of the regular collection and distribution of all State taxes, as well as the (temporary) abolition of tax farming;
(3) Reorganisation of conscription for the army.

In the second document, the *Hatti Humayun*, which was published in June, 1856, special emphasis is laid on the principle of the legal, civic and social equality of all subjects, and the right of admission of them all equally to Government service is recognised. In addition, the religious privileges and special status which had been granted to all followers of Christian and other non-Moslem religions were confirmed.

In this way first the conception and later the actual implements for the construction of a State on the Western model were prepared and the theological despotism of the Islamic State was undermined without any revolutionary changes. Under the programme laid down there was no longer to be any difference, in respect of State law at least, between the new State into which the Turkish Empire was to be developed and its Western models. The process of adaptation in respect of constitutional law alone continued, to be sure, until shortly before the First World War. In spite of this the consequences were quite considerable even in the forties and fifties of the last century. Large-scale reforms were introduced in commercial and criminal law and judicial procedure, which rapidly led to the sifting of the legal material and in part even to the codification of those branches.[12] These were preceded by the first official codification of the existing laws, as well as by a first attempt to establish common jurisdiction over all subjects in the mixed commercial courts (1847).

At that time Turkey had a few outstanding men who were capable of carrying out reforms on this scale. The Turkish statesman Midhat Pasha, who had already distinguished himself by dealing with difficult tasks in the provinces, laid the foundations of modern Turkish constitutional law while President of the State Council, which was first established in 1868.

The development of this constitutional law followed the stages marked out in advance by the reformation of Oriental State structure. Thus the evolution of the *Millet* principle and the expansion of the new institutional view of the State led of necessity in 1869 to the publication of a nationality law. At about the same time (1869–1876) the publication of the civil law provided the basic material for the legal organisation of civic life.

Finally the preparation of a Constitution was all that remained to crown the entire range of reform activities.

The reforms here described were introduced during the reign of the liberal-minded yet fundamentally weak Abdulmajid (1839–1861). On his death his brother Abdul Aziz ascended the throne. After a reign of fifteen years he was deposed; and, after a three months' interregnum during which the ruler was his epileptic nephew Murad V, he was followed by his brother Abdul Hamid II, who ascended the throne on 31 August, 1876.

Meanwhile the condition of the Turkish Empire had deteriorated further. In Europe there was a general conviction that the "Sick Man" had reached the final stages, and that all that was now necessary was a *coup de grâce* in order that he should meet his end. Enlightened Turkish statesmen could see but one way of escape from the situation: the completing of the great task of reform in Turkey by the proclamation of a Constitution, in order to set all the forces of the Empire co-operating in a last united effort.[13]

Midhat Pasha, who was inspired by English ideas, submitted a draft to the State Council in June, 1876, containing the outlines of a constitution. A little later, on September 13, 1876, Abdul Hamid's ascent to the throne served as the occasion for announcing the establishment of a Parliament and the preparation of the draft Constitution; and by December 23 of the same year, under pressure from the Powers, this new Constitution was solemnly introduced.

The proclamation of this new State Constitution by Abdul Hamid in 1876 could be regarded from the outside as a continuation of the policy of his uncle. In reality considerations of foreign policy played a very large part in it. Under the pressure of the Powers the Sultan had introduced it hurriedly in order to eliminate any possibility of intervention in Turkey's internal affairs.[14] At the same time, however, a clear rejection of the Europeanising tendencies of his predecessor was indicated. In the circular note sent by Safwet Pasha to Turkish diplomatic representatives abroad the conformity of the new provisions and of the guarantees for their execution with the divine law was made plain.

Reference was made to the participation of the Sheikh al-Islam and the Ulema in the preparation of the Constitution; as a result of which Moslems regarded the document not as the product of a foreign spirit, but as an expression of their own national thought.[15] The Constitution was no longer a mere promise; it was an accomplished fact, and had become the spiritual property of all Osmanlis. Its further development could therefore be delayed or disturbed only by the will of the entire nation or that of its ruler. It had been neither promoted nor proposed from Europe. Hence, the note ended, the Osmanli Government was conscious of not having given admission to any alien ideas; and it could therefore demand that Europe should place its trust in this most recent creation of the Osmanli spirit.

This trust was demanded although Abdul Hamid already regarded the Constitution with mixed feelings. On considering the fate of the Ottoman realm during the preceding decades, he was compelled somewhat bitterly to reach the conclusion that the increasing Europeanisation of his Empire had actually led to a steady diminution of its area and a reduction in the powers of its ruler. His predecessors had introduced this development with an open approval of Western ideas, and had actively promoted Turkey's process of adaptation to Western State forms. If, in spite of all this, the result had not proved more satisfactory, the path which they had taken must obviously have been wrong; and, Abdul Hamid decided, there would have to be a reversion towards the Orient. It was true that Turkey had been included in the Concert of civilised European Powers; at the same time, however, Rumania and Serbia had won their formal independence, Bulgaria was on the way to doing so, and other losses of territory seemed likely. As a result, Abdul Hamid began to feel inclined to reject the European orientation of his three predecessors, and to shift the centre of gravity of his policy, his rule and the future of the Empire entrusted to him towards Asia.

One of the first steps in this direction was his treatment of the Constitution and its creator, Midhat Pasha. That statesman, who manfully refused to rescind the liberties already granted, was banished; and the Sultan dismissed the first Turkish parliament in February, 1878, after it had functioned for precisely two sessions. The Constitution, to be sure, was not *de jure* abolished, and was indeed printed annually in the State Calendar; but Parliamentary constitutional life came to an end.[16] Only thirty years later was the Constitution restored in connection with the Young Turk Revolution. In the Sultan's letter of August 1, 1908, which followed the Order of July 23, 1908, convening the Parliament, it was stressed that the temporary abolition of the Constitution had been the result of the inadequate maturity of the people. Now, however, the time had come when they could claim the rights accruing to them under the constitutional form of State.

The opening of the Parliament took place on December 17, 1908. The focal point was the speech from the throne delivered by Sultan Abdul Hamid, referring to his unchanging efforts to rule in accordance with the Constitution.

Intrigues and struggles between the parties, dissatisfied cliques of officials and the Ulema led on April 13, 1909, to the outbreak of a reactionary movement directed against the Young Turks and the constitution. This, however, rapidly collapsed, thanks to the determination of the Young Turks aided by the officers of the Third Army Corps. The elected assembly became a National Assembly which could permit itself on 26 April, 1909, to resolve upon and carry out the dethronement of Abdul Hamid. Mohammed V Reshad, his successor and brother, who was summoned to the throne in accordance with the Osmanli law of succession, declared in his letter on this occasion that he had "ascended the throne of his noble ancestors in accordance with the eternal commands of the King of Kings and the provisions of our Constitution, and in general agreement with the Osmanli nation". It was his liveliest wish to secure freedom, equality and justice for all his subjects.

In order to prevent similar events in the future, the House of Representatives provided for a number of precautionary measures in the Constitution. In particular the law of August 21, 1909 established the principle of the sovereignty of the people. During the ensuing period, however, there were repeated grave disputes regarding this principle, based in part upon the infringement of the honour and esteem of the Khalifate which, it was claimed, resulted from it.[17] Even among the Young Turks a feeling finally developed in favour of greater consideration for religious and national traditions. Following stormy debates a change in the Constitution was introduced in January, 1912, in the sense of a return to the Khalif State. However, the differences in the House of Representatives and the Senate, and finally the outbreak of hostilities, delayed any consolidation and further development of parliamentary and constitutional institutions until 1919, when the World War was at an end.[18]

CHAPTER III

CHANGES IN STATE INSTITUTIONS

A study of the constitutional history of the Oriental State offers a particularly favourable opportunity for observing its transformation and its institutions on the basis of constitutional documents. The expressions of the Turkish desire for reform, which often are surprisingly far-reaching in their written formulation, should not, however, lead to the misconception that after the Decree of 1856 the rights therein secured had immediate effect and validity. A large part of the reforms remained on paper. The causes of this lie in the resistance which is always offered to any reorganisation of the political and social power arrangements which have become well established in the existent laws and interests. Beneficiaries by the earlier order who were bound to be affected by the new decrees were able, where proper safeguards had not been provided, to take very effective measures against the execution of the reforms. In addition, a fundamental prerequisite for the execution of such far-reaching reforms in the State was absent; namely, the existence of a sense of loyalty to the State, a conviction of the priority of the common interest; in brief, a feeling of devotion and faith in regard to the State, which could not develop in so heterogeneous a society as that necessarily brought into being by the *Millet* system, feudal structure and Oriental despotism. There will be further opportunity below for dealing in some detail with the inherent defects of the Ottoman State, particularly the deeply rooted corruption and mismanagement in its administration. It is impossible to over-estimate the responsibility of these factors for the failure at many points of the reform programme of the Tanzimat period. In spite of this the developments which began during the period 1839–1876, and were resumed in 1908 after an interval of thirty years, had an epoch-making importance.

To begin with, the renunciation of part of his rights by the chief of the State, who was equipped with the widest of powers, meant the end of the despotic régime in the leading Middle Eastern State. With the exception of a few communities in Arabia, which are, however, patriarchal rather than despotic in character, despotism has now, constitutionally speaking, virtually disappeared. It is true that its successor, the constitutional or parliamentary monarchy, in Oriental lands, in no way adequately fulfils the concept of a constitutional form of Government or one based on co-operation with representatives of the people; and has remained in many respects a paper affair only. But the legal prerequisites for the establishment of the people's sovereignty have been provided beyond any question. There is no reason to underrate the ideological importance of this point.

Apart from the changes in the legal position of the Sultan, which derived from the division of powers, the change in the meaning of his spiritual and religious functions was also extremely far-reaching.

Khalifate and Sultanate

In Article 3 of the revised State Constitutional Law of 21 August, 1909, the connection between the Sultanate and the Khalifate was stressed in the following terms:

> "The High Osmanli Sultanate is united with the lofty Islamic Khalifate and according to ancient custom is held by the senior member of the family of Osman. The Sultan takes oath upon ascending the Throne in the Parliament, or, if it has not met, at its first meeting, that he will honour the prescriptions of the Holy Law and the Constitution of the State, and that he will faithfully serve the Fatherland and the Nation."

The association between the two Powers vested in the Constitution follows a remarkable development. According to the Moslem theory of the Khalifate, first elaborated systematically by el-Mawardi and afterwards taken over by Ibn Khaldun, the Khalif had the following duties to fulfil: the protection and maintenance of religion, the decision of legal disputes, the protection of the territories of Islam and corresponding military measures, the leadership of the Jihad or Holy War, direction of the fiscal administration, and all other affairs of the State.[19]

Hence the Khalif had to carry out both the spiritual and the political functions of the State. In the course of history, however, the office of Khalif did not always share in this association of political and spiritual power. The Abbasids in particular had shifted into the foreground the religious character of their office. This move was even more favoured by the decline in the secular power of the Khalifate. Hence the Khalif is the Supreme Chief of the Community of Believers (*Imam*); and beside this, but separated from it, is the function of the Sultan (*Amir al-'Umara*), who exercises the power of the sword and conducts affairs of State.

But the Arab Khalifate as the highest religious authority did not again achieve real political influence. The descendants of the

Abbasids, who succeeded in escaping from the blood-bath of the Mongols in Baghdad, continued to lead a life of outward brilliance in Cairo, but were really prisoners of the Mameluke Court. The Mamelukes treated the Abbasids with respect, since they provided their rule with a semblance of legality. The Osmanli Sultans eventually excluded the Imamate entirely as an independent institution; the two functions of spiritual Khalif and secular ruler were again united in a single person, that of the Osmanli monarch.[20]

Beyond their own area of rule, however, there was for the greater part only a nominal recognition of the claim to religious control which found expression in this union; although, as the Osmanli dominion in non-Turkish territories was increasingly menaced, the tendency to stress the religious authority of the Sultan as the Protector of all Moslems, including those who were not Turks, was again and again considerably strengthened.[21] The Young Turks, who certainly cannot be held to have shown any particular fondness for theological demands or for the strengthening of spiritual influence in general, also made use of the institution of the Khalifate in order to keep the centrifugal Moslem territories united within the Empire. Thus, for example, the prestige of that institution was used by them during the reign of Sultan Mohammed V Reshad, the successor of Abdul Hamid, in order to prevent the threat of disturbances in the Moslem parts of Macedonia by means of his appearance and presence in person. Despite the clearly recognisable tendency of the Young Turk movement towards freedom and enlightenment, the leaders of constitutional Turkey had not yet departed from the theocratical spirit and habits of the Empire. The form of the dethronement of Abdul Hamid was likewise characteristic. His deposition was legitimised in the eyes of the faithful by the proclamation of a Fetwa of the Sheikh al-Islam, and this intervention in the hallowed order of "Church" and State was justified by the Islamic law itself on the ground that the Sultan had not fulfilled his duties as Supreme Lord of the Faithful.

The Young Turks had incidentally been charged even earlier with the fact that their constitutional reforms, particularly their introduction of popular sovereignty, ran counter to the Osmanli tradition. Such feelings may account for the attempt made in 1910 to do away with the constitutional Law of 1909 on the ground that it meant a breach with the past and, because of its inadequate respect for the dignity of the Khalifate, contradicted the Osmanli religious tradition. The introduction of national sovereignty as responsible State power was held to be dangerous in Turkey on account of the numerous nationalities.[22]

However, the supporters of the above-mentioned Law, in defending it, likewise quoted from the Sharia to the effect that the power belonged to the Islamic Community and not to any individual person. The Sultan was elevated to the rank of Khalif only by the will of the people.

In actual fact, however, public opinion began to favour greater consideration for the religious and national tradition; so that particularly after 1911, a return to the Khalif State in a modernised form was aimed at, in view of the growth of the national movement in the Arab countries and the problem of uniformity within the army. The objective was not a return to the State of the old Khalifate as in the time of Abdul Hamid, but the establishment of a modern constitutional State with pan-Islamist tendencies and headed by the Khalif; that was the outcome of the constitutional struggle.[23]

But these attempts to breathe life into the great Pan-Islamic concept, which circles round the principle of the Khalifate, could no longer heal the inner weaknesses of that institution when the Empire had already begun to dissolve. The first strain to which it was subjected showed that the recognition of the claim to spiritual leadership, which was supposed to be embodied in the Khalif office of the Osmanli Sultan, was a fiction. At the beginning of the First World War Turkey attempted to achieve a single common front of all Moslems, based on the unity symbolised by the Khalifate. That the result was negative is a matter of common knowledge. Arab countries, which were certainly not behind the Turkish heartlands in their faithfulness to Islam, turned against the Khalif and contributed to the undermining of the Ottoman Empire. The national ties of the Moslem peoples, tenuous though they may have been, were already more powerful than the religious bond. National groups who did not belong to the religious community of Islam proved themselves loyal citizens of the Turkish Empire, while Moslem peoples turned against it.

The Moslem Evolutionary Theory of the State

The failure of the efforts to turn the fiction of the religiously based dominion of the Khalifate over all the Faithful into a reality also meant the foundering of the attempt to maintain the identity between political and religious community as the constitutional principle of the Islamic State. The belief that it was necessary to take Islamic teachings as the basis for the reconstruction of the State had still, to be sure, played a part in the State reforms at the beginning of the century. Gradually, however, it became quite clear that even in the Islamic East the newly-developing modern State would have to renounce any insistence on identity between State and religious community, and to recognise the criterion of national affinity. As with the development in other religious systems, the way to this led through the slogan "Islamism *and* Modernism" to a constantly increasing elimination of spiritual influences and positions from the State's life, and their restriction to the purely religious field. That this development was possible in so brief a period and, on the whole, without any bloodshed, is largely due to the Islamic attitude which expressly provides for an evolutionary shaping of the law. This basic conception of the permissibility of adaptation to changes made necessary by time which runs through the entire development of Islamic law, and of which the most striking expression is the consensus (*Ijma*) or approval of the Islamic community, is laid down—a constitutional curiosity worthy of note—in the Constitution itself. Article 118 of the modified Constitutional Law reads:

> "In the preparation of laws and regulations those customs and manners of life as well as religious and legal requirements shall be followed which correspond to the practices and habits of the people and the needs of the time."

The adoption of this evolutionary provision in the Constitution can be explained by the desire to anticipate the possible objections which might be raised, for religious reasons, against changes in and encroachments upon the existing laws. It is clear that the legislator had in mind a similar provision in the *Mejelle*, the Code of Civil Law, which reads literally (Article 39):

> "It cannot be denied that legal prescriptions are subject to changes in the course of time."

Just as this formulation seeks to stress the idea of development in the sphere of civil law, so does the above-mentioned Article 118 set out to make all legal provisions in the Constitutional Law dependent on time. Our appreciation of the scale of this concession, which in principle permits every advance within public and civil law as being legitimized by tradition, is made easier if we deal in slightly more detail with the problem of Oriental legal thought.

Legal Thought in Islam

The legal thought of the Orient differs considerably from that of the West, both in form and content. The basic difference between them is in regard to the function of the State in Oriental as compared with its place in the development of Western law.

Mention should first be made of the personal character of Oriental law already repeatedly stressed. In the West the law has largely been shaped by the State or the territorial association, in the sense of the later logically developed theory of the overriding power of the State as binding on the totality of its citizens; whereas the Orient thinks first and foremost of law *ad personam*. The personality principle, as we might say, divides the subjects of the law in a vertical direction, grouping the population in sections for which differing legal requirements and demands are valid.

In view of the wide expansion of Islamic rule this treatment of the individual *ad personam* had a number of very important consequences for the formal and material law of Islam; and although it has been considerably weakened with time, it has not yet disappeared. Its most important results in the field of State politics were the development of the Capitulations into a tremendous political and economic instrument; the *Millet* Constitution and the dichotomy of jurisdictions into religious and secular, so that usually the spiritual or Canon law was the authority for matters of personal status for members of its own confession.[24]

This difference is supported by others of no less importance. Oriental law is not based on historic analytical thought. It knows nothing of the logical analysis of the legal case and its merits which has gone forward everywhere in the Western world together with Roman law; nor of the artistic construction of legal cognitions and principles to be employed deductively; nor does it differentiate or separate the extremely varied legal material connected with the development of individual, society and State. In the Sharia, the complex of Islamic law, the differentiation in principle of actual departments, which is familiar to us, is not to be found. This inadequate conceptual classification tends in itself to favour an elasticity of interpretation.

To begin with, and in harmony with what we have said above, there is no clear line of demarcation between public and private, or between criminal and civil law. Even in the countries where the Beduin legal tradition as regards actions subject to penalty has not become established, no clear-cut division between criminal and civil law has been made. This differencefinds its counterpart in the Sharia in the antithesis between the claims of God and the claims of men. As a result, the communal life subject to the laws of the Sharia finds the infliction of punishment for various criminal acts such as larceny, highway robbery, incest, etc., extremely limited and of no great consequence for the wrong-doer.[25] The importance of prosecution is considerably reduced by the consideration shown for disposition, for "active remorse", by the difficulties placed in the way of proof, and the meticulous definition of the crime.

In addition to this important difference there is yet another. As a result of the deficient systematic structure of Islamic law already pointed out, the practice of this law has called forth a very highly developed system of casuistry. In countries where the Sharia is current the entire functions of the law are still administered by means of a process of analogy, adequate for most cases, which has already produced large collections of decisions. It is clear that a legal system so greatly dependent upon casuistry must be subject to the traditions which have accumulated in the course of generations, and cannot be expected to handle new legal situations which have developed through legal transactions of a hitherto unknown kind.

Under these conditions it was quite inevitable that, independent of the Islamic legal tradition, there should have come into being a legal system providing for the requirements and new forms of modern economic life. With the growing contact between the Islamic countries and the West in the nineteenth century, and the weakening of relations between Islam and the State, the range of "autonomous" law not based on Islamic doctrine began steadily to expand. Part of the law cases were conducted with a complete disregard of the native legal system, as the representatives of European interests set out to achieve a system of law "transferred" from the West by the establishment of the Capitulation Courts. The legal decisions in these were based on the law of European countries.

On the other hand there developed, within the Islamic legal tradition, a cautious process of extrusion and adaptation based on the liberally interpreted evolution clause already considered above. The development of Islamic law during the nineteenth century, however, proceeded very gradually, and this not without reason; since even up to the present time the social peculiarities of certain regions of Western Asia make every precipitate legal reform seem undesirable. For example, it is unquestionable that the absence of a well-developed civil law considerably handicaps the development of agriculture by modern methods. At the same time there can certainly be no question of any schematic introduction, by a mere drafting of laws.

Thus, for example, it would be possible to expand the opportunities of exploitation in Iraqi agriculture very considerably in view of the large expanse of uncultivated territories; yet it would be erroneous merely to distribute by official decree the land held in State ownership, and to make it the property of individual cultivators. In 1930 an expert on Oriental land law could still state in his report on the conditions of landed property that the reform of those conditions was a prerequisite for the development of native agriculture; but at the same time he added that the greater part of the population were not yet ripe to receive freedom to dispose of their land as they thought fit.[26] But in other countries and other territories, particularly since the First World War, the legal system has undergone modernisation by the introduction of new codes which largely took European examples as their models. In general the legal systems and methods of Middle Eastern countries are definitely passing through a period of transition. The modern legal form of credit transactions and the mobility of capital, especially of company capital, and the securities system, have penetrated into these lands under the pressure of capitalist economic interests. These interests must always and everywhere strive towards a prior calculation of prospects and hence towards an approximation of legal conditions to one another, which in turn involves the creation of the legal instruments indispensable for their efficiency, such as freedom to dispose of landed and other property. In the Orient they either adopt the traditional legal material where it provides a support for them, and endeavour to transform it; or else, in the majority of cases, there grows up alongside the religious law restricted to personal status and the right of succession an autonomous secularised law, which has been taken over from more advanced countries, and which extends its influence over increasing areas of economic and social life, thus securing for the latter further development.

The tempo of this growth was incomparably more intensive in the economic field than in that of public law, where respect for the religious and political tradition exerted a retarding effect. Still, the Young Turk revolution served to mark an acceleration in this process as well, and this showed itself in particular in the development of the so-called "rights of the people".

THE CIVIC RIGHTS OF THE PEOPLE IN THE NEW OTTOMAN CONSTITUTION

The right of participating in and influencing the Government is the first of the newly-won rights of the people which should be mentioned. Until 23 December, 1876, the Turkish ruler was unrestricted in the exercise of the sovereign power falling to him, within the limits of religious law, according to the ancient law of the Osmanli House. The Constitution which he himself proclaimed in 1876, and the later Constitutional changes of 1908, 1909, 1914, 1915 and 1916 considerably reduced his rights as Sultan. The tendency of the reforms, particularly after the Sultan's attempt in April, 1909, to abolish the rights he had conceded, was to replace the constitutional monarchy that had just been introduced by a parliamentary régime, in order to secure a maximum of co-operation on the part of the representatives of the people in the rule of the country.[27]

Although this far-reaching reform, which aimed at a complete division of powers, was partly abolished and the constitutional development was subsequently diverted into a more tranquil course, the rights gained were on the whole retained. The tendencies towards a stronger stressing of the Islamic character of the State which were likewise recognised by the Young Turks and found their expression in the motto "Return to the Khalif State!" did not mean the maintenance of the old Osmanli despotism, but the establishment of a modern constitutional State with the rights accruing to the population in any such community.

Article 3 of the Constitutional Amendment of 21 August, 1909, correspondingly stresses the dependence of the Sultan on the Constitution. This Article reads in part as follows:

> "The Sultan takes oath upon ascending the throne in Parliament, and, if Parliament has not assembled, at its first meeting, that he will honour the prescriptions of the Holy Law and of the Constitution of the State and will faithfully devote himself to the Fatherland and the Nation."

Of no less constitutional importance was the express incorporation of fundamental rights in the new Constitution. It is true that the principle of the personal liberty of the individual citizen had already been adopted in the Constitution of 1876, but the express expansion of the protection of personal liberty by the reduction of the power of arrest, and the securing of freedom of speech in the new Constitution were of great consequence for the one-time police and informers' State of Abdul Hamid. The relevant Articles of the Constitution read as follows:

"Article 10: Personal freedom is protected against every attack. No one may be arrested or punished on any excuse saving on the grounds and in forms determined by the divine and human law.

"Article 12: The press is free within the limits of the law. Journals are not subject to any form of censorship or examination before going to press.

"Article 119: Documents and letters entrusted to the post office may not be opened without the authorisation of an Examining Magistrate or of the Court.

"Article 120: The Osmanlis enjoy the right of assembly and are subject only to law in this regard. It is forbidden to establish associations which have the purpose of endangering the existence of the Osmanli State, to change the form of Constitution or of Government, to call popular movements into existence which contravene the prescriptions of the Constitution, or politically disunite the Osmanli population, or finally such as run counter to morality or public order. The establishment of secret societies in general is also prohibited."

It should further be mentioned that after the Constitutional amendment of 1909, the members of the Parliament were also permitted to propose, introduce and change laws. Apart from this, their salaries were simultaneously raised so high as to permit to all, theoretically at least, the possibility of active participation in the work of Parliament. This meant that the composition of Parliament need not necessarily remain restricted to those representatives who could devote themselves exclusively to politics because they were economically independent.

Of no small potential importance for the education of the public were also the changes introduced in the Constitution in respect of the budget. These provided that the entire budget of the State had to be prepared and published at the beginning of every year. But the value of this measure for the control and checking of corruption must still at that time have been doubtful.

Unlike the constitutions of Western countries, the Oriental constitutional texts of that time were completely silent regarding the necessity of satisfying common requirements through the State. The development of such common requirements and their satisfaction implies conditions which at the turn of the century were not yet present in the Orient. In the nature of things the State can only satisfy those common requirements which are mass requirements; that is, those which imply a certain uniformity of demand. Requirements of this kind are an educational system, public health measures, provision for old age, transport facilities, etc. These demands had scarcely been realised by the populations of Oriental countries at the time under discussion. There was no inducement in this direction. Those cultural, political and economic activities of modern social life, which had already led to the development of requirements of this kind in other countries, were here absent. Whatever was left in the way of common impulse and expression of will deriving from the past had become petrified. As a result the people to begin with gained nothing but abstract rights. Undertakings on the part of the State to fulfil common requirements were not as yet recognised.

The secular importance of the constitutional reforms, despite the merely symbolic value of some of the statutes, has already been remarked upon. The changes in the Oriental State found their most precise expression in the changes of the constitutional documents. First came the creation of the requisite conditions. The feudal State field, so to speak, was cleared by the elimination of feudalism and the subjugation of local potentates, as well as by the extermination of the Janissaries, that convenient instrument of despotism which had become an unbearable power. The introduction of the Constitution itself meant the end of despotism and the participation in the Government of representatives of the people. The encroachment of modern legal thought, the law of nationality, and the article in the Constitution which proclaimed the equal rights and duties of all citizens, laid the foundations for the development of a Turkish nation in a modern constitutional State. The dividing walls which the *Millet* system had raised between the various communities and the nation as such could certainly not be removed overnight; the antipathies, animosities and social differences which had been nourished for centuries on end, the ill-feeling which had developed as a result of political and economic privilege, could certainly not vanish at such short notice. Nevertheless a considerable step had been taken on the road to the homogeneous State inhabited by citizens possessed of equal rights. The relations between State and Church, which had become acute as a result of the reforms, also entered on a new stage. The old associations were still powerful, but the liberation of the political apparatus from association with the spiritual powers had begun, and for a time went forward with tempestuous speed.

In this way the signs of the complex processes which mark the

Oriental State in transformation became increasingly manifest in State administration, the legal system, public affairs and finance during the decades before the First World War. It was an unfortunate coincidence that during that very period the expanding Western Empires were increasing their activities in the region of the Near and Middle East. While the statesmen of the Ottoman Empire endeavoured to steer their country by means of reforms into a new era, the Great Powers discovered the potentialities of the huge territory for economic exploitation; and by means of the continued expansion of their political and economic interests in the Orient they almost succeeded in undermining the foundations of the independent existence of the Ottoman Empire. A support lending no small weight to these attempts was found among many of the non-Turkish elements of the population who, under cover of Capitulations and other privileges, succeeded in extorting for themselves and their national protectors remarkably far-reaching economic and political rights of exploitation.

The obstinacy with which these rights were claimed, and the inadequate driving force of the Young Turk movement in respect of social and economic reforms and measures, may be regarded as the cause of the collapse of this first attempt at reorganisation.

It is a sign of the uncommon vitality of Turkey that, despite extreme pressure from without and grave injuries and defects from within, she was able to salvage the prerequisite conditions for the establishment of an independent State during the post-war period from these decades of trial, filled as they were with continuous warfare.

CHAPTER IV

THE ROLE OF BUREAUCRACY (APPARATUS OF GOVERNMENT)

General Remarks

In few fields of activity did the Orient assimilate itself, formally at least, so rapidly to its Western models as in the bureaucratisation of the State régime and the social organisations.

It was characteristic of the patriarchal structure of State and society as well as of despotism that administrative functions remained largely undifferentiated, and that there were no regulations to govern the handling of administrative affairs.[28] Decisions were largely made *ad hoc.* The discharge of official duties was in the hands not of a trained staff but of personally summoned friends, confidants and favourites of the rulers. The concept of a salaried official class, a bureaucracy appointed under and working in accordance with specific principles, was lacking.

Wherever the modern State system was introduced and the subjects of law and administration were codified or defined in almost all fields, the first result was necessarily in all cases the introduction of a specially trained administrative and legal official class. The rising importance of the bureaucracy in relation to other social classes, and its ever-increasing influence, then followed as necessary consequences from the further transformation of the entire State organism and its functions.

Whatever might be the case elsewhere, this process of the development of a State bureaucracy could not proceed in the Middle East without friction, hindrances and reverses. The distance which had to be bridged on account of differing concepts and institutions was too great. This distance reached from one pole of social organisation, the patriarchal tribal community of the Beduin, to its opposite, the socially atomised industrial proletariat called forth by modern capitalist development.

Hence this process is not a mere repetition of what took place in Europe during the shaping of the modern State.

For one thing, the formation of a bureaucracy and its growth were here vastly accelerated. Developments which in Europe had required a period of centuries were here achieved in decades, indeed in a few years. Further, the necessity of creating everywhere and very rapidly an official cadre coincided here, none too happily, with a vocational concept nourished by the psychology of unearned income (rent) and ambitions for domination, which could look back on no class tradition such as might have provided a counterpoise against these tendencies. Indeed, the contemplative state of mind of many Orientals, with its preference for a course of life requiring no initiative, brought the negative sides of the official career more strongly to the front than in Western countries.

Hence the administrative history of Oriental lands in recent times, especially since the establishment of the new national States, manifests an unbroken contest between the forces and tendencies of the old and the new State administration. The promulgation of modern State law, the revised nomenclature and multiplication of officials and the expansion of the functions of the State have not yet of themselves produced the fundamental psychological changes in the people who constitute the official apparatus, and who must lend to the new States their effective power. This requires a sense of duty to the State which often takes generations to achieve.

Characteristics of the Oriental Administrative Apparatus

Oriental countries had had their official classes before this: there had already been periods, indeed, when their number was by no means small. But there had probably never been any idea of the official as a servant of the State, for whom the aim of such service was paramount to his own personal and material interests. The phenomenon of corruption, which will be discussed in some detail below, is likewise not specific to the Orient as such; but it achieved there a scale and scope unknown elsewhere. The absence of any feeling for the State, the lack of all sense of duty towards the community, a duty related to a renunciation or limitation of the personal desire for property and position, deprived Oriental corruption of the stain of a social misdemeanour and transformed it into a general habit, which appeared in all forms and branches of State life. The almost obligatory custom of making gifts to office-holders is enough to show the virtual absence of distinction between a legitimate payment of taxes and a gift which had the character of a fee. From that point the step to the tacitly accepted official practice of appropriating part of the State income or of permitting it to evaporate *en route*, that is, when sending it to another official quarter, was but short. Nor did the act of offering an official a bribe in order to achieve a specific purpose evoke any scruples on the part of the briber.

We need give no detailed description of the effects that must inevitably follow when customs and views of this kind are found in every sphere of State activity. In its character the State, no matter how various the interpretations of its underlying ideas, is or at least aims at being the embodiment of the fixed and the stable. It is the association which organises the mass, which gives it form, which establishes a legal system, which determines the behaviour of its members. The view that everything can be bought, that everything even in the domain of State life has its price, must make all values highly relative, must weaken all those standards which the State itself has set, must degrade its institutions and in fact reduce it to a pallid fiction or, in the most favourable case, to a veil for a multiplicity of impenetrable relations to the advantage of whoever has most to offer.

The extent of the evil can be shown by a few examples which also give a general picture of the situation at that time. Although the details varied as between the different provinces of the Ottoman Empire, and a tendency to better things could be observed over a number of decades, the picture for the nineteenth century as a whole remains more or less uniform. It cannot be better characterised than by Burckhardt's remark, "An honest governor has no hope of long retaining his office." In his book on Nubia, that author gave a fitting description of conditions at the beginning of the nineteenth century:

". . . The Porte demands supplies and nothing but supplies; and the pasha to satisfy her must press upon the industry of his subject. He who is the well-wisher of his people, who contents himself with the ordinary revenue, and who lets justice preside in his councils will undoubtedly incur his sovereign's displeasure, not because he is just, but because his justice prevents him from plundering and transmitting a portion of the acquired plunder to the divan. To save his existence he has nothing left but silently to resign his unhappy subjects to the rod of a succeeding despot, or to declare himself a rebel and to contend with his rival until the Porte, convinced of the difficulty of deposing him, patiently waits for a more favourable opportunity."[29]

But even where it was not a matter of the financial requirements of the Porte or the provincial authorities, venality and corruption easily found ways and means. The tourist literature of the first half of the nineteenth century is full of reports on the extent of the evil. "As soon as a man becomes a minister or a governor, all his relations and the relations of his relations, all the idlers from his native village, crowd to solicit his patronage . . . He gives them no wages, but they get scraps from his kitchen and 'backsheesh' from his visitors and suitors. As opportunities offer he provides for them, he makes them 'cadis' or policemen or governors of villages, or takes them into his paid service as vacancies occur . . . A man once in the service of a great man, whether hired or purchased, a servant or a slave, gets from thence into the service of the public, and then robs and bribes his way up."[30]

The situation in Egypt before the rise of Mohammed Ali and after his death was even worse. Nobody knew how much was extorted from the fellahin or how much of the receipts from taxation was stolen on the way to the Treasury. ". . . Justice was a matter of bribes, property a matter of favour, life a matter of luck."[31]

Public opinion regarded the dishonesty of officials as a matter of course. What it regarded as ideal was the maintenance of a single tyrant, in order to prevent the rise of many. If the Sheikhs of the villages were left to themselves, they made use of every opportunity to exploit the peasants under their control. Those appointed over them repeated the same process within their domains. Corruption was not their only defect; they were also ignorant. Experience was the official's sole equipment, and it usually taught him how to rob wisely and shrewdly.

Corruption in the Courts was particularly open. The venality of the Judges was notorious, and the results of trials depended almost exclusively on which party offered most. Since the office of judge was open to purchase, it was generally exploited in the most unscrupulous fashion as a source of income. Mohammed Ali had the worst possible opinion of the integrity of judges. He established two new Courts of Justice in Cairo and Alexandria which could pronounce judgment free from the restrictions and bonds of Islamic law, and were composed of members of various nationalities instead of theologians. Their purpose was to decide in commercial disputes, particularly those between Mohammedans and Christians; and they were the forerunners of the Mixed Courts which later became so important.[32]

The procedure and methods of work of the Moslem Courts were very similar in all parts of the Empire. Descriptions by English consuls of those days repeatedly stress the tremendous defects in the legal system. Thus the English consul Stuart reports regarding conditions at Janina in Greek Macedonia, which at that time was still Turkish, that all the courts distinguished themselves by their exceptional corruption and venality. Scarcely any attempt was made to hide the fact that the verdict or decision could be bought. The venal judges worked in two different ways. First came the decision, usually in favour of the party who paid most. Where the subject-matter was rather more complicated, the technique of delay was employed. The Court made whatever decision it desired regarding the time for hearing a case, and often delayed its decision for the sole purpose of gaining time for incidental negotiations in order to ascertain which of the parties offered more for the award.[33]

In the same report the consul remarks that it was by no means the Turks alone who were responsible for this state of affairs. The Christians also bore a considerable share of the responsibility; not only the members of the Courts themselves, but also the entire Christian population which, although they were continually complaining of the injustice of their rulers, were always prepared to profit from the misuse of the law. A consular report from Aleppo expresses itself in the following terms:

". . . If a Turk has an advantage over a Greek adversary in the religious sympathy of his judges, the Greek has generally more to bribe them with, and if a Greek has not the advantage of supporting his case by Christian evidence, he has an equal facility of subpœnaing Musulman witnesses ready to swear to anything for a couple of dollars."

Yet even the consular reports do not always show how corrupt these representatives of foreign powers and interests themselves were. Today it seems scarcely credible that foreign consuls (and not least those of England) openly misused their positions to the advantage of their fellow-countrymen and of their own pockets. Yet several reports of that time give certain details in this respect. Thus, for example, Layard reports in his autobiography that in Salonica most of the consuls lived on the sale of passports and letters of safe-conduct to the local Christians.[34]

In Syria, according to a report of Campbell, the consuls and consular agents had taken an unlimited number of Rayas (non-Moslem subjects of the Sultan) under their protection as agents, interpreters, etc., naturally on the payment of very considerable sums. Certificates were also issued to the effect that goods in the customs houses were intended for the personal use of the consuls, when everyone knew that these goods were for native merchants. The dragomans were mostly rich native merchants who knew only Arabic and were not able to render translation services for the consuls. As consular protection withdrew not only consular staff but also their families and servants from Turkish jurisdiction, many of the native merchants made use of the opportunity to obtain certificates of nominal employment in the consulates for a satisfactory consideration.

The local consuls regarded these practices as so much a matter of course that they reacted with open dissatisfaction to the intervention of the Consuls General called forth by Mohammed Ali, and praised the more pleasant times of Turkish mismanagement as compared with that ruler's incisive measures of reform.[35]

These activities, as already mentioned, were not restricted to the Courts and consuls. There was virtually no domain of State and public life in which anything was to be found that did not have its price. That the Church was not free of this scandal, as was equally the case in Western Europe, is no matter for surprise. Nevertheless the development of the Oriental Churches until the very recent past shows a degree of simony that will not easily find a parallel elsewhere. The English historian Finlay says in drastic fashion that after the Turkish conquest the sale of offices became part of the constitution of the Orthodox Church. In any case it is a fact that for centuries on end every position in this organisation could be bought, from the Patriarchal See to the lowest provincial priesthoods. Here follow a few examples:

In 1583 the brother of a wealthy merchant paid 12,000 ducats in order to be elected in place of the Patriarch Jeremiah II. His successor purchased the office for 24,000 ducats. In 1620 Timothy II was called upon by the Grand Vizier to pay 100,000 ducats because he had created 330 Metropolitans during his eight years of Office. Another Patriarch received a Fetwa from the Sheikh al-Islam, in respect of the succession to a certain bishopric, by means of a bribe which he in turn hoped to regain out of his income. The following interesting statistics compiled by Cobham enumerate the reasons for the 328 vacancies in the Patriarchate of Constantinople up to the year 1884: 140 by deposition, 41 resignations, 3 poisonings, 2 murders, 1 decapitation, 1 blinding, 1 drowning, 1 hanging, and 1 strangling. Of the 328, only 137 completed their office by a natural death.[36]

It is therefore no matter for surprise that a report on the causes of the precarious position of the Orthodox Patriarchate of Jerusalem, prepared on behalf of the British Government after the First World War, exposes and pillories the practices of the Brethren of the Holy Sepulchre with a severity unusual in British official documents.[37]

Malpractices of this kind were not limited to any one Church, but were to be found among all religious organisations, particularly among the Moslem pious foundations and within the Jewish community of Palestine. In the last-mentioned they were found in the *Haluka* or dole system, which contributed to the maintenance of the Jewish population of Palestine until the end of the nineteenth century, the money collected being administered without any form of supervision.

Even an institution of such far-reaching importance for the protection of property and for social order as the system of land registration was found to be a hotbed of illegal practices. According to the report on the administration of Palestine during the early years of the British Mandatory régime, the registration of land had been a source of corruption before the British occupation. "Lands were registered frequently at a fourth or less part of the real area—thus avoiding payment of Land Tax . . . Every form of deceit was resorted to in order to defeat the law and evade taxation."[38]

Evidently excessive avarice constitutes a very important motive in corruption; yet it is not enough to explain adequately the extent and power of this practice. Among the causes for its enormous scope should be mentioned inadequate appreciation of the idea of the State and unrestrained individualistic thinking as elsewhere. Up to the present these traits have prevented the beneficiaries and victims of corruption alike from having any feeling of its illegality. Its maintenance was further favoured by the fact that the officials could frequently hold their offices only because they were able to find resources to purchase them again and again.

Yet these phenomena are not specifically Oriental. In these regions the following fact played an important part: outside the sphere of religion, Oriental society did not establish any criteria of conscience whose maintenance should serve as a highly valued social asset and whose disregard would cause any moral condemnation or, under certain circumstances, a loss of moral and material rights. The respect in which the individual was held was primarily determined by his belief in Islam or membership in one of the Oriental religious communities, which did not depend on a certain social attitude or even on honesty and integrity in matters of public affairs and finance; qualities which were obvious and even second nature for certain classes in the West. Yet such qualifications were the prerequisite conditions for a state of mind which would regard as dishonourable the unscrupulous transgression of self-imposed rules and prescriptions for purposes of personal enrichment. A change ensued only when the idea of the State, which had until then been an abstract concept with no direct effect on or immediacy for the individual, struck root. The supremacy of national ideologies which has been increasingly felt in Middle Eastern territories since the First World War, and the propagation of the idea of the State as the essence of the national form of life, together with Draconian measures on the part of the State authorities, have led to a lesser degree of corruption in these lands. (The recent war, it is true, saw a set-back in the campaign against corruption and a revival of the old evils, at least while it lasted). Above all, the complacency and openness with which corruption appeared in all spheres of the administration and courts is no longer found on the same scale. Where the evil exists it is concealed, and comes to light only in the occasional trials of guilty officials or civilians. An example of the present urgency of the question can be found in the proposals made from time to time, that the Government should ascertain how much property an official possessed before entering on his post. Every official whose property has increased out of proportion to his legitimate income, ought, according to this suggestion, to be punished. The Turkish Government has published certain prescriptions in this regard,[39] yet the success of any such measure must remain questionable so long as there are ways and means of concealing accumulations of property, and, what is more important, so long as the sense of public duty is not strong enough to prevent the evil itself.

The Westernisation and extension of the scope of State functions made the differentiation and expansion of the official apparatus and its activities inevitable. The increase of the Ottoman bureaucracy during the nineteenth century alone is remarkable. The same tendency has multiplied itself in the Succession States of the Ottoman Empire. It is not merely that an extraordinary ramification and specialisation has replaced the primitive division of administration into the four or five chief branches of war and marine, agriculture, trade and foreign policy, internal affairs and education. The administration has also undergone a basic transformation in technique and procedure. Public affairs were conducted for many generations, under the presidency of the ruler or governor, in a public place to which petitioners and observers had free access. Decisions required no preliminary specialist consideration of the case. This enviably uncomplicated form of administration has gradually been superseded in most Eastern countries by the treatment of affairs within and through the Departments to which they belong. A modern Yearbook containing a list of the departments and branches of an Oriental Government will impress the uninformed reader. There is scarcely any difference from the Western countries in respect of the completeness of the individual branches of administration. And in numbers as well the administrative apparatus in the countries of the Orient has now reached remarkable proportions.[40]

CHAPTER V

CHANGES IN LOCAL GOVERNMENT

The General Background

The sources leave very little doubt as to the administrative spirit and integrity of the high officials, supreme judges and divines in a State shaped after this fashion. Hence it is not surprising to find remarkable defects also in the local administration established by law and custom, and in its relations with the central authorities. These defects were bound to lead to grave rifts and cracks in the State structure as soon as the population began to rise against the refusal to satisfy its rights and desires. As for the development of local government, it followed a course parallel with that of the modern State in general.

The structure of political control in the provinces of the Ottoman Empire underwent a thoroughgoing change during the first half of the nineteenth century. The state of things at the beginning of the century constituted the final stage of a development which, like the conditions in other feudal States, led by means of a dissipation of the rights of sovereignty to the virtual break-up of the central authority and its influence in the provinces of the Empire.

The grandees of the Empire, who after the conquest of new territories had been rewarded by the Turkish Sultans with the grant of the taxes from those territories, had in return to provide military aid. For the income from the land tax and other revenue which accrued to them, the feudatories had at first to provide a specified number of soldiers; later they freed themselves from this duty by paying a tribute to the Porte and, thanks to the power at their disposal within their own territories, developed into virtually independent rulers. In this way little princedoms grew up throughout the provinces, and considerable parts of Anatolia, Syria, Lebanon and the Balkan countries became the domains of petty dynasties. Similarly, families in which the honour of tribal chieftainship was hereditary ruled the countries of Iraq and Kurdistan, which were inhabited by tribal confederations. These rights to lordship went far beyond the military fiefs originally provided for in the form of the Turkish *Ziamet* and *Timar*, and practically led to the dissolution of the Empire into a large number of feudal domains independent of or very loosely associated with the imperial centre.

The effect of this state of affairs on the régime in the provinces can easily be imagined. The governors of Damascus, Acre and Baghdad appointed by the Sultan were at the beginning of the century little more than open rebels; those of Antioch and Aleppo were "monsters of cruelty". "In those days putting a wealthy man to death and seizing all his property was an everyday occurrence . . . It had been common for Pashas 'to establish their authority in a new Government' on arrival by cutting off a few heads."[41] It is reported of the last feudal lords (*derebeys*) at Erzurum that they never entered a large town without being accompanied by 500 horsemen. The derebey himself sat in regal fashion on his horse, while the enormous sleeves of his robe reached almost to the ground. At a word from him his followers were prepared to cut into pieces anyone who stood in the way or to carry off a pretty girl to his harem.[42]

There was no influential stratum worthy of the name to face this local despotism. It is understandable that the population of the countryside could not oppose it, yet even in the provincial towns there was scarcely any resistance or organised or persistent counter-pressure against the tyrants.

The first interference with this world of arbitrariness and extreme autocracy on the part of the provincial potentates is to be ascribed to the reformer Mahmud II. The means he employed were hardly scrupulous. In this respect he differed from the preceding despots as little as Mohammed Ali, who was at the same time endeavouring to reform the Egyptian State from the ground up. Such ancient Oriental methods for the removal of political enemies were employed as assassination, murder by poison, or drowning. Property was confiscated, and in addition deliberate slaughter of opponents who defended themselves also served him for the attainment of his objectives. Apart from the fiscal interest which he had in the reform of the Treasury and the eradication of corruption in connection with the taxes, Mahmud's measures were directed first and foremost at restricting the power of the Pashas. Thus the execution of a death sentence was prohibited until it had been confirmed at Constantinople. In addition, local officials were appointed to participate in the administration of the large towns under the direction of the Central Government instead of the notables previously selected by the urban population. Despite great resistance, which often ended in open rebellion, Mahmud relentlessly proceeded to break the power of the great feudal lords and landowners, either by imprisonment, by murder or by threats. The elimination of the Janissaries offered the opportunity to abolish by a daring step the entire feudal system of the Ottoman Empire. In 1831 the great feudatory lords of the State were deprived of their fiefs, State ownership of the land was restored and the former holders were granted an annual income in compensation and settlement. Finally, the introduction of compulsory military service for all Moslem citizens in 1839 established the prerequisite conditions for a people's army capable of fulfilling the functions of the earlier troops who had been levied on a feudal basis.

Organs of Local and Provincial Administration

After the abolition of the feudal system in the more remote provinces and the restriction of the powers of governors in all parts of the Empire through a centralisation of the administration, there remained the wide field of providing for a representation of the population and its interests in the leading institutions of local government. The first steps in this direction taken under Mahmud II made only a slight correction of the existing conditions. Under his successors representative bodies were set up in the provinces, the smaller administrative units and the towns. The laws of 1852, 1858 and 1864 largely provided the foundations for the system of provincial administration existing in the Ottoman Empire up to the outbreak of the First World War. This system was as follows: A Provincial Assembly called *Majlis Umumi* was established in each *Wilayet*, which was the largest administrative unit within the Empire. This administrative Council, which had the character of a provincial assembly of elected representatives, was composed of both Moslems and non-Moslems; and every sub-district had the right to send a representative. These bodies met once a year for a period of forty days at the capital of the *Wilayet*, under the chairmanship of the governor of the province. Two-thirds of the representatives formed a quorum. The functions of the provincial administration included the discussion of such matters as road construction and public works, agriculture, trade and education, so far as these fell within the territory of the province concerned.

In addition to the provincial assembly there were administrative councils under the name of *Majlis Idara* for all the larger administrative units. These corporations had an advisory function and were intended to support the governors in carrying out their duties. Their members were partly elected, partly nominated *ex officio*. Those so nominated included the Mufti and the religious judge, the Treasurer and administrative chief of the district in question. The elected representatives usually consisted of three Moslems and a proportionate number of non-Moslems. The chairman was usually the highest official of the administrative district, who was as a rule the Mutasarrif. The council's functions were administrative and juridical. Questions of taxes, public works, land registration, execution of the tobacco monopoly and the like were among the administrative functions. The legal duties consisted in the investigation of charges brought by the public against Government officials, the bringing of actions against officials and the smoothing out of differences between Government departments; hence they resembled those of an administrative court. The choice of members was made by nomination on the part of the Treasurer and the heads of the various religious communities. Candidates had to be Ottoman subjects paying not less than 150 piastres per annum in taxes who had reached the age of thirty years.

These councils, with largely advisory functions, existed alongside the provincial assembly in every *Wilayet* and in the middle-sized administrative units. Beside them there were district councils under the name *Majlis al-Nahiya* in the small administrative units which were presided over by the Mudir. The Mudir convened four sessions during the year, which usually lasted for a week, and dealt with matters of local importance such as education, road-making, etc.

In the towns there had already been tendencies, under the influence of old Arab ideas, towards a representation of the interests of the population. A developed form of such representation, however, only came about following on the Turkish reform measures in the middle of the nineteenth century. The members of the Municipal Council were elected by direct vote for the period of four years. Their number was from 6 to 12, according to the size of the town. From among the representatives the Government appointed a Chairman of the Council who alone received a salary, all other members acting in an honorary capacity. Half the members were replaced by freshly elected representatives once in two years. Members of the Council had to be landed proprietors. Meetings took place twice a week. The Mayor was the chairman of the executive, and could make appointments with the approval of the

Council. The functions of the Council consisted in the supervision of building, street cleaning, lighting, market control, registration of births and deaths, public health, etc. Every male Ottoman subject aged over 25 years was entitled to vote, if he resided in a town, paid a minimum of 50 piastres in property tax and had a good reputation. The right of being elected was dependent, *inter alia*, on having attained the age of thirty and the payment of a property tax amounting to 100 piastres per annum. The income of the Municipal Council was derived from octrois and other municipal charges.

There was a considerable gap between the *de jure* introduction of the representative bodies and their actual functioning. Contemporary reports, particularly those of independent Western observers, expressed themselves, with few exceptions, in very unfavourable terms regarding the usefulness of the new arrangement. Thus it is reported of the deliberations of the Jerusalem *Majlis* in the middle of the nineteenth century that the true convictions of the members rarely found expression there, "that there is still a lack of moral courage, integrity, sense of honour, love of justice and all other civic virtues. The Moslems are in a large majority. The Christians and Jews are far too cowardly and too few in numbers. The lower rank here are still far too much in awe of the higher. In addition, everybody can be bribed. Votes are seldom taken, for those who dissent prefer to remain silent."[43]

In many cases the existence of the Council provided the all-powerful Pasha with a fresh method for clothing his own will in legitimate garb. Previously the administration of the town could in the last resort appeal direct to the Sublime Porte. "Now the Pasha takes all precautions and does nothing without having the documents signed and sealed by the *Majlis* and it is not difficult to receive documents and seals through his creatures in that assembly. In this way his power has grown even more inviolable than formerly. He does what he likes and merely takes care that his actions are certified as representing the will of the *Majlis*. In this manner he has become even less responsible. Things have remained as they were before. The power has been left in the hands of the mighty Effendis, who continue to look after themselves best, as formerly.[44]

Similar descriptions are found from other regions as well. Thus the British Consul Barker, who was resident in the Orient for more than forty years, sums up his experience as follows: "After twenty years' residence in habitual contact with this Council or

Majlis on public and private business wherever we have resided, we can with truth declare it to have been the most baneful and unfortunate concession, on apparently liberal principles, that could have been made to a country just emerging from anarchy, as the Empire then was.[45]

The difficulties which stood in the way of the co-operation of the population and the establishment of a genuine system of local government in an Oriental country, had already been recognised several decades earlier by the Egyptian reformer Mohammed Ali, who had attempted to overcome them in noteworthy fashion. In 1819 he made the first attempt to subject administrative transactions between the Treasury and European merchants to discussion by a committee of seven persons before they were brought before him for decision. A few years later he introduced larger bodies consisting of the most important civil and military officials with co-opted village Sheikhs in order to discuss with them the measures for the abolition of malpractices and the improvement of the position of the peasants. This Council met night after night in camera for a long time, and was later imitated in Syria on a smaller scale. Some years later again, religious functionaries and representatives of merchants became delegates in the Supreme Council, and the district governors were simultaneously called upon to select village Sheikhs from every district who had to represent the peasants of that district in the Council.[46]

Mohammed Ali's attempts were judged at the time in very varied fashion; either as camouflage for European public opinion or as serious attempts to introduce representative forms of Government. Dodwell is of the opinion that they were neither the one nor the other. In the Middle East administrative affairs were always carried on by a group of officials whose discussions were conducted before the Pasha personally or some other high dignitary. These discussions took place publicly in the presence of a full audience of petitioners and observers. Hence Mohammed Ali merely extended an existing tradition while expecting some benefit for his own administration to result from the cautious application of certain Western governmental methods.

Whatever else may be said regarding the expediency of this form of representation of the population, its educational value for the future was an important factor in the evolution of local self-government. This applies to many other attempts to establish local government bodies and to the work of such bodies, which could be observed in an increasing degree within the territory of the Ottoman Empire from the middle of the nineteenth century onward. Even though these bodies were frequently nothing but a caricature of what the initiators of local government in other countries had had in mind, their influence on the political and social thought of a territory so backward in political consciousness, and suffering from such deep-seated stagnation in public life, should not be under-estimated.

Social and Political Structure of the Population

There were cogent reasons for which the new ideas of self-government could not enjoy any degree of prompt success. Evidence dating from the first decades of the present century still serves clearly to confirm that the real conditions of power and the socio-political structure of the population in the provinces remained unaffected by the reform measures.

Who were the holders of political power, and who exerted the decisive influence on local and provincial administration?

The Palestine Royal Commission Report of 1937 deals briefly with political conditions in Palestine before the First World War. It describes the Turkish régime of those days as a "despotism modified to some extent by the delegation of authority to the leading families in Syria who held estates in Palestine". The situation was not different in Syria, Egypt or Iraq. In the towns the Municipal Councils were the exclusive domain of the urban and rural landlords. In these bodies representatives of artisans or even of workers in general were unknown. These corporations themselves prevented any change in their composition. Without making a breach in this political structure it was impossible for all classes of the population to achieve genuine representation. This conclusion leads us to the question of the type of the classes whose interests were so unequivocally directed in an "anti-democratic" and in a sense also anti-State fashion.

In answering this question, we first meet with the "aristocracy", that materially well-to-do group whom we may regard as the Oriental gentry. In general their material interests were determined by their landed property, which they had originally received as feudal estates or through tax-farming, and afterwards, particularly during the nineteenth century, by skilful exploitation of the distress of peasants and tenants whose land they then acquired by purchase. In addition, this class had an extraordinary influence on the local representative bodies, as is indicated by the following remarks of a contemporary:

"The members of the Mejliss are always the rich (Turkish) landed proprietors . . . They are *de facto* the governors of the country for their own benefit, and they always combine together when any matter is proposed against their collective interests, however secretly inimical they may be to one another. 'We keep the people ignorant and oppressed, in order to be able to govern them, for otherwise how could we govern them?' was told us by Haji Halef Aga, one of the leading members of the Mejliss at Antioch. We could relate many cases of extortion, injustice and violence by this man, always under the legal sanction of the *Mazbatta*."[47]

Whereas the nobility in Western countries frequently served as the protagonists and standard-bearers of the national idea and indeed not infrequently as pioneers of the education and development of the masses, the Oriental noble class in general were opposed to the building-up of a modern State and adopted a hostile or at least an indifferent attitude towards its national function. Their own vested interests, or at best their interest in the prosperity of their clan, left no room for any other considerations and impulses. It nipped in the bud any sense of duty and of service to the State; anything resembling that *noblesse oblige* which was the hallmark of European nobility at the beginning of the evolution of the national State. In Europe also there had assuredly been nobles who watched the growth of the national State with misgiving or indeed with dissatisfaction; since, in accordance with the character of the modern national idea, it would necessarily lead to a diminution of the prerogatives of nobility. Yet many of the Czech counts, the Baltic and Prussian barons, the Hungarian grandees conceived their duty of loyalty towards the affairs of the State and the citizens and peasants of their districts in a manner quite different from that of the feudatories and land-owning class of the Ottoman Empire, who never rose above a restricted clannishness and group egotism.

It is difficult to resist the temptation of ascribing the utter disregard on the part of the nobility for the human requirements of a body social to a fundamental feature of Ottoman statecraft introduced into it in its early phases, namely, the breeding of executive officers and troop leaders from non-Moslem slaves. These were to become the 'human watch-dogs' to keep the Padishah's 'human cattle' in order and his human neighbours at bay. A. H. Lyber (*The Government of the Ottoman Empire in the Time of Suleiman the Magnificent*) and later A. J. Toynbee (*A Study of History*, vol. 3) have dwelt on this significant aspect to explain the extraordinary fact that a tiny band of Nomads, ejected from their native steppe and cast away in an alien environment, did not merely survive but in fact imposed their rule upon a great Christian society.

But we might as well see in this strange instrument of a ruling caste deriving from transplanted slaves one of the main causes for the social weaknesses of the great Oriental Empire. This profession of ruling was to be "reserved almost exclusively for persons who were infidel-born—without its mattering whether their infidel parents happened to be the Padishah's subjects or not—whereas the Padishah's own Muslim co-religionists were ineligible *ex officio religionis*, even if they happened to be the sons of the Ottoman feudal landed gentry who were the Padishah's equals in the sight of God and his companions in arms and even in some sense his social peers. This provision is astonishing because it is an extreme denial of natural expectations to disqualify the members of a conquering community from bearing rule; but, given the ability to enforce this disqualification, as it actually was enforced during at least two centuries of Ottoman history (*circa* A.D. 1365–1565) its utility is manifest. The Ottoman system of training a 'human watch-dog' made such severe demands upon human nature that only an individual who had been torn out of his own hereditary social environment . . . could be expected to submit to it. Now of all the human materials at the Padishah's disposal, the least tractable were the children of his free Muslim feudatories with their pride of race and religion, their local connexions, and their family solidarity . . . Hence the ban upon the admission of free Muslims; and this drastic policy was justified by the sequel; for, when the free Muslims did at last force an entry into the household, the system did break down.

At the time when it broke down through the pressure of the Moslem feudal gentry who wanted to share the privileges of that ruling caste, the latter's influence and methods of domination were already too deeply rooted; the utter disregard for the needs of the population had by then become a firm tradition.

Turning to the second class, that of the intelligentsia, who played so great a part in the formation of the modern European State, it is evident that in the Middle East this group, which was numerically so much smaller, could not exercise anything like the far-reaching influence of the intellectuals in the European national States. The flourishing world of science which had developed in Europe since the Renaissance was not to be found in the Orient. In leaving scholastic and churchmanlike thinking behind, the new scientific approach of the West stimulated minds to unremitting criticism of the spiritual heritage of bygone ages and to fruitful new knowledge. In the Orient the development of this trend of mind was checked by the great influence of the clerical class who were, as a rule, interested in the conservation of religious, political and scientific tradition and made every effort to stifle any indications of the growth of a new concept of State and politics. Here, too, there is a striking antithesis to the clergy of the West with their delight in knowledge and progress, that group which so often has decisively influenced revolutionary thought in the political and social fields. No impulses towards the development of a new State form came from here either.

The difference in the socio-political position of the middle classes is particularly striking. The self-conscious burghers of the medieval towns of Europe, the proud artisans whose guilds largely determined the fate of their towns not only economically but also politically, and their modern successors, the pioneers and standard-bearers of the industrial and civic revolutions, are types who will be sought in vain in the Oriental town. Here citizens and artisans constitute an economically important element in the population, but have no political influence and, even after the great transformation in methods of production has already begun to threaten the structure of Oriental society, show themselves anxiously conservative maintainers of traditional forms of life and economy; incapable of changing their position by their own strength and thereby gaining their due share in the administration of political affairs. The entrepreneurial functions within the Oriental economic society of that period passed increasingly into the hands of elements that were not of local origin, Greeks, Armenians, Jews, and Europeans. Arabs and Turks are seldom to be found as entrepreneurs of the type which in Europe created the conditions for their successful activities, to no small degree on account of their political influence.

Finally come the peasants, who here as elsewhere constituted, numerically speaking, the basis of the population. Until the very recent past if not up to the present time it has been particularly true of them that they have been indifferent if not opposed to the State; that to an appeal on the part of the State to fulfil their duties they reacted with a sense of animosity, fear and an absolute lack of understanding. Everyone who had an opportunity of observing the attitude of the rural population in the Ottoman Empire, was astounded at their extreme political bluntness and their tendency to regard the State as merely an apparatus for the collection or extortion of taxes. The feeling of patriotic devotion towards the State, of the solidarity of all citizens within the framework of the State entity, was entirely absent. Mrs. Finn states in her description of the Palestine fellahin of some two generations ago that neither a sense of unity nor any kind of patriotic spirit was to be found among them. In a Government publication as late as the year 1938 we read: ". . . the Fellah has no trust in any Government. Every action of the 'Hukuma' (Government) is regarded by him as a trick to extort more taxation or to attain some other malicious end".[48]

If such was the situation in an area which has always been relatively open to Western influence, it is easy to imagine the mentality of the peasants in the more remote regions of the extensive Ottoman Empire. This non-political and non-State attitude is even more characteristic of the Beduin population, whose incorporation in the centrally administered State actually constitutes one of the most difficult internal political tasks of the unitary State of today. The passive attitude of the peasants is here transformed into an active animosity, and it has proved necessary to take very incisive steps in order to accustom these groups to any kind of bearable relations to the State authorities.

In this respect important initial measures were taken by the Turkish reformer Midhat Pasha during the second half of the nineteenth century. In Iraq he endeavoured to replace the unproductive efforts of the earlier rulers to achieve the submission of the great Sheikhs by a new policy designed to alter fundamentally the manner of life of the Beduin tribes by means of their settlement on the land. An account of this will be found below (Chapter XXXIV.)

The political régime of the Oriental State was, for the major part of the Islamic period, based on the rule of large landowners over the small landowners or landless classes. The great degree of concentration of landed property in the possession of large landowners has up to the present given the Middle Eastern State the character of a class State, resembling that of the feudal States of Europe during the early Middle Ages. This resemblance can be observed not only in the analogous spiritual foundation, as expressed in the unity of political and religious community, but is found to at least an equal degree in the absence of all political influence, the non-existence of any representation of the cultural and economic interests of the landless population.

This state of affairs applied not only to the relations between the ruling class and the local population in the provinces. It repeated itself in the urban areas, where a small group of landlords directed the fate of the town without any mandate on the part of the great majority of its inhabitants, and also by the relations between the central government and the representative bodies of the distant provinces. As a result, the connections between the masses and their government have remained up to the present exceptionally loose; indeed by their very nature they may be described as exceedingly questionable. The despotic régime of the Oriental State with its oppression and exploitation of the majority of the population called out in the course of time a completely non-political attitude towards the Government and its institutions on the part of the masses dependent on the land. The strong link between the modern citizen and the modern national State, the sense of a personal and collective relation to the régime, its institutions and demands, could not grow on this soil. Indeed, to go further, the national minorities whose members achieved economic power in the towns were of necessity driven to join oppositional currents which worked towards the State's downfall.

CHAPTER VI

PUBLIC FINANCE IN THE MIDDLE EAST

The Inheritance: Historical Survey

A review of the development of State finances in the Islamic Orient must start with an account of the historical and social background. The Islamic State began as a community for war and defence, growing out of an association of tribes and maintained during its early period chiefly for belligerent purposes. A differentiation of State functions began only later and gradually, and even then its scope was restricted to minor and irrelevant interests. The central point of its range of functions during that first stage was territorial expansion, involving the necessity of constant military preparedness.

This aim mainly determined the structure of Islamic public finance in those days. The State budget was largely that of an army, and this to a considerable degree determined the manner in which it was satisfied. The organisation of a military aristocracy shaped the requirements of State and society. The policy of State revenue, i.e., of taxation, was therefore adapted to correspond to this objective. It could not be orientated towards a peace-time economy, as the most urgent purpose of finance, the upkeep of the conquerors, made all other functions appear of secondary importance.

In the reckless pursuit of their financial requirements, the Islamic conquerors frequently did severe harm to and sometimes completely destroyed the sources of taxation. The absence of every responsible interest in the maintenance of taxable capacity and of considerations of fiscal justice towards the taxpayers characterised the attitude of that initial period. This attitude, to be sure, is not peculiar to the Orient alone, but may be found wherever the dictates of permanent preparedness for war have conditioned or now condition the finances of a State. Here, however, it found particularly favourable soil; the overwhelming importance of the warlike Beduin and their leading strata during the early period of Islamic expansion virtually thrust the interests of the settled population into the background.

The countries which became attached as conquered territory to the old original Islamic lands were adopted into the new State association only as members of inferior legal status, like those members of their population who did not adopt Islam.

The Islamic State idea itself was specifically based on this distinction between Moslem and non-Moslem and the principles of differentiation, which played their part also in other branches of State life, had their principal effect on the finances of the State. The defeated non-Moslem peoples were there in order to satisfy the requirements of the military and conqueror class. They had to pay a poll-tax *ad personam* as well as a kind of tribute for the land which they worked; that is, they had to carry the actual economic burden in relation to the Treasury. On the other hand, they were excluded from the advantages and usufruct of the Islamic victories. As against this the Moslems themselves had only to pay the tithe; apart from this they had a legitimate claim to any booty which they might gain during the conquests.

The payments and dues levied on the subject peoples, in so far as they derived from the yield of the soil, became a real charge which, theoretically at least, permanently determined the character of the property. Landed areas which were subject to taxes of this kind were constituted a separate class of land (*Kharaj* lands), which was distinguished from the other categories known as *Osher* lands; the latter were less rigorously treated, and were later recognised as full property, apart from the lighter degree of taxation to which they were subjected. With the continuous expansion of the conquered territories and hence likewise of the religion of Islam, an important change set in. The rapidly growing number of fresh converts wished to secure for themselves the economic advantages associated with the new faith, and in particular to liberate themselves from the heavy tribute through their rise into the privileged caste. The dominant Islamic stratum were not interested in this. But any prohibition of conversion would have contradicted the religious tendencies of Islam, which did not wish to forbid anybody to confess the faith of Mohammed, and offered free admission to all converts. So another way was chosen. The freedom of the upper class from taxation was abolished in order to place old and new Moslems on the same basis in respect of their fiscal duties.[49]

However, being chiefly interested in the later financial history of Islamic countries, we need not go into the rather involved problems of Islamic finance during the Middle Ages. To understand the main lines of recent developments in the Orient and their background, we must, above all, deal with the following questions: Who had the power and authority to impose taxes? And thereafter: What was a taxable object and a source of taxation?

Since the sources of taxation in the agricultural countries of the East consisted chiefly of the produce of the soil, the Islamic ministers of finance had to base their financial policy on this fact. In so doing, they reverted to principles and methods established by earlier administrations. Among these methods a particular place was taken by tax-farming and its peculiar association with the development of the Oriental feudal system. The defectively developed technique of tax-collection always favoured the institution of tax-farming in primitive stages of State and social development. Since the State itself had no suitable instruments available, it transferred the right of collecting taxes to intermediaries, and for this purpose ceded to them part of its power of taxation. In return, the tax-farmers undertook to recompense the State by paying it part of their receipts as a lump sum.

The Islamic authorities took over tax-farming as a heritage from antiquity, and kept it alive together with other antique legacies almost up to the present day. Together with the feudal system of land tenure, which however was abolished in the Ottoman Empire more than a hundred years ago, it exercised a lasting influence on the entire social structure of the Moslem countries. Although the forms of tax-farming changed in the course of centuries, and their development, together with that of the closely associated feudal system, often differed widely from one country to another, their effect on State and society is still observable today.[50]

How was it that these institutions were able to gain so much importance in the Orient? Let us first consider the external factors. For the leader of the State association which had to be financed it became increasingly difficult, as the conquered region grew larger, to find and to supervise responsible Treasury officials and organs for collection in the various provinces and districts. This problem proved all the more important in the wide expanses of Oriental countries, where, in view of the huge distances, the temptation is particularly great for the officials to enrich themselves while collecting the taxes, or even simply not to remit the receipts. One of the means of preventing this was to free the central authority from this function of collecting the money, and to entrust it instead to the administrators in the provinces. This step towards a far-reaching decentralisation was taken, as a rule, by investing the chief of the province with a financial authority of his own. At the same time, however, this prepared the way—particularly at times when the central authority began to shrink—for the advancement of political claims to dominion on the strength of such fiscal powers; though these powers originally derived from considerations of financial technique. This form of relationship between the provincial governor and the central government, which was tantamount to a kind of investiture of the former with the revenue from taxation, constituted one form of the development of a quasi-feudal pattern.[51] Apart from this, however, domains were also directly conferred as fiefs with lifelong and hereditary rights in the land. The following must be borne in mind in order to appreciate the importance of the taxation factor in this connection.

Even prior to the Islamic conquest the administrative apparatus of taxation in the Oriental provinces had been based on the co-operation of the large landed proprietors on the one hand, and of the peasants living together in village communities on the other. The Arabs continued this practice. The new lords became possessed of the land by causing the vacant landed properties to be transferred to themselves as *Muqta* (fiefs) against payment of taxes on those properties; particularly those lands from the one-time State domains which had been occupied by the conquering armies. The form in which the usufruct of these large estates was transferred by the Arab State leaders, was also in point of motive very similar to the hereditary tenure in which fiscal considerations played their part, as in the Byzantine *Emphyteusis*. The question of the nature of the property right in such lands remained of secondary importance. "The State was only interested to see that the rights or the tribute were correctly paid; it did not concern itself with the juridical theory according to which such lands were to be disposed of only as hereditary property, but leased its domain also for short periods or for life." (Becker).

Apart from these lands, which as large estates were subject to the payment of rent, there were also the areas which belonged to the village communities. These bodies were themselves collectively responsible for the payment of the taxes, so that the individual member actually had no possible chance of evading taxation. Naturally the community itself tried to make sure that it would not be injured by the evasion of payment on the part of its members. In this regard the village peasants were at a grave disadvantage as compared with the landed proprietors. The latter, indeed, also had to pay taxes; yet in view of their standing and influence, both in the Byzantine Empire and at all later times, they were assessed at far lower rates when the taxes were fixed. Still more important was the fact that the domains could constitute taxation districts of their own, and hence were not jointly responsible for any non-payment of taxes on the part of their peasant neighbours. For both categories collection of the taxes took place through tax-farming. Since however the landed proprietor likewise collected the land-tax falling on his property from the peasant settled on his land, his attitude tended to approximate to that of the tax-farmer who had leased the collection of taxes from the village communities; it might even come about that the two functions were united, as the landed proprietors themselves frequently took successful steps to acquire this right. The tax-farmer, who was responsible for the payment of a fixed sum to the provincial Treasury and who retained part of the taxes as compensation for his services, became identified with the person of the landed proprietor, who had to collect the taxes on the lands he had received from the State and could call for State protection in return. "In both cases the actual tax-payers were the cultivators; *Muqtaji* and tax-farmers were only the intermediary links between the peasant and the State." The areas of tax-farming and of hereditary lease merged into one another.

The increasing urgency in the financial situation of the State brought about a condition of affairs in which the two last-named groups, the "feudatories" (*Muqtaji*) and the tax-farmers, were finally compelled to render military service in view of their functions as tax-guarantors.[52] The incapacity of the Government to pay the troops regularly out of its revenue from the provinces resulted in military dignitaries being provided in an increasing degree with land as security for their claims for pay. In return they were then obliged to join the army with troops and equipment of their own.

We have now seen how the close connection between tax-farming and the feudal system came about. This leaves the question why tax-farming, which was so closely interwoven with feudatory conditions, remained in existence longer than the feudal system. This question is particularly deserving of clarification since voices were raised very early in opposition to tax-farming in clear recognition of the damage done by that practice.[53] The reasons for its maintenance are not be be sought solely in the geographical and political difficulties, outlined above, which presented themselves when the central authorities wished to collect taxes from an extensive and thinly settled empire. For had this been the case, tax-farming would definitely have been abolished when the modern opening-up of Oriental countries began, more particularly as repeated attempts were made to do away with it in the course of the nineteenth century. Hence it is clear that its utilisation or otherwise by the apparatus of the State depended on other factors as well. Tax-farming corresponds to a specific stage in the development of the State apparatus and bureaucracy; its abolition presupposes not merely a powerful central authority and a well-developed transport and communications system, but also a trained and reliable body of civil servants and a closer relationship between those liable to taxation and the State. During the centuries following the discovery of the sea-route to India, when attempts to revive the barter economy began to increase, the tax-farmers exercised a number of very important functions in the financial system of the State, as storekeepers, transporters, and administrators of the taxes paid by the peasants in kind. Without the tax-farmers the State would have been dependent on the peasants alone, and they were entirely unsuited for any such functions.

Hence the system of tax-farming was maintained until the very recent past. The technique followed was to auction the function of tax-collection to the highest bidder, repeating the process systematically down to the smallest regional tax units, the villages. The increasingly refined extension of the procedure and its development as a profession finally led to a systematic bleeding white of the peasants concerned. In the nineteenth century the abolition of tax-farming was first announced by the Sublime Porte in 1839, but was not achieved. A second attempt to do away with it, made in 1879–80, likewise proved unsuccessful; only in 1917 could the Turkish authorities permit themselves to attack the ancient institution once again. The effect of its abolition on the State machinery can be gauged from the fact that the introduction of tax collection by the State in 1918–19 led to the appointment of 53,000 new officials.[54]

The main features of the financial heritage, as outlined above, may be summed up as follows:—

(1) In its early days the dominant principle of State in Islam, namely the division of the population into two groups, was

also introduced into the financial administration of the Moslem States. On the one side stood the faithful, who enjoyed a series of fiscal privileges; on the other were those who did not participate in the military expeditions but were instead called upon to finance the State household by considerable taxes. The implementation of this principle led to complicated relations in the sphere of property rights and land classification. Later on, the original connection of this classification with fiscal considerations became obliterated.

(2) The most important part of Oriental State revenue almost down to the present time consisted of direct taxes imposed on agriculture, trade and handicrafts. The receipts themselves were for the greater part in kind; a circumstance which involved considerable losses and administrative difficulties for the fiscal authorities, although this form of payment had certain advantages for the peasants. The form of collection was tax-farming.

(3) The financial requirements for military expeditions and for the maintenance of the despotic Oriental Courts dominated the entire taxation policy. That policy was increasingly diverted to tax-farming on a feudal pattern as the money economy of the Oriental State deteriorated. As a result, the feudal system, one of the most important institutions of the State in those days, assumed a predominantly fiscal character. This is also one of the chief reasons for the durability of feudal conditions in the Orient, where they have largely determined the political and social constitution down to our own day. Nothing was more fatal for economic development, particularly in the Oriental town, than the dominant position of the feudal ruling class. At the time when it co-operated with the State, every attempt at developing an independent urban citizenry was nipped in the bud.

Nineteenth Century Reforms

It is doubtful whether anything can have been more inimical to the spirit of Oriental despotism than the submission of public accounts covering the receipts of the State and their employment. For it was an essential element of the despotic régime to be able to dispose of public resources without any interference or supervision. Any admission of financial responsibility, particularly in written form, seemed impossible to the despot. Apart from this, any such publication implied a high level of public accounting and finance. As late as the nineteenth century the elementary requirements even of primitive fiscal book-keeping and financial administration were not satisfied in Turkey. In particular the principle of centralised and co-ordinated fiscal accountancy had not yet been introduced. There were numerous Treasuries, each responsible for its own field, all existing alongside one another, which rendered no account either to themselves or to a central authority. Apart from estimates or occasional notes on the financial position of one or other of these Treasuries, there was an absence of documents which could give a general picture of the state of Turkish finances in those days. Estimates dating from the year 1850 give the total income at between 141 and 168 million francs. Of this amount 50 millions came from the tithe, 46 millions from the land-tax. Hence 96 millions or 60 per cent. were derived from these two agricultural taxes. Indirect taxes produced 34·4 millions and customs duties 19·7 millions. Expenditure was estimated at 173 million francs. Pride of position was held by the items of war (69·3 millions), marine (8·6 millions), and the civil list (17·3 millions).[55] A number of receipts and expenditures, to be sure, were not as yet included in this budget. A decade later a State budget was published for the first time in which income was estimated at 346 millions and expenditure at 327 millions. Here too, pretty much the same distribution of the individual heads of income was given. The taxes bearing upon agriculture far outweighed the others. Of the expenditure no less than 120 millions went on war and marine, 27·7 millions to the civil list and 85·6 millions to public debts. As against this enormous allocation for military purposes and the Court, expenditure for the welfare of the population was almost non-existent. The budgets for trade, education and public works remained at less than 1 per cent. of the total expenditure at the time. That corruption was rooted in the administration from top to bottom has already been clearly indicated.

The state of the Turkish financial administration in itself did not change in any considerable degree till shortly before the First World War, although repeated attempts at a reform were made earlier. The defect ran through the entire apparatus, beginning with the preparation of the budget, which was regarded as a mere estimate with no binding character on the executive authorities, down to the absence of the most essential basic data and evidence for the assessment of the main taxes, tithes and land-tax; for there were no reliable land registers or cadastral surveys. Since in addition, as mentioned above, the principle of centralised Treasury administration was not in force, no central control of income nor any real balancing of the budget was possible. The receipts of a number of branches of the Administration were not even shown, but were used as an internal cover for the expenditure of those branches. A system of sur-taxes supplementary to the main taxes served to provide the means for special expenditures, whose amount was always fluctuating.

What were the financial resources of the Ottoman Empire in the nineteenth century? First came the taxes on the yield of the soil, which had their origin in Islamic law. The two most important kinds of tax, which dominated the financial systems of one-time Turkish countries almost down to the present day, were the Tithe (*Osher*) and the Land-Tax (*Kharaj*).

The *Osher*, or "Tithe", is a tax on the gross yield of the soil. It amounted originally to either 5 or 10 per cent., according as the area taxed was irrigable or not. Both the amount of the tax and the method of collection underwent frequent changes in the course of the centuries.

The *Kharaj* was a land-tax collected from the property of those who did not become Moslems at the time of the conquest or with whom peace had been concluded. Tax rates on *Kharaj* lands were a great deal higher than those on *Osher* lands. As a tax on the yield of the soil the *Kharaj* amounted to between 20 and 30 per cent. of the gross yield, according to the quality of the land. In addition, the *Kharaj* was also levied as a tax on area.[56]

Besides these there was, further, a poll tax, which was levied on all non-Moslems except fire-worshippers and heathens. The amount of this tax was graded in such a way that the rich paid twice as much as those of average means, and those of average means twice as much as the poor. Women, priests, and old people were exempt from this tax.[57]

The State budget was financed, in addition, from a series of other sources, the yields from which did not have the character of taxes proper. Thus the war spoils tax played a certain part. The State took 20 per cent. of all spoils won in war, and employed it for the poor and orphans and for maintaining mosques. The troops divided the rest among themselves.

A further source of income was found in the tributes of the vassal States, the most important of which were Wallachia, Moldavia, Egypt and Serbia. Lastly, a variety of imposts developed on the European model, such as stamp duties, fees and payments for licences, legal and administrative services, etc.

The abolition in 1839 of the feudal system, by means of which part of the State's requirements, i.e. military service and equipment, had been provided by the feudal lords and chieftains, led to a considerable increase in the importance of direct taxation, which thereafter served as the basis of the fiscal system of the Ottoman Empire.

The constitutional reforms of the nineteenth century were aimed at the transformation of Turkey from an Oriental despotism into a modern constitutional State. At the same time they also constituted stages in the transformation and modernisation of Turkish public finances. The principles of the Decree of Guelhane included important guiding lines for the reform of the tax system. The non-Moslems, who felt themselves to be treated in a particularly unjust fashion by the existing taxation system, were promised that as a result of this edict their excessive taxation would be ameliorated. The poll tax was converted into a tax levied on the non-Moslem community as a whole, and its distribution among the individual taxpayers was determined by men who enjoyed the confidence of the non-Moslems. Furthermore, the system of tax-farming was, not for the first time, condemned as injurious, and its abolition was in principle decided upon.

The setback experienced during the Crimean War led to an interruption in the execution of the reform measures. Nevertheless, the reform decree of 1856 again proclaimed new measures in the field of financial administration, and completed certain of the acts envisaged in the Guelhane edict. Its importance lay in the elimination of various defects, particularly in the collection of the tithe, and in the introduction of communal taxation reforms and also of budgetary accounting. In spite of this, extraordinary difficulties had still to be overcome while reorganising and consolidating the financial system. The revenue of the Ottoman State did not suffice to satisfy requirements arising from the modernisation of the administration and the army. If it had, in addition, been true in times of peace that the budget was balanced only by dint of great effort, the frequent war entanglements reduced the Empire to such a state of need that it could not surmount its difficulties save by mobilising extraordinary sources of income. These consisted in foreign loans.

The year 1854 was an important date in Turkish finances; for it was then that Turkey raised its first foreign loan, amounting to

55 million francs. The subsequent epoch is characterised by the fact that with the continuation of this loan policy, which was very unsatisfactory in its financial yield, Turkey's indebtedness, and hence its dependence on foreign interests, which advanced the money, became steadily greater. This is not the place to discuss the external political consequences of this situation. Its effect on the financial and tax administration, at any rate, was very marked. The foreign creditors did not rest satisfied with promises for a regular repayment of their capital and interest, but assured themselves of the fulfilment of their claims by the establishment of a European debt administration in the midst of the Oriental State. This administration, shaped on the Western model, was provided with considerable powers, and by its apparatus supervised the entire financial activities of Turkey; in brief, it functioned as a State within the State.

At the same time, however, it also brought to the knowledge of the local population and the native officials measures and methods which the latter would scarcely have been able to learn in any other way. Although the Moslem State administration continued to operate with its own financial apparatus, it could not ignore the existence of the European Debt administration. The influence here, though slow, was as undeniable as in other branches of public and social life. Mention has already been made of the legal system, where the Mixed Courts exerted an increasing influence on the legal decisions of the local Courts of Justice. The same applies to the school system, in which the modern schools, mostly established by foreigners, stimulated the renewal of the native school system and enriched their programme of study. To regard the financial advisers merely as sponsors of foreign interests would, therefore, fail to do justice to the problems involved in the situation at the time; the financial policy of that régime cannot be adequately appraised, if it is viewed solely from the aspect of indebtedness and the relinquishing of the State's authority in respect of finance.

Despite the extraordinary malpractices which accompanied the raising of loans, the capital import of those times exercised an important function in the development of the Turkish system of communications, in the erection of numerous communal enterprises and the exploitation of concessions. The first stage of the Europeanisation of the Orient was made possible thanks to this influx of capital.

SECTION II

THE MIDDLE EASTERN STATE AFTER THE FIRST WORLD WAR

CHAPTER VII

CONSEQUENCES OF THE LIQUIDATION OF THE OTTOMAN EMPIRE

The First World War established a number of fundamental political facts which altered the State structure of the Middle East from the ground up. At the same time it would be false to regard this transformation as exclusively an effect of the war; indeed, the war may be regarded as merely the factor which started the avalanche. The peace treaties only set a seal on what had long been envisaged in more or less vague contours by the national movements and currents in this part of the world. Hence the significance of that war for the political fate of the Orient lies in the fact that it proved a kind of lever which released the explosive force of the national idea. The victorious Powers, it is true, succeeded in utilising these forces likewise for the attainment of their own objectives.

The following survey does not aim at enumerating all the individual historical data that mark the development of the State in the Middle East following upon the First World War. It is restricted to an analysis of the most important transformations, to wit, the changes in the structure of the State.

Changes in the Political Map as well as in the Composition of the Population

The most decisive event that started the transmutation of the Middle Eastern States was the collapse of the group of Powers to which the Ottoman Empire belonged. When the Armistice of Mudros was signed on October 30, 1918, the framework which held together the centrifugal countries and peoples of that Empire was broken. Some years before, the English, French and Russian Agreement of February 16, 1916, regarding the partition of Turkey had marked out the guiding lines for the reorganisation of the Ottoman area after the termination of hostilities, and had prepared the way for the establishment of the semi-independent Succession States. The first to crystallise was a new Turkish rump State which, with the exception of a small area in Europe, was practically restricted to Anatolia proper. Mustapha Kemal's removal to Ankara, which took place in December, 1919, symbolised the change. His purpose was to shift the centre of gravity of the new State to the centre of the country, which was difficult of access, and away from Istanbul, which had hitherto been the focus of European influence.

The consolidation of this new State, from which the powerful young Turkish Republic was later to develop, took several years. It received its most effective impulse at the time that it was most gravely threatened, which was when the Great Powers on the one hand, and the then ambitious Greece on the other, believed that they could establish a foothold in Anatolia; but by so doing they called out the forces of Turkey to a last victorious resistance.

This victory likewise marked the conclusion of the internal struggle which had meanwhile developed in Turkey between the former holders of State power, who rallied round the Sultan, and the revolutionary leaders of the new Turkey. Thus the Treaty of Sèvres, though signed on August 10, 1920, by the delegates of the Osmanli Empire, was not ratified by the Great National Assembly which opened at Ankara on April 23, 1920, under the leadership of Mustapha Kemal.

The rise of a new Turkey in the old homeland of the Turks was a bitter disappointment for Greece, which had regarded the realisation of its old dream of the establishment of a new Byzantine Empire as already fulfilled. Greece, supported by England, endeavoured to realise its plans by force of arms, but suffered decisive defeats in the famous battles of Inönue and Saqariya. When the repeated attempts to make peace with Greece proved unsuccessful, the Greeks were defeated and almost annihilated on August 30, 1922, at Dumlupinar, and soon after Izmir and Western Anatolia were freed from all Greek troops. Then followed the conclusion of the Mudania Armistice on October 11, 1922, and, on July 24, 1923, the Treaty of Lausanne, which provided the definite foundations for the establishment of the new Turkish State.

The remaining countries of the one-time Ottoman Empire were transformed into a number of new, and for the time being dependent, countries which were placed under Mandatory régime. These were Syria, the Mandate for which was entrusted to France, and the territories of Palestine, Transjordan and Iraq, which were placed under British Mandate. The result of this, reduced to figures, was as follows: the former total area of 1,794,900 square kilometres, with a population of 20·3 millions, was divided among the following territorial units: Anatolia and European Turkey, 763,000 square kilometres; Iraq, 453,500; Syria, 202,500; Palestine and Transjordan, 117,000; other Arab lands, 259,000.[58]

Egypt's status as a vassal state of Turkey, which even before the war existed only on paper, and the legal sovereignty of the Sultan, came to a definite end. Cyprus, which had likewise been bound to the Sublime Porte by the payment of tribute, became a British Crown Colony.

The New Principles that Shaped the Development of the Middle Eastern State After the First World War

The political development of the Middle East after the First World War was largely determined by the realisation of the following three principles:—

(*a*) The principle of nationality;
(*b*) The safeguarding of the interests of the victorious Powers;
(*c*) The realisation of special commitments towards certain nationalities.

What did the establishment of the principle of nationality mean for State development in the Middle East? To begin with, it replaced a large and comprehensive State-mosaic by a number of so-called Succession States in which, at least in part, lived a nationally homogeneous population. The division of a large area into smaller political units led, as everywhere else, to the establishment of new customs and administrative frontiers, within which autonomous cultural and economic interests grew up. It led also to the formation of new State centres which endeavoured to develop a maximum of independent State life in their new territorial units. In view of the wide differences between this development in Turkey proper on the one hand, and in the Arab succession states on the other, we propose to treat these developments separately for the two territorial complexes.

Egypt

Egypt constituted an entity of her own, and the path of her development differed from that of the aforementioned areas. In the degree of her dependence, Egypt occupied a kind of intermediate stage between the independent Turkish Republic and the

Arab Succession States which, by the criteria of international law, were then still considered incapable of enjoying sovereignty.

In Egypt, too, it was the strength of the nationalist idea which finally brought about the abolition of foreign rule within the State. But this was achieved neither by the overthrow of the former régime and a war of liberation, as in the case of Turkey, nor through compliance with the prescriptions of a superior international institution, as in the case of the mandated areas. Egypt's independence was won through a protracted struggle, the outcome of which seemed often enough rather doubtful.

Notwithstanding the many changes in her political fate, Egypt was the only country in the Middle East to succeed in maintaining, in general, her position as a political and administrative unit during the past hundred years. Her relationship to foreign powers during this period underwent numerous and sometimes far-reaching modifications. After acquiring the status of an independent country through the efforts of Mohammed Ali, Egypt was again nominally incorporated in the Ottoman Empire after that ruler's death in 1841. As a Turkish province, she was once more subjected to Ottoman influence, notably in the cultural sphere. Her link with that Empire failed, however, to prevent the military intervention of Great Britain, whose armed forces entered Egypt in 1882, thirty-two years before the First World War. Thenceforward British influence grew until on December 18, 1914, Egypt was proclaimed a British protectorate. During the whole period from the first occupation of the country by British troops until several years after the end of the First World War Egypt was under a dual political régime; namely, an Oriental one which held the theoretical sovereignty, and alongside it a British control apparatus which in fact directed the political and administrative affairs of the country.

These conditions and their background proved most conducive to the development of the Egyptian national movement, which kept on growing until, immediately after the end of the 1914–18 war, it burst into a series of clashes and revolutionary acts. British policy then reached the conclusion that it might be better to protect British interests by the grant of certain concessions rather than to rely on armed power alone. At the end of February, 1922, the independence of Egypt was proclaimed in a unilateral declaration made by the British Government. This put an end to Egypt's status as a protected power; but in regard to a number of vital questions such as, for instance, her defence from foreign attack, and the position of minorities and of foreigners and their separate jurisdiction, matters were left *in statu quo*. This arrangement, by which certain sovereign rights remained in the hands of a foreign power, did not satisfy the Egyptians, and they demanded a bilateral treaty on the basis of full equality.

The struggle of Egypt for full independence continued for fourteen years until the signing of the Anglo-Egyptian Treaty in 1936. During the same period the country was thrown into a heavy and protracted internal conflict which arose around the issue of the constitution and the democratic representation of the people. There were several parties in this struggle: the British Government, the Egyptian King, the various factions and popular groupings and the fairly influential circle of politicians who did not always identify themselves with either the King or the political parties. The many vicissitudes of Egypt's constitutional life and the varying forms it assumed reflect the changing influence of these groups.

It was only at intervals that the Egyptian Constitution of April, 1923, was put into effect, although it continued, theoretically speaking, to be valid until 1930. The popular currents, which found their most vivid expression in the Wafd party and represented the demand for independence from England as well as the claims of the people as against the King and the political vested interests, were gaining in strength, and finally carried their point. Before then the Egyptian Parliament was dissolved again and again: in 1924, 1925, 1928, and 1930. The Constitution was likewise suspended many times until, in 1930, it was altogether abolished and the Parliament dispersed. The new Constitution contained many modifications in the electoral law to the disadvantage of the masses. Theoretically, the new Constitution did not infringe either the sovereign rights of the people or the form of the constitutional monarchy. But the powers under the Constitution were delivered into the hands of the King and of the Cabinet which was dependent on the King.

The intention of the sponsors of the new Constitution was to strengthen the influence of the King, who tended to take account of the British attitude more than did any of the other parties concerned. But shortly afterwards it became clear that there was no ousting the Wafd from their powerful political position. The King could not overcome public opinion, which was sharply opposed to the new Constitution and to the indefinite postponement of the Treaty of Independence with England. In December,

1934, the new Constitution of 1930 was abolished, and the Parliament dissolved. A year later, in December, 1935, the old Constitution of 1923 was again in force. At last the time had come for the conclusion of the Treaty with England. The Agreement, which was signed in August, 1936, marked the victorious conclusion of the first stage of Egypt's struggle for complete independence. Under the terms of the Treaty, England undertook to work for the abolition of the Capitulations. She fulfilled her promise a year later at the Montreux Conference, where the Powers with capitulatory rights agreed to their abrogation after a transitional period of twelve years. Thus ended the period of Egypt's external struggle, and the principle of nationality scored another success.

While assuming all the features of an independent State in her external relations, Egypt achieved no more than a modest degree of stabilisation in her internal social structure and her home policy. Here the heritage of the Oriental régime still largely prevails, and there is reason to believe that this contest between the New and the Old, between the forces of yesterday and those of tomorrow, will continue for a long time to come.

CHAPTER VIII

THE NEW TURKEY

THE EXCHANGE OF POPULATIONS

The measures for the Westernisation of the Middle Eastern State were until the First World War incapable of producing more than an external and at most ostensible adaptation to the European model; though this degree of adaptation in itself constituted a considerable advance as compared with the preceding situation. The overwhelming majority of the population remained entirely alien to the new ideas. They were too strongly tied to their old-established political and religious forms and traditions to be able to constitute a nation in the modern sense of the word. It was here that the revolutionary ideology of the new Turkish leadership came in with a view to bringing about a change. The vertex and the administrative apparatus required to be transformed; over and above this, however, a population was needed capable of understanding the objectives of the new State, prepared to identify itself with them, and to become a willing partner in the foreign and internal policies of its country. The often extreme and intemperate measures which aimed at arousing a new national feeling, a new Turkish State enthusiasm and a new Turkish culture, must be understood in this sense. These objectives are clearly mirrored in the constitutional development of post-war Turkey. Prior to this, however, another undertaking was decided upon which more than any other served to create the conditions for the establishment and growth of a nationally homogeneous State.

This measure, of signal importance for the whole internal and external policy of the new Turkey, was the exchange of populations between Turkey and Greece. Although not the sole case in which one of the complicated national problems of Oriental lands was solved by a population transfer, it was the largest in scope.[59] The Greco-Turkish exchange of population is the logical exploitation of the experience gained by the Ottoman Empire and the young New Turkey in connection with the existence of a large Greek minority within their boundaries. The success of these extraordinary measures was largely due to the fact that the principle of population transfer was made an essential component in the peace treaty between Greece and Turkey. The number of

Greeks who left Turkey during the initial period was 1,300,000; the number of Turks brought back to Turkey was 400,000. Even before the conclusion of the Treaty of Lausanne proper, the obligatory exchange of populations had been provided for in a separate Convention, dated January 30, 1923.[60] The elimination of the Greek population from the territories of the new State solved the grave problems involved in the presence of an influential and numerically strong national group, whose economic alertness and understanding were frequently far higher than those of the Turkish element.

Important Data of the New Constitution

The Great National Assembly of the new Turkish State rightly recognised that without a new Constitution its political work would lack its most important foundation. The Constitutional Committee of the National Assembly therefore immediately began considering a draft Constitution, but owing to the influence of conservative elements could not for a long time come to any unanimous conclusion. Finally, on January 20, 1921, the Basic Articles of the Constitutional Law of "the Government of the Great National Assembly of Turkey" were fixed and adopted. These Articles still bear traces of the efforts to take into account certain traditional and conservative currents. Thus Article 7 provides that in drawing up laws and ordinances the provisions . . . of religious and profane law, as well as custom and practice, shall be taken as groundwork. On the other hand, Articles 1–3 unequivocally state the prerogatives of the Great National Assembly and the sovereignty of the nation.

"(1) Sovereignty belongs without restrictions or conditions to the Nation. The system of government is based on the principle that the people personally and actually direct their fate.

"(2) The executive power and the legislative power are unified and vested in the Great National Assembly, which is the sole and real representative of the Nation.

"(3) The Turkish State is ruled by the Great National Assembly. Its Government bears the name, 'Government of the Great National Assembly of Turkey'."

Though it adopted these Articles, the National Assembly refrained from entirely abrogating the Ottoman Constitution, or from abolishing the Khalifate and Sultanate, the most important institutions of the past. None the less the procedure of the Assembly showed that it regarded itself as entitled to appear as a constituent body; an attitude which was all the more important as at that time the Sultan and his ministers, the actual wielders of State power, were resident in Istanbul and were recognised by the outer world as the Turkish Government. A comparison of Articles 1–3 with the corresponding Articles of the earlier Constitution leaves no doubt as to the seriousness of the will to reform of the new directors of the State.

During the following period a number of further changes, of importance for the future shape of the Turkish State, were introduced, albeit not always immediately incorporated in the Constitution. Thus at the Session of the National Assembly of November 1, 1922, the Sultanate was abolished. On October 30, 1923, the Turkish Republic was proclaimed. On March 3, 1924, the National Assembly resolved to liquidate the Khalifate and to banish the Osmanli dynasty. On April 8 it resolved to close the Religious Courts. All these changes were then included in the new Constitutional Law of May 24, 1924, which was based on the following principles:—

(1) The Turkish State is a republic.
(2) The official language of Turkey is Turkish. The capital city is Ankara.
(3) Sovereignty is unrestrictedly and unconditionally vested in the Nation.
(4) The Great National Assembly of Turkey is the exclusive and legal representative body of the Nation and exercises the right of sovereignty of the Nation in its name.
(5) Legislative and executive power are embodied and united in the Great National Assembly.
(6) The National Assembly itself exercises its legislative power.
(7) The National Assembly exercises its executive power through the President of the State whom it elects and the ministerial colleagues nominated by him. The National Assembly can at all times control and overthrow the Government.
(8) Justice is administered in the name of the Nation and in accordance with its methods and laws, by independent Courts.
(9) In respect of the first Article of the Constitutional Law providing for the republican form of government, no

proposal for any kind of change or modification of this may be introduced (Article 102).

(10) The Constitutional Law of 1293/1876 (a Constitution dating from the time of the Osmanli Sultanate) and the amendments thereto, as well as the Constitutional Law of January 20, 1921, and the articles and amendments added to it thereafter, are declared null and void.

The 1924 Constitution nevertheless still contains certain sections taken over from the past, in which religious organisation and State were linked together. Following on the consolidation of the new State the task of secularisation was energetically tackled. On April 10, 1928, the passage in Article 2 of the Constitution in which Islam was stated to be the religion of the Turkish State, together with the words in Article 26 according to which it was one of the functions of the National Assembly "to enforce the decisions of the Sharia", were abolished. In keeping therewith is the change in the formula of the oath to be taken by the President of the State and the Members of Parliament, which according to Articles 16 and 38 began with the words, "I swear by God". These words were now replaced by the formula, "I affirm upon my honour".

In addition to these reforms introduced into the Constitution itself, a number of other measures along the same lines were adopted with the reorganisation of Turkish society as their aim. These include a number of State provisos against religious practices, such as the abolition of fasting in the month of Ramadan, the introduction of Sunday as a day of rest, the issue of the Koran in Turkish, and the abolition of the tarbush and the turban. The erection of public memorials to the Ghazi (Mustapha Kemal Atatürk, and the glorification of the victorious battles in the war of independence are also noteworthy. These memorials, which offend Islamic tradition by their representation of human beings, have been erected in large numbers, in all large squares in Turkey. In the same way, the use of the picture of the President of the State has been introduced on postage stamps and other State emblems.

If we try to grasp the nature of the new Turkish State, on the basis of its constitutional documents and other reform acts, and with due consideration to the criteria given above as the characteristics of the Oriental State, we may summarise our findings as follows:—

(*a*) The new Turkish State has realised the principle of "territoriality". The population resident within the territory of the State is overwhelmingly Turkish, and regards itself as such by reason of its origin, language and national spirit.

(*b*) The association of religious community and State has been completely dissolved. The Turkish Republic is based on a markedly secular foundation; religious life has been banished into the private sphere, and, by the accentuated negation of all religious tradition, has rapidly fallen to unimportance in scale and influence. The abolition of the institution of the Khalifate as the religious apex of the Moslem community which was based on personal union with the secular ruler, was a logical consequence of this policy of secularisation.

(*c*) The State idea and the meaning of the State for the development of modern society has been pressed home vigorously on the Turkish population. Within a brief span of years the Turkish Government has created a nation; out of a governed multitude it has established State-minded citizens of an aspiring Republic.

(*d*) The Turkish Government remained satisfied with the restriction of its dominion to purely or overwhelmingly Turkish Territory.

(*e*) The replacing of the Monarchy by the Republic simultaneously led to a remarkable shift in the general structure of power relations. True, the replacement of the monarchical apex by a State President provided with dictatorial powers has not done away with all the features of a despotic form of State. Yet the banishment of the Sultan and his Court and the rise of a new official class within the country has definitely deprived the previous ruling classes of their position. At the same time these changes have created the prerequisite conditions for the establishment of a new society upon which the burden of the youthful State shall primarily devolve.

(*f*) Lastly, the abolition of the Capitulations has put an end to the former dependence of the country in the economic and legal sphere.

There can be no doubt that the forces which were able to carry through the immense task of such a regeneration of the Turkish

State could only have been called forth by the continuous state of tension resulting from the threat to Turkey's national existence after the First World War and during the War of Independence. Seldom has a statesman recognised this state of affairs more clearly than did Kemal Atatürk in his speeches to the Turkish nation, in Parliament and on many other occasions, when he constantly advanced the education of the Turkish people to thinking in terms of the State as a primary postulate. The clarity with which this objective is formulated in official accounts is impressive. Thus the *History of the Turkish Republic* issued by the Society for the Investigation of Turkish History contains the following statement:—

"The basic principles of the objectives pursued by the Republic in instruction and education are:—

"(*a*) The raising of nationalist race-minded revolutionary citizens of the Republic who are staunch supporters of the secular State.

"(*b*) A genuine extension of elementary education to the entire population and the instruction in reading and writing of all citizens to the last shepherd living alone in the mountains.

"(*c*) General provision of the new generation at all stages of education with practical knowledge, in order to fit them above all for successful activity in economic life.

"(*d*) To replace the morality in social life which is based on fear and punishment in this or the next world by the true morality and virtue which is supported by the concepts of 'freedom' and 'order'."[61]

There is a remarkable difference between the spirit of this programme, in which a naïve faith and a boundless will to reshape personality by means of education finds its expression, and the fear and concern of the parents of the new Turkish leaders lest their sons studying abroad might have their religious feelings disturbed by the education they receive there. About a century ago, an Oriental despot had found it necessary to punish the wealthy inhabitants of Alexandria for having sent the children of other people, poverty-stricken porters, to study in Paris in lieu of their own sons; today the large-scale appearance of Oriental youths at Western Universities demonstrates better than anything else the transformation of mentality that has taken place within a few generations.[62]

The far-reaching Turkish reforms are in no way underrated, when it is pointed out that even during the period of rapid progress between the two World Wars there remained a broad gap between the programmes and intentions of the reformers and the actual results achieved. The tasks which the youthful Turkish State set itself were not without ambition, and its expectations rather high-pitched. In order to carry them out satisfactorily in view of the "difficult conditions of the modern world", to quote the words used in the Preamble of the League of Nations Statutes for the Turkish Succession territories, a well-informed and educated class of collaborators and officials was necessary. The culture and training which these circles could acquire in so brief a period frequently remained superficial or were limited to the relatively easily appropriated skills in technical subjects and sciences. It will be necessary to wait and see whether the class summoned to lead the Turkish State in the future will develop the capacities needed for the purpose. Other characteristics which strike foreign observers as peculiar or even contradictory are due to the endeavour to set up rapidly fully-developed political institutions which elsewhere were the product of centuries.

The leaders of the new Turkey did not wish to withhold from their new-born nation the political institutions of democracy which had attained their highest degree of perfection in the countries of the West. On the other hand, there was perhaps a danger lest the speedy establishment of such institutions should provide instruments that might hamper the realisation of the Turkish rebirth. On this account the apex of the State was secured an overwhelming influence in the Constitution and the representative bodies of the nation. The establishment of the Republican People's Party as virtually the sole party organisation of voters has the same root. Under the leadership of the party, the voters elected proxies who in turn elected the actual delegates. In 1939, for example, 424 delegates out of 429 belong to the People's Party. The provincial and district administration is likewise closely bound up with the party and electoral system, as the proxies have to elect the Provincial Councils for each district. The Provincial Governors are nominated by the Central Government and are assisted by a Council composed of specialist officials and the Provincial Councils. The organisation of these Provincial Councils resembles their structure in Ottoman times. The same applies with the Village Committees which, as before, remain the nuclei of local administration under the chairmanship of the Mukhtar. The preponderance of the party organisation and its dependence in turn on the Chief of the State has to a considerable degree overshadowed the parliamentary provisions of the system. This is particularly true when the Chief has himself to make the decisions on important issues or for matters in which he takes a personal interest.

It is therefore difficult to offer any exact definition of the character of the rights of the people in the new Turkey. There undoubtedly exist features that bear a resemblance to the position of the leader and the single party of modern totalitarian régimes. On the other hand, the Turkish Constitution, which is influenced by Western European formulas, contains guarantees of "human rights", secures Turkish citizens equality and the right of legal procedure in attempts on freedom and life as well as freedom of speech and of faith. Even the assurance of freedom of association is found, though the formation of trade unions for the protection of the workers' interests is prohibited. Similar contradictions between the ostensible desire to respect certain liberal elements in the Constitution and in political life, deriving from West European tradition, and the maintenance of far-reaching restrictions on personal freedom are to be found in many other fields. Even persons making a flying visit to Turkey can notice them. These contradictions can doubtless not be done away with in the near future, and the Turk who is loyal to his Government can with some justice remark that the existing situation offers certain advantages over the alternatives: which are the establishment of a totalitarian régime on the Russian or Fascist model or the introduction of a democratic-parliamentarian régime after the pattern found in European constitutional States—a questionable procedure in Turkish conditions.

There will be opportunities later for dealing in detail with the economic effects of the new régime. The significant fact in this connection is the adoption of industrialisation as the guiding principle of economic policy, with all the resultant consequences in respect to the spread of political influence, the change in the distribution of population, income and property. At the same time let there be no mistake: the intervention of the State in the economic sphere, in some respects very radical, and its increasingly "étatist" activities do not derive from a specific ideology. The elastic attitude of the State authorities, their economic policy conditioned only by the interests at any given time, has led them to adopt industrialisation as one of the most important means of achieving and maintaining political independence. The forms of the process and the part which the State has assigned to itself therein are in no way identical with Russian patterns and motives, some external resemblance notwithstanding.

Despite certain contradictions, despite considerable inadequacies in the bold reconstruction of the Turkish State, the criterion of its capacity for existence will not be found in the degree of its technical and organisational success. This success is incontestable, and even exacting critics cannot permanently overlook the imposing effect of its achievements as a whole. Far more difficult is the question whether the Turkish State, which, unlike its predecessor the Ottoman Empire, is not cemented together by the bonds of faith and by the respect offered to a ruler over many nationalities, will be capable of living exclusively on the basis of its newly achieved national cohesion and the forces released thereby. This point, however, cannot be answered unequivocally even for contemporary States which can boast a longer period of existence than the Turkish Republic. The new Turkey with her little more than twenty years to look back upon can certainly regard any such issue as premature.

CHAPTER IX

THE ARAB SUCCESSION STATES

A Brief Account of their Formation and Growth

In their present shape, the modern Arab States are of recent date. They came into being, in fact, only after the close of the First World War, with features that were in part still rudimentary. For this reason the transformation of their State structure or State institutions cannot yet constitute central items of our account. What presents itself to our eyes is rather an intermediate State form, a transition stage of State development, as a framework for the emergence of national movements in the earliest phases of semi-sovereign existence within the territories which these movements regard as their potential State areas. Hence in the present phase the history of these State creations can show but little of what has struck us as characteristic of the coming into being of the Oriental State; it is to a large extent a history of the national movement of the Arab peoples.[63] Yet it might be possible to verify certain of our deductions regarding the rise of the State in the Orient and its determinate growth even in these pre-State phases. At the same time the importance of the national idea as the crystallising point of the new State formations will have to be kept in the foreground of our description.

The earliest ideas for a rebirth of the Arab nation and State were conceived, with a clarity remarkable in the conditions then prevailing, by Ibrahim Pasha, the son of Mohammed Ali, rather more than a century ago, on the occasion of his Syrian campaign; though Ibrahim himself was not of Arab origin. The degree to which these conceptions influenced Ibrahim's policy may be judged from their inclusion in his military proclamations and their untiring propagation at every opportunity. These ideas were forced into the background after the collapse of the policy of Ibrahim and Mohammed Ali as a result of European intervention. Yet at the same time the revolutionary attitude adopted by Mohammed Ali and his son with regard to many State functions, and their elimination of many old-established obstacles in the way of progress, did not remain without influence on the advance of the national Arab ideas. The opening-up of an Oriental country to Western initiative and enterprise, for the transfer of the fruits of European research, created many of the more important prerequisites for the subsequent development of an Arab national movement. Together with technicians and engineers, European teachers and missionaries entered the Oriental countries and exerted a far-reaching effect as educators of a generation of Arab intellectuals who afterwards themselves served as carriers and intermediaries of European thought. Naturally, this effect could only be a gradual one; as before, Islam continued as a power of extraordinary resistance which, despite all its elasticity on certain points of doctrine, was not yet ready in general to make concessions to the new forms of thought. This was also the reason why the efforts, made under the maxim of Pan-Islamism to open up the Arab countries and thereby to make the Moslem holy places easily accessible common property of the great Islamic communities, proved so successful. Thanks solely to these efforts the loyalty of the Sultan's subjects, the Arabs included, could be preserved.

The British Ambassador in Constantinople writes that, by the construction of the Hejaz Railway, Sultan Abdul Hamid had secured himself the blind obedience of his subjects to a degree never before achieved, and that he had reconciled them to a despotism which was more absolute than had ever before been known in history. By utilising its strong position, the Ottoman régime succeeded in increasingly introducing Turkish as the language of Government in the provinces, particularly in connection with the reforms which aimed at the centralisation of the administration after 1864. This policy greatly affected the pursuit of the Arabic language and literature, which was the most important medium of Arab national tendencies, and ran counter to the attitude of the foreign teaching institutions and missions, which specifically devoted themselves to the expansion and cultivation of Arabic.

This was the general background for a development called forth in Arab countries through constant touch with the Arabic spiritual heritage which had been recalled from oblivion. The seed thus sown continued slowly but surely to germinate. The foundation in the sixties of learned societies which sought to unite the traditions of the past with modern developments was followed about the year 1880 by the establishment of secret societies in which the less hesitant members of the youthful national movement came together. Even then these secret societies went so far as to distribute revolutionary posters under cover of night. This in itself was a relatively harmless activity, but under the conditions of a despotic espionage régime it entailed some danger for those who did it. In fact the British Consul General at Beirut considered it noteworthy enough to cable to London about one such incident. Antonius, who in his book quotes this report and the text of the telegram, which he discovered in the Public Record Office, stresses the symbolical value of these declarations. The reality of these processes and their actual importance may be estimated at a lower value than that accorded to it in the description mentioned; but at the same time the manner in which the objectives of the movement were formulated is noteworthy.[64] The express demand for the independence of Syria together with Lebanon was already openly stated.

It is clear that the effect of the youthful national movement in the Arab territories was bound to remain restricted to narrow limits so long as the régime of Abdul Hamid continued. For this reason those responsible for the movement endeavoured to continue to disseminate their ideas from abroad, and to create centres which would also work for the further development of the ideological and literary objectives. This led to the establishment of a *Ligue de la Patrie Arabe*, founded in 1904 by Najib Azuri, with the liberation of Syria and Iraq from Turkish rule as its express aim. Literary efforts first and foremost served this purpose. A book entitled *Le Réveil de la Nation Arabe* appeared in 1905, and a journal called *L'Indépendance Arabe* was issued; these set out to draw the attention of European public opinion to Arab national aspirations. These efforts, as well as the attempts made in Constantinople under entirely different aspects, following on the promulgation of the Constitution of 1908, to propagate Arab national aims on the new basis of Turko-Arab co-operation, were important symptoms of the increasingly strong currents that were manifesting themselves in the political life of the Ottoman Empire. Even the suppression of the first Arab society which was established in Constantinople under the name "al-Ikha al-Arabi al-Uthmani" (The Arab-Osmanli Brotherhood) and the at first friendly but later sharply aggressive attitude of the Young Turks towards the Arab National Movement, did not hold back the development. Open and secret societies flourished between 1909 and 1914, and provided the fertile subsoil for the growth of the Arab national ideology, whose existence in the coming war was to prove so important for the political fate of the Arab countries.[65] The ultimate objectives of these movements, to be sure, were not always identical, but they were all carried forward by the same basic current.

A positive judgment may be made regarding that stage of the

movement, without however ignoring the fact that at the same time the various Arab groups which took a leading part in the Arab national movement had to suffer from many fateful defects. Even Ireland, an author by no means unsympathetic to the Arab cause, in his treatment of Iraq's recent history, had to admit the incapacity of the Arab leaders for common action. He considers this to be the reason for the weakness and lack of progress of the Movement up to 1914.[66]

An activity particularly weighty in its effects was undertaken at the end of 1913 by a body calling itself the "Reform Committee", and consisting of 68 members of various religious confessions. This Committee drafted a plan for securing national autonomy for the Arab provinces of the Ottoman Empire, in which the direction of general imperial affairs would be left to the Imperial central authorities. The publication of the plan was received with great enthusiasm in all Arab centres. The Young Turk Government at first reacted with police measures, such as the dissolution of the Reform Committee, but then found itself obliged to reach an agreement on account of the resistance of public opinion, and granted greater powers to the Provincial Councils.

Before this a meeting of delegates from Arab countries had already been arranged. They came together in Paris on June 18, 1913, and prepared a moderate programme of Home Rule for the Arab countries. This programme comprised the following points:—

(1) Recognition of Arabic as an official language.
(2) Increased recruitment of Arabs for public office.
(3) Reform of the Military Service Law.
(4) Improvement in the system of taxation.
(5) Maximum decentralisation and autonomy within the framework of the Turkish Empire.

These demands were moderate and did not by so much as a single word raise the issue of separation for the Arab countries; a moderation which was all the more remarkable since, shortly after the outbreak of the First World War, the spokesmen of the movement raised the demand for independent Arab States as an obvious war aim.

It is useless to seek to discover whether the spokesmen of the Arab Movement would have remained satisfied had there been a stronger spirit of conciliation on the part of the Young Turks, and a greater readiness to accept their moderate programme. The sharply negative attitude of the Young Turks, and particularly their policy of centralisation, favoured a more radical turn on the part of the Arab Movement. Instead of loosening the reins in the peripheral provinces where the desire for autonomy was particularly strong, the policy of the Central Government hardened. The high Arab officials and officers in the service of the Turkish Government who, for both personal and general reasons, would have greatly welcomed a reduction in the tension through a yielding to the moderate Arab demands, reacted in the same way as the local Arab Committees in the provinces, i.e. with resentment and bitterness.

Under such conditions it is not surprising that the separatist wing of the Arab National Movement gladly reciprocated the sympathy which it found in the great British and French Empires, and openly worked towards intervention on the part of those Powers, in the form of an occupation of Arab countries in the event of war. Efforts in this direction had actually been initiated years before the First World War broke out. Naturally they could not be attributed solely to the sympathy felt by the two Great Powers for a youthful Liberation Movement; there were also the interests of power politics which had to be looked after by both Powers in the part of the world where the Arab countries are found. For this reason, as soon as it became probable that the Middle East would undergo a profound political transformation as an outcome of the war, representatives of England and France drew up what is known as the Sykes-Picot Agreement of May, 1916. This agreement provided for a division of the Oriental territories into spheres of interest, and dealt with the extension and character of mutually conceded privileges.

This Agreement corresponded to the traditional division of the spheres of interest. By reason of her possession of India, Britain was the Power within whose territories the greatest number of Moslems lived. Apart from this the key to the control of India from the metropolis consisted in the control of the countries on the routes of access, that is, those territories which lie on the land bridge to the Indian Ocean and the sea routes leading to them: the Suez Canal, Red Sea, Straits of Aden, and Persian Gulf. These motives were to be seen, partly open and partly concealed, again and again in the efforts of British Oriental policy, during the nineteenth and twentieth centuries, gradually to obtain control over the area connecting the three continents of the Old World.

The long-standing cultural interest of France in the littoral of the Levant, going back to the period of the Crusades, had given that country the ambition to strengthen its position as the protecting power of the Christian minorities and, in pursuance of this aim, not to shrink even from a permanent occupation of the Syrian coast.

Arab writers have always regarded the Sykes-Picot Agreement, which became known to the Arab leaders only through the publication of the secret treaties by the Russian Bolsheviks in December, 1917, as an attempt to deprive them of the fruits of their participation in the Oriental campaigns. In actual fact the Agreements arrived at between Sir Henry McMahon, then British High Commissioner in Egypt, and the Sharif Husain of Mecca, on the one hand, and between Sykes and Picot, on the other, do exhibit a certain measure of contradiction to each other.[67]

The Agreement with Sir Henry McMahon constitutes a promise on the part of Great Britain to recognise and maintain the independence of the Arabs or of the Arab countries in certain territories within the boundaries proposed by the Sharif.

As against this, the arrangements of the Sykes-Picot Agreement confirm that the two Powers, France and Great Britain, are prepared to recognise and protect an independent Arab State or Federation of States under the suzerainty of an Arab leader; at the same time they define the boundaries of the proposed new State very differently from what is provided in the McMahon letters, and also fix spheres of interest for the two Powers in which the sovereignty of the Arab population is, to a considerable degree, restricted.

A particularly heated discussion arose over the promises contained in the McMahon letters regarding the fate of Palestine. The full and official text of the letters was finally published by the British Government in March, 1939, after long delays. Had any promises in respect of Palestine been contained in this correspondence, the Arab leaders, as was pointed out in a publication of the Jewish Agency, would have made corresponding demands during the ensuing years 1917–1921. In point of fact, as became evident from the publication, they always expressly recognised the separate treatment of Palestine at that time. Not until 1921, i.e. more than five years after the McMahon letter, was the suggestion made to the British Government that the McMahon undertaking included also Palestine—which clearly shows the argument to be an afterthought. (See also note 67). An additional statement on this subject of dispute was published by Sir Henry McMahon, the author of the famous documents, who had played an essential part as principal negotiator, in the year 1937. In view of the nature of the controversy this statement appears so important that it is here reproduced in full:

SIR,

Many references have been made in the Palestine Royal Commission Report and in the course of the recent debates in both Houses of Parliament to the 'McMahon Pledge', especially to that portion of the pledge which concerns Palestine and of which one interpretation has been claimed by the Jews and another by the Arabs.

It has been suggested to me that continued silence on the part of the giver of that pledge may itself be misunderstood.

I feel, therefore, called upon to make some statement on the subject, but I will confine myself in doing so to the point now at issue—i.e. whether that portion of Syria now known as Palestine was or was not intended to be included in the territories in which the independence of the Arabs was guaranteed in my pledge.

I feel it my duty to state, and I do so definitely and emphatically, that it was not intended by me in giving this pledge to King Hussein to include Palestine in the area in which Arab independence was promised.

I also had every reason to believe at the time that the fact that Palestine was not included in my pledge was well understood by King Hussein.

Yours faithfully,
A. HENRY MCMAHON.

5, Wilton Place, S.W.1.
July 22.

The publication of the Jewish Agency above referred to contains a series of other statements on the part of English statesmen, such as Sir Gilbert Clayton, Colonel C. E. Vickery and T. E. Lawrence, all of which confirm this state of affairs.

The campaign against the Sykes-Picot Agreement was taken up by the Arab leaders immediately after a definite reshaping of the State conditions in the Middle East had been undertaken, and was carried further at the Peace Conference. Simultaneously, however, England and France endeavoured considerably to extend the rights and spheres of influence to which they were entitled under the Agreement. The political struggle between these two Powers, on the one hand, and the attempts of the Arab representatives to have their demands accepted, on the other, characterise this phase of the rebirth of Arab States in the Orient. At the same time it could already be felt that Britain regarded the Sykes-Picot Agreement as less definite than did France, and was endeavouring to persuade France to make concessions in the distribution of the spheres of influence in the Orient.[68]

The achievement of the Arab demands suffered first of all from the fact that there was no closed Arab representation, such as might have been able to speak in the name of a united nation or of an incipient Great-Arab State. At the Peace Conference a delegation from the Hejaz proposed the establishment of an independent Arab Federal State under the leadership of the family of the Sharif of Mecca. On the other hand, the Syrian Arabs, who felt themselves to be an outpost of European civilisation in the Orient, demanded through a Central Committee stationed in Paris that a Syrian State should be established independent of the Hejaz and should stand in some degree under French protection. Side by side with this went the Zionist efforts for the establishment of a Jewish State in Palestine, and the desire of the Maronites of the Lebanon to maintain and extend the autonomy which they had already enjoyed under Turkish rule; as well as the claims of the Assyrians and the Kurds to far-reaching autonomy or even sovereignty within the regions they inhabited.

The final outcome of all these cross-purposes was the establishment under Mandate of the four countries of Syria and the Lebanon, Palestine, Transjordan and Iraq, which were placed under the "trusteeship" of the two great Powers, the first of France, the other three of Britain.

The reason for the establishment of the Mandate system was given classical form in Article 22 of the Pact of the League of Nations, which reads as follows:—

"To those colonies and territories which as a consequence of the late war have ceased to be under the sovereignty of the States which formerly governed them, and which are inhabited by peoples not yet able to stand by themselves under the strenuous conditions of the modern world, there should be applied the principle that the well-being and development of such peoples form a sacred trust of civilisation and that securities for the performance of this trust should be embodied in this Covenant.

"The best method of giving practical effect to this principle is that the tutelage of such peoples should be entrusted to advanced nations who, by reason of their resources, their experience, or their geographical position, can best undertake this responsibility, and who are willing to accept it, and that this tutelage should be exercised by them as Mandatories on behalf of the League.

"The character of the Mandate must differ according to the stage of the development of the people, the geographical situation of the territory, its economic conditions and other similar circumstances.

"Certain communities formerly belonging to the Turkish Empire have reached the stage of development where their existence as independent nations can be provisionally recognised subject to the rendering of administrative advice and assistance by a Mandatory until such time as they are able to stand alone. The wishes of these communities must be a principal consideration in the selection of the Mandatory."

Article 22 contains in a succinct but comprehensive formula the motives which led the League of Nations to establish the Mandatory System. Whereas the fact of the as yet unachieved capacity "to stand alone" made a period of trusteeship necessary, those nations were held in view as Mandatories which were best able to undertake the responsibility involved by reason of their resources, their experience or their geographical situation. Naturally, there is no reference in the official wording to the important interests which influenced the selection of the Mandatories to no small degree.

The Mandates for Syria and Palestine were finally confirmed by the League of Nations on July 22, 1922, after England had received the Mandate for Palestine and France the Mandate for Syria and the Lebanon on April 25, 1920, at the San Remo Conference.

In Article 1 of the Mandate for Syria the function of the Mandatory power is expressly stated to be the taking of measures facilitating the gradual development of Syria and the Lebanon as independent States. In the case of Palestine the objectives of the Mandate are influenced by the peculiar situation of this country as the goal of Zionist desires. The Balfour Declaration promising the establishment of a Jewish National Home in Palestine added here an additional task to the general functions of the Mandate System as stated in Article 22; namely, the creation of such political, administrative and economic conditions as would make possible both the satisfaction of Zionist wishes and the safeguarding of the civil and religious rights of the non-Jewish population. For this reason the State development of Palestine was made dependent, even more than that of the other countries under mandate, on factors which were stipulated by the League of Nations.

Transjordan was included in the British Mandate for Palestine, but in course of time was granted a certain measure of autonomy and received a Constitution. Following on a memorandum by the British Government to the League of Nations, the Council of the League, in September, 1922, accepted the British proposal according to which the articles of the Mandate dealing with the establishment of the Jewish National Home cannot be made to apply to Transjordan. The legal position of Transjordan, which was originally formulated in none too exact a fashion, has in course of time been repeatedly modified. The uniformity of its population and its isolation from developments in the neighbouring countries to the West and East have spared it the tremors which have visited those countries. but have also served to maintain its low level of development, standard of living and public services.

The Mandate over Iraq was also granted to Britain at the San Remo Conference, but in the country itself met with a particularly sharp opposition on the part of the population, which in the same year (1920) went so far as to reach the dimensions of a revolt. Nevertheless the British succeeded in establishing the mandatory régime for Iraq as well, subject to certain modifications which gave consideration to the desire of the Iraqi nationalists for independence.

The Arab nationalists were disappointed by this outcome of their movement, though it was regarded as provisional in character. This is no matter for surprise, as their hopes were directed to the rapid establishment of independent States. They also felt the implication of the immaturity of their countries to be unjustified, after they had maintained such long contact with Western lands and since their spokesmen had enjoyed a Western education and in their political plans were far removed from the ideas of the old style of Oriental State. A constitutional government, the introduction of Arabic as the official language, a modern legal and judicial system, an orderly budget—all these criteria of the modern State appear in the preliminary discussions of the future political condition of the territories, and afterwards likewise in the Constitutions of the Mandatory countries themselves, as basic constituents of the youthful commonwealths. But were all the preliminary requisites for securing the realisation of the high-flown wishes of the Arab politicians actually fulfilled? We believe that the reality will disappoint all those who, starting from the ideal standards of Western State formation, expected a rapid development in this direction to occur in the Arab Succession States.

It should be remembered that important conditions for the prosperity of that complicated and sensitive State organism which developed in the West in the course of generations, are here absent. Quite apart from the question whether the number of those who could seriously be regarded as organs of the national life was not less than the minimum necessary for any establishment of a body politic, an immaturity and multiplicity of political wills was frequently to be found. This heterogeneity and formlessness of political life is due, firstly, to the absence of modern facilities for public life (such as a well-functioning party system capable of providing a political education and training of the will); further, to the elaborate cleavage of the population into national and religious fragments. In Syria, Lebanon and Palestine the Moslem Arabs, Druses, Armenians, Alawites and Jews who struggled alongside the Christian Arabs with varying success for political influence; in Iraq the differences between Shiites and Sunnites and the Kurd and the Assyrian minorities rendered any uniform political expression difficult; apart from the fact that the greater part of the Beduin and their social and national ideas, which differed so greatly from those of the settled population, were a particularly heavy burden on the purposeful advance towards the modern State. In addition, such differences in degree of social development as those between town dwellers and fellahin, settled population and nomads, stood in the way of any rapid consolidation of the State.

Besides this came the fact that the Great Powers which had brought about the liberation of the Arab countries from Turkish domination had to protect very important strategic as well as political and material interests in those countries. Their safeguarding or protection was possible only if they could exercise certain sovereign powers; that is, if decisive State prerogatives remained in their hands.

The legal form of the Mandate served as an ideal basis for the balancing of these interests, which were not always easy to combine; in fact, it was possibly the bridge over which alone any balance of these variegated demands might sooner or later be effected. This basis was to be forsaken only when certainty had been reached regarding the successful completion of the transition stage. By commenting below on certain matters of principle, we now wish to show how the Mandates System was equipped for these functions. Again we cannot offer here anything like a history of the development of the Mandate as an institution.

CHAPTER X

THE MANDATE AND ITS LESSON

A New Type of State

Despite its apparent curtailment of the population's claim to freedom, the Mandate in its official documents shows a fundamentally modern and progressive spirit. The establishment of a régime which, while possessing all the powers necessary for administration, was nevertheless bound by guiding principles laid down by a higher inter-State authority, constitutes one of the most remarkable attempts known to our day at developing a new type of State. Leaving aside the question how far this attempt was successful, it led, to begin with, to the establishment of a type of administration much superior to that formerly usual in the Orient. The setting-up of the Council of the League of Nations and its Permanent Mandates Commission as organs to supervise the Mandatory Government was a conspicuous departure from previous practice: it not only replaced the old autocratic governmental structure, but also established a new authority equipped with wide rights of control over the Mandatory Power.

The possibility that any action on the part of a government official, and in particular administrative measures of internal or external political importance, might not be able to pass the keen scrutiny of the Geneva forum, not only exerted much influence on the administration, as will be shown below; it also paved the way for the development of a progressive Statehood even though certain attributes of Statehood were temporarily withheld. These were the exercise of formal democratic national rights in some of the countries concerned, as well as complete independence in relation to foreign powers. The granting of these two demands might have prevented the attainment of some of the essential purposes set forth in the Mandate; it was therefore not in accord with the spirit of that instrument to bestow them until the primary requirements of the Mandate had been fulfilled. The opponents of the Mandate system, the Arab nationalists in particular, argued that State independence and the unhindered exercise of full national rights could alone be the decisive criteria of the existence of a free State. The mandatory régime, they argued, did not differ in principle in this respect from that of the Ottomans, who likewise refrained from granting to the awakening Arab nation these same rights of State independence and freedom.

In reply to this, however, due emphasis should be laid on the genuinely constructive idea which underlay the Mandate pattern; namely, the creation of a transitional form of State which should allow of the unfolding of the evolutionary possibilities to be found in the individual and collective interests concerned. The aim was in some degree to accelerate a historical process of adaptation which elsewhere took generations and was attended by a very keen collision of antitheses. True, the mandatory system was a compromise rooted in the often conflicting interests of the victor Powers, the demands of the native population based on the promises of the Allies during the war, and the special conditions of individual countries.[69] Its purpose was to bring about in course of time some measure of accord between these different demands. In actual fact the fear, often expressed in anti-imperialist quarters, that the mandate was merely a screen for a veiled annexation, has not so far been justified by the course of events. Neither annexation nor any form of acquisition of "Category A" mandated territories ever came under discussion until the outbreak of the Second World War. Hence the fundamental idea (of the mandate) derived from the Roman legal institution of guardianship and the English conception of trusteeship, has become established.

It is true that some restriction of the original Arab aspirations had become necessary. On the other hand, the existence of such thinly populated countries as unrestrictedly sovereign States is impossible without the support of larger States, which in turn have to be paid for their protection by certain concessions. It is not so long ago that independent State existence was contingent upon military strength and healthy finance.

The guidance of the guardian Powers rendered inestimable services for the inner growth of the new States; indeed such services were recognised by native leaders as indispensable, the more so as new ideas are now beginning to arise which tend to deny the right of small States to an independent existence of their own.

The significance of the Mandate system would thus appear to be that it bridged over a period of development. The question thence arises: At what moment can the objectives laid down in the Mandate be regarded as achieved, and the conditions for the grant of independent status as fulfilled? So far such status has been granted on the lines of the prescribed procedure in the case of

Iraq alone; and even here, before the termination of the Mandate was announced, important discussions took place as to what conditions should be recognised as indicating the attainment of this stage of development. Quite apart from the particular case, these arguments were of importance, in principle, for all the other mandatory countries. Two categories of conditions were established, which were to be regarded as criteria for deciding whether a country under Mandate was deserving of the grant of independent status. The first is concerned with what might be regarded as proofs of the capacity of the population to govern itself. The second consists of guarantees aiming at the fulfilment of its international commitments by every member State of the League of Nations. As W. H. Ritsher[70] justly pointed out, the Mandates Commission, which tested and formulated these criteria without regard to distance and other difficulties, offered an important contribution to the solution of this problem, which is among the most delicate questions of international politics. It reached the following conclusions:—

"The emancipation of a territory under the Mandate régime should be made dependent on two classes of preliminary conditions:

"(1) The existence in the territory concerned of *de facto* conditions which justify the presumption that the country has reached the stage of development at which a people has become able, in the words of Article 22 of the Covenant, 'to stand by itself under the strenuous conditions of the modern world';

"(2) Certain guarantees to be furnished by the territory desirous of emancipation to the satisfaction of the League of Nations, in whose name the Mandate was conferred and has been exercised by the Mandatory.

"Whether a people which has hitherto been under tutelage has become fit to stand alone without the advice and assistance of a Mandatory is a question of fact and not of principle. It can only be settled by careful observation of the political, social and economic development of each territory. This observation must continue over a sufficient period for the conclusions to be drawn that the spirit of civic responsibility and social conditions have so far progressed as to enable the essential machinery of State to operate and to ensure political liberty.

"There are, however, certain conditions the presence of which will in any case indicate the ability of a political community to stand alone and maintain its own existence as an independent State.

"Subject to these general considerations, the Commission suggests that the following conditions must be fulfilled before a Mandated territory can be released from the Mandatory régime—conditions which must apply to the whole of the territory and its population:

"(*a*) It must have a settled Government and an administration capable of maintaining the regular operation of essential Government services;

"(*b*) It must be capable of maintaining its territorial integrity and political independence.

"(*c*) It must be able to maintain the public peace throughout the whole territory;

"(*d*) It must have at its disposal adequate financial resources to provide regularly for normal Goverment requirements;

"(*e*) It must possess laws and a judicial organisation which will afford equal and regular justice to all."

At least as intricate as the formulation of the criteria themselves was the task of finding some manner in which the satisfaction of the principles, vague and abstract as in part they were, could be demonstrated beyond cavil. In the negotiations regarding the withdrawal of the State of Iraq from mandate status, this question was offered for open discussion by the then British High Commissioner:

". . . Is it (i.e. the touchstone of independence) to be some absolute standard evolved from abstract principles, or a relative or comparative standard? In either case what is that standard to be? . . . There are doubtless features in the administration, in the cultural development and in the conditions of life in Iraq which are open to criticism. It is not suggested that Iraq can challenge comparison with the more highly developed and civilised nations of the modern world. It might never do so, even were mandatory control continued for many years. But is such a comparison either fair or necessary? . . . I submit that it would not be right to attempt to argue that Iraq is not fit to function independently merely because the machinery of government there may not run quite so smoothly or so efficiently as in some more advanced or more highly developed State."[71]

It is not surprising that, following on the somewhat cavalier treatment by the representatives of the Mandate Institution of the criteria of maturity that should govern release from mandate status many voices from other camps expressed themselves rather less positively on this point. Thus it was their main argument that criteria which are not fulfilled in a number of already existing States can scarcely be regarded as conditions *sine qua non* for a mandatory country.[72] In actual practice, as we have pointed out, this discussion regarding the termination of the mandate status was brought to a conclusion in the case of Iraq alone. It is scarcely possible to avoid the impression that the generous attitude of those who at the time supported Iraq's rapid liberation from mandate status has failed to produce the results aspired to both for the country itself and for the League of Nations as an institution.

But for the Second World War, the problem of the conditions governing recognition of independence would have been raised in various aspects, and a more satisfactory solution might possibly have been achieved.

Be that as it may, the clarification of these questions in the case of Iraq had the result that the fulfilment of certain demands was established as decisive for the ending of the state of transition. These demands are largely congruent in principle with the functions recognised at the beginning of this book as characteristic of the modern Western State in contrast to the old State of the Oriental variety.

This involves the State's duty towards its citizens of fulfilling a series of functions without respect of person or rank; which in turn involves the following prerequisites: the existence of an organised government and administration, able in particular to maintain public order and security and to provide an impartial judiciary and legal system as well as stable public finances. Other branches of administration such as education, public health and communications must take rank after the above-mentioned services, great as is their importance in the modern State.

The gap between these abstract demands and their realisation in actuality is revealed on a critical consideration of the conditions formulated by the Mandates Commission. Naturally, we should not insist too rigorously on the precise meaning of the terms.

Thus it is obvious that too literal a construction cannot be put on criterion (*b*), namely, the capacity of the State to maintain its territorial inviolability and political independence. Even the most powerful of nations cannot defend itself successfully against a coalition of enemies, to say nothing of a small State against a great Power. For this reason the capacity to maintain independence is contingent not only upon military power but also upon ability to keep up harmonious relations with neighbours and with the international authorities which might guarantee security. It cannot be denied that at this point the elastic interpretation leaves a gap which appreciably weakens the establishment of the criterion in general as well as its significance.

This is also true in respect to the third criterion, maintenance of internal law and order; a demand which is, indeed, quite generally recognised and is indispensable to the existence of any stable government. Yet here also there is a difference of view as to what the people of a country may consider as the maintenance of public order; particularly in cases where a considerable portion of them have been accustomed to regard the absence of a stable central authority, or frequent armed conflicts between the various sections of the population, as in no way irreconcilable with their normal and regular mode of life. This consideration applies in particular to certain of the Oriental countries under mandatory administration which contain among their population a large percentage of Beduin, whose conceptions of stable government naturally differ very widely indeed from those of the settled population. None the less, the most recent developments have shown that even among these elements unequivocal tendencies are establishing themselves towards a recognition of the principles of State existence set out above.

Similarly, the principles of healthy finance, despite some leniency in practice, are likewise becoming increasingly recognised as among the most essential criteria of modern State administration in the mandate countries. The adoption of such principles affects both the discharge of financial liabilities by the State and the administrative structure of the taxation and financial system.

A final condition for the bestowal of independent status is the capacity of maintaining an autonomous judicial and legal system which provides a guarantee of impartial justice. Here, too, important rudiments of the Oriental tradition of the State are eliminated with the fulfilment of this demand. The abolition of the Capitulations for the duration of the Mandate was in itself a beginning, even though it did not as yet definitely remove the institution as such. A series of other measures in the field of jurisprudence had already been introduced in Ottoman times by the codification of the law. The rounding-off and completion of these important legal tasks, as well as the continuous efforts to reform and adapt the judicial system to modern standards, are among the major tasks of the mandatory administration in all countries under mandate.

It would still be premature to attempt to pass judgment on the success or failure of the mandatory system as a whole and the establishment of the new Arab States. The changes in external politics which took place during the inter-war period were so remarkable, while, on the other hand, the heritage of the former régime so retarded State and society, that a final causal attribution of successes and failures is impossible. Yet at the same time, even so benevolent a critic as Ireland, in his book on Iraq, cannot refrain from expressing his misgivings regarding the inadequate progress of that country. Since then the unsatisfactory symptoms have grown even stronger. The low level of parliamentary institutions is even more obvious than it was; the deficiencies in the administration, in the handling of the State finances, etc., are reminiscent of the conditions prevalent in the Ottoman Empire. Anyone who, in contrast to so many champions of the independence of the youthful national States, expresses the view that the "rights of independence" must not take precedence of the "criteria of independence", will in any case treat these symptoms as of very considerable significance; since they are characteristic not only of conditions in Iraq but also, in large part, of the beginnings of modern State life in other Middle Eastern regions.

At any rate, one fact seems incontestable: if the purpose of a modern State is the promotion of the well-being and the material and spiritual interests of the population and the internal and external security of its existence by means of law and armed forces, the new sovereign States in the Middle East can be considered to have achieved these objectives so far only in a fairly limited degree. The standards of justice and administration, the security of life for minorities, and in fact the stability of the Government and of political conditions in general were higher, despite all the incontestable deficiencies, during the period of mandatory rule than they proved to be after it. An almost unbroken chain of Cabinet crises, *coups d'état* and conspiracies and a frequent imperilling of the lives of minorities has characterised the Iraqi political scene since this State was released from its condition of tutelage. Conditions in the Levant States reveal a similar picture of instability. The causes of this development may be appraised from various points of view; but the facts themselves speak all too clearly.

CHAPTER XI

(*a*) POLITICAL RÉGIME AND SOCIAL STRATIFICATION IN THE ARAB SUCCESSION STATES

In the first part of this account of the Middle Eastern State we have dealt with the most important characteristics of the political and social structure of the old Ottoman Empire. The change of régime in the new Turkey has doubtless exerted a far deeper influence on the social structure of its population than have the new régimes of the mandatory countries on that of theirs. The Turkish Government aimed consciously at these social transformations, and applied every method, including some very drastic ones, in order to alter the existing social mentality and the relative weight of the various classes in the State. Indeed, it went further, endeavouring to create a new type of citizen, who would be in a position to take over new functions in the State.

The situation in the Arab countries is different. It is true that here, too, with the new Constitutions changes were introduced in the structure of the administration and the Government apparatus. Equally, there were shifts in the ruling political forces, in the distribution of the burden of taxation and in administrative competencies. In addition to this, the activity of a staff of higher officials coming from the Occident was a factor in shaping political life.

All these innovations, however, were only outward, and hardly penetrated to the social and political consciousness of the population. Indeed, it must be stressed that the mandatory Powers themselves were not interested in the introduction of far-reaching reforms. Their interest obviously lay in fostering good relations with the dominant classes who enjoyed advantages under the old social and economic order. Characteristic of this attitude, for instance, is a remark in the Report of the Palestine Administration to the League of Nations for the years 1920–1925. This Report remarks incidentally: "Apart from a few cases in which it seemed clearly advisable it was not regarded as desirable to introduce rapid changes in the methods of administration to which the population had adapted itself." It is therefore not surprising to find that under the surface the old forms and foundations of political and social life often continue to exist, and to meet all new issues and problems with the traditional reactions.

This becomes particularly clear when we consider the reality of political life in the light of the composition of the bodies supposed to represent the interests of the population. The first impression is, that those classes who are at present in an overwhelming majority, the fellahin and workers, have still, as before, neither influence nor weight in these representative bodies. Egypt, Syria, the Lebanon, Iraq and Transjordan are all agrarian in structure. The majority of the farmers everywhere are fellahin and fellahin tenants. Some of these countries have long had Parliaments or other such bodies, representative either of the whole country or of special districts. However, neither the fellahin nor the workers are represented on a scale corresponding to their numbers. As a rule the Parliaments are composed of representatives of other classes, and in some cases the workers and fellahin are entirely unrepresented. This situation is no accident, for so far there are only the modest beginnings of an organisation of the population on the basis of clear-cut economic associations or class interests. Nowhere has the rural or urban working class as yet come forward as a tightly knit political group, sending its representatives to Parliament and making effective demands there. The same is also true of the small peasants.

On the other hand merchants, officials, and members of the liberal professions are usually associated with the large landowners in a kind of community of interests. In these groups spokesmen of genuine national currents are already to be found alongside those who represent naked class interests. Here too, however, the associations between the various groups are still often loose. The community of interests often dissolves, and their supporters then join some fresh party grouping which accepts one-time members of other parties without any qualms of conscience.

Economic or social political principles or programmes, such as condition the political parties and organisations of the West, are not to be found in any like form in Oriental countries. Personal following plays a great part in them. It is in the main the ruling families that have great influence, more particularly their heads. The power of such associations is stronger than the recognition of any programme of principles and practical objectives laid down by any party. For this reason likewise, the composition of the membership of the parties, if such somewhat casual associations deserve that name, is elastic, and very frequently has no relation with the economic position of their supporters.

Characteristic light on these conditions is thrown by a note in the Egyptian journal *El-atnin w'al dama*, issues no. 405–407, regarding the composition of the Egyptian Legislative Assembly in 1914. Most of its members belonged at that time to the same families who to this day provide the members of the Senate and Parliament. The journal states with quite comprehensible exaggeration: "It is truly no sign of national or democratic spirit when a family is represented in Parliament or the Senate by five delegates."

Modern economic development in these countries has not so far succeeded in destroying hitherto existent personal links and relations or in creating a system of parties and classes on the Western model, in which the material position of the party member constitutes a primary motive in the party's formation. This is specially true of those districts which have not yet been industrialised, such as Arab Palestine, Iraq, and those other parts of the East which have a similar agrarian structure. In Palestine, for instance, there were in February, 1930, no less than 17 "parties and loose groups of a somewhat party character", seven of which had a certain nucleus of members. These included the National party, the Peasants' party, the Liberal party, the Husseini party and the Nashashibi party. These names, however, tell us nothing regarding their programme. Some of them, indeed, clearly show that they are mere associations of followers of the great families of the country. Others only wear their resounding names as an empty ornament. As an Arab journal remarked, some of these parties never even survived the day of their establishment. Political life in the Levant States or in Iraq is equally amorphous, showing a semi-feudal structure of political parties closely resembling that of Palestine.

(*b*) THE WESTERNISING OF ADMINISTRATION

The anti-Turkish propaganda of the Great Powers, and their aggressive attitude in regard to many features of the Turkish régime, was largely nourished by the defects of the Turkish administrative system, which were well known abroad. For this reason the world was justly curious to know how the mandatory Powers would exercise their functions. The forms by which onetime Turkish countries were to be ruled by the Great Powers France and England were, for the most part, laid down in the texts of the mandates. The repeatedly stressed purpose of mandates, namely, to take over the administration "for those peoples who are not yet able to stand by themselves under the strenuous conditions of the modern world" and the administrative legal provisions deriving from that purpose brought about for the administration of mandatory territories a singular régime which is a novelty in the sociology of the State. But we are not here concerned with an analysis of the consequences in the field of foreign policy, or of the motives or interests which led the powers to establish the mandates; our immediate subject is the Westernisation of the administration, the transformation of the State apparatus which was necessarily put under way by the introduction of the mandatory régime.

An attempt has already been made to define the traditional Oriental administrative atmosphere in the fields of legislation, ecclesiastical and tax administration. All accounts on this subject by contemporary observers combine to give an idea of the immense difficulties with which every European power which might try to introduce a new system of administration in these territories had to reckon.[73]

Britain's experience in the field of administration conferred upon her certain qualifications and gifts necessary for carrying out such delicate functions. During the decades before the First World War her practice had already begun to introduce in her colonial territories a system of administration based on participation of the local leaders. This tendency has been taken up in particular in the British mandated territories. At the same time, the idea underlying the mandate itself played an important part in shaping their administrative régimes. The institution of the Mandate, derived from the principle of guardianship, conferred upon the League of Nations a right of control in various forms. Thus the mandatory Power is required to submit an exhaustive annual report on the administration of the mandated territory to the League of Nations, which has this report examined by the Permanent Mandates Commission of the League in the presence of an authorised representative of the mandatory Power. Further possibilities of control are that the Permanent Court of International Justice may be called upon to decide in cases of dispute, and that the populations of the territories have themselves the right of appeal by petition to the Council of the League. Legal experts are at variance as to the exact scope of these rights, but there are practically no affairs of the mandatory Power pertaining to the mandated territory that are not subject to League control.

For the spread of Western administrative technique it was important that, according to Article 22 of the Covenant of the League of Nations, the European mandatory Power should itself render advice and assistance in all administrative branches in the mandated territories entrusted to it. In practice this has had the result that in all these countries an administrative apparatus has been developed, whose higher ranks and organs are filled entirely by representatives of the mandatory Power. This has caused the administration to become far more Europeanised than was the case in any other Oriental countries, to a degree extending far beyond the administrative sphere and affecting the public life of these lands. At the same time the possession of these key positions secured the mandatory Power a position of great political scope within the administration of the country. With this structure it was easy for the protecting Power to secure its own interests, and it is only natural that where the interests of the mandatory Power and those of the native population collided, conflicts should frequently develop.

In the Middle East countries not under mandatory rule, the European director or adviser of important State departments also played, and in part still plays, an important rôle. Since the days when Mohammed Ali summoned French and English experts and officers to Egypt to carry out his reform ideas, the European counsellor has become a familiar figure in Middle Eastern State administration. Even in countries with very pronounced feelings regarding the independence of their State structure, such as Turkey and Persia, the part played by Europeans as advisers on and initiators in the shaping the new State and the new economy can scarcely be over-estimated.

Foreign influence and ideas proved of particular importance in the sphere of State finance, bringing about there a change in structure as well as in sources of income. The new Turkish financial policy after the wars of liberation, for instance, rejected in principle the receipt of foreign loans. At the same time, however, it had to introduce drastic innovations in the system of taxation in order to finance the far-reaching reconstruction plans of the new régime. These included the abolition of the *Osher* and of fees on changes of ownership by inheritance. On the other hand, the Turkish Government introduced an Income Tax, an Inheritance Tax and a Turnover Tax, all innovations in Oriental States. Apart from this, a series of improvements in the technique of tax collection and assessment for already existing taxes were announced. In this way the Turkish taxation system, so far as its legal foundations were concerned, was largely adapted to European models.

Among the financial reforms which were introduced in the other succession States of the Ottoman Empire, mention should first be made of the Income Tax. This tax has been introduced in Iraq, Egypt, Transjordan and more recently in Palestine as well. Despite misgivings and the sceptical comments regarding its introduction in countries with so low a tax morality, it will become established as a permanent source of income for the Government, aided by the expansion and variegation of the vocational structure of the population.

A further important innovation in the financial system of these countries is the regular payment of considerable sums as concession fees and royalties by companies which exploit local mineral resources. Whereas the activities of foreign capital in Eastern countries were in the past frequently accompanied by simultaneous pressure on the native Treasury, that department has now become an important beneficiary of such undertakings. The high fees charged for the acquisition and utilisation of concessions form an appreciable part of the total receipts of Oriental budgets.

Loans received from abroad are arranged for on favourable conditions which, when the mandatory Power acts as security for interest and repayment, scarcely differ from the conditions of loans to large States. Naturally this also did away with the great loss of such capital as was formally retained as profit by the houses of issue which arranged the loans.

Important improvements have likewise been introduced in the taxation and budgetary technique of most Oriental countries. Of these the chief are the unification of the agrarian taxes, which in the past usually consisted of the threefold Osher, Werko and Cattle Tax, on the basis of a uniform tax on yield, the transition from the *ad valorem* to the differential tariff system, and the establishment or expansion of audit departments. The liquidation of the dual tax administration, which had given foreign Powers far-reaching though sometimes justified rights of intervention, established the sovereignty of Oriental financial systems, and thereby created the conditions for an independent financial and fiscal policy.

The problems which had developed for the legal system have already been treated. All that we need remark here is that even from the formal viewpoint important changes have been introduced. In the mandated territories the new Administration has effected a reorganisation of the courts, which has been of primary importance for economic development. The division of the jurisdiction into secular and religious, so characteristic of Oriental countries, has, it is true, been maintained. But the uniform direction and control of the entire legal and court system by qualified foreign jurists has done much to raise the standard of justice. In particular the administration in territories under British influence has tried to place the native judges in a more satisfactory material condition in order to counteract the tendency, general in this profession in the Orient, to raise income by foul methods. That corruption has not vanished from State life should be no matter for surprise; its roots go back through centuries, and its elimination within any brief period of time is impossible.

The development towards a further improvement in the quality and quantity of administrative technique had already set in before the First World War, and has progressed rapidly since. Should it persist, it will prove stronger than many other factors in determining the future State and social life of the Orient. The reasons for the expansion of bureaucracy in all parts of the State machinery have already been mentioned, and there are no grounds for anticipating any change in this tendency. The new Oriental State apparatus is subject to the same laws as the modern State machinery in the West. A deterioration in the morale of the bureaucracy can, therefore, have none but fatal consequences for the development of the Oriental State.

PART TWO

THE AGRARIAN SOCIETY OF THE MIDDLE EAST

SECTION I

STATIONARY AGRICULTURE

CHAPTER XII

THE HERITAGE CONDITIONS OF LAND TENURE

General Features

The first impression which the onlooker receives on coming into contact with the rural life and forms of agrarian society in Middle Eastern countries is one of broad external similarity or even uniformity. Even though pronounced differences may exist side by side within each single country, according to the nature of its soil and water supply, the aridity of the climate, with its long rainless summer and the need for artificial irrigation in rainless areas, has produced similar conditions of vegetable life and of production over wide zones of the Orient.

To this must be added a number of other factors of social, political and juridical nature which have also tended towards uniformity, such as the Moslem code and philosophy of life, Islamic legal institutions, and the effects of the feudal social order with the specific forms it takes in the countries of Hither Asia. In addition there was the Ottoman régime, which for centuries had grouped these areas together, endeavouring to impose upon them both its rulers and its political and administrative institutions, and, finally, the links of language intensified by the religious factor which brought the peoples of these lands closer to each other. All these factors have tended to create, in spite of the differences that exist, a social structure permeated by many similar elements.

Nevertheless we must be chary of inferring a general uniformity in the stratification and development of this society, or of applying stock explanations and sociological formulas accepted in other spheres. Thus we must take into account in the first instance the social divergences which exist between fellahin and townsfolk, landowners and tenants, settled population and nomad elements. More important as a factor of deviation are the differences which result from the prevailing systems of agriculture conditioned by nature, that is to say, between areas of irrigated agriculture and dry-farming. The religious and national stratification has an even greater bearing on this question.

National and religious groupings in the Orient have determined the differentiation of society far more than in European countries. It is true that the tendency to a class division on economic grounds is to be found here also; so far, however, these factors have not been able to remove the old-established traditional bars between the national communities, or the stationary structure of the Oriental agrarian society, built as it is on a number of basic facts operating throughout the entire Middle East.

For anyone with a sense of history visiting these lands for the first time this impression of an arrested development, of a gap in the course of historical progress, or, indeed, of a retrograde movement, was the essence of an experience which henceforth was irrevocably bound up with the word "Orient". As a matter of fact, impressions of this kind applied to all Oriental countries, with the exception of the parts settled by Europeans. Up to the years following the First World War the Oriental town presented a characteristic picture. There was a centre whose buildings, constructed in a spurious Oriental style and mostly serving commercial purposes, conveyed a certain bigness of conception ; around this centre there was a criss-cross of streets whose ugliness and dilapidated appearance increased with their distance from the main thoroughfares. Only the market-places and the mosques ranked as worthy presentations of native architecture and were in better structural condition. But here too, time and again, in the immediate neighbourhood of noble edifices one would note with surprise the very low state of housing and building conditions with a correspondingly inferior standard of living, a fact which can hardly be explained solely by the generally prevailing poverty. For has not the Orient everywhere and at all periods been able to boast of accumulated property and wealth to an extent quite unknown to the Western world before the capitalist era, and do we not find even to-day hidden away in the crooked lanes of the poorer quarters of the towns buildings and palaces of almost fabulous beauty and orderliness?

In the villages also, similar almost insufferable contrasts were to be found: a stately dwelling, generally situated on high ground, the property of the local sheikh, with round about it a conglomeration of miserable dilapidated clay or stone hovels whose primitiveness almost beggars description. According to all our sources the forms of settlement established many centuries ago throughout most parts of the Orient show no appreciable difference from those of to-day, just as agricultural practice has undergone no important change. The thousand-year-old Eastern nail-plough still leaves its trail across the stony fields; still can the ox be seen turning the old water scoop-wheel, or sometimes even, as in Egypt, the fellah himself at the *tambur*, the Archimedean screw, and the *shaduf*, the simple wooden lever for lifting the water; as in former days he threshes the corn with the threshing-board, and is everywhere living a life of almost unsurpassable frugality based on exploitation both of the soil and of human exertion. It is a way of life which can only be interpreted through the extreme traditionalism which supports it—a traditionalism which has invested the agriculture of the Orient with its own specific stamp.

In these spheres the mind does not see further than the narrow confines of its surroundings, and behaviour seldom budges from the paths prescribed by custom and doctrine. This impression is further confirmed by the picture conveyed to us by the constitution of economic society in the Middle East. Thus, in many districts up to the outbreak of the First World War and even to-day the predominant feature of Oriental economy, especially of agrarian economy, its principal sector, was the conspicuousness of the connection or union of man and soil, the chief factors of production. By various legal institutions a large part of the cultivable land was withdrawn from free disposal on the market. Foremost among these ranks the *Waqf*, which immobilises land in favour of religious institutions. As a result of the establishment of the *Mushaa*, the Arab system of common ownership, the individual peasant is allowed only a share in the land possessed by his village, not the right of individual property in land. These restrictive ties were further seen in the lasting effect of the feudal social order which turned the individual tenant into a helot at the mercy of the landowner; and in the economic disfranchisement of the peasant and the artisan, which ruled out any inner and positive relationship to the State or the ruling power.

What are the reasons for these stationary conditions? This question, already raised in the Introduction to this book, calls for further elucidation. Whereas we have already analysed the persistence of political and State institutions, the problem of the stationary character of the economic forms remains to be dealt with. As in other parts of the world, the development of these forms is due not only to social and historical, but also to natural factors. The specific forms of Oriental agriculture, especially its stationary character, must therefore be explained both by the sociological and the climatic and geographical conditions obtaining in this area. The following chapters will, therefore, be devoted to a survey of the agrarian and sociological factors with their historical aspects, and above all of the conditions of land ownership with thereafter a discussion of the connections between natural conditions and Oriental agriculture.

Historical Summary—Early Times

In the Middle East, and especially in the Moslem world, conditions of land ownership have been shaped by the heritage of history, which here more than anywhere else in the world still remains a living force. The sociologist or land law expert, therefore, if he wishes to understand the complicated land questions to be met with in these countries to-day, must pay considerable attention to the historical element going back to the Middle Ages if not to late Antiquity.

In the following sketch an attempt is made, so far as space allows, to outline these historical elements, with the object of showing to what a remarkable extent the heritage of the past still colours modern land legislation, and at the same time how most of the laws relating to land ownership have emerged from the peculiar conditions of this agrarian society, besides throwing fresh light on the motives for some of the far-reaching changes introduced in recent times.

All historians clearly recognise that conditions of land ownership are a factor of central importance for the whole course of ancient history. That "the distribution of land is the foundation of every system of State" is emphasised by Mommsen in his essay on the *Italische Bodenteilung und die Alimentartafeln* (Italic Land Distribution and the Alimentary Tables).[1] This sentence may well be supplemented to the effect that the distribution of land forms not only the foundation of every State system, but also of every pre-State community and social group. Real or alleged injustice in the distribution of land was always the prime motive for serious social warfare in ancient times. Division of landed estates and remission of debts was the ancient battle-cry which excited revolutions and wars in the Greek cities.[2]

In the matter of land ownership the Oriental countries, ruled as they were to a great extent by theocratic, or at least hierarchical constitutions, differed quite appreciably in ancient times from the countries of Southern Europe. Whereas in the latter private ownership and the amassing of individual landed estates predominated, in the ancient State systems of the East there was an unmistakable trend towards authoritarian control and even authoritarian appropriation of landed possessions by a central body, by the head of the State, or symbolically by the Deity itself.[3] But in this case—despite the many forms of abuse to be found—we are struck by a certain understanding of the special nature of the relationship of man and soil, the gist of which is crystallised in Jewish lore in the assertion of a prior right of ownership on the part of the Deity—in addition to the right of usufruct on the part of the cultivators—and finds expression in the Oriental code in peculiar legal and political consequences up to the present day.

However, in attempting to make deductions as to the original conditions from the forms which now obtain, we must guard against jumping to conclusions. The development of land law institutions in Oriental countries, as in all other parts of the world, has been neither uniform nor continuous. New political and social developments and new religious conceptions have had their effect on the land laws, and on the other hand the conditions of land ownership have in their turn affected the course of political development.

It is obvious that the roving desert nomad has a different relation to the land from that of the resident fellah in the village, that the conception of ownership of the large landed proprietor living in the town differs considerably from that of the small village tenant, that early Moslem ideas as to the importance of individual and collective land ownership are by no means in harmony with those of the modern Islamic world. The famous controversy on the origin and extent of private land ownership is brought no nearer to a definite settlement by the material at our disposal regarding conditions in the Orient. At the same time the existing clues make it easier for us to gain some idea of the nature of ownership as obtaining in those days, particularly in regard to the question whether it was private or collective.

Light is also thrown on the predominance of tribal ownership as one of the most important forms of collective ownership. Evidence for the existence both of collective and private landownership can be found in very ancient times. We have reports from Babylon that in the time of the Kassites (*c.*2000 B.C.) and again later (*c.*1500–1200 B.C.) cases of clan ownership of land were not infrequent. It is evident from the contracts of purchase in those days that the clans cultivated their land possessions collectively, and that the population likewise was grouped under collective labour organisations for the purpose of constructing roads, work on fortifications, canals and sluices, etc.[4] This compulsory work ("liturgy") is manifestly connected with the land; from the documents which have come down to us from those times we may infer the existence of collective ownership which took the form of clan holdings in land. The right of the individual member of the clan in respect of its sale and inheritance was abolished.

The prevalence of collective ownership in Babylonia is remarkable inasmuch as from the earliest times private ownership was also known there and apparently, despite the advantages of collective land ownership in such a typical flat irrigation country, managed again and again to re-establish itself during times of prosperity.

Although we can also find evidence of private ownership in ancient Egypt as early as the time of the Middle Kingdom, all such ownership is actually an exceptional transfer of royal rights which after the triumph of the Theban Dynasty became invalid. The Pharaoh became the owner of all the land in Egypt.[5]

Incidentally, the temples also played an important part in shaping the conditions of Egyptian land tenure; under Ramses III they already owned 15 per cent. of the cultivable land. It is true that the temples had State lands in their possession at an earlier period, which they forfeited, but it is only at the end of the Middle Kingdom that they gradually became the determining economic factor in the country. The importance of the various temple centres can be clearly seen from the data setting out the property owned by the temples. Thus, the temple of Edfu (New Kingdom) owned land to the extent of 36·5 sq. km.; this figure is, however, far surpassed by the Theban estates, which comprised no less than 2,393 sq. km. and 81,322 bondmen.[6]

The conditions obtaining in Biblical Palestine were no doubt very different. For lack of other sources we must base our deductions in this connection on Biblical accounts. For the period dealing with the entry into the Promised Land there are numerous indications which point to the existence of a highly evolved tribal organisation which also covered conditions of land ownership. The prevailing system was that of clan holding as practised by the Beduin; should any violation occur through disposal by sale, the property in question could be saved for the clan by the right of re-purchase. The details given in Num. xxxiii—liv state that the land is to be inherited by lot according to families (clans), the large families receiving a large inheritance, the small families a correspondingly smaller one. The importance attached to the preservation of the clan property is evident from the account dealing with the question of the inheritance of the daughters of Zelophehad (Num. xxxvi). Here the guiding principle was that the daughters should be free to choose their future husbands, provided that they married into one of the families of their father's tribe. Similar conditions are disclosed by the account in Jeremiah xxxii and Ruth iv.

Jeremiah as the principal heir of his family is morally bound to buy the property of his cousin, who wishes to sell his field. Boaz cannot acquire the property belonging to Ruth in right of her late husband until her near kinsman has declined to make use of his right of redemption. This tie between the land and the kin is enforced even against the king. When Ahab wished to purchase Naboth's vineyard, offering him a more valuable piece of land in exchange, Naboth refused to sell on the ground that the transfer of inherited property was contrary to the law of God. The institution of the Jubilee, in conception a magnificent embodiment of the inalienability of kin property and in its simplicity a remarkable anticipation of all later ideas of land reform, aimed at nothing else but the preservation of the original kin inheritance; a consideration for the person of the former or new owner was certainly not a particular motive in this institution. In general a period of fifty years was so long that the original seller who had the right of repurchase was hardly likely to be still living or economically active. Although a complete elimination of further disposal was not possible so long as the right of pre-emption could be renounced by the kin, nevertheless as a rule, in conjunction with the aforementioned institution of the Jubilee, the return of all purchased property to the original family or kin of inheritors was envisaged.

The question whether and to what extent the law was carried out in practice has been the subject of much discussion. The fact that such a law was made, however, is proof in any case of an extraordinarily keen sense for the need of safeguarding the inheritance and so for the importance of equitable distribution of the land in general. With increasing settlement the legal forms of tribal organisation gradually disappear in Palestine. Their place is taken by forms of village land tenure. As a result the social conscience of the population slowly outgrows the rigid claims of tribal tradition as represented above all in the injunction regarding the return of all alienated family and kin property to the original owners.

The wandering tribal association becomes a society of peasants, primitively organised, yet settled, the peasantry—and this applies particularly to those who returned from the Babylonian exile under Ezra—thereafter a class deeply influenced by the urban civilisation of the Land of the Two Rivers. Despite all the exhortations of their leaders the germs of town culture soon developed to so formidable an extent that the old social constitution deriving mainly from patriarchal foundations could no longer hold its ground.

A particularly noteworthy attempt to stem this overpowering development which was destroying the elements of the old rural tribal life is to be seen in the movement of protest led by Jonadab, the son of Rechab, who called for a return to the simple customs of the desert. The Bible relates how the Rechabites agreed to plant no vineyards, nor to build permanent houses, nor to drink wine, nor till the field, but to content themselves like true shepherds with milk and meat. (Jeremiah xxxv, 6ff.). It is almost certain that this ascetic movement may be regarded as a protest against the importance accorded by the settled population to private land ownership and the evils connected therewith. But this attempt, a last heroic effort to revive the ancient Israelite tribal constitution, quickly faded away; only a few lines in the Bible story inform us of the decline. In the Talmud, where we find many details on the conditions of agriculture of that time, there is a complete absence of reference to the common tribal or family ownership of the rural population. Individual forms of ownership with a distinct differentiation in the categories of lease appear to have been general.[7]

Whereas there is a rich store of literature on the general political and legal conditions in the East during the Middle Ages, the precise sources of information on the nature of land ownership conditions during this period and the beginning of modern times are but scanty.

Characteristic of conditions in the Byzantine Empire—apart from the amassing of big estates in few hands—was the grouping of the small peasants liable to pay rent and interest in tax-debt collectives as an alternative to their relinquishing their property or selling the fertile part of their holdings to the large landowners whose domains enjoyed substantial tax privileges and exemption from the *Epibole*. The collective tax debt at that period, called *Epibole*, i.e. the obligation on the part of the landlord to pay the taxes on the adjoining properties abandoned as a result of arrears of taxes and poverty, represented a kind of collective ownership on the part of the community in respect of taxable property.[7a] The object of this institution was to make all members of the community liable for the debts of every individual member, a procedure resorted to up to quite recent times and, as will be seen, forming a determining factor in some Oriental countries in the recreation of collective ownership.

The Early Islamic Period

With the conquest of the Orient by the Moslem armies a transformation in the conditions of land tenure set in which has made its effect felt on the land laws of Eastern countries up to the present day. It is true that the Arabs often refrained from interfering in the prevailing conditions of farm management. The existing peasantry was allowed to remain on its land and even encouraged to continue its accustomed activities. On the other hand, the landlords, mostly of Byzantine origin, were expelled or killed, the conquerors thereby obtaining free disposal of the ownership of their estates.

The major portion of the land thus confiscated became the property of the Moslem community, later to be bestowed on favourites and deserving generals. The introduction of a new system of taxation brought with it remarkable forms of legislation and taxation such as were met with only in the Moslem world. The application of the new Moslem political theory led to a differentiation of the population in respect of their rights in accordance with their religious belief, the followers of the Prophet being given a markedly favoured position. This discrimination made itself felt economically in the distribution of the burden of taxes. Seeing that the structure of most Oriental countries was agrarian and the State's revenue derived predominantly from agriculture, the ever-growing financial needs of the young State had to be met by agricultural taxes; such taxes were assessed at a much lower rate for Mohammedans than for non-Mohammedans. According to early Moslem writers Moslem landowners were liable to payment only of the modest *Osher*, a tax on the yield of the land amounting to 5–10 per cent. according to whether the land was irrigated or unirrigated; in the case of property whose owners were left in possession though they had not accepted the Moslem faith, the quite oppressive *Kharaj* was levied, a tributary tax of 20–50 per cent. on the gross yield.[8]

Thus through the medium of tax differentiation in respect of landed property the religious cleavage of the population introduced in the occupied countries by the leaders of Islam in its early militant stage was perpetuated in the land laws. For this reason we find Moslem land legislation and Moslem authors far more concerned with questions arising out of the tax classification of the land than with the complicated problems of agrarian rights on which the development of land legislation turned in other countries.[9] Questions of collective ownership, right of inheritance, tenant rights or the fundamental attitude to private ownership in general are treated as secondary.

CHAPTER XIII

AGRARIAN INSTITUTIONS OF MIDDLE EAST COUNTRIES

Categories of Land in Islamic Law

In accordance with the fundamental traditionalism of Moslem doctrine the tax categories instituted in the initial stages of the Arab conquest, *Osher* and *Kharaj*, remained in force over a long period, despite the political and social changes which have since continually swept over those countries. Originally, any land which paid the *Osher*, the tithe (single or double), was classed as *Osher* land; this applied above all to property whose owners had embraced the Moslem faith at the time of the conquest or which had been distributed among the conquerors. All other land was termed *Kharaj* land, and was liable to the payment of the tribute known as *Kharaj*. Both categories of land comprised cultivated and uncultivated areas, private and public. In the course of time the original fiscal criterion of classification came to denote also a difference in conditions of tenure. Whereas originally all land apportioned to individuals, whether *Osher* or *Kharaj* land, was regarded as the private property of the owner, the right of private ownership was subsequently denied to owners of *Kharaj* land. The *Osher* estates retained the status of private property (*Mulk*), whereas the peasants occupying *Kharaj* land were given only the status of hereditary tenants of the Crown on State land (*Miri*).

The expansion of ownership rights on the part of the Crown was much facilitated in the countries under Moslem rule by the fact that the old pre-Islamic conception of the State as supreme owner found points of contact in the Moslem world of ideas, and with the Moslem conquests was transferred into the legal notions of the Arab and Turkish countries.[10] In practice, as a result of these legal notions, the ruler or the State, as the case might be, acquired immediate possession of estates whose owners were killed; moreover, with the theoretical recognition of the right of supreme ownership in respect of many areas which for the time being remained in the hands of the conquered inhabitants, there was the further chance on the death of the owners, who had only the status of Crown tenants, of recovering such lands for free disposal. Thus, in time, the extent of these State lands steadily increased. In

Iraq, for instance, as late as 1931 the bulk of the cultivable land was State property.[11] The Ottoman government regarded Mesopotamia as conquered territory wherein, except for the rather restricted areas expressly recognised as private property, almost all the remaining land became State land.

The idea of supreme ownership on the part of the State and consequently the dual conception of ownership under Islam emerges also from the fact that, contrary to Roman law, where a distinction is made between ownership and usufruct, a twofold right of disposal of ownership is admitted, viz. one in respect of the land itself and one in respect of its yield. Thus in the countries which fell into the hands of the Arab conquerors there developed several specific forms of ownership which in Moslem legal practice have retained their validity side by side up to the present day.[12]

Consequently, a house and the site on which it is built may belong to different owners. There are further various degrees of ownership. There is the unrestricted right of land ownership known as *Mulk* which allows the owner to dispose of his property without any qualification. There is again the conception of ownership which covers *Miri* land. The owner of such property has outwardly all the status of a quasi-owner; he may sell, let, mortgage, give away or otherwise dispose of his land. Irksome restrictions arise, however, in respect of the right of inheritance; *Miri* land cannot be freely bequeathed by will, but failing the recognised heirs the succession reverts to the State, although the original restriction of the right of inheritance to the sons of the testator has in the course of time been extended. The "State" or the head of the State has reserved certain rights of supervision which cannot be applied to land in private ownership (*Mulk*). The theory of *Miri* land is based on the assumption that the State has conferred the land for the purpose of cultivation and production. The recipient must cultivate it, and thus be in the position to remit a share—later called tithe, although not identical with the original *Osher*—to the State as tax. In addition, the validity of any transfer of *Miri* land is dependent on the nominal consent of the State.

The Ottoman land law of April 1858, which represents the first codification of land regulations under Ottoman law, enumerates the following categories of land tenure, incorporating at the same time many of the existing legal traditions:

(1) *Mulk*, full right of ownership, property which like movables is in the possession of private persons.

(2) *Miri*, property of which the *rakabe*, the *nuda proprietas* belongs to the sovereign, whereas possession and extensive rights of usufruct are vested in the private owner.
(3) *Waqf* land, belonging to endowments and pious institutions, for which the rights regarding ownership and usufruct are subject to important restrictions.
(4) *Metruka*, land intended for public use, streets, public places, etc. corresponding to the *res publicae* in Roman law.
(5) *Mevat*, "dead" land, *res nullius*, land for which no owner exists and which is not under cultivation.

This list does not include one of the most remarkable forms of property in Oriental countries, *Mushaa* land, an institution deserving of special treatment.

Collective Land Ownership (*Mushaa*)

In some of the principal Middle Eastern countries even to-day collective land ownership (*Mushaa*) is very widespread, in part in genuine form. It is met with above all in the Levant States, Palestine, Iran, Turkey, Arabia and Transjordan. In the many agrarian reforms introduced since the beginning of the 19th century as a result of the infiltration of European ideas into the Orient, the problem of collective land ownership and its adjustment to the new conditions occupies an important, if not a central position. Most illuminative in this connection is the discussion on the origin of communal ownership as existing to-day in Moslem countries, a question which arose in particular over the collective forms in North Africa. The French colonial administration took up the view, which was also applied in legal practice, that in the North African countries and especially in Algeria the original law of landownership did not recognise private property, and that the natives were not owners of, but only usufructuaries in the land and, therefore, could claim no special protection in respect of their right of ownership. This theory, which for easily comprehensible reasons was very welcome to the French colonial administration in its land policy, was based, on the one hand, on the old Moslem conception of the State's supreme right of ownership, and on the other, on the primitive forms of ownership as practised by the nomads who in their early stages of settled life were content with common grazing and possibly also with the primitive cultivation of their lands without claiming or determining individual ownership rights. Opponents of this view point out, however, that the idea of collective ownership on the part of the tribes, in Algeria for instance, was introduced only in 1901 and had not previously existed there. They maintain moreover that the agrarian-communistic constitution was imposed on these tribes for fiscal reasons, a fact which is confirmed also in the case of many non-Oriental countries where communal forms of land ownership and usufruct existed or still exist. "As far as North Africa is concerned, the land classed as collectively owned, the so-called *terresars* or *sabega* as well as its Moroccan counterpart, has nothing in common with agrarian collectivism, but is a creation of the Turkish or Moroccan system of government. The aggregate condition to which they revert when the government pressure ceases is the régime of private ownership by individuals or individual families.[13]

As against any generalisation on the part played by the Government in this connection it is not difficult to find examples both in the East and in Europe where the State has interfered in the very opposite direction; the formation of individual ownership was by no means always favoured, let alone effected, by the usufructuaries but, like collective land holding, was imposed on them from without. Similarly the attempts made by the Turkish Government to curb the authority of the feudal lords and large landowners in the second half of the last century frequently failed owing to the attitude not only of the overlords but also of the indolent fellahin population.[14]

In the countries of Western Asia, especially Syria and Palestine, conditions were no doubt essentially different from those in North Africa. Thus Bergheim writes in 1891 in a survey of land ownership conditions in Palestine, in respect of the Turkish reforms which were introduced 28 years previously and particularly affected the land constitution, that they were carried out against the wish and will of the people. Their enforcement cannot, however, have been everywhere equally vigorous : the Ottoman land code, for instance, theoretically prescribes the dissolution of the institution of *Mushaa*, i.e. common land ownership:

> "The whole land of a village or of a town cannot be granted in its entirety to all of the inhabitants, or to one or two persons chosen from amongst them. Separate parcels are granted to each inhabitant and a title deed is given to each showing his right of possession." (Art. 8).

In practice, however, the institution of the *Mushaa* has survived in large measure up to the present day, although the reasons which at the time induced the Ottoman government to abolish it have since then been considerably strengthened. For details of the trend of development during the past decade cf. Part II, Section II.

WAQF

Among the specific institutions of Oriental agrarian society there is one which calls for particular emphasis: the immobilisation of the land or the returns therefrom in favour of religious or public utility institutions, the *Waqf*. The *Waqf* represents one of the most important restrictions on landed property which Oriental land law has devised. The meaning of the word *Waqf* is to cause to rest, to halt, to bring to a standstill. *Waqf* property is withdrawn by its endowment from the right of free disposal on the part of the individual in favour of a charitable purpose, or, as was later the case, of a stipulated usufructuary.[15] To become *Waqf* property signified economically that the private and consequently the marketable value of the property concerned is limited, if not annulled, in accordance with the provisions of Moslem legal tradition. The usufruct (*usufructus*), the use of the produce, is reserved, in keeping with the principles of the foundation, mainly for religious purposes.

As the object to be endowed must be of substance and bring returns, *Waqf* was predominantly real estate; the beneficiaries were as a rule institutions such as schools, libraries, mosques, etc. The endowments were originally dedicated to such religious and charitable purposes or were used for the maintenance of needy members of the family, whether children and grandchildren or other relatives. By means of evasion, mostly by the transfer of the property to a third party who would then register it as *Waqf* property in favour of the owner, endowments could be arranged in favour of the person of the endower.[16]

The origin of the *Waqf* system is attributed to the Khalif Omar. Here, too, an institution which according to tradition is purely ideological in conception is in practice made to serve quite different purposes. Omar, the companion of Mohammed, guided by the old ideas of divine ownership, left large parts of the conquered territories to God, i.e. the Moslem community. "The interest, i.e. the yield from the land, should belong to man, the capital to God."[17]

The immobilisation of land, however, is no Moslem invention. Similar legal forms were already in existence in the Byzantine era.

In the former Byzantine countries of Hither Asia which the Arab conquerors occupied they found institutions for the community (i.e. for the benefit of churches, monasteries, orphanages, etc.), a practice which they took over for their own ends. These bestowals invested the property concerned with the character of inalienability.

The establishment of *Waqfs* occurred in the first century of Islam mostly from religious motives, but was later superseded by a powerful movement for the immobilisation of real estate actuated by motives deriving from entirely different sources. Of the religious origin of the institution which conferred on the *Waqf* properties a generally accepted status of immunity, the founders still remained conscious. For it was indeed the prerequisite for the large-scale use of the *Waqf* as a means for securing at least rights of usufruct. The insecurity of landed property, which was particularly exposed to confiscation on the part of rulers, provincial despots and feudal chiefs, led to an ever-increasing conversion of privately-owned land into *Waqf* land in order to assure to the owner or his family the usufruct of the property.

That land sales were rendered more difficult by this transformation did not matter. In actual fact, many families have succeeded in preserving the core of their possessions by the establishment of a family *Waqf*. Not in every case, however, has the status of the land been respected; many abuses crept into the administration of the *Waqf* and have remained to this day. Another motive for the creation of *Waqfs* was the dislike of the clause of the Koran which conferred rights of inheritance also on female successors. Through a *Waqf* it could be stipulated that male heirs only should be entitled to inherit.

In view of the absence of any modern system of education and instruction controlled or guided by the State, the institution of the *Waqf* has fulfilled a great mission in disseminating learning among the Muslim population. It has likewise performed an important task in the field of social welfare, at a time when no one else would have cared.

On the other hand, great disadvantages attended the *Waqf* system. The huge agglomeration of vast possessions as "mortmain" property without any efficient control proved a grave impediment to the management of the land animated by the interests of the peasants themselves. All the phenomena familiar to us as symptoms of decay in large landed property are present also in the case of *Waqf* property: neglect and impoverishment of the soil, corruption of the administrative organs, bad management, indebtedness on the part of tenants or workers. Some changes, it is true, were introduced after the sixteenth century, by granting hereditary lease rights in *Waqf* lands with a view to arousing more interest in the management of the land. These changes were not without success. The new inheritable rights were an imitation of ancient forms of tenure which had already proved their value in the Byzantine period, in the management of Church land.

On the whole, the evils of the *Waqf* system far outweigh its possible advantages. Nowadays, when owing to the development of a powerful central State authority and modern conceptions of the duties of the State in relation to the peasant landed property in most Moslem countries is safeguarded and the religious motive has receded in importance, the *Waqf* system has become completely obsolete and superfluous. Its shortcomings were, however, not confined solely to the Mohammedan institutions. They were scarcely less in the management of Church property, especially that of the Eastern Orthodox Church, where abuses in the accumulation of lands were the subjects of censure as early as the time of Nikephoros II Phokas. Up to the present abuses of this nature have been an inseparable concomitant in the management of Oriental church property. Nikephoros was obliged, like his predecessors, expressly to forbid his abbots to acquire property, even when freely bestowed in order to curb the senseless accumulation of treasures by the monasteries.[18]

About a thousand years later a commission appointed by the British Government to examine the accounts of the oldest Christian Church body found itself obliged to report that there were grave abuses in the management of its affairs. The difference between the eloquent appeal of the Emperor Nikephoros and the sober British report is solely a matter of style. So far as contents are concerned, the finding and reproaches are nearly identical.[19]

To sum up, it may be said that the principal effect of the *Waqf* system and its variations is to be found in the favoured position it affords to those living on the receipt of annuities, such as the officials appointed to manage the *Waqf* properties, or the occupants and functionaries of the religious institutions, or finally the members of the endowers' families themselves. Especially did the *Waqf* donations made for the purpose of safeguarding family possessions lead indirectly, and subsequently even directly, to the growth of an idle beneficiary existence to a degree almost beyond belief. This state of affairs corresponded on the other hand with continuous and spreading impoverishment among the actual cultivators whose task it was to maintain such sinecures.

The agrarian institutions dealt with so far are not by themselves enough, however, to give agrarian conditions in Oriental countries their specific character. It was, above all, the prevalent form of feudalism together with the above institutions that helped to mould the stationary agrarian economy of the Middle East.

Oriental Feudalism

At all periods of the Moslem era conditions in the Orient have been characterised by an extraordinary prevalence of large landed proprietorship, which at times has been the most widespread form of land ownership. For the existence of these conditions a variety of reasons is jointly responsible. Apart from the trends of more recent date, which will be gone into in detail later, feudal grants of land for the purpose of securing the military services of those on whom it was bestowed were made at an early period.

In all countries the characteristic principle of feudal land tenure was the separation of the rights of ownership and of usufruct. But this criterion applies also to conditions of large land ownership not deriving from genuine feudal origins. The term "feudalism" in the narrow sense designates a system of land ownership based on a certain form of personal relation between overlord, landowner, and cultivator, with recognition of mutual obligations and a clearly defined allocation of land.

In the Orient also a feudal system of this nature came to assume extraordinary proportions. Feudalism was a factor of no less importance for the course of history in the East than was its counterpart in the West. The effects of this feudal system, however, are, to this day much more tangible and apparent in Middle Eastern countries than in other parts of the world.

From the economic point of view a fief in the Orient was likewise an intricate system of rent-ensuring rights—as a rule over landed properties whose possession guaranteed a materially independent seigniorial existence. From the sociological standpoint, however, Oriental feudalism differs very substantially from the European form both in origin and effect.

What is the reason for the establishment of feudal conditions? "The normal purpose of the feudal system is the creation of horsemen through the grant of land and seigniorial rights to people prepared to act as vassals." (Max Weber). This definition is based in the first instance on conditions in the West. There feudalism was mainly an attempt to solve the problem of military preparedness, i.e. the establishment of an army and its adequate equipment, in a State built on the basis of a natural economy. In view of the fact that neither the central authority nor the individual rulers had the ready money at their disposal, the acquisition of mercenaries against payment in cash was out of the question. The problem of equipping an army had to be solved by an apportionment of the burden of armament, i.e. of keep and equipment, among those who produced both these items as part of the natural economy process of that time. Thus the feudal nexus came into existence, which by the grant of land and manorial rights secured the services of knights and men-at-arms. As soon as, in the development of economic forms, tendencies towards an exchange economy appeared, new trends were to be noted in the feudal system also. The feoffee became an official. Where the exchange economy is undeveloped or occurs only sporadically, officials and soldiers are procurable only by the grant of land.

As against this, conditions in the Moslem Orient appear in a entirely different aspect. Islam as heir to Antiquity took over the developed forms of exchange economy which so fully characterised the general economic life of that period.

In the Omayyad and Abbasid States the government revenue and taxes were paid predominantly in the form of money, the customs receipts in money and in kind. Officials and soldiers received money payments besides food rations in kind. Money circulation and transfer was likewise based to a large extent on the forms of an exchange economy; thus cheques and bills of exchange were customary both in commercial and State dealings and State clearing, although barter transactions also were frequent. One of the chief forms of monetary transactions was tax-farming as handed down from ancient times.[20] The need to finance the troops led as a rule to the direct method of tribute-collecting through the central Government or the central tax administration being supplemented or replaced by a decentralisation of tax collection, one of the principal prerogatives of the State. The reason for these drastic and in part long-lasting changes in the administration of State powers lay in the increasing decline of the centralist State organisation. The State could no longer exert its authority in the outlying provinces, a weakness from which the local representatives of State power, the tax farmers and seigniors on State land, benefited. Originally the tax-farmers and the owners of domains conferred for life known as *Muqta* had in most cases no military obligations. In return for certain services, generally of a military nature, they were rewarded with rights to land or tax farming on the strength of State title-deeds. They had the *beneficium*, but not the *homagium*.[21]

It was only when the State was no longer able to pay the troops in cash that the military, in order to satisfy their needs, encroached generally on the existing system of benefices. The Treasury, which had not yet come to dispense with the revenue from taxes and tributes owed by the tax farmers, large landowners and feudal guarantors, lost more and more ground. The chiefs of the troops, in default of another alternative, were invested with the lands, whose revenues could be used directly for the maintenance of the troops.[22] It was out of the grant of the tax-farming from the bestowal of conquered territories on the Arab grandees that there grew up the Arab feudal system, which both in origin and character differed so remarkably from its Western counterparts.

The fact that the rate of tax farming was reckoned in money, that at the time of its assignment a fixed annual sum was agreed upon, also determined the character of the bestowals, and with lasting effect. The question of revenue dominated these institutions to such an extent that the personal-feudal relationship to a certain fief was no longer of any consequence, but only the receipts, no matter what form they took. It must, therefore, cause no surprise that endowment in the Moslem countries included also the assignment of commercial and industrial rights of usufruct based on the exploitation of urban trade concessions.

A contributory factor in this trend of development was the fact that the beneficiaries on whom the Moslem rulers bestowed their grants settled down in the towns and were necessarily interested in the sources of taxation to be found there.

Whereas the growth of feudalism in the West was conditioned by the natural economy then prevailing in conjunction with the social conceptions of vassaldom and homage inherent in the idea of chivalry, Oriental feudalism represents, as Becker in particular, and before him Prutz, have shown in dealing with the feudalism of the Crusaders,[23] so to speak, a system of military beneficiaries engendered by the decay of the tax system and by the need for military equipment of a State relying on a money economy. The elaboration of the conceptions of class honour and allegiance produced in the West a way of thought which made these qualities the very essence and indispensable substratum of feudal society, using them as a touchstone of the worthiness and rectitude of the member of this society, i.e. of the liegeman bound to allegiance. Feudalism in the Orient knows little if anything of this social ideology, this mutual tie which formed such a vital factor in European feudal conditions. The bestowal of fiefs in the Orient was based either on tax farming direct or on a subsequent legalisation of the State revenue already usurped by the potential feoffee. It was represented by a benefice measurable in figures, but not as a rule by an equivalent for personal services, such as is envisaged in the *homagium*; hence it fostered the development of a far more calculating approach to the concept of feudalism in those invested and of a much more labile relationship to the concrete fief itself and to the tasks and duties it entailed in relation to the bestowed lands and their population.

The results of the Eastern feudal system are twofold. They consist, on the one hand, in an unusual impoverishment and deterioration of the agricultural population which saw in their masters, both sovereign and landlord, only the representatives of an oppressive fiscal régime which had no interest in the fate of the peasant. On the part of the large landowner also the relationship was not that between the lord of the manor and his ancestral soil, but that of the rent-receiving capitalist and a feudal way of life under which the land represented to him only a source of income or often a mere object for speculation. Descriptions of the lot of the fellah in Arab countries as recorded in various centuries testify unanimously to a state of extreme economic and moral degradation which reduced his actual position in many cases to that of a forced labourer crushed by his debts. Even after the abolition of the feudal system in 1839 nothing much was changed in this respect. Urban and rural capitalists exploited the new possibilities of acquiring land and occupied in fact the position of the old landlords, even if they now did so without the feudal background. (*Vide* Section II).

The mentality of the Oriental grandees deriving from the system of benefices and differing so widely from the social values of the European feudal classes could not produce personalities who would play a part in the establishment of the Arab and Ottoman commonwealths such as did those who contributed the keystones for the reconstruction of Western States. The great State reforms attempted by the Ottoman rulers failed owing to a lack of understanding, and often also to the actual resistance of the Oriental feudal class.

Had there been—as was the case in the West—a citizen class fit to be considered an ally of the reform-minded few at the court of Constantinople, this might have caused a change in the general cultural development of the East. But a citizen class of this nature was lacking. The industrial revolution did not reach the gates of the Orient, or, if it did so, it was in a fundamentally different version, and thus the urban sector which in the West was the scene of that bloodless economic and social revolution remained under the shadow of feudal domination. Whereas the European urban centres, with the exception of the Italian towns, flourished and prospered only after repelling and overcoming feudal influences which had long been attempting to gain a foothold there, the Oriental town was dominated by the feudal class, represented by the landlord who derived his rental income from rural estates. This class was above all interested in maintaining and extending its dominant position in the town and in suppressing that very element which in the West was the medium for free progressive cultural development. In the West, by ousting the influence of the feudal class within its precincts, the urban citizenry became finally the most influential class in the modern capitalistic State.

Types of Farm Management and Land Occupation—Distribution of the Income from the Land

In contrast to the conditions prevailing in the majority of the European countries, centralised management of large estates is the exception in the Orient. Compact individual country estates, the property of princes or lords of the manor, so typical of Europe since the early Middle Ages, and the system of direct labour on them, is in fact rarely met with in the East; the country nobles prefer the town as their permanent place of residence. Even newly-arisen large landowners have up to the present made no appreciable changes in the methods of decentralised management and cultivation of their estates common in these zones since ancient times.

Absenteeism occurs in the East in a particularly unsympathetic form. All pride of possession and pleasure in the upkeep of one's estate is lacking: a deep-rooted spirit of matter-of-factness pervades conditions of large ownership where personal relations are almost completely lost sight of. Characteristic of the prevailing state of affairs is the following comment by a good judge of such conditions:

"Should one enquire of the landowners (some of whom do not know the exact locality of their estates) as to the value of their lands, they will answer without exception that they are the best in the district; should one enquire as to the profits from the crops, they will give incredibly high figures, at least so long as they do not suspect that this question harbours a fiscal motive, in which case the yields are always nil."[24]

The actual management of the larger estates and the distribution of the income from them usually takes the form of share tenancy. Where rent is paid in kind, the advantages of the tenancy system under the conditions of Oriental agriculture are self-evident. It lessens the risk both for tenant and landlord in times of fluctuating prices, even if in the long run it offers the landlord greater advantages than the cultivator. The system of share tenancy may appear in many mutations and variations of relations between owner, tenants, and peasant workers regarding the rate and nature of rent, etc. Sometimes the tenant cultivator becomes a partner in the exploitation of the land; sometimes his position resembles that of a wage-labourer. The rent is paid in cash or kind amounting to from 25 to 50 per cent. of the crop or its value in cash. As regards the size of individual farms, there is no lack of variants here also, due to the nature of the lands to be cultivated, local traditions, and fiscal conditions. Thus on irrigated land the small holding prevails, while on unirrigated cornland the farm unit may be of substantial extent.

The following paragraphs will serve to illustrate the conditions existing in the principal agrarian countries in the Middle East.

Egypt

Within the agrarian economy of the Orient as a whole the types of cultivation in Egyptian agriculture deserve special attention. In the standard of development of its irrigation, and the intensity and value of its agricultural production, Egypt ranks first among the Middle Eastern countries.

The manifold forms of land tenure to be found in Egypt may be classified under two main categories: ownership occupation and the estate system. Ownership occupation or direct management of estates is confined principally to two cases: the very small farm and the large-scale estate with direct labour as represented on the one hand by the owners of parcellated farms consisting of a few feddans, and by the large estates mostly run by very wealthy landowners and land companies organised as limited companies on the other. The direct management of large estates in Egypt, as in other Oriental countries, is not, however, very common. Properties of this kind are especially to be found in the Delta; they are characterised by the extensive use made of modern agricultural machinery and by substantial capital investment. The management of such estates, in view of the large amount of working capital entailed and the requirements of a farm largely based on machine labour, must necessarily be on centralistic lines. The administration of the estate lies in the hands of farm inspectors; the distribution of profits takes the form of dividends or interest to the shareholders and debenture holders of the company. But the life of such societies, apart from cases where State domains are concerned, is limited. Generally the establishment of such companies had as its object the development of new land acquired at cheap rates and its successive disposal in small lots to the fellahin at remunerative prices.

Ownership cultivation is far commoner in the case of the small parcellated farms. The area occupied by such small holdings is estimated at no less than 40 per cent. of the total cultivable land in Egypt. In view of their limited resources the farms managed by the fellahin themselves must necessarily be of small dimensions. As the water buffalo, the working animal in general use on such farms, costs from £E15 to 17, the fellah hires an animal for the principal working season at a high rate, amounting to 2–3 shillings per day. The combined labour of a family of 5 or 6 persons is as a rule not capable of properly cultivating a plot of more than 4 to 6 feddans. Assuming an annual return of £E10–15 per feddan, it is easy to see how extraordinarily low are the total receipts, which must cover the cost of implements, seed, cultivation, and all other expenses and the maintenance of the family. If, in order to acquire the land by purchase, the fellah has undertaken the payment of heavy interest on the sum advanced for the purchase, he can meet these obligations regularly only by dint of the greatest exertions. In many cases the high assessment of the rent for the land he has acquired brings him to such straits that the land finally reverts to the creditor.

In cases where it is not a question of farming one's own land, the usual forms of lease found also in other Oriental countries predominate, above all the share tenancy for rent, which is often paid in kind. Owing to the steadily increasing commercialisation even in agriculture and the great importance of cotton, an export product quoted on the international exchanges, the payment of rent in cash is coming more and more into use.

The lease of land in return for a fixed sum of money is usually undertaken by proprietors of large or middle-sized estates in the following form: lots comprising an area just sufficient to occupy the full labour of a family, i.e. 4–6 feddans, are leased to a fellah family. The period of the lease is usually one year. The supervision of such estates divided into individual leasehold farms is as a rule undertaken by an agent on the spot, who represents the landowner. The task of this agent is to supervise and arrange for the distribution of water and the cleaning of the canals, as well as all other communal affairs. The cost of keeping the canals in order falls as a rule on the tenant; but there are numerous variants as regards the allocation of these and other costs of cultivation and irrigation. The annual rent which is payable in a fixed sum amounts on an average to £E10–12 per feddan; it rises to £E15–20 for first-grade land and sinks as low as £E4–6 for mediocre land north of the Delta. The landlord can generally reckon on a gross income of 10–15 per cent., while the value of the land is put at £E60–100 per feddan. (All figures are pre-war).

Payment of rent is generally made in the following manner: one-third is collected at the beginning of the harvest of the winter crops (May), and the other two-thirds after the cotton harvest (September).

Turkey

Although a greater contrast in natural conditions than that between Egyptian and Turkish agriculture can hardly be imagined, the forms of landownership and land tenure even in the extensive agrarian economy of Anatolia still show features in some respects similar to those of Egypt. The number of large estates in Turkey remains far below the actual number of medium-sized and small farms, as is likewise the case in other Middle Eastern countries. Roughly 97 per cent. of the existing farms are peasant farms. They may be divided into large, medium-sized, and small peasant farms, according to the area. The average size of a large peasant farm was, according to Dr. Kazim Köylü, 26·1 hectares, medium-sized farms 12·1 hectares, and of the small ones 4·7 hectares. Of the remaining 3 per cent., 5,700 (or 2·3 per cent.) are medium-sized estates comprising between 50 and 500 hectares, whereas the large private estates, or rather blocks of large property, whose number was last estimated at 418, are said to contain over 1,500 hectares per establishment.[25] Unfortunately detailed information on the conditions of agricultural land tenure in Turkey is scarce, as Turkish statistics, otherwise well developed, do not throw much light on this point. The larger estates, where privately owned, are but seldom managed by their owners, who prefer either to entrust the task to a responsible administrator who in his turn engages hired peasants for a fixed period and sets them to work at the owner's expense, or the share-cropping system is resorted to, in which case the owner or large tenant leases the land to a number of peasants who in return for land and seed deliver to the landlord one-third to one-half of the harvest.

Cases where large estates are centrally managed as one big unit are likewise rarely met with in Turkish agriculture. The mismanagement which obtained for centuries in the internal administration of the Ottoman Empire discouraged in the past any incentive to progress. Characteristic of the low state of development in Turkish agriculture is the extremely small share of land which is brought under cultivation. Kazim Riza, of the Agricultural College at Ankara, declares that an estate is often considered properly managed when hardly 10 per cent. of the land is under cultivation. In fact, certain landowners are content with the yearly hay crop from the land. Another still more extensive form of utilization consists in leasing the land as pasture, a custom likewise very widespread.

Agricultural labour conditions in Anatolia vary considerably with the part of the country concerned. As regards both the pattern of labour obligations—there are monthly, yearly and daily contracts—and the form and rate of wages there exist great differences, which are again determined by the conditions of production prevailing in the various districts. In East and Central Anatolia, where the population is sparse, workers are employed on a wages-in-kind basis. But labour requirements are only partly satisfied by hired workers. In the coastal areas, where intensive cultivation, and often also horticulture, is practised, the employment of many hands is necessary. These are supplied by the peasant's family, and in part by gang-labour for cash.

The most intensively cultivated part of Anatolia is the West, especially the coastal districts in the neighbourhood of Izmir (Smyrna). Here the demand for labour for the cultivation of the various commercial crops (raisins, tobacco, figs and other fruits) is so great that there is often a considerable labour shortage, and high rates of cash wages are paid. Similar difficulties obtain in procuring workers for the cotton fields in the Adana district.

Iraq

The forms of farming and cultivation in Iraqi agriculture are governed to a wide extent by the uncertainty of conditions of land ownership and land tenure. As up till recently the bulk of the land belonged to the State, modern forms of agricultural exploitation based on the existence of private ownership could make but limited headway. In the none too extensive literature on conditions of Iraqi land tenure the insecurity of ownership conditions is a point which comes in for continual criticism. The authors, themselves usually Government officials, stress the fact that even in those cases where the landowners seek to prove their claims to their land by virtue of Tabu titles, this is still not sufficient reason for recognising these claims as legitimate. In many cases the landowners have acquired their title-deeds at a very small cost by none too scrupulous methods, and they are often not in a position to prove the legality of these claims, whereas the actual cultivators of the lands in question can point out that they and their forefathers have worked them for many years past.[26]

The predominant mode of farm practice and land occupation is the share tenancy system. The usual variations within this system occur in Iraq also. The cultivator cannot lay claim to any right of ownership or occupation in respect of the land; but he receives a varying share of the crop, from 30 to 50 per cent. As a rule under such arrangements the responsibility for the maintenance of the irrigation system falls on the landlord or large tenant. The share system is still favoured in those districts where the owners of the land for lack of capital are not in a position to offer cash wages to the workers they need.

In view of the marked differences in the systems of cultivation in Iraq the forms in which the tenant and the agricultural workers share their interests show marked divergences, although the facts themselves, above all the principle of the share system, have been prevalent for generations. In the spring of 1933 the author was able to note the following distribution of the crop yields in central Iraq. Of the total harvest the Government receives 10 per cent., the Government-recognised landowner or the large tenant (or lessor) claims as his first share 7½ per cent., the head (*serkal rais*) of the fellahin group who cultivate the land (the position of *serkal rais* is often hereditary) receives 2½ per cent. Of the remaining 80 per cent. the said large tenant receives a further 40 per cent., whilst the fellah who actually cultivates the land is entitled to the remaining 40 per cent., from which, however, a further small percentage is deducted for local expenses. In many cases the large tenant is at the same time the creditor who supplies the sub-tenant on credit with seed and often with implements, from the time of ordering until harvest, claiming the return of the sums advanced at a high rate of interest when the harvest is disposed of.

Social conditions in agriculture are much more backward in Iraq than in other Middle East countries. Iraq is a classical example of the dangers which threaten the progress of a country when its population is deficient. The shortage of labour, especially for the cultivation of large irrigated stretches, is so acute that it has led to the institution of quasi-compulsory labour on the part of the fellahin together with the abolition in fact of their right to freedom of movement. On a large estate north-east of Baghdad the administrator was in the habit of hiring through the *serkals* as many fellahin as he needed for the cultivation of his lands. These workers were also personally liable for the advances they received, and could not leave their place of work without permission. They are at the mercy of their creditor, who, with Government aid, can have them brought back if necessary. For the management of the large estates the availability of such hired labour is almost a *sine qua non.* If the fellah were able to find a permanent place of settlement the labour problem in many districts would be insoluble. Thus, the large landowner can obtain workers who are not yet tied to a place of settlement, even if the means resorted to are none too scrupulous.[27] On the other hand the sub-tenants in the districts where the cultivation of the date palm predominates have old-established claims on the landlords which go considerably further than the short-term commitments imposed on the landowners in the corn-growing country. The cultivation of the date palm is a lengthy process. The landowner must, therefore, endeavour to maintain the interest of the tenant or fellah in the proper care of the plantations for some considerable period. Thus, in the Basra district a tenant is given an area of 8 *djarib* (1 *djarib* = 3·988 sq. km.) which he must improve and plant with date palms in the course of 4 to 5 years. The share of the tenant is then often as high as 50 per cent. of the crop. When the owner wishes to dismiss the tenant, he must pay him 18 per cent. of the value of the trees, including those that are not yet in bearing. Where the cultivation of the plantations is done by hired workers, wages are paid either in cash (three shillings a week per worker pre-war rate) or in kind. In addition a special sum may be claimed for extra work such as the cleaning of the canals. The worker also receives annual presents in the form of clothing, whose value may be put at about £P2–3.

The division of the crops, however, not only differs from one part of the country to another, but is subject to modification in the same district as a result of changes in the social and political régime. At the same time the share that comes to the fellah remains almost always unchanged: the modifications affect the distribution of the shares due to the other interested parties. Although, for instance, the Government share on Government land which amounted before the British occupation to 45 per cent. was reduced to 30 per cent. and even less, little advantage, if any, accrued to the fellah. The calculation and division of the harvest according to a detailed scheme would in view of the primitive conditions prevailing in Iraqi agriculture only help to complicate matters for the fellahin; consequently in the course of time the payment of two-thirds of the harvest to the *serkals* came to be recognised as the customary ratio, out of which the *serkals* have to provide for all Government taxes and the share due to the proprietor. In the case of fertile land the fellah's share is still less; it then falls to as little as 25 per cent.; for apart from the major payments he is liable to a number of minor payments and obligations which have to be met in accordance with custom. Thus, a fellah cultivating land which is under the control of a *serkal* must hand over to him a certain sum as the price of security; moreover he is also obliged—a strange survival of feudal traditions—to buy a gun which he must use according to the *serkal's* instructions.

Finally, he is encumbered with a number of smaller obligations in the form of presents, mostly to the *serkal*, in return for certain "communal" services rendered by him and his assistants. These cover certain perquisites (in kind) due to the scribe, the man in charge of irrigation, for guests and the coffee-maker. It is not surprising, therefore, that in such circumstances the income of the actual cultivator of the land may hardly suffice in practice to provide him with the barest existence. Examples of the manner in which the harvest is divided, taken from official reports, reveal that the annual pre-war income of a fellah family of 6–8 persons averaged between £10 and £20; whilst the incomes of the landowners amount frequently to a hundred times this sum or more. The situation is aggravated still further by the fact that the seed and money loans necessary for the cultivation of their farms are advanced to the peasants by merchants who make use of the opportunity for their personal enrichment[28].

Syria, The Lebanon and Palestine

In Syria the common system of land tenure apart from ownership occupation is likewise a form of share tenancy, i.e. the so-called *métayage*. The landlord can terminate the agreement of lease yearly; the tenant himself has no claim whatever in respect of the land he cultivates. The rent is as a rule paid in kind, the usual terms being 45 per cent. of the crops for the fellah, 45 per cent. for the landlord and 10 per cent. for the Government.

The estates belonging to the large landowners comprise as a rule extensive stretches of land, some of which cover an area of thousands of hectares. Small property is to be met with for the most part only in the coastal regions and in the mountainous parts of the country. The large private estates are most common in Syria and in East and North-East Lebanon, where they are farmed on extensive lines by means of the *métayage* system. The tenant who lacks the resources necessary for intensive cultivation uses the traditional methods of extensive farming; the landowner (in the case of Government land, the lessor), in view of the heavy capital outlay to be financed by him in case of intensification, cannot decide on such a radical change in the system of cultivation.

In Arab Palestine also share tenancy continues to play an important part. Here, too, we have to distinguish between leasehold proper, i.e. the leasing of the entire land by the absent landlord, who is not a resident of the village, to independent tenants and a kind of sub-share tenancy, when the resident owner or occupier of a larger estate hires so-called *Harrats* who cultivate the land in return for payment in kind and whose status nearly equals that of agricultural workers with certain perquisites or free lodging and a small share of their own in certain crops.

In such cases where an absent landowner leases his land to fellahin he will often grant them, apart from free accommodation, a completely free hand in the management of the land. Again, these estates are not administered as economic units. The land is shared out to villages composed of individual leasehold farms, while the peasants pay the rent to the large landowner. The rate of rent charged is not always equal; up to recent years it was customary for the tenant to hand over to the landowner 20 to 40 per cent. of the harvest (in Arabic, *chums*, i.e. $\frac{1}{5}=20$ per cent.) in kind. With the increased infiltration of modern economic forms in Palestine the change-over from rent paid in kind to cash rent has already begun. Up to the time of the sharp fall in prices the rate of 100–150 mils per dunam corresponded to the value of the rent when paid in kind.

Also among the larger tenants themselves it is, as already mentioned, often customary to engage *Harrats* when the extent of the leased lands exceeds the area they can work themselves. The *Harrath* then receives one-quarter of the harvest and pays his respective share of the rent and the *Osher*. He is also obliged to contribute to the costs of harvesting the durrah and the summer peas. The number of agricultural farm units in Palestine is estimated at about 70–80,000; the average size was as a rule 100 dunams, but there are not seldom larger units, though, following the increase in population and the intensification of farming, the trend is clearly towards smaller holdings, particularly in the irrigated and irrigable areas.

Conditions of land tenure in Transjordan correspond in general to those in Palestine so far as the hill districts are concerned. According to the Annual Report of the Mandatory to the League of Nations, 1938, the distribution of 15,960 individual holdings was as follows :

CLASSIFICATION OF HOLDINGS IN TRANSJORDAN

Owners		Approx. Areas in Dunams
No.	Per Cent.	
12,649	79	up to 66
2,082	13	66 – 133
750	5	133 – 200
479	3	over 200

Summary of the Social and Economic Features of the Stationary Agriculture of the Middle East

Conditions of land ownership in Middle East countries as they exist today were determined in greater part by the Moslem land laws: conditions of land tenure and the social structure in agriculture are the heritage of the feudal or quasi-feudal past in the Orient. The development of Moslem land law took place principally during the centuries following the Moslem conquests. Despite all the differences which have cropped up in individual institutions and in various countries, the following general features may be taken as characteristic of the legal thought of Islam as applied to agrarian law and its effects on the social and political conditions in Oriental countries:

(1) Moslem land law assimilated the old Oriental conceptions of supreme ownership on the part of the ruler or the State. The State possessed, in one form or other, a kind of supreme right of disposal. Even if this state of affairs was not noticeable in times of State weakness whenever important dynastic or State interests were at stake, the right of disposal invested in the Crown or the State in relation to the possessor of land was energetically upheld. The abolition of the feudal system in the Ottoman Empire in 1839, which against only slight compensation re-established the State's right of ownership in respect of former feudal property, was achieved by decree from above, not as in France and other Western countries as a result of social pressure. True, subsequently also, from the sociological standpoint, the dominating position held and asserted by the landowners for centuries past continued in regard to both the peasantry and the townsfolk. The reforms introduced in the taxation and agrarian system created opportunities for further appropriation of peasant land as well as new possibilities of purchase and leasehold which were quickly seized upon by the large landowners and urban capitalists. Thus, as will be shown in due course, a new class of landowners came into existence, whose origin was, however, divorced from any feudal background.

(2) Another peculiarity of Moslem land law was its recognition of various claims of ownership in respect of one item of immovable property. As a result of the manifold aspects of ownership and its "flexibility" the institutions of the *Waqf* and *Mushaa* spread to an extraordinary extent, involving further restrictions and splits in land ownership rights. It is true that special conditions favoured the spread of these institutions, but they could not possibly have attained such remarkable proportions without the peculiar conception of property rights emanating from the Sharia. Their chief economic effect was seen in the encouragement of the accumulation of large landed property in the hands of a few landowners coupled with increasing neglect of cultivation and corruption of management.

(3) The thought and outlook of the men responsible for State policy and administration in the Moslem countries was permeated to a wide extent by fiscal and feudal motives, so much so that the requirements of the State became identical

with those of the administration and the army, that is, of the predominating strata in these spheres, to the detriment of all other spheres of public life. Land legislation, too, was far more influenced by the necessity of financing State requirements than by the motives which are normally responsible for the shaping of land law conditions. It attempted, in the first instance, to solve the financial and legal problems of the Moslem community, thereby neglecting important questions which are prominently treated in other legislative systems, such as rule of succession and collective ownership.

(4) The relation of the landowner to his estate was from the beginning that of a pensioner or a beneficiary. Arab and Turkish feudalism is, despite certain variations, essentially a special form of reward for meritorious service to the State, no matter whether in the capacity of warrior or other State official. The *homagium* is absent, as are likewise the other criteria of a landed aristocracy of feudal origin. The fact that this class chose to take up its residence in the towns led to the spending of this rent income in the towns, usually on consumption goods, at the cost of the rural district, which had to deliver the means for this life.

(5) The position of the farmers was in theory perhaps more liberal than in many European countries before the emancipation of the peasants: this notwithstanding the despotic features which the Middle Eastern State régime never attempted to conceal, and in spite of its tolerance of many institutions such as slavery, which was abolished in the West generations before its legal repudiation in the East. This liberal line followed by the law was in practice, however, unable to prevent a degree of economic enslavement and extortion such as was scarcely surpassed in the West even in the worst periods and countries of peasant oppression in Europe. True, the degree of personal servitude borne by the Oriental peasant was as a rule less than that of his European brother; in the districts under Turkish rule especially, he possessed a certain measure of personal freedom. On the other hand, in a number of Arab countries the fellah was so utterly degraded that, in comparison with his, even the position of a serf could be considered preferable. The slave had a master whom he served with his person only; the fellah was bound not only in person, but

often with his whole establishment, his family and his farm stock to a master who had the right to whip him, throw him into prison or, under the Mamelukes, even to kill him.[29] As late as the nineteenth century the forcible enlistment of workers, carried out in brutal fashion in the villages of the countries of irrigation for the repair of the dikes or construction of roads (*corvée*), was widespread.[30]

The bleeding of the peasantry by the continual brutal application of the tax screw and their unworthy treatment by the landowners and the State has engendered in the bulk of the rural population in the Oriental countries an attitude of extreme indifference, if not of hostility, to the State and its demands. The "apolitism" of the Oriental masses caused by the circumstances described above is the heritage of those centuries. It is one of the principal problems in connection with the reconstruction of the young national States of the Middle East.

CHAPTER XIV

NATURAL FACTORS IN STATIONARY AGRICULTURE

In the preceding chapters we have dealt with conditions of production in themselves, the outcome of recent social history. These, however, form but a part of the many factors which have helped to shape stationary agriculture in the Orient. Natural conditions are of no less weight in this connection, and although these may vary in degree according to the prevailing level of social and technical development, they invariably exercise a decisive effect on the process of production.

The foremost of these natural factors is to be found in the local climatic conditions.

Climatic Conditions, Past and Present

From ancient times there has been no change in regard to the fundamental fact that agricultural practice in every phase and detail is absolutely dependent on climatic conditions: system of cultivation, selection of crops, form of tillage, method of sowing, treatment of the crops, harvesting. In view of the undeniable reduction in the extent of the cultivated area in Oriental countries as evidenced by the many remains of agricultural installations from ancient times (aqueducts, irrigation canals, winepresses, etc.), the question of the climatic conditions in those days has been a matter of much speculation. In discussions on this point, particularly where Palestine, a country which has always attracted the attention of the civilised world, is concerned, the view is often expressed that a change in the climate must have occurred since olden days, especially in respect of the rainfall, which would seem to have declined. To this diminution in rainfall is attributed the state of desolation which prevails over wide areas. This view is based on the frequent references in ancient documents to the fertility of these zones, with which present-day impressions are in striking contrast. The apparent decrease in the cultivated area and the settled countryside in general, the effects of erosion in the hill country and the large proportion of desert and steppe existing today all appear to point in this direction. In spite of this it will be found on closer examination that these retrograde phenomena cannot be explained by changes in climatic conditions.[31] The range and distribution of the principal crops and generally the zone of vegetation in the Orient, a matter which is above all determined by climatic conditions, is known to be the same today as it was in earlier times for which we have data regarding the existence of these very crops. The zone of the date palm, particularly as regards its northern limit, corresponds closely with the accounts given in ancient sources. The olive tree was already found in antiquity in the same regions where it grows today.

The same applies to the other crops on account of which Palestine, for instance, was regarded in the Bible as blessed: wheat, barley, figs, grapes, pomegranates, olives.[32]

Over and above these immediate proofs this congruity in respect of climate is confirmed by the fact that rain measurements in the period of the Mishna show the same results as today, and that the level of the Dead Sea, apart from slight fluctuations, has remained the same since ancient times. If there had been, for instance, any considerable increase in the climatic moisture since then, the Dead Sea would have experienced a tremendous swelling and flooded the Wadi Araba to the south beyond the existing bed. Consequently, the Gulf of Aqaba would have extended northwards deep into the Ghor. In point of fact, however, all the water marks on the banks of the Dead Sea indicate that the fluctuations in the water level in historical times could not have exceeded more than a few metres.[33]

Thus, it may rightly be assumed that the great changes in the agricultural landscape of the Middle East are not attributable to climatic changes, a fact which is of importance for an understanding of the social and historical development of these countries.

Climatic Factors

The principal climatic factors determining the process of agricultural production and the specific forms of local vegetation are as follows:

1. Amount and intensity of warmth.
2. Conditions of rainfall and moisture.
3. Relation of rainfall to average yearly temperature (Rain Factor).
4. Periodicity of climatic events.
5. Air currents.

1. Amount and Intensity of Warmth

Despite considerable differences in individual regions, a fairly

DIFFERENCES IN TEMPERATURE BETWEEN COASTAL AREAS AND THE INTERIOR

Name of Station	Altitude in metres	Mean Annual Temperature (degrees Centigrade)
TURKEY		
Istanbul	20	14
Ankara	905	12
Izmir	5	18
Isparta	1030	12
Riza	75	14
Erzurum	955	6
SYRIA AND LEBANON		
Beirut	70	21
Jezzin	1000	16
Latakia	70	19
Aleppo	390	18
Damascus	725	18
IRAQ		
Basra	—	24
Baghdad	35	22
Kirkuk	330	19
CYPRUS		
Larnaca	10	20
Nicosia	169	19
PALESTINE		
Tel Aviv	30	20
Jerusalem	790	17
Jericho	-260	23
Amman	780	17
EGYPT*		
Alexandria	30	20
Cairo	20	21
Assuan	100	26

* In Egypt the heat increases in a southerly direction proportionately to the distance from the sea.

uniform scale of temperature appears to prevail in the countries of the Middle East, which permits the cultivation of plants of the temperate and sub-tropical zones. The main divergences in this scale are caused by differences in altitude, latitude, distance from the sea, and exposure to air and wind currents. Typical is the drop in temperature between coast and hill-country, a phenomenon particularly striking in the coastal countries of the Mediterranean, but evident also in the land of the Two Rivers and in the countries bordering on the Black and Caspian Seas.

Differences in temperature coupled with humidity conditions determine the external pattern of the agricultural scene. Some of the vegetation flourishing in the profuse oasis valley of Upper Egypt would suffer seriously in Alexandria under the influence of the Mediterranean winter climate. The banana and date plantations in the Jordan Valley and in the Syrian and Mesopotamian plains, and even the widespread citrus groves, may be sought for in vain in the ruder mountainous country of Palestine, Lebanon and Kurdistan.

2. Conditions of Rainfall and Moisture

(a) Rainfall

The moisture requirements of the vegetable world can be satisfied from various sources, the chief of which is the rainfall. In many important parts of the Middle East this function is supplied by water taken from the rivers and to a lesser extent by underground water and springs, though these are often locally of vital importance.

The rainfall is distributed very unevenly between the various districts. It is concentrated on a number of tracts in the neighbourhood of the sea and on numerous mountain ranges of Anatolia, Syria and the Lebanon, Palestine and the Kurdistan-Iranian highlands. Whereas the coastal countries of Asia Minor on the Mediterranean, particularly the Anatolian and Syrian coasts as well as those of the Black and Caspian Seas, receive very considerable amounts of rain which sometimes exceed the average amounts for European countries, wide areas in the interior of Arabia, Central Anatolia, Egypt and Southern Iraq are left practically without rain. The table on page 145 illustrates the large difference in rain supply and shows without need for further comment which regions are dependent—even for crops whose need for water is minimal—entirely on artificial irrigation, i.e. on water supplied or regulated by the hand of man. The rule is that tracts receiving less than 200–250 mm. rain per annum need irrigation. Naturally also districts with a rainfall of 250–300 mm.—which is just sufficient for the cultivation of barley, and, when distributed over favourable intervals, even for the growing of certain vegetables for a short season—differ externally from those with a higher rainfall. The unirrigated plains near the Lake of Tiberias or in the vicinity of Beersheba present a different picture as regards vegetation from the valleys in the hill-country of Palestine. The same applies to the steppe country in the interior of Anatolia as compared with the district round Izmir (Smyrna). Even slight differences in rainfall have a far-reaching effect on the natural vegetation of the various zones.

Whereas zones with up to 300 mm. rainfall have a steppe-like character, a rainfall of over 400 mm. is sufficient, if evenly distributed—as in the principal areas of cultivation in Palestine, Syria-Lebanon, Transjordan and Anatolia—for the traditional cereal crops of those countries (wheat, barley, durrah, sesame, maize) and the large number of plantations with relatively moderate water requirements (wine and fruit-growing). However, the cultivation in these districts of crops which demand horticultural treatment and consequently a more intensive water supply, can only be carried out given the pre-conditions for additional, i.e. artificial irrigation.

The dew which falls regularly in the littorals of Western Asia and their vicinity plays an important part in meeting the water requirements of the vegetation. In the dry season it fulfils to a certain extent the function of rain.

(*b*) Artificial Irrigation by Rivers and Canals

In districts where the rain is not the principal source of moisture, primary importance attaches to the water-courses. In the two classical lands of river irrigation, Egypt and Mesopotamia, agriculture is as dependent on their river systems today as it was in ancient times. This applies to Egypt even more than to the land of the Two Rivers, whose north and north-eastern areas receive no inconsiderable rainfall. In central and southern Mesopotamia, however, as well as in Egypt as a whole, cultivation stands or falls with the possibility of utilising the water-courses for irrigation. Likewise in Syria and Turkey irrigation by rivers plays some part: but there it is confined, as compared with the aforesaid lands, to relatively small areas. The form of settlement and the density of the agricultural population is also greatly 'nfluenced by the type of irrigation, as in Egypt and Mesopotamia, where the irrigated areas have the character of large self-contained oasis zones and border directly on the desert or steppe, the area thus settled carrying a very dense population and differing sharply in this respect also from the unsettled area. In other parts of the Middle East with more plentiful rainfall the settled population is spread over the whole area, the inhabited and less inhabited districts forming a kind of intermingled whole. These variations in the distribution and density of the population give rise to great differences in the political and social fabric of the countries concerned.

(c) Irrigation by Underground Water and Springs

Underground water owes its origin and replenishment as a rule to the rains. It is particularly important for the cultivation of the soil in those rainy countries where a transition from extensive to intensive farming is desired, i.e. in lands where the rainfall, although adequate for normal tillage, is not sufficient to satisfy crops with greater water requirements. The tapping of the underground water resources is achieved by means of wells ranging in depth from a few metres to many hundred; the water from these, formerly raised by animal, or sometimes by human, labour, is today in the more developed countries obtained by motor power. Such installations play a special part in the zones suitable for citriculture. Citriculture in fact acted here as the pacemaker of modern underground water-raising. At the same time the raising of underground water by means of the time-honoured, primitive field wells, which will be described in more detail later, has retained its place in all Middle Eastern countries up to the present day. Under the same head comes the use of spring water as practised where distances are short. An intermediate form of water-conduit exists in Iran. The mountain rivers formed during the spring as a result of the spring rains are conducted—so far as they do not drain away in the karst formations—by gravitation via underground canals and shafts to the fields to be irrigated; there the water is conveyed to the surface if necessary by means of winches and used for the irrigation of the fields.

3. The "Rain Factor"

An expedient for the classification of the various areas according to their climatic conditions is provided by the formula of the "rain factor", introduced by the agronomist, R. Lang.

ARIDITY RATIOS (RAIN FACTOR) FOR THE MIDDLE EAST

	Mean Annual		Aridity Ratio
	Rainfall (mm)	Temp. (°C)	Rainfall / Temp.
EGYPT			
Alexandria	188	20	9
Cairo	29	21	1
Assuan	1	—	—
PALESTINE AND TRANSJORDAN			
Tel-Aviv	550	20	27
Jerusalem	614	17	36
Jericho	150	23	7
'Amman	306	17	18
CYPRUS			
Larnaca	473	20	24
Nicosia	379	19	20
SYRIA AND LEBANON			
Beyrouth	864	21	41
Jezzine	1,409	16	88
Aleppo	376	18	21
Damascus	178	18	10
Der-ez-zor	171	20	9
IRAQ			
Kirkuk	420	19	22
Baghdad	168	22	8
Basra	176	24	7
TURKEY			
Istanbul	740	14	53
Ankara	359	12	30
Izmir	698	18	39
Isparta	566	12	47
Riza	2,570	14	183
Erzurum	548	6	91

It represents the relation between the annual amount of rainfall and the average annual temperature.[34] On the basis of this index figure the principal Middle East countries may be relatively easily classified according to the respective climatic constellations. Although the method itself is only a rough-and-ready one, it suffices to determine on general lines which places belong, for instance, to the dry climate zone. A rain factor deriving from the relation $\frac{460 \text{ mm.}}{20° \text{C}} = 23$, thus remaining below 40, indicates that the climatic conditions of such an area constitute it a dry climate; at the same time there may be many variants within the margin up to 40. On the other hand, a rain factor of over 40 means that the area in question cannot be considered as having a dry climate even when adjacent zones register other rain factors.

In calculating the ratios of rainfall to average yearly temperature for representative points in Oriental countries we find that the greater part of the Middle East falls within the "dry climate" class, i.e. that the natural rainfall does not suffice in view of the high average temperatures to produce the conditions of a wet climate. This leads us to significant deductions regarding the two agricultural systems possible in these countries; dry farming and irrigated farming. In the former the moisture requirements must be covered by the rains which fall during the rainy season, even when the process of growth does not coincide with these months, and this necessitates a conservation of the rainwater in the soil during the dry months. In irrigated farming the method of cultivation is based entirely on the artificial supply of water.

Those zones or tracts in these countries (other than Turkey), for which the rain factor exceeds 40, form so to speak climatic islands and, where the excess is considerable, reveal an essentially different form of vegetation. They approximate closely to the conditions of "Wet Agriculture". This demarcation, as already stated, leaves all niceties out of account and serves merely as a general guide for the broad purpose of orientation.

Rain Factor		Nature of Climate
0 – 20	...	extremely dry
20 – 40	...	dry
40 – 80	...	dry – moist
80 – 140	...	moist
over 140	...	very moist

4. Periodicity of Climatic Events

The course of Oriental agricultural work is shaped to a marked extent by the periodicity of climatic events, which as compared with northern countries is particularly conspicuous. The regular annual overflow of the Nile in late summer due to the rains falling in the districts of its source, and the floodtide of the Mesopotamian rivers in the spring, have always been the central regulators of agricultural activity in Egypt and Iraq. Up to the present day the overflowing of the Nile is celebrated in the capital as an important annual event and national festival marked by ancient traditional rites.

The rainfall in the various Middle Eastern countries with a dry climate occurs with but slight fluctuations always about the same season, so that here also the course of the year is demarcated by the rainy and rainless seasons, and thus agricultural activity falls into corresponding working periods. Likewise the dew occurs so periodically that it can be depended on as an item in the water economy of the vegetable world. Finally, the increasing warmth, reaching its culmination in the summer months and—as is proved by observations over many years—registering a remarkable regularity in its maxima and minima, exercises, as a result of this periodicity, a decisive influence on the choice and succession of crops and farming practice in general.

Even those climatic events which are injurious to the growth of the crops, such as hot winds (*Khamsins*), occur regularly every year at definite times, as a rule in May and October.

5. Air-Currents—Winds

Air currents in Oriental countries are a climatic factor with considerable influence on vegetation and agricultural practice.

In the first place, the sea wind exercises a significant function as carrier of air with a high humidity content. Its effect penetrates far into the countryside when the current is not held up by mountain barriers. In the latter case the sea air rises and deposits its moisture in the form of dew, mist or rain. The difference between the dampness of the air in even neighbouring places is often extraordinarily marked, as can be seen from the following table:

Relative Humidity of Air (Mean)[35]

Tel Aviv—Jaffa .	May, 1938	80 per cent.
Lydda Airport .	" "	69 " "
Jerusalem . .	" "	62 " "
Jericho . .	" "	47 " "

The distance between Tel Aviv and Jerusalem is less than 50 km. as the crow flies, that between Jerusalem and Jericho barely 25 km.

During the summer months the cooler sea breeze which in many coastal districts of Asia Minor is sucked inland through the heating of the outer crust of the earth is an important factor in regulating the daily temperature. Man and beast welcome it with gratitude as an alleviation of the inland day heat. Mention has already been made of the often very extensive damage to the vegetation done by the hot winds from the East. When of longer duration these may even cause the destruction of entire crops.

Reference must also be made in this connection to the regular use of the wind for agricultural purposes. In the corn-growing farm using traditional working methods, the wind fulfils the function of separating the wheat from the chaff. The winnowing peasant throws the threshed corn into the air; the wind carries the light chaff to one side, whilst the heavier corn falls vertically to the ground.

Steppe Character of the Oriental Landscape

One of the most typical results of climatic conditions in the Middle East is the steppe character of a large part of these areas. Since the word "steppe" is often used in an ambiguous sense, it will be as well, using Humboldt's definition, to describe under that name such tracts as owing to inadequate natural precipitation are devoid of forests, but show a vegetation covering about half the soil and consisting of rough grasses, shrubs or scrub, including isolated clumps of trees. As soon as the vegetation of such an area covers appreciably less than half the land, such country may according to the usual botanical terminology be described as desert.

The steppe country is recognised today on the strength of the generally accepted findings of Ratzel, Hettner and Hahn as an area offering—apart from the oasis zones—the most favourable living conditions for peoples of a certain standard of development, pastoral tribes, hunters and collectors of roots and seeds. Virgin forest and highland are difficult to traverse, and mostly deficient in food and game, whereas steppe and parkland is easy of access and survey and relatively well equipped with nutritious plants, fruit and seeds, edible roots, and particularly fodder plants for grazing animals. The steppe landscape of Hither Asia fostered the development of pastoral peoples, especially that of the wandering shepherds who predominate in these countries.

The survival of these nomadic tribes up to the present day is due to the fact that their hosts could rove the vast Oriental spaces and preserve their form of life not bound to "time and space" inasmuch as everywhere, even in summer, the vegetation ensured the satisfaction of the minimum requirements of their mounts.

A further consideration helps to enhance the importance of

the steppe in this connection. The steppe formations of the Middle East are particularly suitable as areas of transit for certain means of communication, especially for beasts of burden and carriage. As compared with wooded and mountainous districts they have the advantage of offering fewer obstacles to travel. Over and above this, their favourable position as a bridge between West and East was a valuable asset. Traffic between the two halves of the Old World had to cross the steppe lands of Hither Asia.

The exact demarcation of the steppes is a matter offering no little difficulty. True, the results of botanical research, especially the ascertainment of the species of plant typical of the steppe flora, offer important clues, but the boundaries are indefinite in view of the often very narrow extent of the main vegetation zones, particularly in Syria, where the steppes encroach on the area of the original forest land. Moreover the differences in rainfall offer a good criterion for the demarcation of the steppe character of an area, although even here the margins are apt to overlap. Nevertheless, it may be assumed that districts receiving on an average 200–300 mm. of rain have a steppe character, whereas tracts with rainfall under this figure may be regarded as desert and districts with 400 mm. and over as areas of original forest.

The Soil and its Specific Properties

It is not within the scope of this work to give any detailed description even of the principal soils in the countries under review, or to expatiate on their importance for the agrarian economy of the Middle East. Nevertheless, attention must be drawn to certain specific properties of the soil which have a lasting influence on the system of cultivation in these countries.

We will first mention one advantage which modern soil research has shown the soil of the steppe country to possess. Climatic conditions make it particularly rich in phosphorus and potash, although poor in nitrogen. For this reason the fellahin and semi-nomads who grow corn on the steppes of Syria, Anatolia and Mesopotamia dispense as a rule with manuring the soil; for apparently some natural renewal of the plant-food takes place, without human aid. A much less desirable effect of the dry climate is the excessive formation of salt, from which agriculture in Oriental countries is apt to suffer greatly. The formation of salt soils is due, according to Sigmond, to the climatic conditions prevailing over wide areas in the Middle East, as a result of which, on the one hand, the dry climate causes a considerable evaporation of water, and on the other, the irrigated soil is at times saturated with water from above or from underground sources. The same effect of the dry climate, which in regard to the preservation of the nourishing substances stored in the soil of the steppe zones is favourable in its action, causes in the case of alkaline soils and artificial irrigation an increasing insalination of the upper soil strata. It is only in the dry climate that the salts brought about by decomposition are not washed into the subsoil; the capillary movement of the soil solution upwards to the surface results in a separation of the salt by evaporation. In the case of strong evaporation at the surface the salt-containing soil water is drawn upwards, leaving its salt content in the upper soil levels. Whenever the salt formation is particularly strong an efflorescence of the salt on the surface of the soil can be seen and a distinct salt crust is formed.

Soil with such strong salt pans naturally renders any form of cultivation impossible. The salt-forming process suffices even in its early stages to kill off existing crops.[36]

In Egypt the area of salt land unfit for cultivation in the Delta alone is estimated at 1,200,000 feddan. These lands can be brought under cultivation only if systematic large-scale washing-out operations are employed, whereby the salts are removed in solution by the drained-off water. The insalination of the land in Egypt has become an acute problem since the reform of the irrigation systems. The threat to soil productivity by the increasing salt content is regarded as one of the gravest problems in Egyptian agriculture, and some experts consider that the price thus paid for the extension of the cultivated area by the new irrigation methods will make it a doubtful bargain.[36a]

Summary: The Importance of Natural Conditions in the Shaping of Middle East Agrarian Economy

The facts presented in this chapter should clearly demonstrate the outstanding importance of natural conditions for the specific structure and forms of Oriental agrarian economy. Nowhere is the power of the forces of nature more distinctly manifest in the shaping of the landscape, in the harsh transition from sown to desert, in the effect of the sun's heat, in the blessing of water, than in these zones. Where else do the oldest sources speak of the violence of weather, heat and cold, of flood and drought with such impressiveness and sincerity as if written only yesterday! The geographical distribution of the crops in Middle Eastern countries is even today practically identical with that of ancient times, at least to a far greater extent than in Europe.

Not only the intensity but also the very regularity of climatic phenomena is of particular importance in this connection. In the fully arid districts such as Upper Egypt year after year passes with only occasional rains; on the other hand, with the certainty of a law of Nature comes the rise and fall of the river which irrigates the surrounding plains. In the half-arid districts the climate for ages past has been determined by the unshakable succession of winter rains and summer drought. Even periods of emergency, caused by shortage of rain or *khamsins*, occur with some measure of regularity. The rhythm of this process could not fail to strengthen the already existing disposition of the peasantry towards the preservation of the established order of things. Conditions in the desert and steppe belts which cover such a wide area in the Middle East have likewise imposed on the social groups living there, the nomadic pastoral tribes, definite forms of economic and social life which, thanks to the immutability of natural conditions in the steppe country, have so far proved extremely static.

The nomadic life of the roving Arab, Kurd and Turkmen pastoral tribes has had a marked influence on the shaping of the cultural and political history of the Middle East. The ever-present threat to the cultivated zones from the existence of nomad predatory bands on their borders tended again and again to dampen the incentives to progress on the part of the settled population. On many occasions the incursion of these pastoral tribes has led to the destruction of whole areas of cultivated landscape. The pressure exercised by these tribes was so strong that their way of life managed by diverse channels even to touch and influence the manners of the settled population.

In contrast to the zones of "monotonous" climatic influences are the areas where the rainfall is distributed over the entire year and which consequently allow of a much greater range in vegetation. As a matter of fact, the changes occurring in the course of centuries in the realm of cultivated commercial crops in Europe are incomparably greater in scope and significance than in Oriental agriculture. Whereas in Europe these changes in the forms of vegetation often resulted in serious upheavals in the whole agricultural system[37], the pattern of the agrarian economy in the

Middle East has during the same historical period remained practically unchanged. The tiller of the soil, so long as he was content with a minimum of needs, could eke out his scanty existence and overcome even lasting disturbances caused by human agency with relative speed.[38]

But when searching for the factors responsible for the stationary character of agrarian society in the Middle East, consideration must also be given to a series of other points, including the already-mentioned effect of the geographical position. Besides, attention should be paid to certain characteristics peculiar to the forces of production in Oriental society, such as the qualifications of the Oriental worker, the primitive nature of his tools, the scarcity of capital and population growth.

CHAPTER XV

OTHER FACTORS OF STATIONARY AGRICULTURE

The subsidiary factors which have likewise contributed to shape the stationary character of Middle Eastern agriculture are:

(1) The unfavourable conditions for mass transport obtaining in some of the territories concerned;
(2) The traditionalist attitude of Middle East society and accordingly certain specific qualities of the Oriental worker;
(3) The nature of the agricultural implements and tools;
(4) The scarcity of capital;
(5) The growth of the population.

(1) Lack of Facilities for Mass Transport

From the standpoint of commercial goods transport a number of Middle Eastern countries are at a disadvantage. The large areas in their interior which would be suitable for corn-growing are as a rule separated from the sea by mountain ranges. It was only with the construction of railways and modern roads at the turn of the century that the Anatolian and Syrian districts were slowly developed and their production made available for the world markets. The river-ways in Egypt and Mesopotamia indeed offered certain facilities for goods transport, but the primitive vessels used could not cope in speed and tonnage with the demands of mass transport. In wide areas of Asia Minor cultivation was artificially restricted because the problem of transporting the increased production could not be solved. Owing to this isolation arising from the lack of communication during the past centuries, agriculture in the Middle East, apart from the coastal districts, was not only confined to production for the home market, but also was deprived as a whole of all incentives from without. New types of crops, which about that time were already tending to change the very foundations of agriculture in the West, were unknown in the Orient.

(2) The Oriental Worker and His Specific Qualities

These external factors are supported in their turn by others deriving from social causes. Traditionalism, which is the natural attitude of pre-capitalist and in particular of agrarian society "in original and undeveloped circumstances"[39] has probably nowhere attained greater proportions than in the Moslem East. The leaning towards the continuation unchanged of traditional methods of work and a way of life inherent in a peasant society was particularly reinforced by those tendencies in the Mohammedan religion which likewise inclined in this direction. Moreover the physiological and psychological qualities of the Oriental peasant developed in the course of centuries in common with his style of life and work—and especially his working mentality tended to the same end. The result was a tenacious clinging to traditional forms of production, coupled with the display of at times extraordinary powers of endurance on the one hand and the lack of all initiative and incentive to innovation on the other. Thus, this question of the particular qualities of the Oriental worker is obviously one that calls for closer consideration.

In view of the apparently clear-cut impressions of the qualifications of the Oriental worker, there is a temptation to generalisation which may easily lead to false conclusions. Expressions such as Oriental indolence, Oriental tempo, suffice to show in what direction this generalisation tends to run. But this complex problem cannot be adequately sifted without answering some preliminary questions. First: Is there such a thing as a uniform standard of Oriental labour? Further: To what extent are we justified in regarding these real or alleged specific working qualities of the Oriental as a temporary or chance product, and to what extent are they permanently connected with special climatic, geographical and more deeply rooted historical and religious factors?

As to the existence of a generally representative type a distinction must be made between the worker recruited from the non-settled population and the settled worker. The inner relationship to work, to regular activity repeated day after day and binding the worker to a fixed place of work must necessarily differ as between the nomad, who places the highest value on a roving, untrammelled existence, and the settled Oriental; even if the latter's devotion to regular and specialised work has not yet attained the standards current in the West.

First let us consider some of the impressions gathered from a closer observation of the non-settled population and its suitability to the modern process of production in industry and handicrafts.

The overwhelming majority of writers whose experience has been gained by direct contact arrive at a negative opinion. C. S. Jarvis, for many years Governor of the Sinai Peninsula, describes characteristic experiences in respect of the attitude of the Beduin Arab to the needs of civilisation and the possibility of acquiring those needs by means of work. Writing on the young men from Beduin tribes employed by him temporarily during the First World War in the workshops of the Royal Engineers, he says:

"They learned carpentering and blacksmith's work with amazing ease, becoming quite expert in a year and receiving rates of pay that meant unlimited wealth to a nomad, but none of them stayed the course. Invariably, after eighteen months or two years, these budding craftsmen would disappear from their benches without previous warning and would later be discovered tending a flock of sheep in the desert for which they were being paid, if they were lucky enough to extort their wages at all, at the rate of £1 a year instead of the £6 a month they had been receiving as workmen."[40]

Jarvis himself offers an explanation which is given with variations in many descriptions of Beduin life. The desert Arab hates civilisation, because it means that he must live in a house and cannot wander at will; the observance of a time-table and the acquisition of certain habits which curb his freedom seems to him unbearable.

Apart from this motive of extreme emancipation from human needs the working mentality of the Arab is affected also by other considerations deriving from his aversion to any kind of subjection, such as is necessarily connected with all work undertaken for others. Bertram Thomas, likewise a thorough judge of living conditions among the Arabs, goes so far as to find the reason for the proneness of the Arabs to slavery in this aversion to self-labour:[41]

"The answer to the question 'Why do the Arabs want slaves?' is in part sociological, in part economic. Slavery is a traditional part of the social structure. It is congenial. The peninsular Arabs are in the mass far too proud to work as servants, far too independent in spirit to obey a master, so that the well-to-do have either to do their work themselves or to resort to slavery. This is why, among a poor people, having little more than a subsistence culture, all attempts at the suppression of slavery have hitherto failed."

Lastly reference must be made to the views expressed by Doughty, who in his description of conditions during the second half of the nineteenth century is never tired of relating the frugality of the Arabs and the independence thereby obtained, which causes them to decline all work—even in their own districts. Doughty, who made no special study of this particular problem, does not fail to point out on several occasions that certain works such as the construction of desert forts, and the building of wells on the pilgrim route, were done by Christian masons. "It is remarkable that all the Hajj road Kellas are said to have been built by Nasâra (Christians) nearly to Medina."[42]

It is self-evident that this sovereign, conscious or unconscious rejection or contempt of regular work will not be found to the same degree in a settled population in a state of advanced urbanisation. The very housing requirements arising from the settlement process and the refinement of habits of life (clothing, food, etc.) call for a settled and specialised artisan class.

This applies equally to the rural sphere. However, there exists both in Oriental handicraft and agriculture a marked divergence from the working mentality observable in modern countries of production. A clear indication of the differing attitudes is provided by the relation of a large part of the peasant and working population to the machine or the improved technical means of production. A Turkish village in the western provinces of Anatolia received, for instance, before the First World War a seed-cleaning machine. According to a report by Kazim Riza of the Ankara Agricultural College, it was left unused and unusable in a corner of the village.[43] The same applies to the use made of other machines.[44] A number of interesting facts have been collected by A. Rühl in regard to conditions in North Africa:

"What efforts the French have made in order to raise technical standards in Algeria, and how slight are the successes so far ! The Algerian peasant was made acquainted with the deep-cutting French plough, but even today scanty use is made of it; in the Kabyle country a school of handicrafts was founded where the young men could be instructed in smithery, carpentry, repair of weapons, etc.: it was burnt. In Constantine the government placed at the disposal of the local tanners 100,000 Fr. for the purchase of machines; furthermore it offered to provide people to train them in the running of the plant and to supply tannin at cost price: not one would have anything to do with it. Among the Flittas a high officer had small houses with stables built for some sheikhs in the hope that the others would then copy them; these erected their tents close by and left the houses intact."[45]

As regards the most recent times the following remarkable experience in the new Turkey testifies to the lack of willingness on the part of the workers to subordinate themselves smoothly to the new industrial working tempo:

". . . The present body of miners is recruited from the peasants, of whom only 15 to 20 per cent. are regular workers, whereas the rest work only temporarily in the mines. These people come to the collieries in order to earn enough money to fulfil some definite wish of theirs. They want, for instance, to raise enough to pay their taxes or meet their most essential and simplest needs. They work for 15 to 20 days, at best one to one and a half months, and as soon as they have earned the necessary money they return to their villages . . .
". . . The output of the workers is with us so slow, that it permits of no comparison with European conditions. Whereas the output of European miners, according to the degree of development and the geological nature of the mine, varies from 1,100 to 1,700 kg. daily, it amounts in our case to 830 kg. at most . . .
". . . The peasants (whose needs for centuries as a result of various economic and social influences do not exceed the minimum) are more or less uninterested in earning money; they have in fact not even any desire to do so."[46]

Even the far-reaching reforms introduced by the new régime in an attempt to influence the inner attitude of the workers towards employment in the factory by offering improved living conditions, served but to reveal the whole complicated nature of these working conditions:

"As a typical example we may quote the reluctance on the part of the workers to adapt themselves to the social reforms introduced for their benefit by the "Türkis" company. Many of the workers objected for days to the three-course meal served to them for 7·5 Kurus because they alleged it was not to their taste, and the factory was obliged to risk being without personnel for weeks if it insisted on sending the workers' clothes to the cleaners and the workers themselves to the bathing establishment. Sometimes the workers would leave their spring beds at night, spread the mattresses on the floor and sleep on them."[47]

It would be premature, however, from these examples from the present and the recent past, which could be multiplied at will, to infer any fundamental difference as compared to conditions in Europe before the period of industrial capitalism. Sombart, who in his chief work deals at length with the question of the disposition of the workers, has collected a wide range of examples which in point of fact indicate a similar attitude on the part of the European workers of that period. We will content ourselves here with two quotations dealing with conditions in England and Holland.

"England: All observers of the conditions of the workers in the seventeenth century agree that the worker accommodates himself to work only in the direst emergency, when he will work only just enough to procure his barest existence. For this reason the cheaper the cost of living (and the higher the wages) the lazier he is.

"Holland: . . . Throughout the whole summer in the surrounding villages there are alternately Kermesses for which a number of waggons stand at the gates in order to convey the weaver with wife and child to the pleasant village. On arrival there, all is jollity and mirth, and I need not say that the exultant worker after having drunk and danced lustily has very little if any inclination to work on his return home, and prefers to let everything be rather than to curb his passions."[48]

It appears, therefore, that between Eastern and Western mentality, so far as it represents the typical attitude of the worker in the pre-capitalist epoch, there is no fundamental difference. In both cases—except perhaps in the Beduin world—it is the subsistence motive which determines the relation to work. The aversion to any unnecessary exertion—from the standpoint of the satisfaction of the minimum living requirements—and the readiness to while away the greater portion of the day in idleness and torpor, exchanged at times for considerable physical and mental exertions for some other, perhaps religious, purpose, is an expression of the same difference of values as that which divides the medieval world from that of the twentieth century.

The psychological attitude of the Oriental worker and producer has its counterpart in the nature of the implements and means of cultivation employed in the stationary agriculture of the Middle East.

(3) Implements and Means of Cultivation

The productivity of soil and labour in agriculture is determined by the form and nature of the implements employed. The principal implement in Oriental tillage is the plough. The forms of the Eastern plough more than any other implement of cultivation demonstrate the conservative spirit of the Oriental peasant. Wherever we look, in Palestine, Syria, Turkey, Egypt, Iraq or Arabia, the plough modified from its ancient basic form, the nail-plough, still dominates the scene as the first agricultural instrument; thanks to its simple construction, it enables animal power to be used for efficiently increasing the fertility of the soil. This primitive plough consists of the share with its arrow-shaped iron point, whose length and thickness varies with the district, the beam to which the share is fixed, the handle which guides the plough and which is attached to the beam should the latter not serve this purpose, and finally, the shaft-like draught pole by means of which the plough is connected to the yoke of the draught animals. The various parts are joined together by ropes, clasps, wooden or iron bolts and rings.

The Oriental plough which in various forms is today in use on the fellah farms in Oriental countries is—except for small improvements—the rude plough of antiquity known to us from the Bible or from pictures on Babylonian seal cylinders. The plough of Western and Central Europe is a complicated instrument in comparison. Close to the ploughshare which tears up the earth in almost horizontal clods a knife is attached which cuts the soil vertically, and to this a mould board which turns the furrows was subsequently added. Thus the ploughing need be done in one direction only, and the fields can be divided into strips, whereas with the Oriental plough the work must be done in a criss-cross fashion in order to obtain any real breaking up of the surface soil. Naturally the primitive plough can only stir the soil on the surface and does not reach very deep. The normal tillage obtained hardly exceeds 10 cm. (about four inches), whereas the European plough can easily turn a furrow of 25–30 cm. (10–12 inches) and the machine plough can reach any depth up to 80 cm. (32 inches). Notwithstanding its primitive form and output the native Oriental plough fulfils its function under the existing conditions and is in every way equal to the work demanded of it. The shallowness of tillage is in fact essential to the successful cultivation of cereal crops. If the surface soil were stirred to a greater depth, the evaporation of its moisture content would merely be accelerated and intensified; shallow surface ploughing serves to preserve the moisture content of the subsoil. Moreover, the simple and uncomplicated construction of the plough enables the peasant to guide and transport it with ease, to manipulate difficult and stony places in the fields and, if necessary, to repair or replace its parts himself. In Egypt, according to Strakosch, the light wooden plough has the advantage that it does not turn up the soil, so that its already low humus content, which would soon be entirely used up by exposure to the dry air, is retained. Then there is also the low purchase price to be considered. The cost of an Arab plough amounted in Palestine in 1930 to 400 mils (= 8 shillings) that of an Egyptian plough to 200 mils, as against a price of £1·5–2 for a European plough. As an item in the dead stock of the fellah farm this expense would contrast most strongly with the total value of the equipment, which hardly exceeds £P10.

However practical and adequate this Oriental plough may be for the very unpretentious fellah mode of farming, it is, on the other hand, little suited to cope with the increased demands of an intensified cultivation and thus to obtain the optimum yield. It is an ideal implement of cultivation so long as the main conditions of farming under which it is used remain unchanged.

The same applies to the tools in use for sowing and harvesting, such as the leather seed funnel which is attached to the plough at the time of sowing, the cart with disc wheels destined for transport to and from the field, and the threshing sledge which is made to glide over the crop collected on the threshing floor in order to thresh the grain from the dry haulm, etc. Finally, all irrigation implements show the same features of utter simplicity and a fair degree of efficiency if properly operated. All these utensils have undergone scarcely any change, and they render the fellah the same important services today as in earlier times. Their continued use derives from the happy combination of (*a*) simplicity of construction, (*b*) ease of handling and (*c*) adequate fitness for their purpose. It is true that these implements—with a few exceptions such as, for instance, the wind-wheel in which a gratuitous natural power is utilised—call for the continuous application of human and animal power in a trying climate, and are, therefore, serviceable only in those places where human and animal labour are of little account. As soon as the value of labour, in particular of human labour, rises, the use of such implements proves to be irrational.

Thus we come to the function of human labour in the primitive Oriental agriculture in general. The part played by human labour even in extensive cultivation is very considerable; it is still more marked on the intensive and especially the irrigated farms. Here man is not only the conductor of the process of production, but at the same time its chief physical instrument. On his physical efforts depends the decisive part of the process. Starting with the preparation of the bare ground, clearing away the stones, manuring and ploughing, up to the harvesting in of the threshed corn, in every phase of production the share of human labour is of vital importance. Even where animals are used, as in ploughing, or turning the *Saqia* (water scoop wheel), the use of the implements without the continuous and strenuous participation and co-operation of the peasant himself is unthinkable. Outstanding is his share in the common work of tillage, in threshing and winnowing, and particularly in the old methods of irrigation by means of such primitive implements as the *shaduf* and the *tambur*. Nevertheless, the productivity of such labour is slight; it amounts at most to a fourth or less of the returns obtained in Western countries. The existence of the agricultural worker and the fellah is rendered possible only by the fact that he can live with a minimum of expenditure. His standard of living is characterised by the absence of all higher requirements. Seeing that the economic conduct of the peasant is determined by the one purpose of securing a subsistence rather than by the idea of gain, the limit of his efforts is usually fixed by the amount of work necessary to secure his minimum needs; it is only in rare cases that he is lured by the prospect of higher earnings into changing his traditions of work and expenditure.

There exists a close connection between the level of the technique of production of an epoch and its cultural standard. The low level of the pre-capitalistic Oriental rural society is reflected in its low degree of productivity. In keeping with the simplicity of the implements and the "instinctive" use of old-established methods of work is the low record of output which is barely enough to supply the primary consumption goods. But it is not the standard of technique alone which determines the share of the producer in the yield of his land. This share depends also to a large extent on the general social and economic conditions which determine the distribution of the product of the society. At the same time the principal factor still remains the low standard of agricultural productivity. Calculations undertaken for the purpose of obtaining comparable data relating to the net product *per capita* in Western and Eastern countries reveal the wide difference which exists between the two zones even today. If we distribute the net agricultural yield over the number of earners we obtain a production value *per capita* of persons engaged in agriculture in Middle East countries (with the exception of the Jewish sector in Palestine) equivalent to 90–186 units, i.e. one-fourth or one-third of the figure established for those Western countries where the actual technique of production is still far from being fully developed.[49]

(4) Scarcity of Capital

Although itself the result of the aforesaid combination of circumstances, the acute lack of capital in Middle Eastern agriculture contributed in its turn to uphold the stationary character of the agricultural economy. This shortage of capital is due in part to the low productivity and in part to the distribution of the returns from cultivation, which by virtue of the land régime existing for centuries past deprived the actual cultivator of his full rights, both socially and economically. The usufructuary who received an essential part of the revenue from the land in the form of rent and interest on the sums advanced to the tenant consumed this share more often than not outside the agricultural sector.

(5) Growth of Population

Last on our list of subsidiary factors determining the stationary character of the agrarian economy in Middle Eastern countries is the trend of the population movement. The stimuli to overcoming stationary phases of economy which often originate in an intensive increase in the population, began to make their influence felt only with the increase in the population at the beginning of the nineteenth century. Comparison of the trend of growth in the Middle East countries with population figures in Europe or in the principal countries of immigration overseas indicates—so far as the figures available allow—that although the relative increase was very considerable in the Orient also, the absolute figures are far behind the corresponding data for the West. As can be seen from the following table, the population in the countries enumerated increased from 10 millions in 1800 to *c.* 25 millions in 1900, i.e. by approximately 150 per cent, which is certainly a substantial rise. The absolute increase of *c.* 15 million for a vast area which could easily accommodate several large European states does not approximate to the increase in population in a single one of the large European states over a similar period. No further explanation is needed for the fact that an increase of more than 250 millions recorded in Europe during the nineteenth century, when it went hand in hand with the industrialisation of Western and Central Europe, must have had an enormous influence on conditions in European agriculture.[50]

	1800 Population in millions	1900 (estimated)
Palestine	0·3	0·6
Iraq	1·0	2·0
Syria	0·8	2·4
Egypt	2·5	10·0
Turkey (Anatolia)	5·5	10·0

As against this the slight absolute increase of population in the Middle East represents but a weak stimulus, whose effect cannot be compared with the dynamics of the population movement in Europe.

So far we have treated a number of single factors operating within the agrarian society of the Middle East; we must now turn to the consideration of the agricultural systems in these zones as a whole and their interdependence in order to explain the nature of this society and its power of endurance.

CHAPTER XVI

PRINCIPAL SYSTEMS OF FARMING IN ORIENTAL STATIONARY AGRICULTURE

THE PROBLEM OF THE "ASIATIC AGRARIAN SOCIETY"

The diversity of types revealed by Oriental agriculture can hardly be reconciled with the picture of Oriental or "Asiatic Agrarian Society" which figures so prominently in historico-economic and sociological discussions of Middle Eastern problems. The notion of a specific structure of Oriental agrarian society is used in a number of extremely stimulating accounts, based in their turn on arguments formulated by Marx and Engels, in order to prove how the development of certain political and social forms in the Middle East is the inevitable result of natural conditions, i.e., in the first instance, of the need for artificial irrigation over large areas.[51] Likewise in the exhaustive historical and economic studies of Max Weber the whole ramified agrarian problem of the Orient, including its political structure, is intimately linked up with the conditions of irrigated farming. However appropriate it may be to schematise when it is a matter of visualising and interpreting connections on broad lines, nevertheless it does seem as if in the works of the said authors the picture of Oriental agrarian conditions is in some respects distorted, at least where the period since the Middle Ages is concerned. Not only has an appreciable part of Oriental agriculture nothing whatever to do with artificial irrigation, but it represents dry farming in its original form. Other districts which are artificially irrigated obtain their water requirements by means of locally developed sources of supply, and are thus excluded from the scope of conditions responsible for the prevalence of large-scale irrigation farming in the Orient. If so, then significant conclusions in respect of the social and political structure of the Oriental countries of today are unsubstantiated, based as they are on the alleged predominance of irrigated agriculture both at the present time and also apparently for certain periods and districts in the past.

According to the respective objects in view, which may be either to counter the water shortage by economy in use and avoidance of wastage, or to supplement inadequate moisture or water by artificial watering, or, in cases of over-abundant rainfall, to remove the surplus moisture, the systems of cultivation and of tillage in particular may be classified as follows:[52]

(1) Dry farming.
(2) Irrigated farming.
(3) "Wet" farming.*

In the case of dry farming, especially in the Middle East countries, we have a further subdivision into

(*a*) Cereal cultivation.
(*b*) Unirrigated plantations.
(*c*) Natural grazing.

Variations are also to be found in irrigated farming: besides the artificial irrigation of cereals and garden or field crops the irrigated cultivation of fruit trees (oranges, bananas, dates) plays an important part in many districts. Unirrigated and irrigated plantations are often combined on individual farms. As may be seen from the following table, the preponderant part of the cultivable area of the Middle East is dry farming country, although from the standpoint of value the volume of production from the irrigated districts is disproportionately greater.

Areas and Value of Crops in the Middle East (Estimated in 1937)

Country	Cultivable Area	Cultivated Area	Irrigated Area	Gross Value of Crops	of which Irrigated Land
	sq. km.	sq. km.	sq. km.	(million £)	
Egypt . . .	34,000	24,000	23,000	75·2	75·2
Turkey . .	300,000	87,000	4,000	48·2	8·1
Iraq . . .	92,000	13,000	7,000	15·5	10·7
Syria and Lebanon* .	61,000	16,000	2,100	10·4	3·0
Palestine . .	12,000	9,000	400	7·0	4·0
Five above countries .	499,000	149,000	36,500	156·3	101·0

* Including the Alexandretta district.

We will now turn to the consideration of the relevant features of the two principal systems of agriculture in the Orient.

---

*Wet Farming

Wet farming calls for but cursory mention here, as it plays no decisive part in Oriental agriculture as a whole. Its distinguishing

DRY FARMING

Dry farming, throughout historical times the indigenous system of agriculture in the Middle East, an offspring of the steppe country and often called steppe farming, has resulted for the plants which thrive in this part of the world in a natural selection based on a maximum of resistance to drought and a minimum of soil cultivation and care. In arid districts which offer no possibility of artificial watering and where the periodic rainfall is stored up in the soil, dry farming is the only way in which the production of crops acclimatised to such conditions is made possible. Where conditions are still less favourable, as for instance in the steppe districts of Anatolia and the border districts of the Arabian peninsula in the north, it becomes necessary to intercalate a bare fallow and to sow only every second year. During the fallow year all the rain which falls must be stored in the soil, losses through surface drainage and evaporation being as far as possible prevented. This reserve then serves to supplement the rainfall in the year of cultivation; the crops have thus the available rainwater of two years at their disposal.[53] The fallow-corn rotation of crops is in many parts so widespread that the rate of rent is calculated not on the calendar year but on the harvest year, in this case a two-year period. Howbeit, these zones which are so meagrely provided for by nature represent within the total area of Oriental dry farming but a fraction of the total area under corn. In the Levant States, Palestine, in most of the rainy districts of Mesopotamia, and in Turkey the winter rainfall suffices for the normal rotation of two crops. Dry farming is essentially an extensive form of agriculture. The amount of labour expended, the methods of cultivation, the

---

feature is the predominance, over long periods if not permanently, of precipitation over evaporation, i.e., a surplus of water in the soil (Christiansen-Weniger). Where such conditions obtain the chief task is to provide adequate drainage in all places where the level of free water in the soil is too high and the surface soil receives an excess of water from below. This applies particularly to those areas where as a result of inadequate drainage facilities swamps are formed, as commonly happens alongside riverways and in low lands and particularly on the shores of the Mediterranean where the action of the sea in conveying sand towards the coast causes the silting up of the river mouths. After systematic drainage operations which vary from place to place the flooded areas are frequently turned into valuable farming land.

implements and working animals employed, and lastly the harvest all point in this direction. The peasant's principal preoccupation is by means of frequent ploughing and harrowing to bring the surface soil to as fine a tilth as possible and to take every care lest by too much loosening of the subsoil its moisture content is drawn to the surface and allowed to evaporate.

This form of tillage corresponds to the amount of human and animal power available on the peasant farm. As a result of the peasant's frugal way of living, a certain standard of expenditure has been developed which has remained the same for centuries. The question of subsistence centred in the harvest from the fields (cereals, vegetables, olives); the cattle kept were working and not dairy cattle. Neither did they have any particular value as producers of manure. The position of the livestock in Oriental farming is, therefore, quite different from that on the peasant farms of the West, where the intimate combination of stock-breeding with crop production is conspicuous. It is true that the plough and its use is a product of the steppe; but the central position which the breeding of cattle and especially of dairy stock came to occupy in Europe has not been attained in the East up to the present day.

Besides the ox, the camel, horse and mule are put to the plough; in so far as meat and milk are consumed small cattle, sheep and goats, or in any case, the camel takes over the rôle of meat supplier.[54] Attempts on a large scale to develop the qualities of the cattle to anything approaching the European standard have not as yet been successful; dry farming offering no possibilities of cultivated pasturage. Oriental cattle are not a record-breaking stock; in respect of feeding, housing and care they are just as modest as their masters.

A comparison of the cattle population per 1000 inhabitants and per 1000 hectares for the Oriental countries and Europe shows the striking difference in the livestock position which exists even today when attempts to introduce European pedigree and cross-bred animals have been made in the East to an increasing extent. Where the importance of livestock on the farm is so neglected it is obvious that a further factor in progressive agriculture must be lacking: the enrichment of the soil with animal manure (see Table, p. 169).

Lastly, dry farming has a large measure of mobility which serves to demonstrate the "extensive" features of this class of agriculture in a particularly striking form.

This refers not so much to the nomad farming as such—in

which, as in the steppe districts of Mesopotamia, the land is cultivated until it is exhausted, when new lands are taken in hand—but also to the sedentary peasants who in many districts show an inclination to periodical shifting of their places of habitation. The reason for this movement is to be found in the climate, which renders the living conditions in the summer, in the higher mountain regions for instance, considerably more favourable for the stock than in the hot and dry lowlands. The inexpensiveness of his farm equipment, both live and dead, makes it easier for the settled peasant to abandon his place of habitation in favour of a fresh one, so that such cases of migration occur for relatively trivial reasons (political pressure, oppressive taxation, and so forth).

In respect also of the marketing of its products, the Oriental system of dry farming differs from more developed types of agriculture, and especially from most forms of irrigated farming. Its very choice of crops and the limited yields confine it mainly to the provision of the peasant's own needs. The crop which the peasant can obtain with one team suffices to cover his own requirements and to defray the taxes on the lands, occasionally leaving something for sale, but on the whole in the sparsely populated zones it does not go beyond the narrow margin which keeps the producer tied down to subsistence production.

Work in the village is organised on individual lines, according to families and individually-owned farm units, even in those villages where the land is held in common.

While nature's gifts—rain and warmth—exercise their vital functions with unfailing constancy, the simplicity of the work and its relative independence of external factors, have here created a significant form of the great Oriental agrarian society; a form unique in character and determined by other laws than the system of farming dependent on the mechanism of irrigation.

For this reason the political consequences of this set of production conditions differ considerably from those resulting from irrigated farming. The peasant who lives and works under such circumstances, manifests a larger measure of independence and freedom, less need for territorial and State organisation and less dependence on the markets. On the other hand, capital formation, the spread of urban civilisation and more refined ways of life proceeds in these districts at an incomparably slower rate than in the zones of artificial irrigation.

LIVESTOCK PER 1,000 INHABITANTS

	Palestine 1937	Egypt 1935	Syria & Lebanon 1936	Turkey 1935	Cyprus 1936	France 1935	Denmark 1935	Holland 1936
Cattle and Buffaloes .	124	115	136	365	104	374	829	303
Sheep . .	149	90	665	768	838	228	47[4]	77
Goats . .	258	46	552	587	720	31	8[4]	16[5]
Horses .	14	2	21	37	12	67	140	35
Donkeys .	66	49	32	60	119	5	—	—
Camels .	20	10	52	6	2	—	—	—
Poultry .	1,893	1,251[1]	2,559[2]	1,125	?	2,115	7,888[4]	3,279
Production of hens' eggs .	77,143[3]	47,550	42,303	65,067	?	125,800	386,400	218,300

[1] 1929.
[2] Based on official figures of 8,574,000; the *Statistical Yearbook* of the International Institute of Agriculture at Rome gives, however, a figure which is less than half the official one.
[3] Per 1,000 of Jewish population the production is 100,000. In addition to the local production 65,714 eggs per 1,000 of the total population were imported.
[4] 1933.
[5] 1930.

IRRIGATED FARMING

In extremely arid regions with no rainfall, irrigated farming offers the sole possibility of cultivating the land; in those districts where there is also a certain amount of rainfall, it makes possible the cultivation of crops which require large amounts of water and would not grow without the extra water. Thus it helps to extend the scope of the cultivable crops and spreads the period of cultivation and harvest over the whole year.

Whereas in the autumn and winter months the fields in the rain zones of the Middle East are hardly distinguishable from those in northern latitudes, the farm landscape in the Oriental world during the warm, rainless seasons has a distinct note of its own due to irrigation. To whatever spot the cunning hand of the peasant conducts the water, there we find the luxuriant fertility of the oasis; while hard by, almost without transition, begins the sun-scorched and arid realm of the steppe and the desert.

The Prerequisites of Irrigated Farming

The prerequisite of irrigated farming is the availability of water in adequate quantities. On the extent to which water is available depends the regional organisation and technique of irrigation as well as the quantities which can be allowed to the individual peasant. It is also most important whether the water in question comes from surface watercourses or from springs or underground sources. River water as a carrier of valuable deposits can exercise an indispensable function in enriching the irrigated land. The lie of the land is also of considerable importance for the methods employed in irrigation. The flat country in the plains is the most favourable, but slopes and terraces are also used to no small extent in Eastern irrigation districts for the cultivation of irrigated crops.

The importance of irrigation consists not merely in its effect on the water content of the soil; it also produces changes of a biological, physical and chemical nature which may have a far-reaching influence on crop growth. Naturally the structure and composition of the soil itself plays an important part in the choice of crops. Light land, above all alluvial lands in the coastal plains, calls for different crops from the heavy land in the river basins and in the mountains. Great importance attaches further to the alkalising effects of irrigation, which in certain parts of the Orient have resulted in serious insalination and sterilisation of the soil. With the judicious use of irrigation it may be possible to avoid the damage of this kind which may easily occur. However, the questions arising in this connection are among the most difficult and as yet unsolved problems of applied soil science in the Middle East.

The peculiarities resulting from the special needs of artificial irrigation have created within this form of farming a fundamentally different ratio between farm labour and land unit to that in the extensive zones of agriculture which receive their water requirements without the aid of man.

This rough sketch should serve to show that even within the sphere of irrigated farming in the Middle East there exists a great diversity of zones of cultivation varying with the structure of the soil, level of the land, origin and distribution of the irrigation water, etc.

One of the first points that strikes us when looking at the map is the large area over which the irrigation districts are spread, leaving out of account the compact areas of Southern Iraq and Egypt. In all other countries, in Syria, Palestine and Turkey, in Iran and even in smaller places such as Cyprus and Lebanon we find a considerable number of irregularly distributed districts, most of which are very limited in extent. Relatively wide areas are to be found in the coastal plains and river basins, and even here not always in one connected block. In addition, innumerable other irrigation fields of smaller, sometimes very small dimensions are dotted over all these countries.

Howbeit, the socio-economic and political importance of these districts cannot be measured by their geographical dimensions. The economic weight of the irrigation sector in respect both of productivity and population capacity is many times that of the other, unirrigated, areas. From the above table (p. 165) we learn that in 1937 no less than 64·7 per cent. of the total value of the crops—which amounts to £156·3 millions in the five countries enumerated—derived from irrigated cultures, although the area under irrigation remains below a quarter of the total area cultivated.

Irrigation and the Agrarian Society as a Whole

The important position occupied by irrigated farming in the agrarian society of the Orient, particularly as compared to dry farming, emerges fully only after a closer study of the various types and their common features. We are struck, above all, by the fundamental dependence of this form of farming on certain very definite natural facts.

Apart from the basic fact that in important areas of the Middle East artificial irrigation is the essential condition for the growth of the principal crops, the water serves as a means of conveying valuable deposits to the fields. Richthofen, Wittfogel, and others who have studied the conditions in the irrigation districts of China and India with a vast amount of discernment and knowledge of their subject, stress above all the great importance of this manuring function of artificial irrigation.[55]

Willcocks, who before the First World War made a thorough investigation of the irrigation conditions in Mesopotamia on behalf of the Turkish government, states in his report that at high tide the waters of the Tigris contain more mud than those of the Nile and are especially rich in phosphoric acid. At low water, the content of solid matter in the water of the Euphrates amounts to approximately 1 kg. per cubic metre, whilst at high tide the content of sand and other deposits is as high as 25 kg. per cubic metre. In contrast the Seine carries in normal times 0·715 kg. per cubic metre and 0·500 kg. at high level, the Nile as a rule 1·500 kg.[56]

In Egypt the question of the extent to which the waters of the Nile carry mineral food substances is of particular importance. The conversion of the entire irrigation system from basin irrigation to canal irrigation introduced during the nineteenth century caused a marked reduction in the amount of solid matter deposited. When irrigation is carried out according to the basin system, the water flows straight from the Nile and remains for some two months in the large shallow basins prepared before the river overflows; a large part of the solid fertilising elements being deposited on the fields. After the water which has not filtered into the soil or evaporated has been drained off, the fellah sows his seed directly in the mud which has remained behind and which contains the valuable plant food. When canal irrigation is resorted to, the Nile water previously dammed up in large lakes or reservoirs, where it has already to a large extent become settled, is conducted several times during the year, by means of canals to the fields; its enriching effect is thus but a fraction of that obtained by basin irrigation.

As long as the sowing was absolutely dependent on the overflow of the Nile, the cultivation of the fields was carried out but once each year. The plant-food substances taken from the soil were replaced by the mineral elements contained in the Nile sediments; the balance between extraction and renewal of the plant-food remained intact. How the change in irrigation methods effected in recent years came to upset this balance will be dealt with later. The vital dependence and interrelation of irrigated farming with certain natural factors can be seen not only positively in the decisive function of the water conveyed to the crops and its content of solids, but also negatively in those cases where natural forces are allowed to get out of control and to devastate whole regions of cultivated land.

In the larger stream and river valleys, the rising of the spring tides which flood the old river and canal beds brings about a significant change in the pattern of the landscape. The impact of the water-masses cuts a new path, causing substantial changes in the banks and bed of the water-courses as well as in the depth of the bottom. Such deviations may in course of time assume great proportions. Thus, in the case of Egypt for instance, according to old sources the Delta once began 7 km. north of Cairo; today this point is 21 km. distant. The Delta's rate of advance is calculated at 7 metres per annum. The changes which in the immediate vicinity of harbours caused a shifting of the Mediterranean coast-line are also known to us.

Of no less consequence are the inundations which occur from time to time as the result of heavy rainfall in the districts forming the sources of the Nile, which have at times wrought grave havoc both to the natural landscape and to the works created by the hand of man. To forestall such natural phenomena the construction of dykes was taken in hand quite early; but the dykes alone do not guarantee the security of the settled countryside if at the same time mass-levies cannot be immediately mustered in order to repair the expected cracks or breaks in the dykes. In Charles-Roux's *Le Coton en Égypte* we find the following dramatic description:

> "In 1874 the annual inundation occurred with devastating effects; the sheet of water, cutting like a sickle, felled whatever it reached: sugar canes, cotton-plants, maize floated at the mercy of an uncontrollable current, while 700,000 fellahin urged by an heroic sentiment resolutely confronted it with their arms and chests. For thirty days, with their feet in the water, a burning sun overhead, these men struggled to consolidate the sides of the canals and to rebuild their crumbling banks. When at last the Nile resumed a calmer course, the workers returned to their villages with no recompense other than the satisfaction of having saved the country from destruction."[57]

Though the Nile floods do not every year attain such dimensions, it is nevertheless necessary to be on guard during the flood period. The number of those called up to protect the dykes runs into hundreds of thousands, and often only by dint of supreme effort are they able to save the land from the gravest damage.

Similar conditions obtain in Mesopotamia. Here, too, during the course of centuries the accumulation of solid matter, the raising of the river-beds and the innumerable inundations have caused continual changes in the course of the rivers and canals. Moreover, as a result of the deposits from the streams the land throughout historical times has been continually encroaching on the Persian Gulf. It is assumed that about A.D. 400 the sea reached approximately to the spot where today the first junction of the Euphrates and the Tigris occurs, i.e., some 50 km. from the present delta. About 2000 B.C. both rivers discharged themselves into the Gulf still widely separated from each other. At the present time, the annual gain of land is said to amount to between 10 and 40 metres. During flood tide the two rivers convey 10 cubic metres of deposit into the sea.[58] The flow of the river varies according to whether the waters come from the mountains of Kurdistan or Anatolia; when the high water period of both rivers coincides, the annual spring flood assumes the dimensions of a catastrophe; but even in normal years the waters of the two rivers overflowing their banks cover the Mesopotamian lowlands to a breadth of many kilometres.

Directly connected with the periodic inundation is the extensive formation of swamps characteristic of southern Mesopotamia. Wide stretches along the Euphrates as well as the whole lower Tigris are permanently covered with standing water. Although the high rate of evaporation during the summer reduces the water level, this does not suffice to clear the swamps failing human intervention. These swamps can be drained by the work of man alone; they are, so long as they are not rendered sanitary, veritable hotbeds of disease and a danger to the health of the population in the surrounding areas.

The principal social and political consequences of large-scale forms of irrigated agriculture consist in the growth of administrative and political systems aiming at the firm direction of the whole population of the area concerned and their co-ordination or subjection to the requirements of irrigation control. The vital importance attaching to the regular working of irrigation in normal times, the necessity for allocating the available water to the various fields and for adjusting cultivation to the irrigation methods, the immediate muster of large masses of people in order to prevent such ever-recurring natural catastrophes as high floods, breaks in the dykes, washing away of the river banks—all this gave an impetus towards central control of population and means of production and found its natural expression in a despotic form of government. Wherever people were not thus firmly tied to the conditions of large-scale irrigation, i.e., in the dry farming regions and the steppes of Anatolia, Iraq, Syria and Palestine, despotic régimes could only be established with much greater difficulty. Here the individual peasant was less dependent on the central authorities, who had no function to fulfil in respect of the maintenance of his production.

Irrigation as a Factor in the Economy of the Individual Farm

The fact that large sections of Oriental agriculture are dependent on artificial irrigation does not as yet shed light on the importance of the various irrigation systems for the individual farm. In order to arrive at more concrete conclusions in this connection, it will be expedient to make a distinction between the central installations and plants coming under the general classification of irrigation systems and the local measures serving to irrigate the individual fields. Even where a large-scale irrigation plant exists, the watering of individual farms is by no means superfluous. The small farmer must see that the quota of water allotted to him actually reaches the various places at which it is needed, even when fully confident that enough water will be at his disposal from the central source.

Between the two great irrigation economies of Egypt and Mesopotamia, both of which are based on river systems, there exists a remarkable similarity of social features. These, however, must not lead us to minimise the appreciable differences caused by the different periods at which the floods occur in the rivers of the two countries. Whereas the Nile flood takes place between August and October and the winter crops can be sown on the still moist soil, the flood tides in Mesopotamia coincide with the spring months, March, April and May, the season immediately followed by the scorching Iraqi summer which withers every blade that is left unirrigated. Thus, for the arid regions of Mesopotamia artificial irrigation during the summer months by means of an extensive canal system was always the condition of regular cultivation of any kind. Whenever the canal system fell into decay, agriculture was ruined. In Egypt, on the other hand, owing to the fact that the natural Nile flood and consequently the inundation of the fields occurred regularly in the autumn, at least one crop could be produced yearly, for which the climatic conditions prevailing during the spring and summer were irrelevant. True, the cultivability of Egyptian soil was thereby limited to one crop each year. It was only after the construction of the great flood dams that in Egypt also the sowing of summer crops, and over and above this any regular cultivation during the entire year, became possible.

As is apparent from this comparison of Egyptian and Mesopotamian conditions, the differences between the various irrigation systems have a considerable bearing on the conditions of production within the individual irrigated farm; nevertheless, conditions in the two countries mentioned, where water requirements are supplied by central watercourses, reveal far greater resemblance as compared with that form of irrigation based on local sources of water (springs, subsoil water, or small rivers). Subsoil water is made available by means of animal or motor power on the spot and even the utilisation of rivers and springs bears but a local or regional character as compared with the major forms of irrigation in Egypt and Mesopotamia.

The relatively large sums required even for the opening-up of local water sources necessitate the co-operation of entrepreneurs with substantial capital backing. The independence afforded by a local water supply invests the farms irrigated in this manner with a more individual note than typifies the other forms which draw their requirements from a stream system covering the whole country.

The individual character of this locally restricted form of irrigation is most striking in certain half-desert areas of the Middle East, especially in Turkestan and Iran. Instead of a continuous stretch of country under irrigation the landscape here is split up into numerous small irrigation oases. The same applies in a sense to the districts on the west and south coasts of Asia Minor, and in the Syro-Palestinian plains where irrigation can be obtained locally by means of wells or from rivers without the need for its territorial organisation on a large scale.

Nevertheless, certain forms of co-operation or co-operative exploitation of the water are called for in all districts of artificial irrigation inasmuch as, even where such supplies are limited, their opening-up and utilization exceeds the physical strength and absorptive capacity of the individual farmer.

To the problems thus arising must be added the control of the underground water level. Wherever the volume of available water supplies is not determinable from without, as in the case of underground water, not only are the interests of individual farmers at stake, but also those of all the neighbours and often of even more distant villages. A lowering of the underground water table by excessive lifting of water in one place will affect all the wells in the same district. Thus irrigation economy even when of local extent entails the co-operation of those who need the water.

Where the water available is sufficient to satisfy all requirements, the forms of co-operation are relatively loose. In cases where the water is rationed it is usual to find co-operative water associations which in the Syrian and Anatolian villages, for instance, are established on very similar lines and regulate rather rigorously the distribution of water to their members. It is in such cases only consistent that the right of the individual member is not

AVERAGE PRICES OF CULTIVABLE LAND

	Irrigated	Non-irrigable
	Prices in Turkish gold pounds per Dunam (1 Dunam=0·1 hectare)	
SYRIA AND LEBANON (1936)*:		
Lebanon	2·5–10	0·5
Bekaa	3 – 9	1
Vegetable plantations near big towns	40 –80	—
State of Syria	2	0·2–0·6
	* Prices in 1936 under the influence of depression.	
	Irrigated	Non-irrigable
	Prices in Pal. Pounds per Dunam	
PALESTINE (1936):		
Southern Palestine (more than 40 km. from Jaffa–Tel Aviv)	4·5	1 – 4
Coastal plain	10 –30	5 – 8
Hill country	5 –15	2 – 5
	All irrigable	
	Prices in £E. Per Feddan=0·42 hectare	
		M. Dunam
EGYPT (1937):		
Upper Egypt	98	23·4
Middle Egypt	143	34
Lower Egypt	98	23·4
	Easily irrigable land before cultivation	Land distant from water
	per Djarib=0·4 hectare	
IRAQ (1935):		
Basrah district	£7·5	£0·75
	Irrigable land	Non-irrigable
	In £T.	
TURKEY (1935):		
Adana district	Annual rent paid for one Dunam 10	5

to a definite quantity as such but is assessed according to his share in the irrigated land of the village. In this way, the danger that in the frequently occurring times of water shortage the weaker elements might be at a disadvantage is obviated. The water associations are usually responsible for the distribution of the water, and also for the maintenance of the communal irrigation canals and dams. In Turkestan, for instance, the whole population was liable for the annual maintenance of the irrigation installations. The Khan supervised these works in person. For the actual construction of the canals the inhabitants were mustered in huge numbers.[59]

The fact that a field within the area of an irrigation system had a definite right to water resulted in the value of the lot being determined by the quality of its water rights. Similar criteria for assessing the value of irrigable land exist in all irrigation areas. The often very considerably higher value placed on irrigable land is not confined to such land as actually possesses irrigation rights, but covers all land for which the possibility of irrigation may be presumed to exist without this being actually proven in each case. Illustrative of this trend are, for instance, the marked price-differences for agricultural land in Palestine and Syria. Un-irrigable is valued as a fraction of the price of irrigable land.

Traditional Implements of Irrigation

The various systems of irrigation, whether based on the exploitation of local underground resources or springs, basin or canal irrigation, do not render superfluous the use of implements for the individual transport of the water to the fields. In Egypt, as in many Mesopotamian water courses, the water level is often several metres below the level of the fields to be irrigated. In addition, the varying height of the water surface which in many places may cause differences up to 8 metres in the water level makes the use of implements for raising the water essential. Also in those cases where local water supplies or smaller water courses are tapped, these must generally be first raised and then distributed over the fields.

As compared to the system of agriculture based on rainfall, a supply independent of man's effort, the introduction of irrigation implements adds a new and vital factor to the individual farm economy. The following is a list of the traditional implements for water lifting in common use in the main irrigation areas of the Middle East.

List of Traditional Irrigation Implements in Use in Middle Eastern Countries

Local Name	Description	Lifting Height	Lifting Capacity per hour	Remarks
		(metres)	(cubic metres)	
nattala .	straw mat basket with four cords attached.	1	5	Very simple. Needs two workers to dip the basket into the water and swing it out.
badala .	a wooden trough composed of three boards, 2·5–3 metres long, closed at one end and open at the top; fixed through a cross-bar to two posts; for plunging one end into the water to fill it and then to discharge the water through the other end.	0·3–0·5	7	
tambur .	archimedean screw.	0·75	15–25	Needs two workers, as capacity with one is not efficient.
shaduf .	wooden lever. A long lever is fixed with a cross piece on two posts or earth-pillars. On the short arm of the lever a counterpoise is fixed—as a rule a ball of mud or of stone—and a dipper with a skin bag hangs down from the long arm.	2–3	8	
saqia .	a set of horizontal and vertical wheels driven by bullocks or oxen and driving an endless rope, carrying earthen pots or buckets.	3–8	15–40	In addition to the usual form of saqia in Egypt, there exist varying types in other Oriental countries
noriah .	somewhat resembles the saqia, but is driven, as a rule, by water power and, therefore, used in river irrigation.	3–5	15–20	Frequent in NorthernSyria and Anatolia
tabut .	resembles the saqia, but instead of the rope and buckets, the wheel has a stiff hollow rim divided into compartments.	1–3	10–30	

Every form of work with the traditional implements of irrigation has one thing in common; it demands an exceptionally heavy measure of physical exertion. The amount of work is not only very considerable in the absolute sense—raising several cubic metres per hour under the climatic conditions of a warm climate means a highly intensive form of labour; it also makes heavy claims on the farmer's time and that of his helpers.

Irrigation work calls, however, not only for much time to be spent in operating the implements, but also for a particularly intensive preparation of the plot to be irrigated. In addition to a thorough levelling of the ground, mounds must be raised round the various beds according to local needs, and in the case of canal irrigation furrows must be carefully drawn and, generally, great attention paid to keeping the ditches open. In Iran, where many villages are dependent on artificial irrigation and the settlements are often situated 10–20 km. distant from the foot of the mountains, it is customary—in order to avoid their being washed away by the torrents of rainwater rushing down from the slopes—to convey the water to the villages by means of underground channels called *qanats*. *Qanats* vary in length from a few yards to 40 miles. These shafts which often go down to a depth of 40–70 metres are dug along the slopes, from which tunnels branch off to the villages. For the difficult work connected with this procedure only primitive technical means are available. The earth accumulated from the digging of the tunnels is conveyed at the cost of much drudgery by means of skin sacks and rudely constructed tread winches through shafts upwards to the surface. According to E. Noel 20 million working days per annum are spent on the maintenance and reconstruction of *qanats* in Iran.[60] Although terrace cultivation based on irrigation calls for other methods of operation the amount of labour entailed in this case also is extremely great.

Wherever we observe such excessive demands for labour arising from the method of cultivation of the soil, we discover a relation between the unit of land and the number of agricultural workers which is characteristic for all areas of irrigation. Irrigated farming is the domain of the small farm. Although large landownership is not uncommon in countries of irrigation, the predominant unit of cultivation from ancient times to the present day in all areas of irrigation throughout the Orient is the small-holding. Even the introduction of labour-saving mechanical implements at the beginning of this century has not caused any appreciable change in this fundamental relation. Wherever irrigated farming is carried on in the traditional forms and human labour is in the centre of the irrigation process, the very act of irrigation is bound to cause a specific prolongation of working hours.

The need for an additional expenditure of labour results in the production costs per unit of land being much heavier in the case of irrigated than of unirrigated crops. This extra labour is compensated for, however, by an increase in the yield which on an average considerably exceeds the yield per unit of land in dry farming. Detailed figures for the production costs in irrigated farming are rare, but wherever records are available the share derived from the need for irrigation represents a prominent item. Calculations of production costs made in Turkey in respect of the rice crop showed that the necessary expenditure on additional labour for irrigation amounts to 37 per cent. of the total expenditure per dunam. For cotton the costs amounted, according to another calculation, to £T11·5 per dunam, whereas unirrigated crops required only £T6.[61]

In keeping with the varying expenditure of labour is, as already mentioned, the varying yield per unit of land. Whereas Oriental dry farming can show wheat crops of 500–1000 kg. per hectare (10 dunam), irrigated agriculture boasts of 1800–2500 kg. The figures for barley are 900–1,300 kg. as compared with 2,000 kg. on irrigated land; for beans 1,600 kg. as compared to 2,800 kg., sesame 900 kg. as against 2000 kg., cotton 150 kg. as against 500 kg. Moreover several important crops such as oranges, rice, sugarcane, bananas, can only be grown by means of irrigation.[62]

Plans in respect of the costs of settlement in Palestine were based on similar experiences. Both capital investment and current expenditure per unit of land are considerably higher in the case of irrigated than of unirrigated crops; but they bring correspondingly higher yields.

In the irrigated zones in the hills the extra labour is chiefly entailed by the construction of terraces and their upkeep—apart from the further work necessitated by the bringing of the water; in this respect there is no difference between irrigation in the flat country and in the hills. The irrigation network in the mountains is characterised by the huge built-up terraces, which extend in Palestine, for example, to a height of 700 metres, in the Lebanon to 1,800 metres, and in southern Arabia up to 2,000 metres.

The descriptions of the working methods employed in the agriculture of Southern Arabia are largely identical with the accounts given of the mode of work on the terraced farms of Syria, Kurdistan and Turkestan. They demonstrate in a particularly striking manner the immense labour effort involved in this type of agriculture. As cultivated land on slanting ground is always faced with the danger that sudden rain floods may sweep away its layer of humus, the slopes are broken up into terraces which as mentioned above sometimes rise to astonishing heights. Each terrace is built horizontally and separated from that immediately underneath by a strong stone wall. The latter is plastered with earth to prevent the water from flowing off.

W. B. Harris at a certain place in the Yemen counted 137, C. J. Cruttenden in front of Metne as many as 150 terraces, one above another, on a single hillside, with a stone wall nine feet high, whereas the arable strip was only six feet wide. Every space that is in any way accessible has been and continues to be exploited in this manner, by century-old methods. The landscape thereby acquires a unique character. Regarded from below and on the same level the hills with their black or grey terraced walls, bleak and stony, have the appearance of gigantic amphitheatres, but from above the eyes revel for miles in the green of the crops.

Terrace cultivation is also carried on in Baihan, in Awaliq, at a height of 7,000 feet, as well as in Wadi Do'an and Wadi Baqaran and in Wadi 'umen Girge near Mukalla. It demands a laborious and assiduous cultivation of the soil. The torrents in the hill country do not carry with them the fertile alluvial slime which they do in the plains. Consequently, the humus content of the soil on the terraces must from time to time be removed, and manure is carried by the peasants in baskets from a central heap on to the fields over neck-breaking and often perilous tracks. As the layer of earth is often only one or two feet deep, ploughing must be done with special care. The fields need to be well manured, especially for coffee, for which purpose the necessary animal manure is collected in large heaps in the vicinity of most towns, rendered odourless by a covering of light earth and conveyed in baskets to the terraces for miles around. Besides animal manure ashes are also used. The terraces are also fed by canals, which supply them with the water stored up by the weirs.[63]

Similar accounts are given us by Rathjens and Wissman regarding Sana:

"The waters in the spring valleys at the western edge of the depression are, of course, likewise constantly used for the irrigation of the fields which in the narrow valleys decorate the slopes in the form of ingeniously arranged terraces. The most fertile of these oases are the slopes of the Jabal Hatte, two hours south-west of Sana, the valley of Dhula, two hours north-west, and above all, due north, the Wadi Dhar with its royal castle, the summer residence of the King. Veritable forests of fruit trees here provide their welcome shade, and apples, pears, quinces, peaches, apricots, plums, almonds, cedro, lemons, walnuts, figs and twenty sorts of grapes besides the katbush, are cultivated, whilst on the fields seed-time follows harvest with three crops during the year. Particularly common are the plots of lucerne which people say can be cut every four weeks."[64]

W. H. Ingrams, in his report on economic conditions in the Hadhramaut, states that, soil in the villages being very scanty, it was necessary in many cases to bring earth from distant places for building the terraces. The size of the unit varies from five to a thousand square yards.

On the basis of the foregoing the qualifications and interdependence of the chief agricultural systems in the Orient may be summarised as follows:

1. As regards the natural conditions, it appears that in historical times no climatic changes have occurred likely to have exercised a decisive influence on the spread of natural flora or cultivated crops. Neither in temperature nor in other natural phenomena affecting agriculture such as sandstorms, hot winds, the annual rise and fall of the great Oriental river arteries, are any changes to be noted. The changes that have occurred have their origin in the acts of man, of which both the positive, such as the construction of dams and canals, and the negative, the destruction of such works, have had history-making results. Under the Ottoman régime we find, particularly in the irrigation areas situated in the outlying provinces of the Empire, that only the barest attempts were made to reconstruct the former installations for the exploitation of natural forces.
2. In the domain of dry farming the prevailing form of land possession is the large landed estate where the land is leased to tenants for cultivation. Centrally managed large estates are rarely met with. In keeping with the capital-and-labour-extensive form of management is the sparse occupation of the unit of land. The area belonging to the individual farm, although varying with local conditions, is usually sufficient, yet less than that attached to the farmsteads in Europe run by their owners. The equipment of these farms in the way of live and dead stock is primitive,

production being generally confined almost exclusively to the satisfaction of the farmer's own needs. Cattle serve first and foremost as working animals, and not as producers of milk. Poor quality of land, low yield per unit of land, crude farming equipment and the poorest accommodation for man and beast are the characteristics of agricultural life in the domain of dry farming. Isolation from without and shortage of capital favoured clinging to tradition and frugality among the dwellers in these regions.

3. In the domain of irrigated agriculture matters are very different. Here the prevailing unit of farming is of very modest size. The large landowner or the large tenant who has managed to secure for himself the right of usufruct over wide stretches of land is the actual master of the peasants who earn their livelihood by dint of toilsome manual labour on their small irrigated plots. The equipment of these small irrigated farms—and likewise the yield per unit—is considerably more generous than in dry farming, owing to the disproportionately larger number of working processes (lifting and conduct of the water, etc.). At the same time the usually large outlay of labour required prescribes, when the traditional implements of irrigation are used, a definite size for the individual holding which amounts per cultivator to but a fraction of the area usual in dry farming. The irrigation farmer, if he musters all the members of his family in full force, cannot cultivate more than a certain area. Also the degree of isolation from possible markets is far less in the river districts owing to the availability of the water courses for transport; furthermore, many crops are grown here which are destined not for home consumption, but for sale.

4. Thus the utmost importance attaches to the differences in methods of cultivation, average area of land per farm, yield per unit of land, and in the general economic and administrative structure between both systems of agriculture. The irrigation farmer, owing to his dependence on the regular supply of water to his land, forms part of a system which controls and rules him, politically and socially, to a far different extent from the farmer in a dry farming district.

5. On the other hand, irrigated farming was likewise not free from the shackles of the generally backward and impoverished Oriental economy. Despite its advantages from the

standpoint of larger yield per unit, the productivity or output per worker employed was no larger than in dry farming. Here, too, the hand of the landlord weighed heavily on the tenant or small farmer and allowed him no more than was necessary to satisfy his meagre requirements. The peasant was thus condemned to a miserable and degrading standard barely reaching subsistence level. The potential forces of man and soil could find no outlet; the vast potency inherent in irrigated farming was not able to free the peasant from his indifference and stimulate him to greater economic activity. Although the constancy of certain natural factors (tidal irrigation) guaranteed a minimum livelihood, the peasant was afflicted, on the other hand, by many negative concomitants of the primitive irrigation system, such as the formation of swamps, the spread of infectious diseases, malaria, worms and intestinal troubles, insalination of the soil. It was owing to such circumstances that in this sphere also, though it embraced such important possibilities of development, there was no sign of that new approach which in the same period was instilling fresh life into Western agriculture through the medium of chemical and technical discoveries in the realm of modern soil science. Both in the domain of dry farming and in the zone of irrigation the agrarian society of the Middle East remained a stationary, stunted system of production. In the following chapter we shall show how and in what measure this picture is changing as a result of the infiltration of modern influences into the Orient.

SECTION II

AGRICULTURE IN TRANSITION

CHAPTER XVII

CHANGES IN CONDITIONS OF LAND TENURE

The transformation of economic and social systems is a continuous process extending over long periods. The historical course of events admits of no abrupt turns, no immediate disappearance of old forms which from one day to another, without warning, lose their validity.

It is only in statistical and in part in sociological abstraction that such processes can be described in concise form. Unfortunately, figures to illustrate the structural changes in Middle Eastern society are available only for the most recent decades, while for the first phases at the beginning of this century and the progress of the transformation process in the nineteenth century but few statistical data exist. In view of the economic and technical innovations and the changes in the political and social world panorama since the beginning of last century it is evident that this period must have a marked bearing on the process of change already in its inception in the agrarian society of the Middle East. This process, which was begun as early as the first half of the nineteenth century, experienced in the years before and after the First World War a stimulus which exceeds all previous phases in intensity and has not yet reached its peak.

Despite the inadequacy of our statistical material we must attempt also to trace the changes that occurred in the earlier phases, for it is here that the key to the course of later developments is to be found. At the same time we can dispense with repeating the data on natural conditions, as these show no changes even at the present day. The changes to be seen in conditions of land tenure, methods of production, markets and communications appear, on the other hand, all the more significant.

The Re-emergence of the Large Landowner in the Nineteenth Century

In an earlier chapter we have pointed out the ambiguity of the term "feudalism" and decided on a narrower and more precise interpretation, viz., that the divorce of occupier and owner is not enough to constitute a set of conditions which can be called feudal. The large landed estates prevailing today in the Middle East countries derive in the exact juridical and sociological sense only to a small extent from the large property-holdings established in feudal times. They are predominantly the product of the shifts in proprietorship and the legal interference in the conditions of land tenure which took place in almost all those countries during the nineteenth century. Economists and social historians, it is true, have been in the habit of using the term feudalism as a kind of general denominator for every category of large land-holding, those forms, that is, where possession is in principle separated from occupation. The Marxist school likewise uses the word in a similar sense:

> "The most important characteristic of the feudal social order is that specific economic form where the feudal lord, the landowner, appropriates the unpaid product of the immediate producer, i.e., in the form of rental in kind. It is these very relations between the owner of the means of production (in this case the land) and the immediate producer that constitute the factor wherein we find the inmost secret, the hidden foundation of the entire social order and consequently also of the specifically feudal form of State."[65]

However, as already mentioned, we shall use the word "feudalism" in this context only where the right to landed property was actually constituted in the form of a fief or similar title.

The legal rights deriving from the Oriental feudal system retained their validity in the Ottoman Empire up to the beginning of the nineteenth century, when they were abolished in quick succession by various legislative devices. The course of such changes in the various countries was not uniform. In the first decades of the century the rulers of these countries, Sultan Mahmud II for the Turkish provinces, and Mohammed Ali and his son Ibrahim Pasha for the Arab lands of Egypt, Palestine and Syria, under the influence of the progressive ideas of the time, initiated far-reaching reforms in the political structure and conditions of land tenure of their respective realms. Mohammed Ali after an examination of the title-deeds abolished in 1811–1814 the property rights of the *Multazim* who had hitherto held large estates in fief and distributed the land under a kind of hereditary lease in small lots to the fellahin who in future were to pay their taxes direct to the

State. In 1838, the rights of the large landowners in Syria and Palestine were similarly cancelled in favour of the State, and in 1839 the Sultan issued a general order abolishing or redeeming all military and tributary fiefs in the rest of Turkey, the State becoming the owner of the redeemed land.

It would be wrong, however, to assume that with the passing of these measures the heritage of the former Oriental land régime had been actually abolished. For this the steps taken, well-intentioned as they obviously were, were too juridically one-sided; they did not touch the basic problem, the position of the fellah, but at best only effected an exchange of the previous over-lords for the nominal rule of the State while the factual rights of possession were as a rule appropriated by new classes. The fellah, the actual cultivator of the land, gained neither in political influence nor economically, but was obliged, besides toiling as before for his scanty livelihood, also to find the means to pay his taxes and rent. He also remained helpless before the attempts to create a new landowner class which began in the nineteenth century, especially with the increasing affluence in the Oriental towns.

Conditions in Syria and Palestine

Accounts of the "land hunger" on the part of wealthy sections of the town population in the countries of the Middle East all read alike. In many cases there was a genuine desire to acquire an estate near a town, in others it was just the fact that the dealers in the towns who had transactions with the peasants foreclosed on the mortgaged lands when the peasants got into arrears with their payments. Thus, regarding conditions in Syria we read as follows:

> "Entire villages in the Syrian plain passed in this way, piece by piece, into the hands of the notables; the large properties which surround Homs and Hama, in fact, have no other origin. In these places the inhabitants were not expropriated but remained as share tenants. They have retained their old mode of exploitation of individual or common land and the old parcelling-out into narrow strips. The seizure by the notables did not destroy the village community but merely reduced it to servitude."[66]

Another occasion of the revival of the large landed proprietor in the nineteenth century was the clause in the new Turkish Land Code by which all land in the villages, even when it was no longer represented as Tabu tenure, had in future to be entered in the land register. In many cases the heads of tribes or clans, or the village sheikhs, had the previously unregistered property, including the collective *Mushaa* lands of the groups under their charge or the lands of the village community, entered as their own personal property, thereby acquiring the status of large landowners. The fellahin often declared themselves agreeable to this procedure either because they hoped thus to obtain a consolidation of their rights, which had not always been undisputed, or because they did in fact recognise the village sheikh as the privileged local leader and magnate. Similar in a certain respect were the cases in which the Government, after repeated futile attempts to induce the peasants to have their plots entered in the land register, had these lands put up for auction. The villagers who had refused to comply with the Government's demand, partly from fear of the possibility of higher taxation, with the sale of their lands lost their rights of ownership and remained on as tenants on the lands farmed by them. A famous example of large landownership being established in this manner is the case of the Sursuk family, the former owners of lands in the Valley of Jezreel (Arabic: Marj ibn Amir) in 1872:

"The villages in the Valley of Jezreel suffered formerly from frequent raids of the Beni-Saker Beduin who claimed a kind of protector rôle and extorted from the fellahin heavy services in return. In 1872 when the Government tried in vain to collect the taxes from the economically depressed villages of the Valley of Jezreel, the Greek banker Sursuk purchased the whole area, 70 square miles in extent, for about £18,000, of which, however, it is said that only £6,000 found its way into the Government Treasury. Sursuk, however, was not content with the right of ownership over the lands, but also acquired from the Government the tax farming of the area, so that he had a double source of income at his disposal. The fellahin paid one-tenth of the harvest to the Government, one-tenth to him as landlord, besides ten Mejidiyyas (about £2·5) for each feddan (4,226 sq. metres) of land. In addition, he found a further very profitable source of income in acting at the same time as moneylender to his own tenants and holding their securities at his own disposal. Thanks to this status of landlord, tax collector, and creditor he became the real ruler over this stretch of country, a potentate with whom no one could compete. The annual revenue that Sursuk obtained from the Valley of Jezreel was valued at no less than £20,000. Nevertheless, writes Oliphant, even these grotesque conditions of exploitation offered the fellahin certain advantages inasmuch as the landlord, thanks to his powerful position, was able to protect the villages under his control far better from the tyranny of the roving Beduin tribes, government officials, and malevolent neighbours than the "independent" fellahin could do if left to their own resources."[67]

Iraq

The emergence of the present-day large landed proprietor in Iraq proceeded, save for individual exceptions, on the whole on similar lines to those in Syria and Palestine. The variations in topographical and natural conditions help to account for the differences which exist between the northern and the southern parts of Iraq.

In the southern parts of the country, where tillage was carried on predominantly by the nomad tribes, the traditions and practices of the old Turkish feudal constitution were more in evidence. Sale and purchase even of State land had gone on for generations without the cognisance of the central Government, which in these regions was obliged to leave the exercise of authority to a large extent to the provincial rulers, usually the leaders of the large tribal associations.

The influence of these tribal groups changed with the personalities at their head and with other circumstances. In any case, the Ottoman Government was not in a position to exercise a systematic control over the *Miri* land in its possession. Thus the idea took root that the members of the tribes and their sheikhs were the legitimate owners and rulers of large provinces.

With the abolition of the feudal régime it became necessary to put conditions of ownership and land tenure on a new basis despite the many difficulties involved. How could the registration of the land, control over the institutions dealing with land affairs, etc., be put into effect in view of the social forms and habits of life of a nomad population, its primitive cultural level and standard of needs? However, it was the very existence of these handicaps that urged the statesmen of that period to win over the population to the principle of settlement. The establishment of a new and stable State régime was a hopeless task if the Beduin element could not be successfully incorporated within this framework by direct or indirect legal measures aimed at binding the nomads to the soil.

The chief incentive for the change of conditions of land tenure is represented by the land laws introduced by the ingenious land reformer Midhat Pasha in 1868. He hoped to solve the problem of land ownership by the distribution of land to the actual cultivators on a kind of hereditary lease while retaining the State's supreme right of ownership.[68] An important provision of the reforms stipulated that the new deeds of ownership could be obtained by the new cultivators only if they undertook themselves to defray the costs of the irrigation or drainage of their land. This provided the moneyed landowner with a welcome loophole for extensive acquisition of property, while the poor peasant had to be content if he could establish himself somewhere as tenant. Nevertheless, if the reform could have been sensibly carried out, it would have meant a great step forward in the agricultural development of Iraq. The well-conceived attempt at reform failed, however, because the Turkish Government did not possess the necessary experience for the execution of such a far-reaching measure; no doubt the will was also lacking. The weak response which the proposed new order evoked among those immediately concerned likewise contributed no little to its failure. An undertaking begun under such discouraging auspices—sabotage by a part of the officials and opposition by the landlords—could but increase the general uncertainty prevailing in regard to conditions of Iraqi land tenure. Thus a situation obtained offering great opportunities to all those desirous of exploiting them for their own personal gain. Members of leading families acquired title-deeds over large stretches of land which had hitherto been regarded as the collective domain of the tribes. The establishment of sheikh families as new large landowners led in time to come to serious conflicts between the tribes and the holders of the new title-deeds in which both parties claimed rights of possession in respect of the same land, conflicts which were repeated, often with the use of force, up to the present day. The total effect of these violent disputes was only to increase the predominance of the already powerful large landowners who as a rule knew how to secure for themselves a more juridically satisfactory position.

These tendencies towards the accumulation and new formation of large landed property were fostered in some degree by a certain technical factor. In view of the difficulty involved in these vast and sparsely populated territories in arranging a direct allotment of land to each individual fellah, the Government were obliged to avail themselves of the help of middlemen. The most appropriate authorities for this purpose were obviously the sheikhs or the leaders of the fellahin groups, the so-called *serkals*, who disposed of a following of active farm labourers. By resorting to such middlemen and recognising their status the Government itself helped to create the prerequisites for the establishment of an influential class of landowners, no matter whether these middlemen were directly interested in establishing themselves as landowners or whether by distributing the plots they had opportunity for enrichment.

The emergence of the large landed proprietor in the northern parts of Iraq occurred on the whole in conditions analogous to those described above, if in a less pronounced form. The village population lived as a rule under the leadership of a local Agha who was intermediary between the village and the central authority insofar as the latter could exercise any influence. This local chief was responsible for the collection of the tithes and other taxes and the settlement of differences in respect of land within his area so long as these conditions of village seclusion were not changed. With the growing power of attraction exercised by the towns new social concepts assailed the world of the village; above all, the relations between the village head and his community underwent a change: the local chief became often an absentee landlord. The introduction of compulsory registration of land ownership made it possible for the sheikh to have the village lands registered as his personal property, although the peasants originally undertook the cultivation of the lands with the same title as the sheikh.

Particularly conspicuous shifts in the relations of ownership occurred when, as a result of the mortgaging of encumbered lands to town merchants and the subsequent reversion of such lands, a new landowner element entered the village circle. Whereas the connection between the villagers and the sheikh or village elder, despite all the despotism of the latter, was based on a certain loyalty and recognition of their mutual interests, the emergence of a new interested party from the town denoted a serious disturbance of the hitherto closed circle and made possible the accumulation of large properties in the hands of one person regardless of the former nature of ownership relations.

Egypt

In Egypt also the general Arab concepts regarding the character of land ownership up to the middle of the nineteenth century had favoured the retention of that form of land tenure in which the cultivator had but slight claims on the land, whereas the community or its symbolic representative, the head of the State, claimed the actual right of ownership. The peasant, by paying the land taxes, acquired only the right to cultivate the land. Thus in Egypt, also, the institution of tax farming, originally granted as a feudal privilege, was widespread; the leading Mameluke families bequeathed it from father to son. The tax-farmers (*Multazim*) had, in addition, a claim on certain tax-free land and the right to conscript the inhabitants of their districts for gratuitous work on such land (*Corvée*). The tax-free land itself, called *Wasiyya*, became the private property of the family when tax-farming was made an hereditary privilege. A further group of landowners was made up of higher officials and officers to whom land had been promised in the name of the Sultan, which was likewise exempt from taxation.

The Egyptian reformer, Mohammed Ali, who wished to turn Egypt, then stagnating in Oriental torpor, in a few years into a modern State, rightly directed his efforts for reform at the root of the evil: the privileged position of the large landowners. Mohammed Ali first of all abolished those privileges which were exploited by their possessors as most serious abuses. Only part of the taxes paid by the fellahin found its way into the coffers of the State. After an examination of the validity of all title deeds, which served as a basis for the claims on the land entrusted to the tax farmers for the purpose of tax collection, all such claims were one after another declared invalid during the years 1808–1814. Those tax farmers with a loyal past were indemnified by the grant of a life pension, the taxes from then on being collected direct by Government officials. The success of these measures lay first in the liberation of the country from the oppressive claims and privileges of the tax farmers, so that the way was clear for further reforms. The fellahin, owing to the merciless exploitation by the *Multazims*, had neglected the cultivation of large stretches of land. In the ten years 1798–1808 alone the cultivated area is said to have declined by two-thirds.[69] In 1813, Mohammed Ali, who by annulling the title deeds of the tax farmers and the confiscation of their private land possessions (*Wasiyyas*) had become the owner of practically all the land, had a general land survey carried out and arranged at the same time for the distribution of the cultivated areas. The fellahin received on an average between three and five feddans, which were entered in the register of lands in their name. This registration did not represent any grant of ownership, inasmuch as it had been expressly stated that the ownership of all the lands was reserved for the State. The peasants received solely the right of usufruct, but on the other hand could not sell or mortgage their land. The State reserved even the right of expropriation without compensation. Mohammed Ali did not content himself, however, with this rearrangement of title deeds, but intervened also in the cultivation of the land. He compelled the peasants under threat of punishment to bring the untilled land once more under cultivation, and established a monopoly of the trade in agrarian products.

The effects of Mohammed Ali's reforms were twofold. On the one hand the development of individual ownership was encouraged despite the remaining restrictions on the transfer of land. The peasant, who, in contrast to the practice prevailing under the Mamelukes, could sell or otherwise dispose of his harvest, either to private purchasers or at fixed prices to the Government's temporarily established storehouses, increasingly tended to regard his land as belonging to himself. In accordance with this tendency the peasants who cultivated the land received the right to encumber it or transfer it to a second party by means of a certificate (*Hoja*) from the local sheikh or by verbal agreement before witnesses. In the case of non-payment of taxes a tenant might lose his property, but he could recover possession on payment of the arrears. Mohammed Ali himself, in order to encourage the working of uncultivated land, had earlier invested wealthy notables with land as their personal property. Such land, which was declared exempt from taxation for ten years, was distributed on condition that it was brought under the plough.

On the other hand, in the same degree that we find this tendency towards the individualisation of landed property originally belonging to the sovereign making general headway, the abuses common to this process are also rife, especially the accumulation of property in the hands of a few. From the very start when the general survey of the land was carried out—an undertaking which could only succeed given wholehearted co-operation on the part of the officials—serious irregularities came to light. Apart from the fact that the surveyor personnel was insufficiently trained, the inspectors were accessible to the bribes of the wealthy landowners, especially the old *Multazims*; consequently, many of these remained in *de facto* possession of their influential position and were able to use it for the accumulation of landed property. Moreover the above-mentioned lands which had been declared by Mohammed Ali to be family property were soon involved in this speculative traffic in land, and although Mohammed Ali endeavoured to prohibit the transfer or sale of such property out of the family of the original owner, he was eventually obliged to withdraw his opposition to this practice.

Of no less consequence were the many abuses committed by the sheikhs of the villages, who had been allowed a right to co-operate in the transfer or mortgaging of land. In order to guard against such malpractices, a decree was passed in 1854 to the effect that in future every transfer of land must be effected by contract and registered by the local district court. Notwithstanding these and other indisputable measures of progress the fellahin could not improve their circumstances, inasmuch as the burden of taxation was not appreciably lightened in the years that followed, and the frequent calling-up of the fellahin for military service and gratuitous forced labour absorbed a considerable amount of their energy.[70] The effects of Mohammed Ali's reforms were largely frittered away. In order to stimulate the interest of the fellahin in the preservation of their property, which under such conditions naturally flagged, a further law was passed (also in 1854) to the effect that the tenant rights which had hitherto been granted for life only could be inherited by the next of kin.

In 1858, the principle of descent was confirmed and at the same time both sexes were given equal rights in this respect. This was followed by a number of further improvements in matters of administration, all aimed at stabilising the rights of ownership and usufruct. But it still took a number of years, i.e., until 1871, before the right to acquire full ownership of their estates was granted to landowners. This law, which was known under the name of *Muqabala*, owes its existence to the financial difficulties of the Khedive Ismail. Every tenant who paid the taxes on his land for six years in advance received full right of ownership therein, and in addition a permanent reduction of the land tax by 50 per cent. A considerable part of the privately owned land in Egypt passed into the hands of its present owners on the strength of this law.

A fact which had a great influence on the structure of Egyptian land tenure and the size of the average farm was the increase in the population. The number of inhabitants, estimated in the thirties of last century at 3 millions, had risen a hundred years later to 16 millions ; this increase is reflected—notwithstanding the extension of the cultivated area—in the steady reduction of the area in possession of the private owner. During the period for which statistical data are available, i.e. from 1896 to 1939, the aggregate number of owners rose from 767,260 to 2,481,250, i.e., after allowing for duplications, approximately threefold.

The disappearance of the old agrarian constitution in Egypt paved the way for the entry of foreigners into the ranks of Egyptian landowners. Mohammed Ali in his time, in order to encourage the cultivation of the land, had distributed uncultivated stretches (outside the surveyed areas) tax-free to wealthy Egyptians and foreigners on condition that the land should be brought under cultivation. In 1842 he was obliged to allow the owners to regard such land as their private property with power to dispose of it as they thought proper. In this way foreigners became to no insignificant extent the owners of Egyptian land, despite the fact that originally, by the Capitulations, although foreigners could settle in Egypt and engage in industrial activities, they could not acquire land. The acquisition of land by foreigners was further facilitated when in 1858 they were allowed by Sayyid Pasha to bid for land put up for auction on account of non-payment of taxes or abandonment by the tenant. The right of foreigners to purchase *kharaj* land was confirmed in 1867 by an Imperial decree from Constantinople, thus giving foreigners the opportunity of acquiring land in all provinces of the Ottoman Empire. According to the latest statistics, the amount of land owned by foreigners in Egypt totals 404,000 feddans.

Changes in the Waqf

In a period of general slackening of the traditional ties of ownership, an institution such as that of the Dead Hand could not remain unchanged in view of the difficulties it caused for the handling of land affairs such as administration, taxation, mortgage and inheritance. Nor is this surprising when we remember that the extent of *Waqf*-owned property in former Turkish territory alone is estimated at no less than three-quarters of the total cultivated area. In Egypt *Waqf* property comprised in 1927 one-eighth, in Algiers about the middle of the nineteenth century one half, in Tunis in 1883 one-third of the cultivated land.[71]

Mohammed Ali, as the first agrarian reformer in the Orient, did not exclude the *Waqf* institution from his plans of reform. He confiscated at the same time the *Waqf* estates known as *Ar-rizaq al-Abbasiyya* and compensated the former beneficiaries.[72] In the subsequent years the remaining *Waqf* properties were repeatedly subjected to administrative reforms; in more recent times, after the first World War, some fairly radical proposals envisaging a dissolution of family-endowed lands and their transfer to private ownership were put forward. Ali Shamsi Pasha, a prominent Egyptian politician, demanded expressly either a radical change in the *Waqf* system or its complete abolition, as it constitutes in its present form a grave obstacle to all progress. The large number of people sharing in the usufruct of *Waqf* property is generally the cause for its desolate state. "If you see a building in ruins, you know immediately it is *Waqf* property."[73] A similar tendency towards the secularisation of *Waqf* property by breaking up mortmain estates and the transfer of part of their property to the communities and public undertakings made rapid headway in the New Turkey.

Less radical in their scope are the measures introduced by the

Mandatory administrations in Palestine, Syria, Lebanon, and Iraq inasmuch as they were bound by the statutes of the Mandate to manage the *Waqf* properties in accordance with the decisions of the Sharia and the endowers. In Syria, a special department was created under the Mandatory Power itself for the direct supervision of *Waqf* estates. Similarly in Iraq, these matters were entrusted to direct Government control. In Palestine, after the First World War, a Supreme Moslem Sharia Council was established which also managed matters connected with the *Waqf*. But in these countries also the *Waqf* institutions are being more and more undermined. Recent decades have thus seen an appreciable decline in the importance of the *Waqf* institution; the trend towards the reduction of its influence continues; the area of *Waqf* land possessions is steadily declining as a result of these tendencies, while at the same time its revenue has likewise fallen to a marked extent. Although in certain countries the disposal of these funds, especially where it is in the hands of politically active cliques, exercises a significant influence on local politics, the institution as a whole, so influential in the past, is fast receding into the background.

Collective Landownership (*Mushaa*)

A similar process of dissolution obtains in respect of another important institution of land tenure in the Middle East, viz. collective ownership. Attention has already been drawn to the inclination on the part of the legislators in Oriental countries to bring about the abolition of collective ownership. These tendencies have everywhere grown in force since the First World War. What with the growing intensification of agriculture and the rise in population figures in the Middle East lands the necessity for the apportionment of collectively owned land and the creation of peasant farms on individually appropriated land became more and more urgent. The application of additional efforts and labour for the improvement of his holding appears to the peasant only justifiable if such expenditure, no matter whether in the form of labour or capital, remains in his possession and he runs no danger of forfeiting the advantages thereby attained by a change of the plots; such a change resulted from the drawing of the lots when occupied on a collective basis. In most Oriental countries the Governments have, therefore, in the interest of agricultural development, exercised pressure in order to expedite the *per se* complicated procedure of establishing individual ownership of land and settling the disputes between the parties concerned. Nevertheless, the tempo of this process is still slow. Immediately after the First World War, for instance, in Palestine nearly 60 per cent. of all villages were registered as "undivided"; in 1932, despite the speeding up of the procedure of distribution, they still numbered 40 per cent., although the reasons which had induced the Ottoman government at the time to proceed with the abolition of *Mushaa* property have since then been considerably strengthened.

CHAPTER XVIII

CHANGES IN AGRICULTURAL SYSTEMS AND METHODS

Most characteristic of the transformation in the agricultural system of the Middle East countries is the fact that the individual peasant-farm is as a rule but slowly affected by the changes which occur in the field of land legislation and agricultural technique. The fellah's farm is predominantly based, as heretofore, on the use of the old traditional implements and devices; his methods of tilling the soil, raising cattle and poultry, harvesting his crops, etc., are in the main those practised by his forefathers, his standard of living—in spite of some occasional improvement—is still far lower than that of the townsman. Many of the facts given in the first section regarding the methods of production in stationary agriculture, more particularly in dry farming, still hold good in respect of present-day conditions notwithstanding the introduction of minor innovations. This synchronism of stationary and dynamic elements is an outstanding feature of the Oriental agrarian society of today. On the other hand, most important changes have occurred in agriculture as a branch of national economy, in its share of total production, area under cultivation and structural development.

Egypt

The most far-reaching changes in agricultural methods are to be found in the irrigated farming sector, and especially in Egypt, the chief agrarian country of production in the Middle East. The incentive thereto was provided by the discovery that Egyptian soil was suitable for the cultivation of high-priced varieties of cotton. The cultivation of this commercial crop, first sponsored by the far-sighted Regent Mohammed Ali, of which the exports increased two-hundred fold in a few years (1821–1824) made cotton the central product of the country and the backbone of its economic and financial system. Agents who represented foreign capital and other interests had been the Pasha's chief advisers on this question, and were able in subsequent years to assert their influence in the direction of changing over and adapting Egyptian agriculture and its principal source, the waters of the Nile, to the requirements of cotton growing. The first steps in this direction undertaken almost exclusively by the State, i.e. by Mohammed Ali, began as early as the first half of the nineteenth century with the building of canals and of the Nile barrage north of Cairo. The most important canal was the Mahmudiyya canal, built in 1819 by a levy of 250,000 workers as a means of transport to Alexandria, but at the same time as a valuable factor in irrigation.[74] The purpose of the Nile barrage was to maintain the level of the waters in the Delta area at such a height that in the summer even in times of water shortage all canals could be provided with adequate irrigation water. Soon after its construction in 1843 it was allowed to fall into decay, and was not repaired until 1890. Its reconstruction on a large scale dates from recent years. This period also saw the rapid development of the modern Egyptian irrigation works, above all of the Nile dams, which completely revolutionised the productive capacity of Egyptian agriculture. Before the introduction of this system of Nile barrages irrigation in Upper Egypt was carried on by means of the so-called basin system. Over 200 basins, each comprising on an average 7,000 feddans and separated from one another by earth mounds, were filled at the annual rise of the Nile flood with 1–2½ metres of slimy water. When the water after standing 30–40 days had drained away, the winter seed was sown in the still moist mud. In all districts where the basin system was used, only one sowing could be as a rule made and one harvest obtained yearly, inasmuch as the seed was directly dependent on the previous moistening of the soil. The crops grown were the typical winter crops: wheat, barley, beans etc. It is here that the ingenuity of the modern engineers, by constructing the Nile dams, produced one of the chief instruments for the reform of Oriental agriculture. The damming up of the summer Nile water in artificial lakes and its regulated distribution over the whole year made possible the fundamental change-over from a system of agriculture limited to a single winter crop to all-the-year-round cultivation. This made possible repeated sowings during the course of the year, above all the growing of the important summer crops such as cotton, sesame, etc. The water stored up by the dams does not reach the field—as in basin irrigation—through natural flooding, but is conducted in rotation to the fields requiring irrigation by means of a ramified and co-ordinated system of canals.[75] The area of crop, therefore, always exceeds the area under cultivation.

Naturally this radical change of system also brought difficulties and dangers in its train. Whereas in the case of the basin system fields and villages were sometimes flooded at times of exceptionally high water, the damage thus caused was limited, since at the time of the inundation the fields were not under crops. Moreover, the force of the flood-waters, thanks to the horizontal run-off, could not inflict damage of any great consequence. Very different are the conditions in the canal system. Here the water required for irrigation is carried exclusively by means of canals which are not capable of holding the swollen water of the Nile at flood tides and are often severely damaged or destroyed by their impact. In addition, the fields themselves suffer serious damage in the event of high water which, under a system of permanent cultivation, catches the crops in full growth. Lastly, the already-mentioned danger of insalination as a result of the uninterrupted irrigation and the lower content of minerals in the stored-up Nile water represents no negligible disadvantage as compared with the previous system. Nevertheless the advantages accruing to the general economy of the country are so important that they far exceed these drawbacks. The following table illustrates the extent of the cultivated and crop areas in Egypt at various periods; it shows the rapid development of the crop area, i.e. the total area consecutively sown in the course of one year.

CULTIVATED AND CROP AREA IN EGYPT[76] IN FEDDANS

	1835	1877	1907	1937
Cultivated area .	3,500,000	4,743,000	5,403,000	5,283,000
Crop area .	1,856,000	4,762,000	7,662,000	8,358,000

The general expansion of both cultivated area and crop area made possible by the systematic development of modern large-scale irrigation led to a corresponding increase in the volume of production. The intensive cultivation of cotton brought Egyptian national economy into the closest relationship with world economy. The increased production of Egyptian cotton, which became a summer crop, brought the summer crop yields up to a figure far in excess of previous records, but the winter crops also show appreciable increases. Thus Egypt acquired the position of an important agrarian producer on the world market. With the rise in the return obtained for the produce of the Egyptian peasant came a corresponding increase in the purchasing power of Egyptian economy as whole. But one important fact must not be overlooked in this connection. The share falling to the individual Egyptian peasant or agricultural worker in general as the result of this magnificent development has hardly increased during these 40 years. For it must be remembered that during this same period the Egyptian population showed a quite exceptional increase: it rose from *c.* 8 millions in 1888 to 16 millions in 1937. To maintain the level of the extraordinarily low share in the agricultural output on which the fellah could count 40 years ago, there should have been, in accord with the population increase, a doubling of agricultural production. This was not secured. But this remark is not intended in any way to disparage the achievement as such, for thanks to it very important sources of income could be created from agriculture alone. For a country with so very high a birth rate as Egypt this result proved invaluable.

The establishment of facts and figures regarding the transformation process in most other countries of the Middle East is possible only to a small extent in view of the fact that the territorial changes resulting from the First World War have made pre- and post-war statistics practically impossible of comparison. Nevertheless the fundamental facts are in every case similar: in the sphere of irrigation—in no small measure under the influence of Egypt's example—important projects have been inaugurated, which serve to increase the production capacity of the various countries. This applies above all to Iraq, and to a lesser extent to the Levant States and Turkey. In Palestine Jewish colonisation has led to an intensified development of underground water resources.

Iraq

In Iraq the preparation of comprehensive irrigation plans had already begun in Turkish times; but only one project was actually carried out, the Hindiyya barrage on the Euphrates. The other plans did not get beyond the blue-print stage. After the First World War the new administration took steps to promote the planned development of the irrigation system, to restore the existing net of canals and to carry out two important new projects: the Habbaniyya dam and the larger barrage near Kut on the Tigris, the biggest installation of the kind in Iraq. Apart from these two works which regulate irrigation on the basis of a country-wide plan, motor pumps were installed in large numbers during the period between the two wars. Before the First World War there were 166, with an aggregate of 1,276 h.p., most of them in the Baghdad district. On the eve of the Second World War the number had risen to 2,467 with 76,000 h.p. The chief result of the introduction of motor pumps is the extension of the area under summer crops, especially in those regions where the natural tidal irrigation was inadequate. Marked development in the cultivation of cotton also is to be observed during this period: the harvest rose from 60 bales in 1920 to 20,000 in 1937.[77] Of all Middle East countries Iraq has still the largest irrigable land resources.

Palestine

In Palestine, where visible water sources are rather limited, the discovery of large subterranean supplies is particularly significant. The exploitation of underground water in districts formerly considered quite unsuitable for cultivated crops has influenced settlement plans and farming methods to a far-reaching extent. Irrigation technique is likewise on a very high level. The number of modern, power-driven wells amounted in 1939 to 1,350; their lifting capacity to 103,000 cubic metres per hour or 750 million cubic metres per annum.[78] As a result, it has been found possible to reduce the basic farm unit per family and thereby to increase the general settlement density, i.e. the number of settlers per unit of area. Through these revolutionary changes in irrigation conditions in the plains of Palestine, where ample supplies of underground water are available, this sector of agriculture is today more "capital-intensive" than any other agrarian district in the Middle East.

Jewish agricultural colonisation in Palestine has also developed new social forms of settlement. A considerable number of Jewish settlements in this country have been established on a collective basis, i.e. in the form of communal villages, where land, animals, farm implements and machinery, houses and stables, in short all production goods are common property. The provision of food, clothing, child education, washing and mending, etc., is likewise undertaken for all the members collectively. The importance of these collective settlements does not lie in their numerical strength, though that is by no means negligible. They now comprise more than 30,000 souls.

There are varying degrees of collectivisation in these settlements; some of them give the members more individual freedom in matters of child education, personal inclinations, etc., some less. The structure of the settlements likewise differs, according to the share of non-agricultural sources in their income. These sources comprise, *inter alia*, industrial activities such as workshops and factories. But the main point is the creation of a new form of social economy, where all members are of equal standing and decide by common agreement on their economic and social fate. In these days of general crisis in social and economic development, this collective venture means the opening of a new chapter in the history of agrarian society, and perhaps of social history as a whole. In the other Oriental countries the schemes for the extension of irrigation have not yet gone beyond local or district projects. During the Second World War there has been, it is true, a certain expansion of irrigated farming caused by acute supply shortages, particularly in the Jezira district in Northern Syria and in the Lebanon, but it is not yet possible to say whether these beginnings will be continued in times of peace and developed into large-scale irrigation schemes on a country-wide basis.

In Turkey comprehensive projects have been prepared, especially in the southern districts where ample river water is available. This applies particularly to the utilization of the Euphrates, Tigris, Wehan and Sehan; but the northern water-courses of the Saharia and Kizil Irmaq are likewise earmarked for development under Turkey's modern irrigation programme.

Dry Farming

Relatively less conspicuous are the changes introduced in dry farming, although in most recent times they appear to be increasing in scope. The introduction of agricultural machinery produced changes in all Middle Eastern countries, representing innovations of considerable significance. The use of tractors and combines brought in its train the advantages and disadvantages familiar to us from other countries: shortening of the harvest season, improved cultivation of the land, better treatment of the crop, on the one hand; frequently higher production costs and correspondingly heavier overhead charges on the other. As compared with other agrarian countries in the Middle East, the changes seen in the non-irrigated sector of Palestine are probably the most outstanding. Here is to be found, side by side with the extensive and primitive system of tillage with its scanty yields patterned on the needs of the fellahin, a highly intensive, technical and rational form of agriculture, economical both technically and rationally. Novel types of farm organisation have been developed, new both in their social and agricultural structure. The use of modern technical devices has advanced to such a degree, especially in the settlements of the Jewish colonists, that sceptical voices are already being heard warning against too rapid expansion. Here the machine has almost completely ousted hand labour in cereal production. Tractor and combine, i.e. the combined reaping and threshing machine, replace the draught animal and human labour, thus making it possible to overcome the regularly recurring difficulties involved in harvesting by reason of climatic factors and labour shortage. The import of dairy cattle from countries of record herds has raised the standard of milk production to a remarkable extent and enabled dairying to develop into an important branch of modern Oriental agriculture.

Similarly directed efforts, if not equal in intensity, yet sufficiently pronounced, are under way especially in Turkey. Agricultural policy there was carried out at a slower pace, and therefore progress in the sphere of the individual farm is relatively slight. The authorities, however, have paid much attention to the education of the peasants, and by providing instruction by permanent inspectors, establishing agricultural colleges and experimental stations, have endeavoured to effect an improvement in their knowledge and methods. The official encouragement given to the founding of co-operative societies must also be mentioned. An interesting agrarian and socio-political experiment is the creation, in 1940, of four agricultural zones, each containing 5,000 villages, on lines analogous to the Russian combinates. Each of these zones was allotted 50 tractors in the hope that on the strength of preliminary experiments the corn harvest would be substantially increased. Incidentally, the Turkish Government itself is obviously not interested in effecting a complete collectivisation of agriculture, but bases its policy above all else on the fact that by collective efforts greater productivity can be achieved. Thus no peasant is allowed to "pool" more than a fourth of his land in the collectively ploughed area, so that he may not lose his pride and interest in his farm property.

The tempo of progress in all Oriental countries, where the population itself is often far from wholeheartedly behind the idea of progress, depends largely on the attitude of the Government authorities. This initiative on the part of the State made itself felt relatively late in the sphere of agrarian economy, and success, owing to the difficulties encountered in the effective formulation of the necessary measures, particularly as affecting conditions of land tenure, came but slowly. Nevertheless, another essential condition of any fundamental agrarian reform has been duly recognised, viz. the creation of a progressively-minded and sympathetically interested type of peasant by means of appropriate education and guidance. In many of the reports issued by the commissions appointed to investigate the position of agriculture in Oriental countries, educational and economic measures were recommended which have in part been realised. Reference must be made in this connection to the continued extension of the agricultural training system by the establishment of agricultural schools, research centres and experimental stations, museums, and so forth. Parallel tendencies in this respect are seen in all Middle East countries. Apart from periodical events such as exhibitions, which are most valuable as a means of conveying new impressions and methods, nearly all States in the Middle East today have established their own special institutes for the study of agricultural and allied problems.

Before summing up, we wish once more to revert to the issue of productivity, the most concise expression of productive capacity in agriculture. We have already enlarged upon this question above, and have found that the output per unit of land is much greater in irrigated than in dry farming. (Cf. p. 181). But even in the latter a large increase in productivity is still possible if full use is made of the results of theoretical and practical research. A comparison of average figures for agricultural productivity or net output per unit of land illustrates the conspicuous difference between the two types of agriculture. The figure is 128 International Units in Egypt as against 43 in Iraq, 41 in Turkey, and 40 in Syria.[79] The high figure for Egypt should not mislead us as regards the technical level of Egyptian agriculture. It is, in fact, only a different expression for the far larger amount of labour invested per unit of land or the much higher capacity of irrigated farming for absorbing people at a very low level of subsistence. It is worth mentioning that both factors, the high productivity and the high population density per unit of irrigated land, are responsible for the steady increase in land prices in all irrigated zones.

As to productivity per worker, the important fact should not be overlooked that farms or districts where no radical change has occurred in working methods generally fail to show any progress. As against this, a considerable advance is noticeable in all cases where new means and methods have been introduced to raise the output (selected seeds, improved cattle, rational manuring, etc.). Reports by agricultural research institutions in Egypt point to the important rise in the average output per unit achieved in such cases. This increase exceeds two kantars for cotton, one ardeb for wheat, 1·75 ardeb for barley, 1·2 ardeb for lentils.[80] Similar encouraging results were obtained by the rearing of pure-bred cattle and the introduction of Leghorn poultry. These achievements have perhaps not yet reached outstanding proportions, but it may safely be assumed that given reasonable conditions, there is likelihood of further improvement.

Of particular importance for the extension of agricultural production was the opening-up to traffic of districts situated on the periphery of the Oriental agrarian sector. In view of the fact that the price obtainable by the agricultural producer is largely dependent on the cost of transport while, on the other hand, his produce becomes marketable only if means of transport are available, there is no further need to emphasise the huge significance of the means of communication for agricultural production. The increase in production—both absolute and in relation to the land-unit—goes hand in hand with the development of communications. Before the First World War the railway was the principal means of communication. This meant at the same time a slower tempo of development inasmuch as the construction of railways called for much capital. Today the motor car—thanks to the important services it renders without much capital investment—is assuming this function to an increasing extent, especially in intensive agriculture where perishable goods (milk, butter, fruit, eggs) are produced.

True, all these developments and achievements are for the time being confined to the sphere of improved production. The solution of marketing difficulties has not kept pace with expanded production; in fact the shaping of the market situation in the years preceding the recent war renders the demand for internal and external regulation of the market more and more imperative. Whereas in Palestine, for instance, the lowering of production costs per unit is of vital importance for the further expansion of production in the newly-settled areas, in other Oriental countries this problem has not arisen with the same force. The level of production costs is determined above all else by the cost of labour. As labour is cheap and the climatic qualities of the Oriental zones favour the raising of a variety of high-priced crops for export, the expansion of agrarian production continues. This goes hand in hand with the growing of crops produced for generations: cotton in Egypt, citrus fruits in Palestine, Egypt and Syria, tobacco, stone fruits, raisins and figs in Turkey, dates in Iraq. The incentives are the said efforts to raise the standard of living, the necessity of feeding the rapidly growing population, and, last but not least, the sympathetic attitude on the part of the State, which from the beginning of this century has tended to permeate the whole of the Middle East. European and overseas markets in the course of the next few decades must count on the supply of high-priced agrarian produce of the Mediterranean zone through the Oriental countries in payment for their imports of capital goods, raw materials, machines, armament requirements, etc. The Middle East will thus become a new international centre of production pivoted on such branches as are climatically favoured. But with such a revolutionary change in structure and dependence on international markets, sensitiveness to breakdowns in the marketing mechanism will be extremely acute. In the past, crises in the demand for cotton, cereals, dates, tobacco, citrus fruits, etc., were among the gravest mishaps affecting agriculture in all these countries, and they are liable to return if there is no decided and co-ordinated policy of cultivation and marketing.

. . . . . .

Any attempt at summarising the principal features of the transformation process of Oriental agriculture is bound to ignore many particular discrepancies and deviations. The general lines of the picture, however, show uniform traits, especially in cases where similar natural conditions determine potential prospects and actual development.

There is, to begin with, the growing individualisation which underlies all shifts in land ownership and land tenure. The removal of restrictions and ties, such as *Mushaa*, *Waqf*, the abolition of the remains of the feudal land régime, etc., coincides with a marked increase in the number of small and minute farms, which is accompanied by a notable growth of large landed property. Although relations between the small farmer and the large landowner are no longer permeated with the deeply rooted spirit of servility, there is still an absence of that security and equality before the law which characterises such relationship in the principal Western countries. In particular the flagrant inequality in the structure of land tenure continues unchanged. The position could be remedied only by a determinate land policy. Up to the present none of the Arab countries, whether those formerly controlled by the Western Powers or the new independent Governments, have been able to decide on such reforms. Agrarian reforms liable to prejudice the interests of the landowning class will certainly not be introduced so long as the composition of the

Government bodies is dominated by these interests. Tentative reforms are to be found only in Turkey, but even here they have not been able to get beyond modest beginnings. Without the development of truly democratic forms of government, or intervention from without, no radical changes in conditions of land tenure can be expected; the same applies to the standard of living of the bulk of the agrarian population, which remains close to the minimum.

In the sphere of production, the main progress has taken place in irrigated agriculture. Apart from the enormous extension of the irrigated area, the replacement of flood irrigation (basin system) by canal irrigation has rendered perennial irrigation possible. The huge investments involved in this change have been effected by foreign capital, which has found its compensation in the increased yield of commercial crops, notably cotton.

The most conspicuous criterion of irrigated farming is the excessive splitting up of the land into tiny plots. The small-holding has thus become the most common type of farm unit. This development is called forth by the great increase in population and the large demand for labour per unit of land, the ultimate result being a high density of the working population on such land. At the same time, the economic weight of irrigated areas by far exceeds that of unirrigated zones of similar size, owing to the larger yields of the former. Likewise, from the viewpoint of world economics and colonisation the significance of irrigation areas is incomparably greater than that of unirrigable land.

The administrative requirements of large-scale irrigated farming, which in the past called for far-reaching supervision and control on the part of Government, have become more refined, thanks to modern developments in irrigation technique and the use of new devices for the centralised direction of the irrigation apparatus. This has permitted the abandonment of many means of despotic control which had once been indispensable for maintaining and regulating irrigated agriculture.

We are thus able to point to the following significant trends in the transformation process of Middle East agrarian economy:—

(*a*) All efforts directed towards increased exploitation of development potentialities are, and will continue to be, focussed on irrigated farming.

(*b*) The population increase, calling as it does for a further expansion of irrigated agriculture, is bound to lead to a continued reduction in the size of the individual farm unit, where there is still a margin of land available, or else to migration to the towns. Simultaneously, conditions of land tenure and land ownership will become more flexible.

(*c*) The necessity of procuring foreign capital for developing the local economy will be effective also in the future in favouring guidance on the part of foreign Powers, particularly in areas of large-scale irrigation.

(*d*) Notwithstanding the fact that in their economic undertakings in the Middle East the foreign Powers have been governed primarily by capital interests, the latter have become important factors in promoting local agriculture. To secure their investments, both past and future, the Powers will have no alternative but to participate in the coming economic development of these countries.

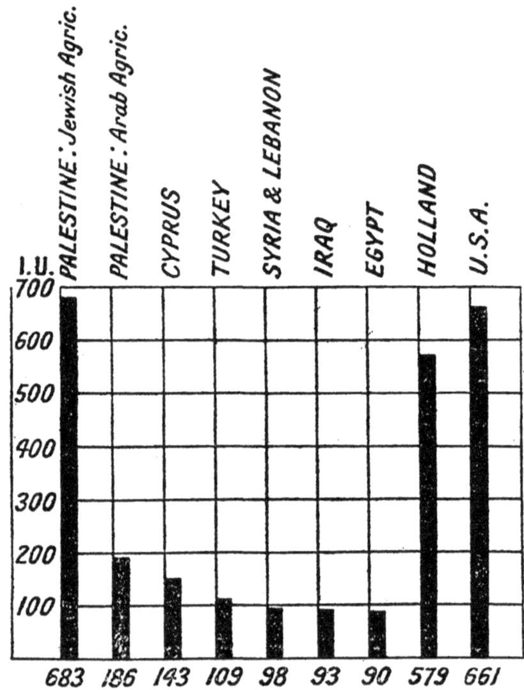

NET PRODUCTIVITY PER MALE EARNED IN AGRICULTURE, 1934–35

Crops in international units (one I.U. approximately one dollar)

PART THREE

THE INDUSTRIAL REVOLUTION IN THE MIDDLE EAST

SECTION I

THE PRE-INDUSTRIAL PERIOD

CHAPTER XIX

GENERAL FEATURES

The Meaning of the Industrial Revolution

The transformation of industrial production in Europe as the result of the introduction of the machine has come down in social history under the name of the Industrial Revolution.

It may well appear open to question whether this term, representing as it does a specific historical and sociological phenomenon in the industrial development of Europe, can be applied to conditions in the Orient. Differences of time and place prevent any strict repetition of the social process and consequently preclude the analogous application to conditions in Oriental countries of criteria and maxims based on Western experience. It is only insofar as the results of the industrial revolution derive from drastic technical changes and are thus moulded by the inevitable consequences of mechanisation that they must also follow in the East. We will deal, therefore, in the first place with those developments which are traceable essentially to the introduction of new and revolutionary methods of production.

How exactly, from this aspect, did the Industrial Revolution affect the development of industrial production in Europe? Let us see what one of the most discerning analysts in this field has to say on this point:

> "The machine which forms the starting-point of the Industrial Revolution replaces the worker handling a single tool by a mechanism operating simultaneously with a multitude of the same or similar tools and driven by a single motive power, whatever its form."[1]

It amounts, therefore, in the first place, to a technical change in the production process, its mechanisation, which results in a far-reaching release from the bonds of human labour, i.e. its quantitative limitations and its specific mode of operation. The chief effects of the use of the machine were first, a vast increase of output which—provided there was no immediate jump in consumption—led to the reduction or release of workers, a result which was often the prime motive for the introduction of machinery. The second effect was the splitting up of the production process itself into a number of phases often isolated from each other. The old method of manufacturing an industrial article in the workshop stage by stage is disrupted by the use of the machine. The watchmaker, for instance, who in former centuries was able or even obliged to make every individual part of the watch himself, today obtains these parts ready-made from the factory where, as a result of many manufacturing processes, they are produced by machines which in their turn are made in some other factory. The motors driving the watch-making machines, the transmissions, the belts and finally the packing implements, are again produced in special establishments. In short, the whole complicated apparatus of modern industrial manufacture represents for almost every class of goods a series of phases of production which with increasing mechanical and declining manual labour tends to be extended more and more. This extension of the production processes is the characteristic feature of our modern completely mechanised system of production which is shifted further and further away from the consumer in ever more specialised phases of the production process. At the same time the products themselves are classified increasingly from the standpoint of their destination, viz. into goods produced to serve the manufacture of other goods (machines, raw materials) and known as production or investment goods, and those destined for the direct use of the consumer and called accordingly consumer goods.

With the progress of mechanisation the sector of the national economy devoted to the production of investment goods gains in importance. This tendency derives from the growing demand for machines, fuel and raw materials required for the maintenance of the whole production process, principally coal, oil, iron, metals, fibre. Industrial technique, in order to escape from the restrictions inherent in the use of organic power producers, started to rely on iron and coal as primary sources of material and energy. Dependence on animal power or plant growth today sets no limits to the scope which science considers essential to the satisfaction of man's demand for goods. Animal power, from the very onset of industrialisation, has almost everywhere been dispensed with, for the introduction of the steam engine multiplied the output of such primitive motive powers. The replacement—partial or complete—of wood and water by coal and mineral oil brought about a further multiplication of the amounts of energy hitherto available. Many of the important fibrins formerly obtainable as raw materials from natural sources only have in the latest stage of technical development been replaced by materials produced industrially by highly complicated chemical processes and thus completely freed from the limitations of organic growth.

Thus today the production goods industry, so far as values are concerned, has come to comprise the bulk of industrial activity.

Turning now to consider the immediate social consequences of the industrial revolution, the release of the workers, already mentioned, appears to be the biggest attack yet made on the statics of the social order as hitherto existing. This release was not uniform in all branches of industry; it followed the actual change-over of production to a mechanised basis which was introduced at very different periods. Important dates in this development were the years 1735 and 1740 when coke was first produced from coal. In 1784 the puddling process first came into use. The three most important discoveries in the field of the textile industry were the flying shuttle (1733), the power loom (1785), the spinning jenny (1767). In 1769 came the discovery of the steam engine (Watt), crowned by the opening of the Stockton and Darlington railway. "The power-loom", writes Lipson, "was introduced only gradually, yet it set the pace, and the ability of the power-loom master to undersell the hand-loom master forced the latter to cut the rates of payment. Machinery was thus the great 'screw', and the ever present menace of its introduction sapped the weavers' power of resistance. The fate which befell the hand-loom weavers overtook also the woolcombers, though the latter did not succumb without resistance."[2]

This resistance, however, tended but still further to aggravate the position of the hand weavers and combers. The data at our disposal which throw light on the extent of the release of the workers point to the occurrence of really effective, if locally unco-ordinated, movements. There was not only unemployment—as a direct result of the new production methods—for the now superfluous hands; side by side with this went the elimination, that is, the final ousting of the artisan worker who formerly, even when dependent, had a secure sphere of work and living space. The mechanisation of production had as an immediate effect not only a considerable decline in the future demand for labour; even when this demand increased, it was invariably marked by violent fluctuations, so that no permanent fixed relation was possible as between place of work, employer and employee. The independent worker found himself a "free" worker, free in the sense of "vogelfrei" (outlawed); his freedom was the freedom of the proletarian obliged to sell his labour at any price, and often even deprived of all possibilities of casual gain.

True, the Industrial Revolution had not only these negative results to show. The mechanisation of the manufacturing process reduced the price of the individual article, and thus offered thousands the possibility of enjoying the benefits of cheaper production. The standard of living of the masses in the age of industrialisation indisputably shows a considerable increase, particularly since, thanks to the organisation of the workers, and to modern social legislation and insurance, the worst evils accompanying the growth of the industrial working class have been obviated. The raising of the standard of living acquired special significance wherever the intermediate stages of social disintegration which elsewhere preceded the improved conditions of today could be overleapt.

As a further effect of the Industrial Revolution mention must be made of the steadily increasing urbanisation of the last hundred years. All industrial countries have experienced this growth in population in the urban districts, a phenomenon which is closely connected with increasing technicalisation. The massing of industrial enterprises in the towns is due to the fact that there the new factories are favourably placed as regards labour, transport and consumption, three prerequisites which are all present when such enterprises are established in the towns; the result was an ever-growing influx of people into the already existing centres of industry.[3]

Thus, the process inaugurated by the mechanisation and specialisation of production had far-reaching repercussions. Tending as it did to devaluate the function of the individual worker, it led to the dispossessing of the artisan class as a whole; with the mass production of the means of production (machines, implements, etc.) entirely new alignments emerge as regards its aims. The social consequences of the increasing commercial exploitation of the new technical achievements culminate finally in class-division as between entrepreneur and workers and in over-urbanisation as a result of industrial concentration.

The Problem of Capitalism in Oriental Countries

All those who believe in the universality of socio-economic laws will be prepared to apply the scheme in question also to the later industrial developments in Oriental countries and to defend this line of argument despite certain divergences due to special conditions of time and place. They will, therefore, be prepared both to admit as regards the past a causal connection between the social changes and the technical processes analogous to that noted in European countries, and in respect of the future to cast a prognosis based on Western experiences.

This attempt at analogy, however, is confronted quite unmistakably with another reality. The divergences between the development of the two spheres of culture are not due to temporal causes alone. The phenomenon of free industrial capitalism is confined to the Occident, i.e. to Europe and North America, to a sphere of culture which, owing to a series of specific features more than accidental in character, is marked out as unique in social history. The temporal rift here becomes the expression of a basically different cultural evolution. At a period when the phenomenon of modern capitalism was moulding the face of society in the West, we find in Oriental countries widespread stagnation and the absence of all signs of even an approximately parallel or similar development. If the present appears to be making up for much that we recognise as characteristic of modern capitalism, this must not lead us, because of similar external symptoms, to expect further development on completely corresponding lines. Industrial capitalism came into existence and was developed in Europe, where it assumed such mighty proportions, under entirely different conditions. Neither in respect of its promoters nor of the origin of the capital with which it was financed, nor of the attitude of the State, is any comparison between industrial capitalism in European countries and the industrialisation of Oriental lands possible.

Capitalism in the West owes its existence, *inter alia*, to the influence of a class of citizens endowed with specific virtues as organisers and entrepreneurs, a class which did not exist in the East. The rational-scientific technique which formed the starting-point for the profusion of industrial discoveries in the seventeenth, eighteenth and nineteenth centuries, remained unknown to Oriental civilisations.

The formation of capital in the West, quite apart from differences in the degree of its intensity, benefited production to a far greater extent; furthermore, the industrial pioneers used the new capital to expand production still further, although clearly aware of the risks involved. On the other hand, fortunes deriving from production in Oriental countries weak in capital backing were spent as a rule on personal consumption, often in the form of foreign luxury products.

The population conditions in the densely inhabited European countries proved a great stimulus to industrial mass-production, whereas in the Orient the sparsely settled districts with their population of extremely low purchasing power and markets often swamped with European products, offered but slight scope for local industry. For this reason the industrial capital which in the nineteenth century was invested in certain branches of Oriental economy was mostly of foreign origin. The promoters and owners of the funds were foreigners, and had no interest in any widespread industrialisation of the country of their residence. They also claimed for themselves monopoly rights and market privileges which the expanding European industrial economy very definitely refused to concede at home.

When eventually young national States replaced the Ottoman Empire, these States, realising that they alone could fulfil this important function, assumed the rôle of industrial initiators, and in part even that of actual entrepreneurs. Thus in certain countries there arose a kind of monopolistic State industry or State-controlled industrialisation which differs both in aim and achievement from industrial capitalism in the West.

This limitation, however, does not answer the question of the place which the industrialisation process in the Orient occupies in modern world economy. Where does this development stand as regards its general form of organisation, its stage of intensity and economic activity?

The term "form of organisation" is used here in the sense employed by Wagemann to indicate the rules and principles according to which the forces of the national economy, production and consumption are co-ordinated, in short the prevailing economic system; "stage of intensity" means the volume of productive forces and circulation of goods in the widest sense as applied per unit of area and population of a given economic territory.

Form of Organisation

From the beginning of modern times up to the middle of the nineteenth century Middle East economy, both as a whole and as regards most individual economic enterprises, had the character of a subsistence economy, i.e. production was regulated mainly by the home demand. There were partial exceptions; production for the home market in some cases being switched over without any transition from a developed domestic market direct to foreign markets. This change-over could be effected as a rule only by means of a mercantilistic policy on the part of the State in relation to the fellahin producers.

The normal subsistence economy in the Middle East countries has been characterised up to the present—and in many districts so remains even today—by collective ties; landownership relations in particular were permeated by collective forms handed down from olden times, for which interesting analogies can be found in the land laws of primitive communities in other parts of the world. (Vide Chapter XII). In the case of the individual producer, scarcely a trace can as yet be found of the rationalised capitalist spirit. Conjointly with the time-honoured working traditions extra-economic factors, social and religious, helped to preserve the static character of economic society in the Orient.

The structure of this subsistence economy, which characterizes both agriculture and industry, begins from the second half of the nineteenth century to disintegrate, in some countries more quickly, in others more slowly. Its place is increasingly—in the case of some branches of production exclusively—occupied by the acquisitive economy centring on the market, although for a long time interspersed with enclaves of subsistence economy.

The period from 1918 onwards reveals in some countries, especially in the field of industrial goods production, the entrance of a new principle of organisation, that of State or quasi-State initiative and control. The State becomes production-minded and, what is more, itself founds industrial enterprises. Two motives lie behind this policy. On the one hand there is the desire to diversify home production in order to minimise the danger of periods of depression and to lessen dependence on imports from abroad. On the other hand, the need is felt to increase production for export in order to be advantageously placed for the exchange of goods.

Thus a decisive change occurs in the motivation and direction of commodity production; an economy catering solely or mainly for the needs of the producers themselves becomes a State-directed economy aiming at production for the market; out of the isolated, almost anarchic, economic activity of pre-State days arises modern exchange economy backed and directed by the State.

Degree of Intensity

It is far more difficult to judge the economic system of the Middle Eastern countries by the degree of intensity or the stage of development achieved by them. The difficulties lie in the complex socio-economic structure of this part of the world, to which must be added the lack of data necessary for a complete analysis. Determining factors for the establishment of the stage of intensity are the scope of the country's assets in respect of workers and capital equipment, the level of production technique, the degree of industrialisation and the intensity of the exchange of goods in the home and foreign markets.

Wagemann has drawn up the following criteria: population density, use of machinery, density of communications, industrial workers' quota and foreign trade *per capita.*[4] On the basis of the key data assembled by him four stages have been established, namely, the high capitalistic, the semi-capitalistic, the neo-capitalistic, and the pre-capitalistic stage. In 1930, Europe (Russia excepted), the U.S.A. and Japan belonged to the high capitalistic stage; Russia and Asia to the semi-capitalistic; Australia, New Zealand, Canada, South Africa and Central and South America to the neo-capitalistic, and the remaining territories to the pre-capitalistic stage. This classification is not very refined, though it offers in broad outline a fairly instructive picture. To render it more complete, it appears desirable to supplement these criteria with a few others of importance, such as national income, capital investment, productivity, State finance and growth of population. Density of population in respect of the total area may lead to incorrect conclusions in this context and has therefore been omitted. The table on p. 222 compares these key figures with those of Western countries and illustrates the stages of development in the Oriental zone.

This classification leaves out of consideration one significant feature which obtrudes in Oriental lands. The figure for agrarian output per unit of land varies extraordinarily as between the individual areas, being very much higher in those where agriculture is based on irrigation than in agrarian districts dependent on rainfall (vide Chapter XVI). In the former we therefore find a stage of exploitation (i.e. density of labour and population per unit of land) which, despite the extremely low productivity per earner, points to a high degree of utilisation. Human labour may be said to have assumed here the rôle of capital investment. To

COMPARATIVE DATA ON MIDDLE EASTERN COUNTRIES

	Egypt	Syria & Lebanon	Iraq	Turkey	Palestine		
					Total	Arabs	Jews
Density of traffic— Number of motor vehicles per 10,000 persons (1938)	21	30	19	6	62	—	—
Railway lines— length in km. per 10,000 persons (1938)	3·1	3·9	3·3	4·2	5·2	—	—
Import per head in £ (average 1935-8)	2·19	1·84	2·83	1·07	10·52	4·07	24·85
Export per head in £ (average 1936-8)	2·10	0·95	1·16	1·21	3·60	2·60	8·73
Volume of Foreign Trade	4·29	2·79	3·99	2·28	14·12	6·67	33·58
National Income in £ per head (1936)	12	13	10	19	26	16	46
State finance (1938-9)– revenue in £ per head	2·323	0·894	2·119	3·286	3·958	2·6	12·1
expenditure in £ per head	2·494	0·788	2·198	2·958	3·870	—	--
Agricultural productivity in £ (net): per male earner (1934-5)	18	19·6	18·6	21·8	35·4	29·6	74·2
per Hectare cultivated land in £	25·6	8	8·6	8·2	7·8	—	—
Density of population (1939)— per sq. km. total area	16·7	18·8	8·16	22·94	55·6	—	—
per sq.km. cultivable area	490	62·7	40·2	58·3	125·1	—	—
Import of machinery, apparatus, electrical goods *per capita*, average 1936–8 in £	0·156	0·111	0·254	0·160	0·770	—	—

throw this peculiar feature into relief, the population density per unit of cultivable land has been included in the table. Eastern countries with scanty capital resources but with modernized irrigation, such as Egypt, ought therefore to be classed under "Labour-intensive semi-capitalism."[5]

According to these categories our Middle Eastern countries, with the exception of Palestine, should be classed as semi-capitalist

STAGES OF ECONOMIC DEVELOPMENT ACCORDING TO KEY FIGURES (PRE-WAR(

	Middle East Countries (incl. Arab Palestine)	Other Semi-Capitalistic	Neo-Capitalistic	High Capitalistic (Mature)	Palestine Jewish Sector
National Incom (£) per Head . .	10–19	5–20	35–80	70–130	46
Capital Investment (£)per Earner .	106*	125–200	750–1000	1000–1250	463†
Agric. Productivity per male Earner (in Intl. Units .	90–186	70–200	1000–2400	400–1000	683
Growth of Population (per 1,000) 1931–1935 . .	16–25	10–15	8–10	0·8–7	21
Density of traffic (*a*) Number of lorries per 10,000 Inhab.	0·5–5‡	0·6	27	70	25¶
(*b*) Railway lines—Length in km. per 10,000 Inhab. .	3·1–5·2·¶	1·8	21·8	13·6	—
Volume of Foreign Trade per Head .	2·8–6·7	1·5	17	17·4	33

* Egypt only (1937) excluding communications.
† Refers to the period 1920–1940; excluding communications.
‡ Not including Palestine.
¶ Average for Jews and Arabs.

or pre-capitalist countries. In any case they have not reached the degree of intensity of high capitalism, i.e. levels typical of high capitalist or mature countries, in respect of capital investment, labour expenditure, national income, communications per head of population, etc. Palestine is the only country presenting, mainly in its Jewish sector, the picture of an economy approaching that of the developed communities of the West.

Having thus determined the place of the Oriental economy of today in recent economic history as compared with that of other economies and thereby obtained certain clues for the pursuit of our study, we now come to our principal task, viz. the delineation of the industrialisation process in the Middle East in its various stages. The period covered extends from the end of the great stagnation which closed with the Napoleonic expedition up to the Second World War. We must deal widely with the general social conditions which are reciprocally bound up with the infiltration of industrial capitalism. Before defining the individual phases of this process, it will be relevant to give some data on the basic conditions of population and standard of living which constitute the decisive factors in the development of industrial production.

Distribution of the Population over Town and Country

The meagre statistical data which throw light on the population conditions in Middle East countries in the eighteenth and nineteenth centuries are not suited to serve as a basis for the calculation of rates of increase, or an analysis of the population problems of that epoch. They are, however, useful for forming a picture of the general population structure, and above all of the distribution of population over town and country. As far as the majority of these countries are concerned, it appears that the number of inhabitants in the large towns certainly increased considerably in the course of the nineteenth century; the ratio between urban and rural population, however, shifted only gradually but not fundamentally in favour of the town.

The following figures give some idea of the size of the more important towns and their total population. We begin with Egypt:[6]

Year	Total Population	Cairo	Alexandria	Joint population of the two towns
1848 .	4,543,000	254,000	143,000	343,000 = 8·8%
1897 .	9,715,000	570,000	320,000	890,000 = 9·2%
1937 .	15,905,000	1,307,000	682,000	1,989,000 = 13·1%

In the case of Syria and the Lebanon we likewise find a relatively small increase in the ratio of the urban to the total population. At the beginning of the nineteenth century the town of Beirut may have contained scarcely 10–12,000 inhabitants, the Lebanon as a whole only 300,000. A similar ratio existed between the population of Jerusalem and that of all Palestine; the respective figures are in this case 12,000 for Jerusalem (1814) and *c.* 300,000 for the whole country, i.e. 3–4 per cent. as Jerusalem's share. Towards the middle of the century the share of both centres still remains considerably under 10 per cent. of the total population,[7] and it is only at the turn of the century that the population figure for Beirut shows a sharp rise, while Jerusalem even at that period continues to stagnate. Whereas for lack of data we are unable to draw up comparisons of this nature for other districts in even so rough a form, there are certain pieces of evidence which lead us to infer at least similar tendencies. Thus, the town of Haifa, which today numbers 120,000 inhabitants, had about 1880 only 5,000, the town of Ankara at the turn of the century scarcely 30,000 as against 160,000 today. In Iraq about 1900 Baghdad with 145,000 inhabitants contained, as the only town with over 100,000 inhabitants, approximately 7·5 per cent. of the total population. The percentage of the total population living in the cities in the various parts of theOttoman Empire is thus seen to be extremely slight, and it scarcely changed during the course of the nineteenth century. How did conditions in the West compare with this?

In Europe, the number of persons living in the towns with over 100,000 inhabitants about 1800 formed 3 per cent. of the total population, whereas about 1900 it had already risen to 13 per cent.[7] For individual countries the figures are still more striking, as may be seen from the following table:

PERCENTAGE OF THE TOTAL POPULATION LIVING IN TOWNS WITH OVER 100,000 INHABITANTS IN:

	1800	1900	Increase in % (1800 = 100%)
England and Wales	7	37·6	537·1
Netherlands	7	22·3	318·5
Germany	1	15·6	1560·0
France	2·7	13·8	511·5
Russia	1·6	9·3 (1910)	518·7

The table shows at the same time that the urbanisation process with all its consequences for the way of life, direction and extent of goods production at the close of the nineteenth century was incomparably more advanced in Europe than in Middle Eastern countries where only the first signs of urbanisation had become evident.

URBAN LIVING CONDITIONS (EXPENDITURE AND MODE OF LIVING)

There are various reports available on living conditions in Oriental towns prior to the beginning of industrial production. For Cairo, for instance, we possess a survey dating from the third decade of the nineteenth century compiled by Lane who was a very reliable observer of contemporary conditions.[8] According to this report, the annual budget of a well-to-do family of 4 adult persons amounted to not more than £E27¼, i.e. somewhat less than £E7 per person or approximately 2 piastres *per diem*. The composition of the list of necessities is noteworthy seeing that it shows that the principal article—bread—is not obtained from the baker; the baker receives the flour from the private individual to whom he delivers the finished loaf against a fixed charge for baking (See table at end of Notes to Part III, p. 413).

Of the total number of 240,000 inhabitants that Cairo, according to Lane, was said to contain at the beginning of the thirties, 80,000 were male adults. Of this number we find 20,000 accounted for as domestic servants, 15,000 as simple workers and porters, 30,000 as dealers, 10,000 as artisans, and the remainder as military and officials. The number of artisans, estimated at 10,000, is more likely to be too high than too low. This figure, however, indicates the insignificance of this element *per se* and the slender scope of industrial goods consumption in the capital and its hinterland.

In respect of an urban centre in Northern Syria, Aleppo, we have the report of a contemporary author, the French Consul Henry Guys, towards the middle of the century:

> "Like all oriental peoples, the inhabitants of Aleppo lead a very monotonous life which is only rarely interrupted on the occasion of events which occur every year, i.e. their two feasts, the departure of the pilgrims for Mecca, their return, etc. Apart from this, they are extremely systematic, and one day in their life is spent more or less the same way as the whole. Those who have a profession, begin their work in the morning, and those who have not, spend their time lying on their couches if they live on their income, or in cafés waiting for chance to offer them means of subsistence."[9]

Living expenses are put by Guys at 30 centimes per diem in the case of the poorer classes, at 50–75 centimes in the case of the middle and wealthy classes per head per day. The rent paid by a family of 6–7 persons amounts to £5–6 per annum, the wages of a domestic servant to Frs. 1–3 per week. This modest way of life in the Syrian towns has lasted, incidentally, down to the present day. Ruppin writing in *Syrien als Wirtschaftsgebiet* ("Syria and Its Economy") of conditions in 1915, says that it would be difficult to find in any other part of the world towns of 70,000 or 80,000 inhabitants with a fair amount of industry and considerable Beduin trade in which the population spends so little over and above the most essential necessities of life as in Homs and Hama.[10]

This appears moreover to be confirmed by the fact that in

1835 the *maximum* of Firde, a kind of income tax in Cairo, which in normal circumstances should amount to about one-twelfth of the income, was fixed at 500 piastres, corresponding to an income of £60.[11] Even if we allow for a good deal of evasion, the figures indicate a very low level of income.

Thus we have a picture of a static economy in which the predominant part of the total population, the rural element, itself produces it own means of subsistence as a rule without the need to purchase, besides making or having made a considerable part of its industrial commodities such as shoes, fabrics, utensils in the villages.[12] Also their dwellings are "autarkically" constructed *in situ* without recourse to products from without. Such features are preserved to a wide extent in many otherwise highly developed villages of the present-day Orient, where a number of articles of daily use, such as baskets, mats, pitchers are produced; likewise in these countries the preparation of olive products, spinning and weaving are still familiar domestic occupations.

To the fact that this economic structure is predominantly agrarian and self-supporting must be added the low standard of living of the urban population. The demand for luxury goods which in European countries was caused by the nobility, the courts and the urban patrician class and achieved great importance for the maintenance of a flourishing industry, was largely lacking in the East, or was confined to the few places where the Sultan and his Pashas resided. Thus from this quarter also there could come no strong incentive to the renewal of production or its cheapening by machine processes.

After this outline of the background we will now describe the forms and the nature of non-agricultural production in Middle East countries in the first half of the nineteenth century.

CHAPTER XX

THE DEVELOPMENT OF NON-AGRICULTURAL PRODUCTION FROM THE END OF THE EIGHTEENTH CENTURY TO THE DEATH OF MOHAMMED ALI (1849)

General Conditions of Non-Agricultural Production

In the field of industrial goods production actual changes occur in a more conspicuous and less gradual fashion than in any other economic sphere. But here, too, we find that in economic history there are no clear-cut discontinuities. True, the early attempts at industrial *mass*-production, which might serve as a turning-point, date from the first third of the nineteenth century; but notwithstanding the introduction of the first machines in the Middle East, we find, holding their own in important branches of industry down to this very day, technical and organisational forms of labour and production which have been unchanged for centuries and belong in all respects to a pre-capitalist stage.

What was the status and quality of industrial production in these countries at the turn of the century in the light of contemporary reports? The end of the eighteenth century brought the Orient for the first time for centuries into closer contact with Europeans and European ways of life. This impact tended to have a fateful reaction on the vitality of local industry, although the effects were not always uniform. Between conditions in the Arab and non-Arab parts of the Orient there were considerable differences. The former had till then remained on the whole far more isolated from Europe than the Balkan and Anatolian districts. Furthermore, the various national groups and races of the Oriental world differed markedly from each other in both ability and taste. Early writers noted that the autochthonous Arab nomad population possessed no high skill or interest as artisans and craftsmen, and were dependent to the widest extent on non-Arab workers.[13] We already find Ibn Khaldun struck by differences in this connection which he repeatedly and quite unreservedly stresses. The Arabs brought no artisan or handicraft tradition with them to the countries in which they settled:

"The practice of the arts is in general very limited in the countries where the Arabs are indigenous and in the areas which they have conquered since the promulgation of Islam. Consider, on the other hand, how the arts are flourishing in the countries inhabited by the Chinese, the Hindus, the Turks and the Christians, and how the other nations derive goods and foodstuffs from them."[14]

Cairo and other Arab towns owe their notable buildings and outstanding achievements in the arts and crafts to non-Arab artists. But even if we must, particularly in the early period, concede a long preparatory spell for the education of an Arab artisan stock, there still remains sufficient evidence of an inferiority in the mentality of the Middle Eastern worker. This applies to industry and agriculture alike. Lane, whose observations have a reputation for particular conscientiousness, described about a hundred years ago his impressions regarding the working mentality of the Egyptian:

"Indolence pervades all classes of the Egyptians, except those who are obliged to earn their livelihood by severe manual labour. It is the result of the climate, and of the fecundity of the soil. Even the mechanics, who are extremely greedy of gain, will generally spend two days in a work which they might easily accomplish in one; and will leave the most lucrative employment to idle away their time with the pipe . . .

"It is seldom that an Egyptian workman can be induced to make a thing exactly to order: he will generally follow his own opinion in preference to that of his employer, and will scarcely ever finish his work by the time he has promised."[15]

Lane qualifies his remarks only in respect of such workers as, for some reason or other, are obliged to undertake severe manual labour, such as boatmen, porters, and the like.

In the course of time, and under the influence of the spread of Mohammedanism, which caused the foreign workers to assimilate with the Arab sections of the population, skilled workers came to be found also in the Arab countries, especially for the products of the textile and metal trades, always highly prized in these lands. On the whole, however, the standard of industrial production in the towns of Egypt, Syria and Iraq remained inferior to that of the Turkish towns.

The position in Egypt at the end of the eighteenth century is described by Volney, who complains of the decay in the Nile country, in the following words:

"The most simple arts have fallen into a kind of dotage. There are carpenters, locksmiths and primitive gun-making trades. Ironmongery, haberdashery, gun and pistol barrels come from abroad. One can scarcely find a watchmaker in Cairo capable of repairing a watch, and if one does, he is a European. The jewellers do not know how to set a diamond properly; the powder is coarse, sugar full of molasses and, if white, beyond price. The only objects having any quality are the silk fabrics, and although less fine, they are dearer than those of Europe."[15a]

Girard, likewise, stresses the sad plight of industry at the time of Napoleon's expedition:

"Confined to articles of current use, it is satisfied to work up—more or less badly—clay from the Nile, sand, saltpetre, plant-juice, animal faeces, dressed tanned skins, sheep's wool, sugar cane, in short, all such materials as are to be found in the country."[15b]

Of the situation in Aleppo in the first half of the nineteenth century, we are told that it owes its former rise as a commercial and industrial centre to the fact that it was able to serve as entrepôt for the commerce between Europe and Asia; thus the town benefited by the decline of Palmyra and Baalbek. This prosperity, writes Guys in 1854, lasted until 1775, although it had already begun to feel the effect of the discovery of the sea-route round the Cape of Good Hope; the great decline setting in only subsequently.[16]

Industry in Aleppo is, therefore, confined almost exclusively to the production of simple articles of daily use; the number of persons engaged in handicrafts in the town has thus fallen from 16,000 to 1,116.[17]

The general state of industry at that period cannot be adequately portrayed without drawing particular attention to the part played by European competitive goods. Whatever sources we use, we cannot fail to find, even at that early period, complaints about the devastating effect of the cheap European machine-made products which were then for the first time making their appearance to a major extent on the extra-European markets. It was the period when European industry went marching forward unhindered. Native industry was at once exposed thereby to appreciable losses. The introduction of British-made India textiles put more than ten thousand workers out of employment in one year. The silk factories had to register a no less acute set-back.[18]

Acording to a report by Campbell for the year 1836, Syrian factories turned out *c.* 1,200 kantars of native silk fabrics in the workshops of Aleppo, Damascus, Tripolis, Hama, Beirut, Deir el-Qamar and Sidon. But all these native products have had to yield to the British manufactured article.[19]

In a review of the situation in Aleppo, the already-quoted French Consul Henry Guys stresses the fact that the poverty of the population with its continuous increase must be aggravated inasmuch as the import of British and Swiss fabrics would result in the total ruin of the native weaving industry.[20]

The Orientalist Alfred von Kremer, who visited Damascus in 1850, reports that the sole cause of the decline of the once important Damascus silk-weaving industry is to be found in the import of British and Swiss made goods. These goods, he writes, are a quarter cheaper than the Damascus silks, though far less durable; they are bought by the poorer classes, who, as a result of their increasing impoverishment, gave up the better and more expensive qualities to purchase the cheaper grade goods. The Turkish Government, according to Kremer, encouraged the import of the foreign-made fabrics to a degree such as is usual with other Governments only for the products of their own subjects.[21]

In Turkey proper the decline of native industry, although brought about in the first instance under the influence of European competition, had already begun towards the end of the eighteenth century. In Scutari (Albania) the number of silk workers dropped from 600 in 1812 to 40 in 1821, in Trnovo (Bulgaria) the number of artisans fell between 1812 and 1830 from 2,000 to 100.[22] In the town of Ankara, which at the end of the eighteenth century produced—and for the most part exported—more than 25,000 bales of woollen fabrics, the export fell in 1836 to less than 5,000 bales.[23]

This trend was aggravated by the gradually developing competition of the machine-equipped factories newly established in the Oriental countries themselves. Thus Vambéry writes of conditions in the old weaving centre of Bursa in Anatolia that the famous industry of silk brocade production had been brought to a standstill as a result of the establishment of European looms under European management.[24]

Although the position of the merchants and many independent artisans was still tolerable as, thanks to their private fortunes and property, they had resources at their disposal enabling them to outlast the crisis, that of the workers was very bad. The description of Egypt given by Napoleon's French scholars' expedition estimated that in 1800 in Cairo two-thirds of the working proletariat dwelt in diseased quarters, slept on mats, lived on raw vegetables and let their offspring run about practically naked.

The stagnation in the position of native industry caused by the competition of imported industrial goods and the beginnings of local production and its helplessness stand in curious contrast to the strenuous activity with which in those days the European industrialist strove to beat his new competitors. There this rivalry tended to encourage technical progress to an undreamt-of extent, a process which in many cases ran parallel even to the interests of the competing producers. In the Orient the opposite was the case: the local producer, helpless as he was, was ruined by the competition.

Character of Industrial Production in Middle East Countries up to the Middle of the Nineteenth Century

Place of Production

In accordance with the general lay-out of the Moslem town, the trade and industry of that period centred in the *Suq*, the bazaar quarter with the adjoining business thoroughfares. The residential quarter of the town is as a rule separated from the business centres, and there we find the area split up according to nationalities into national or racial quarters; sometimes these are again subdivided into business and residential sectors. Where, for instance, there are Arab, Armenian and Jewish quarters, one can frequently find separate Arab, Armenian and Jewish shoemaker bazaars. But there are occasionally "mixed" bazaars also where all races are represented.

As a rule the bazaars form a conglomeration of blocks of building which the outsider will find most difficult to identify. The whole area is traversed by lanes which are the actual theatre of commerce. These alleys are roofed over and form at times a whole series of market halls which in their present shape, as seen in the large urban centres of the Orient (Damascus, Constantinople, Baghdad) are of more recent origin. In some of the Oriental towns the older form of Arab bazaar with the original architectural structures is still in good preservation; here the alleyways are narrower, and the stands and booths are formed by spaces in the masonry mostly in the form of open vaults (Jerusalem, Aleppo). In the alleys which are roofed over the light trickles through from above through openings in the vaulted roof.

The individual *Suqs* consist of the workshops and booths let into the buildings on both sides of the alleyway, mostly cubical rooms without any internal divisions enclosed by a back wall, two sides and a vaulted roof, the front which opens on to the street being fitted with wooden or iron shutters. In the booths where a handicraft is carried on, this is usually done in the back part of the room, whereas the finished goods are laid out in front on a kind of counter or displayed from the walls of the booth so as to catch the eyes of the passers-by.

Lines on which Production was Organised

The structure and organisation of industrial production was not uniform.[25] One fact above all others determined its form: the manufacturing process was as a rule based on manual labour. The artisan, either alone or with assistants, executed his work by means of simple tools and instruments; his methods of work were also simple; the capital required, provided he did not accumulate an extensive stock of raw materials or finished goods, was slight.

Work was carried out either in the form of:

(*a*) wage work paid for as such by the individual customer who often supplied even the raw material (wool, cloth, flour), taking an interest in the process of manufacture, or

(*b*) price work, when the customer selected from the finished goods those which suited him.

In the State factories, and also in those cases where the State supervised the production of artisans working, not in State factories, but for the State, the State took over the finished article; the individual artisan was at times forbidden—as during the Government monopoly of Mohammed Ali—to sell his goods direct.

Reports on the immediate organisation of production differ. Whereas Clerget regards wage work or work for a customer as the normal type of handicraft work, Junge (for Turkestan) and Schurtz (for North Africa) give the production of goods for stock or free sale as the rule.[26] In the Jerusalem bazaar, for instance, goods are made both "to order" and for free sale up to the present day. Probably both forms are to be found everywhere, just as we everywhere find besides artisans who produce their goods on the spot and sell them to customers or work for "stock," shopkeepers who offer for sale goods not of their own manufacture. As long as the expansion of industry was restricted by guild regulations, the difference in the orientation of the producer, i.e. whether he worked for the market or, if needed, for a particular customer, was of no account. It became important only when the artisan ceased to be a workman and was exposed to the temptation of combining the management of his enterprise, employing several hands and working capital, with his personal functions.

The implements and tools which were at the disposal of the artisan in past times are to be found even now in many of the bazaars of Oriental towns. The motive power used, insofar as any regular process of manufacture was concerned, was human and animal power. Motor power, after a brief interlude under Mohammed Ali, made its reappearance in Egypt relatively very late. The working utensils were simple, often primitive in form. The time required for the production of an article was not measured. Dexterity and skill, in knitting and weaving especially, but also in metalwork, played a large part. The necessary capital requirements were insignificant, as the total turnover was very small. The most important question was the procurement of raw materials; the wages of the few workmen, so far as they received any cash wages worth mentioning, likewise remained at a very low figure in accordance with the general standard of living and price level. The following details concerning the cost of raw materials, of manufacture and of a finished article are taken from the report by Guys on conditions in Aleppo in the forties of the nineteenth century, and are not without interest for a judgment of the size of capital investment and the extent of handicraft production in those days.[27]

Among the important "industries" in Aleppo in 1844, there were 337 factories and 1,691 smaller workshops with 4,481 workers, which term covers probably all those engaged in them, including the independent artisan himself. The gross value of production amounted to frs. 4,477,065, i.e. frs. 998 or approximately £40 per worker. These statistics enable us also to estimate the average sum to be counted as "added value" *per capita* per worker. It amounted to no more than frs. 259, i.e. only £10.5 for the year under review. Even if we put the purchasing power of money at that period considerably higher than today, besides assuming that a part of the work was seasonal in character, the amounts are remarkably small and reveal an unusually low standard both as regards production and living in the industrial occupations. True, it is difficult to decide whether the figures given by Guys, very detailed for Oriental conditions, can be regarded as an adequate basis for such calculations; however, the stress laid by the author, himself a statistician, on the care with which the material was collected, justifies us in treating this notable study with less scepticism than many other data of that period. In any case, these figures as well as others tend to establish the fact that even in those cases where the producer was both worker and owner of the raw material and accessories—as opposed to job-work where the artisan approaches more closely to the type of the mere wage-earner—the turnover and value of production was very limited, and there could be hardly a question of mass-production.

A certain capitalistic element enters into this early form of industrial production owing to the fact that the settled artisan, who is tied to his place of work, is unwilling to give up his domicile in the centre of the town. Thus, the owners of the land and houses where the artisans work are able to exploit their monopoly of location stand, which indeed they have fully done. The owners of the bazaar booths and land or of the right of usufruct in them, are frequently wealthy notables or sheikhs who for years have enjoyed this lucrative form of capital investment. In no rare cases the actual owners of these properties are the *Waqf* authorities, a fact which has favoured the conservation of this form of economy to no small extent. The amount of capital actually invested in the primitive building is of no particular significance in this connection; what counts is rather the possession of land in a favourable business locality.[28]

The Entrepreneur

In the industrial production of the Middle East during this period the artisan represents the typical entrepreneur. He employs as a rule one or more journeymen and apprentices; the friendly relations generally existing between them are engendered by the rules of the Moslem guilds which, besides laying down the specific working conditions for individual trades, regulate also the relations between master and workman as well as their relations towards other trades.

In addition to the artisan, the State, through its own factories, played from time to time an important rôle as industrial producer, particularly in the silk-weaving, sugar and arms industries. The continuing military enterprises undertaken by the Turkish rulers secured for the Army factories in Turkey in the seventeenth and eighteenth centuries a leading position in the industrial sector of the country. Cannon foundries, canvas looms, dockyards as well as factories making goods for indirect war needs (paper, leather, textiles) were run by the Government, and from their surpluses the civil population also was supplied. These concerns, after their decline in the eighteenth century, experienced a revival under Selim III in Turkey and Mohammed Ali in Egypt. It was then a case of larger establishments run under the supervision of Government-paid experts and involving considerable capital investment.

Organisation of the Labourers

The organisation of the workmen in Moslem society, although not yet adequately studied, is one of the most remarkable chapters in the social history of the Orient. Elements of religious and professional tradition interspersed with local political and economic usage here form a unique social pattern which—allowing for all local variation—differs considerably as a whole from the traditional picture of the European guild.

As far as the outward aspects are concerned, there is a series of parallels to the history of Western guilds. As a matter of fact, elements out of European corporations, especially after the conquest of Constantinople by the Turks in 1453, were adopted: many of the rules as to acceptance of members, limitation of the number of workshops and artisans in each town, *Gedik* rules for the execution of work, besides some features in the organisational structure resemble the Western guild and company system. The differences in the ideologies of the various trades and their social attitude as compared with their European counterparts are so marked, however, that important clues emerge showing how different was the course of development taken by industrial development and enterprise in the Orient.

Take, first of all, the constitution and structure of the Moslem guild (in Arabic *Sinf*);[29] which came about in all Oriental countries in a kind of hierarchical order.

As the common head of the artisans' societies, and ranking in certain respects above the individual heads of societies, in some places there was the "Sheikh of Sheikhs"; in others this supreme function was fulfilled by the Chief of Police or the officer in charge of the general control of the market, the *Muhtasib.*[30]

At the head of the individual guilds there was usually a Sheikh whose appointment was confirmed by the Government, and who possessed far-reaching authority within the guild. His functions consisted in the management of the guild, i.e. in convening and presiding over the meetings and festivities, the performance of the common devotions, in assessing and collecting from the individual members their respective share of the Government guild tax (imposed on the guild as a body). Likewise the guild authorities had the right of imposing light penalties, fines, besides the responsibility to a certain extent for the preservation of peace and order among the guild members. It was further customary to choose from among the oldest members of the guild special functionaries who had to fulfil the task of reader as well as acting as liaison officer between guild and Government. In Mecca the sheikhs of the various guilds were appointed by the Government and were authorised to accept members and exact from them the oath of allegiance.[31] As regards the exercise of the trades, there were, as in the European guilds, rules governing technique of production, the keeping of trade secrets, the admission of apprentices, the election of masters, and so forth. The settlement of these details was, however, evidently on the whole much less strict and precise than in the craftsmen's societies in European countries, where much more emphasis was laid on the maintenance of their monopolies of production and sale. On the other hand, the ideology of the Oriental guilds contains many mystical and religious features; this is obvious from the great importance attached to the ceremonial acts and celebrations so markedly permeated with religious elements.[32] According to Thorning, the close connection between the craftsmen's guilds and the Dervish school of thought is unmistakable.[33] The Dervishes drew their recruits up to quite recent times mainly from the ranks of the artisans who only from time to time attend the ceremonies of their order.

The term *Futuwwa*, which frequently crops up as signifying the craftsmen's societies, was originally used to define an ethical quality which may be interpreted as self-denial, also as asceticism and escape from the world, altruism in regard to earthly and heavenly goods. This ideology of world renunciation, to which Sufi mystical features are not foreign, excludes from the societies within its domain flagrant sinners and dishonest people; it allows, however, of the admission of slaves, eunuchs and even non-Moslem members such as Jews and Christians. The contrast to this composition of the *Futuwwa* societies as associations which included also persons elsewhere regarded as *déclassés* is particularly apparent when compared with the German guilds of the Middle Ages, where the journeymen of the same trade formed their own societies even if they were occasionally affiliated to their actual guild. The Moslem world knows of no such organisation of journeymen.

The emphasis laid on religious and social elements serves to show that the origin of the Moslem guilds derives from a movement whose character lay originally outside the economic field; the *Qarmats*, among whom, besides mystical and revolutionary features, the elements of an organisation on the lines of a brotherhood constituted the bond of union.[34] To what extent, in contrast to the European corporations which were brought to ruin by the rise of capitalism and the incipient technical revolution, this specific Moslem quality is responsible for the decline of the Moslem guild organisation, cannot—on the basis of the material available—as yet be clearly established. But apart from the powerful repression of the acquisitive instinct by the idea of subsistence, based on religion, advocated by the Moslem guild, other important factors are to be found which in any case were not favourable to an expansion of industrial activity. A large part of the workshops and premises in which the artisan's trade was carried on was *Waqf* property, and so inalienable; it formed a vested interest on the part of the *Waqf* beneficiaries who were averse from any innovation or progress likely to prejudice their revenue. The office of market inspector, or *Muhtasib*, likewise originally a purely canonical institution, after a temporary slackening off in the twelfth century, was reintroduced by the State for political reasons in order to keep the guilds (which especially in Egypt, Syria and Turkey were suspected of *Qarmatic* and revolutionary leanings) under close supervision.[35] In view of the fact that the State and the local authorities in these countries were to a large extent hand in glove with the feudal landlords, the Moslem guild in past centuries was an association of elements "socially" supervised, at times oppressed, and in no respect on a par with its mighty sister organisation and its weight of influence on the development of the European town.[36]

CHAPTER XXI

THE ATTEMPT OF MOHAMMED ALI: THE FIRST INDUSTRIAL REVOLUTION IN THE MIDDLE EAST

Conditions of industrial production in the Middle East at the turn of the eighteenth and during the first third of the nineteenth century were determined by

1. The predominantly agrarian character of the population in general.
2. The widespread custom amongst the agricultural and, to a certain extent, the urban population also, of providing itself with consumer goods of its own.
3. The gradual shrinking of local handicrafts in line with the general economic decline of the Middle East as a result of
   (*a*) the diversion of traffic routes (new sea route to India, growing importance of the Western Hemisphere).
   (*b*) the increasing competition from European production.
4. The stagnation and alienation of production technique and loss of initiative in trade and handicrafts.
5. The decay of vocational organisations (guilds and the like).

It is only when this background is clearly visualised that the approval and achievement of Mohammed Ali can be duly appreciated. Mohammed Ali, whose importance in the shaping of modern social history in the Middle East has not so far met with the recognition it deserves, converted by the reports and recommendations of the members of the French expedition on the magnificent achievements of Western civilisation, became a convinced and staunch supporter of its methods. Seized by a feverish determination to westernise his country, in the sphere of industrial production also he subscribed completely to belief in the power of European technique. The lure of the ideas of the European technicians and organisers who arrived in Egypt from the time of the Napoleonic expedition and their theoretical and practical demonstrations, must have been extraordinary. In a report on the sessions of the *Institut d'Égypte*, the contemporary historian Abdur-Rahman al-Jabarti sums up these impressions of his fellow-countrymen as follows: " We have been shown other experiments, all of them as extraordinary as the first ones, so that people like ourselves could neither conceive nor explain them."[37]

In view of the general stagnation and the improbability that the Egyptians would of their own accord make profitable use of the ideas infiltrating from Europe, the conviction grew in Mohammed Ali that active intervention on the part of Government in the sphere of industry and education was imperative. The mentality of the Oriental at that time did not hold out much hope that he would be able to overcome all the difficulties confronting the revival of industrial initiative, let alone the introduction of European production methods on his own account. This could be achieved only by some dominant body invested with extensive powers. Thus, the State itself, i.e. its ruler, embarked in grand style on an ambitious programme of economic and political activities and took on a number of national-economic functions direct.

As the principal instrument in this policy Mohammed Ali turned to the establishment of trade monopolies and State industries. The problem of securing the necessary experts was solved by engaging foreigners. Thus, he did not hesitate, for instance, to summon hundreds of foreign workers to Cairo and to take into his service at high salaries a vast number of European experts and officers as managers of factories, schools and institutes.[38] Their gradual replacement by native personnel was envisaged, and several hundred young Egyptians were despatched to European schools and institutions.

The whole structure of Mohammed Ali's work in the economic and social-political field reveals quite distinctly the outlines of a State-capitalistic undertaking: production monopolies were instituted in nearly all branches of the textile industry as well as for other articles such as glassware and cast-iron goods. Particular attention was devoted to the establishment of State factories for cannon, rifles and other metal articles. Also many other plants were constructed on his initiative, under the guidance of European experts, and appeared within a brief period to effect a fundamental change in the entire pattern of production, industry and handicraft in Egypt. If Mohammed Ali's plans had been realised, Egypt as far back as the middle of the nineteenth century would have become the foremost industrial country in the Orient.

History of Mohammed Ali's Experiments

Mohammed Ali's plan as a whole was undoubtedly assisted by the old Oriental ideas of the sovereign's unlimited right of disposal over all the property in the country, both movable and immovable. Mohammed Ali, after having summarily annulled by decree the rights of the large landowners over their own land, in 1816 declared all existing branches of industry Government monopolies. Yet at the same time the process of manufacture itself was not interfered with. The artisans remained in their workshops and were allowed to continue with their production, but had in future to apply to the Government for their raw materials and likewise to deliver the finished goods at the prices fixed by the Government. The Government reserved to itself the sole right of sale of the total production. Goods which before sale did not bear the Government stamp were confiscated.

At this period, in other parts of the Orient also the system of monopolised handicraft production had found a footing. The Porte, in the part of the Ottoman Empire under its sole control, had for fiscal reasons introduced monopolies which were mostly sale monopolies; owing to the extraordinary abuse on the part of the monopoly holders they soon, however, fell into discredit. In Turkey these sale monopolies were usually granted to individual persons for high licence fees. In Egypt too, under the influence of the Turkish example fiscal interests came to play an important part; in fact, Mohammed Ali's monopolies brought the Treasury substantial revenues. The prices of raw materials could be kept low inasmuch as the Government obtained these materials (cotton, wool, silk, etc.) at the maximum State-fixed, i.e. bargain, prices from the producers. It sold them to the artisan at much higher rates while paying him for his finished product merely the Government-fixed maximum price. In selling the finished product, the Government made a further profit in that it sold for high prices the goods obtained at cheap rates.

This fiscal success, due as it was to an unscrupulous commercial manipulation, was yet clearly only one of the motives of Mohammed Ali's industrialisation policy. The Pasha was interested also in the technical development of local production. Up till then (in contrast to what had been possible abroad during this period and even earlier, thanks to the introduction of machinery) industrial production in Egypt had been practised on the old lines of manual labour. Mohammed Ali, beginning in 1816, established a number of new enterprises which, if we ignore the question of the motive power used, might be classed as modern and well-equipped establishments when compared with handicraft concerns.[39] Among the first of such enterprises were two woollen goods factories in Cairo; these were followed by iron foundries, a sugar refinery, a glass factory in Alexandria, arms factories as well as the construction of an important arsenal for shipbuilding which in the years from 1829 until shortly before 1840 so efficiently replaced the Egyptian warships destroyed in the battle of Navarino that the Egyptian Navy became once more the strongest sea-power in the Eastern Mediterranean.

Particular importance must be ascribed to Mohammed Ali's initiative in the field of the cotton industry. Although the cotton plant had long been known in Egypt, the rise of this crop to become the predominant branch of the country's economy is his work, to which he was stimulated by the suggestion of a French engineer. After successful experiments in the cultivation of a selected variety of cotton fibre, planting was carried out at a rapid rate, while at the same time the erection of a number of cotton spinning and weaving mills was started: two in 1821, four in 1824 and four in 1825, to be supplemented in the following years by further establishments of the kind. In 1828 a quarter of the cotton crop was already being absorbed by the local factories. The annual manufacture of cotton goods amounted in 1833 to a total of no less than 2 million piq, yarn production amounting in 1837 in 29 establishments to 50,000 kantars. The Egyptian factories were able at the time to cover the home demand for cheap cottons to a major extent, a notable achievement as compared with the situation a hundred years later, when, in spite of the improved machine production, only a fraction of the country's needs was met by the home product.

In keeping with Mohammed Ali's general policy aimed at making the Egyptian State as far as possible independent of external factors, even as regards the supply of important war materials, was his interest in the development of iron and metal works, quite unusual at that time. In 1820, in the Bulaq quarter of Cairo, a foundry was erected after the plans of an Englishman where practically every class of foundry goods could be executed. The works contained eight furnaces and could turn out 50 cwt. of castings per day, including machinery, looms, spinning machines, and even repairs to steam engines and essential parts of the arsenal.[40]

Thus, the Pasha, by sheer force of will, subjected all important branches of industry to his radical plans. These ideas of a forced development of a country's production power, i.e. a development imposed from above or outside, did not remain confined to Egypt alone. In Syria the champion of industrial reconstruction was not Mohammed Ali himself, but his son Ibrahim Pasha; he, too, was obviously ruled by the view that a carefully thought-out plan was needed in order, by exploiting the country's existing natural possibilities, to raise the prostrate agricultural and industrial production. In this connection he attached particular importance to the education of the population, to the spread in all classes "de l'esprit d'entreprise, d'esprit d'initiative, source durable et féconde de toute activité sociale et économique."[41]

Accordingly, Ibrahim, in contrast to his father's tactics in Egypt, attempted to realise his industrial plans in Syria less in the form of State undertakings than by encouraging and awakening industrial initiative. Thus, he was instrumental in establishing textile factories and exploiting the mineral riches in the mountain ranges of Syria, leaving further steps to private action. The first of such enterprises were a woollen goods factory in Tyre, silk mills in the Lebanon, modern oil presses in Tripolis and some mines in the mountains.

In the opinion of the British Consul Werry, then resident in Syria, the most important results of the Mohammed-Ali-inspired administration of Ibrahim were: the establishment of the security of property, liberty of religion, of life and speech, fair distribution of taxation and, on the whole, under the prevailing circumstances a rather far-reaching approximation to that state of freedom which an independent Government should offer its subjects. In many respects he found the administration so vastly improved as could never have been expected. But, he adds, the people do not know how to value it.[42]

In order to convey some idea of the extent of Mohammed Ali's work, it will suffice to mention that the number of workers engaged in Egyptian factories during the years 1830–1840 amounted to over 30,000, the workers in the arsenals to 5,000, and that the capital invested in machinery and plant is estimated at no less than £12 million. In 1836, 95 per cent. of total exports came out of the Government's stores, whilst 40 per cent. of the total imports came into the country on the Government's account.[43]

The Failure of Mohammed Ali and its Lessons

In appraising this first large-scale plan for the inauguration of the industrial revolution in the Orient, our interest centres not merely in the fact that the originator was sorely disappointed in his expectations, but at least to an equal extent in the reasons for this lack of success. In the numerous accounts of this period we find a number of causes given which in part were correctly diagnosed by Mohammed Ali's contemporaries themselves. Dodwell gives us the following illuminating picture of the immediate causes leading to its failure: "Many of these activities were based on false notions. The more elaborate factories were a failure. The machinery was neglected, the running parts left unoiled, the management ignorant and careless. Oxen provided the driving power, whereas of course the Nile itself should have been harnessed to the work. The fellahin detested the unaccustomed regularity of toil and had to be gathered, as the army conscripts were, by force." The Pasha, Bowring observed apparently in accordance with contemporary notions of Europeans about industrial attempts in Oriental lands, "takes hands from the fields where they would be creating wealth, to employ them in . . . factories where they are wasting it."[44]

But the critics even then were not content merely to criticise; Dodwell goes on to record a more objective appreciation of the Pasha's intentions: "But wasted as much of his endeavour was, it is worth noting with respect because it marks a modification of the Pasha's conceptions of his duty. He began by seeking only to raise money. He ended by seeking, however mistakenly, to develop and civilise the country. In this matter he was carried away into an excessive and unwise imitation of the West; but he had come to be something far nobler than the greedy adventurer seeking nothing but his own power and wealth. Even his monopolies had their good side. He may have squeezed the fellah, but he squeezed him less closely than the foreign merchants would have done, had they been left free to buy and sell as they pleased, and the burden of mercantile advances would have been yet heavier than the arrears of the Pasha's revenue.[45]

Today we should go even further in positively appraising the main intentions of Mohammed Ali's industrialisation plans. Only a man with a rare foresight and daring could then conceive of and attempt the industrialisation of an Oriental agrarian country, in spite of the formidable difficulties which everywhere arose.

Apart from the internal shortcomings of many of these undertakings, there were undoubtedly some other factors which would have sufficed to unseat the new local production, even if it had been run under better conditions. First, there is the problem of the bureaucratic management of such enterprises by officials of the State, and, allied thereto, comes the general question how to procure the entrepreneur personalities, to say nothing of the lower personnel who must possess the necessary qualifications for the modern production process. Egypt had neither the factory managers nor the skilled workers. Both categories were at that time lacking. The European experts often came too late to save a badly-run undertaking, or were inadequate in numbers to meet the demands on them. The lack of managerial and practical-technical experience in modern production methods, particularly under the special climatic conditions of the Nile country, was bound to have a prejudicial effect; the schooling which the early stages of industry in Europe had provided for exponents of industrial development, had here no counterpart; the lack of personal interest on the part of the officials in contrast to the incentive of entrepreneurs acting on their own initiative, was plainly in evidence, and its traces were seen in the poor technical and economic success of the undertakings. Crouchley stresses these negative aspects.

"Indeed it appears doubtful whether the industries were ever run at a profit. It is true that some of his accounts appear to show a profit on sale. Thus in 1837, it was stated that the cost of manufacture of cotton cloth was 49 piastres per piece, and the cloth was sold at 110 piastres per piece. But in the accounts of the factories it appears that the calculation took into consideration only the cost of the raw material and the wages of the workmen, without any allowance for overhead charges, rent, loss of material in manufacture, interest on capital and depreciation of machinery, plant and buildings. When properly established by an expert economist, the account showed that even cotton goods were being produced at a loss. Dr. Bowring found in 1838 that cotton cloth produced in Egypt cost 8·7 piastres per yard, whereas English cloth of the same quality could be bought in Egypt at 7½ piastres per yard. Even this did not take into account the enormous cost of the new factories, machinery, spare parts, to say nothing of the restriction of agriculture because of the men employed in the factories."[46]

Again we may arrive at different views as to the reasons for the failure, but whatever these deficiencies were, they could have been overcome in the course of time, had not a political factor interfered in a decisive fashion with the industrial plans. This was the inevitable clash between foreign and local interests; for Mohammed Ali, who had already appropriated the whole of the agricultural land and its returns, was about to make himself the owner of non-agricultural production, and thus the sole regulator of the country's total circulation of goods. In this, however, he was encroaching on the sphere of interests of foreign powers who were interested in the sale of their goods and the purchase of certain raw materials from Egypt. Egypt represented an important market for the products of the new English and continental factories, and this position was seriously threatened by the Pasha's bold experiments. Interference with the liberty of trade had already led in Turkey to vigorous intervention on the part of British diplomacy. There it was the Turkish monopolies which had become very remunerative, if extortionate, instruments of an unscrupulous financial régime.

"It made no difference what were the previous rights under treaty to the foreign merchant; he had to submit to any terms the monopolist extortioner imposed before he could sell his goods.... The system was more favourable to the foreigner than to the native, but undoubtedly restrictive, and in some cases prohibitive, of trade. Ponsonby declared that by its means the Porte has evaded or broken through a large part of our commercial rights. This information at once roused the British lion in Palmerston, who demanded immediate redress.... Two days before (i.e. April 14, 1838) he had repeated the ingenious argument that, as Mohammed Ali was the 'universal monopolist' in Egypt, the abolition of monopolies would hit him much more than it would the Sultan. And he added that, if the Sultan abolished them in his empire, the British Government would expect and require similar abolition in Egypt and Syria. These were strong words for even Palmerston to use."[47]

The result of this intervention was the treaty of 1838, based on the Capitulations which guaranteed the foreign subject freedom of industry and shipping. It led to the abolition of most of the monopolies: in Turkey in 1839, in Egypt in 1840. Whereas the consequences of the treaty are considered as fortunate for Turkey, they were greeted in Egypt with severe criticism. This criticism was but another expression of the latent conflict between the expansionist tendencies of Mohammed Ali and the economic and imperialist interests of the West. This view obtrudes all the more seeing that before Mohammed Ali hardly any attempt was made by foreign powers to claim the rights arising out of the Turkish capitulations in Egypt itself. "Life has been too insecure, trade too irregular, the beys too rebellious, and the European trade with Egypt too insignificant for France or England to attempt to stand upon their theoretical rights."[48]

The reason for the intervention of the Great Powers was certainly not the desire to re-establish generally the security of trade, but the economic policy of the Pasha—dangerous for British interests. British intervention broke the Pasha's spirit of initiative in the industrial field once and for all. Even as early as 1840, two years before the final ratification of the treaty, a number of factories which could not show a profit were closed. When the treaty came into force, nearly all the other factories followed suit. A few years later the ruins of factories and rusted machinery were the sole indication of what was left of the first industrial revolution in Egypt.[49]

The reasons for the collapse of the Pasha's programme of industrialisation are to be found in various fields. They may be summed up as follows:

1. Shortcomings in the internal management, faulty economic calculation in the majority of undertakings, inadequate qualifications on the part of the personnel; lack of engineers and masters, lack of technical experience as regards the industrial production process in Egypt.
2. Difficulties of marketing and commercial policy; competition of cheap European goods.
   Political intervention on the part of export countries in favour of competition goods.
3. Sociological shortcomings:
   Absence of entrepreneur qualities in the Egyptians of that period.
   Arbitrary treatment of private trade interests by the State (inadequate protection of rights and property), clash between the liberal tendencies in industrial practice in Europe and the State-capitalistic planned economy of Mohammed Ali.

As long as these causes and deficiencies were effective, a development such as that witnessed in Europe was not possible. Mohammed Ali's attempt in itself proves that the more important prerequisites for a successful industrialisation must be present simultaneously in order to achieve the desired result. As matters stood the most essential conditions were lacking. The only chance of success, in these circumstances, lay in an attempt by the head of the State himself to solve problems of industrialisation by a planning policy pursued along almost modern lines, and for this purpose to employ all material and personal means at his disposal.

Although this industrial revolution from above failed, the lesson it imparted to the workers and engineers in the factories, the first direct contact on the part of the native Egyptian population with the production methods of the new Europe, did not pass without reactions. It was on these experiences, both technical and administrative, that subsequently, in the second half of the nineteenth century, the second attempt, this time a successful one, was made to equip the country with a modern apparatus of industrial production.

CHAPTER XXII

THE INFLUX OF EUROPEAN CAPITAL AND ENTREPRENEURS (1850–1914)

The Background

From the middle of the nineteenth century a new epoch in industrial development begins in the Oriental countries. Technical improvements, particularly in methods of communication, the construction of railroads, the development of regular steamship lines, the establishment of telephone and telegraph services, are in the air; these, combined with the economic and political ideologies of liberalism tending towards the abolition of customs barriers and the creation of wide economic areas, bring the world closer together both in space and spirit. Distant countries belonging to a foreign sphere of culture, such as those of the Near and the Far East, come within the orbit of this contraction of the globe, just as *vice versa*, in the West, the spirit of enterprise stretches forth desirous of taking part in the development of these hitherto closed areas.

The economic repercussions of these tendencies for the group of countries under review led also to a new situation as regards production of goods. Whereas this sphere for the past hundred years had been characterised by a period of unusual stagnation, the new situation differed from the preceding one in that it united within itself two apparently mutually conflicting movements of vast political and economic dynamics, both deriving from outside sources: one the exceptional increase in the import of industrial goods in Middle Eastern countries, the other, the growing number of large-scale undertakings with foreign capital which begin to crop up throughout the Middle East, predominantly in the field of transport and production. Egypt had, as we have seen, already known such a period of company promoting some decades earlier, but in the Egypt of Mohammed Ali ownership of capital and control of the enterprises remained in the hands of the Government, whereas the large undertakings inaugurated during the new period in all parts of the Ottoman Empire were almost all foreign in character and formed owing to the Capitulations quasi-autonomous enclaves within the indigenous economic body. The legal and political status of foreign capital interests as well as the rights deriving from the possession of foreign nationality ensured them a privileged position.

Into what channels did the foreign capital flow, and in what form was it active?

The foreign capital which after the middle of the nineteenth century sought an outlet in the Oriental countries chose very definite spheres of activity. Not all propositions which appeared economically or otherwise interesting came within the scope of its consideration. First and foremost, in accordance with the actual meaning of the term "opening up" or "development", projects coming under the head of transport and communications were favourite objects for its activity. The following summary covers the principal fields in which foreign capital operated.

1. TRANSPORT AND COMMUNICATIONS

The aim of these projects was the opening-up of countries and areas to international traffic and home needs as well as the satisfaction of the communal transport requirements in the larger towns. The desire to expedite and cheapen the increased international exchange of goods and to create all communication prerequisites for the exploitation of the natural resources of an extensive region led to a rapid extension of waterways and important railways in the whole territory of Ottoman Turkey. Of the various nations concerned, the British were mainly responsible for the development of the Turkish railway system in that early period. The granting of a concession for the line running from Smyrna to Aydin in 1856 was followed by the grant of similar rights to a French company for the Smyrna-Kassaba line which was later extended to Manisa. Probably the British originally harboured plans reaching further afield and envisaging the opening-up of Anatolia and Syria, but owing to their participation in the Suez canal scheme and the construction of this sea route, they dropped these projects. Germany's appearance on the scene in 1888 gave the development plans of the Great Powers a strong political turn. The objections raised by Russia on the one hand, by the French and at first by the British also on the other, led to repeated tension and delay in the execution of the ambitious German plans.[50]

The authority for the pursuance of the German plans was vested in the Deutsche Bank, which stood at the head of a German syndicate interested chiefly in the development of the projected railway routes running through Anatolia to Mesopotamia. The Bank in 1888 obtained a concession valid for a period of 99 years for the construction of a railway-line between Scutari and Izmid and its extension to Ankara. The Bank was offered revenue guarantees backed by the Turkish Treasury. During the period 1893–1902 the Bank acquired further concessions for the construction of railway lines to Kayseri, Konya and Baghdad, at the same time incorporating concessions in respect of the exploitation of the mineral resources covering a zone 20 km. on both sides of the railway as well as water power, river shipping and construction of harbours.

These activities, promoted by European capital, represented a combination of financial and political interests, in which the banks became the principal agents of the new economic imperialism; by sending leading bankers on missions to the countries concerned, they entered the field quite openly. Without the backing of their own Government, foreign capital would never have been able at that time to realise plans of such far-reaching political and economic significance. It is not within the scope of this work to go more closely into the history of the various projects.[51] It must be emphasized, however, that these ambitious plans were conceived in the full realisation that any industrialisation calls for a well-developed system of communications: firstly, in order that consumers may be supplied with the industrial products, secondly in order to facilitate the transport of raw materials to the places of work. It is only by means of such a system of communications that the desired penetration of the newly-opened region may be effected: delivery of the goods imported and the despatch of important raw materials and minerals for export. The construction of the railways was encouraged by the guarantee of a minimum revenue per km., which usually formed an essential clause of the building agreement conceded by the Ottoman Government.

2. Undertakings on the basis of Concessions

In the second instance it was the so-called concession enterprises that attracted foreign capital. These comprised establishments founded in order to supply the population with articles of daily use and public services, such as water and gas works, local tramway, port and shipping facilities—enterprises as a rule necessary for the fulfilment of communal functions. Consequently these could be run with slight risk, if even this risk were not entirely obviated by guarantees.

3. Virgin Production

A third field of activity for foreign capital was found in virgin production. Here we find companies interested in the exploitation of mines, the development of cultivable land, irrigation schemes, plantation of market crops, etc.

As regards the extent of foreign capital activity, precise figures in respect of foundation, year and capital invested are available only in the case of Egypt, where official statistics can be consulted.[52] According to the statistics in 1914 £E92,039,000 of paid-up company capital was controlled in 1914 by foreign interests, i.e. 91 per cent of the total capital of £E100,152,000 invested in joint-stock companies at that period. This imposing figure does not include the sums invested in the Suez Canal Company, of whose capital a sum of £E16,218,000 was invested by foreign countries or shareholders, or the substantial sums invested by a number of private firms and open trading companies belonging to foreigners. Lebon & Co. alone, a firm maintaining gas and electricity works in many Egyptian towns, represented according to Roux a capital investment of approximately £E4 millions. To this must be added the very considerable sums of capital operating in the branches of the foreign banks, the sums invested in loans on property and in real estate companies as well as the many short- and long-term credits granted to other branches of Egyptian economy. In view of the undeveloped state of local capital formation and the practically insignificant participation of Egyptian entrepreneurs in the important development process which their country underwent, it is no exaggeration to state that the control over the entire communication system, industry and trade, was in the hands of foreigners.

In spite of the lack of precise statistical data in respect of conditions in Turkey, it is safe to say that Turkish economy was likewise dominated by foreign interests. Almost the whole of the export and a substantial part of the home trade was in the hands of foreign subjects or at least of non-Turks by race. Banking was controlled by foreign capital. All transport enterprises of standing, both the interurban and the local traffic services, were owned by foreign companies. The exploitation of mineral resources was undertaken by foreign financial interests. At the beginning of the First World War, private investments owned by nationals of the three great Powers, France, Germany, and England, totalled 1,686,000,000 frs. The significance of this figure as regards the Turkish economy as a whole can be seen in its proper light only if we bear in mind that industrialisation in this country had still made little progress. The fact remains that in both Turkey and Egypt alike the economic superiority of foreign interests was

PRINCIPAL FOREIGN CAPITAL INVESTMENT IN TURKEY[53]

	French: Francs	British: Francs	German: Francs
Public Debt	2,454,417,377	577,499,821	867,583,506
Private Enterprises	902,893,000	230,458,675	552,653,000
TOTAL	3,357,310,377	807,958,496	1,420,236,506
	French Per Cent.	British Per Cent.	German Per Cent.
Public Debt	60·31	14·36	21·31
Private Enterprises	53·55	13·66	32·77
TOTAL	60·08	14·46	25·42

COMPANIES CONTAINING CAPITAL FROM ABROAD WORKING IN EGYPT[54]
(TOTAL PAID-UP CAPITAL AND DEBENTURES)

Companies	Paid-up Capital and Debentures		
	1883	1902	1933
	£E thousands	£E thousands	£E thousands
1. Mortgage Companies	3,826	10,525	44,310
2. Banks and Financial Companies	1,843	2,174	5,085
3. Agricultural and Urban Land Companies	—	2,395	6,745
4. Transport and Canals (not including Suez Canal)	62	3,645	4,445
5. Industrial Mining and Commercial	669	5,903	20,780
TOTAL	6,400	24,642	81,365
Suez Canal	15,615	18,350	20,930
GRAND TOTAL	22,015	42,992	102,295

bound to lead to political control. Turkey, in losing its economic independence, had sacrificed its political independence also.

How was it possible that foreign interests, bound as they were to clash with those of the sovereign Turkish Empire, could increase to such an extent and at such a pace? In order to answer this question, let us review the political, economic and sociological conditions of this process, where important clues are to be found.[55]

Political Conditions

The commercial and political agreements already mentioned above, which the Porte concluded with England in 1838, and whose validity was later extended to Egypt also, already reveal an element of weakness in the political attitude of Turkey. On the strength of the Capitulations and the rights thereby conferred on foreign subjects as regards freedom of trade, the Turks could be forced to surrender important local industrial and economic interests in order to allow foreign products to enter the country with the least possible hindrance.

The exploitation of these privileges proved at this juncture more than ever advantageous to the interests of the European Powers. The new system of machine production depended to a far greater extent than the previous methods on open markets, on the continuous capacity and readiness to purchase on the part of the importing countries. Foreign industry could establish a market only in those countries where the population was not self-supporting, and where people would readily buy the foreign goods. The opening of the Oriental areas was achieved despite the initial resistance of the countries concerned. The right to pursue a sovereign economic policy, i.e. to increase the customs tariff without first obtaining the consent of the foreign Powers, was the chief bone of contention in this connection. In almost all sovereign countries a preferential treatment of local producers—by exemption or reduction of machinery tariffs and taxation of foreign imports—was usual. Up to the seventies the Turkish producer could not enjoy such rights, and even their subsequent recognition was merely theoretical, the Turkish Government hardly making a claim under this head.

A further political factor favouring the influx of foreign capital was the claim to consular jurisdiction. The establishment of foreign industrial and concession companies could thus be effected as if it were done on transferred native territory, i.e. on British, French or German soil. Every transaction effected within this sphere came under the law of the home country of the company or entrepreneur concerned. Thus, actually, the capital and functionaries of the foreign companies enjoyed the legal security and jurisdiction of a European State, and were able to make good their claims at any moment despite opposing local interests.

Another factor which must not be underestimated is to be found in the increasingly expansionist policy of the Great Powers which coincided with the evident decline of the "Sick Man on the Bosporus."[56] His dominions were bound to offer a magnificent field for such foreign enterprises as felt themselves secure in the support of a strong Power. These considerations would often enough lead the Governments themselves to inaugurate the activities of their respective subjects. Once privileges were granted to one foreign group, other groups operating in the same field and belonging to different Powers immediately began to agitate, and seldom failed to obtain similar privileges for their projects and capital interests.

The insistence on these rights, whose fundamental socio-economic significance for Turkey's economic future was scarcely recognised at the time,[57] paved the way for the economic vassalage of the Ottoman lands in relation to Europe. This intrusion became more and more manifest as from the middle of the century, with the growing importance of the raw material supplies from the Orient on the one hand, and the expanding markets developing there for industrial goods from Europe on the other.[58]

Economic Conditions

What made the Oriental countries so attractive for the industrial entrepreneurs from Europe was firstly the possibilities they offered for the development of an interesting market, the needs of which must increase with the growing contact of the population with Europe; secondly, the rich sources of raw materials; thirdly, the extremely cheap labour, and fourthly, the immediate economic advantages, such as exemption from taxes for foreign undertakings, State-guaranteed returns and similar privileges of an economic nature to be met with as a rule only in colonial and semi-colonial countries.

As regards the first point, the extent to which the absorptive capacity of the Oriental countries for industrial products increased, has demonstrated quite clearly the chance that existed for local production, however limited. Egypt, the only country for which continuous data are available, shows, for instance, in the course of the nineteenth century a multiplication of imports *per capita* of the population: in 1801, the import value *per capita* amounted to £0·1, in 1907 to no less than £2·3, more than a twentyfold increase. Even if we allow for the changes in money values, this increase is a very substantial one. But even this latter figure was, according to the experiences in respect of the growth *per capita* of import and consumption of industrial goods in Western countries, capable of still further expansion; an optimistic estimate of the further development (in view of the simultaneous rise in exports and the enormous increase in population) was therefore justified, even economically.

The plentiful natural sources of raw materials open for development in the Middle East countries included (besides mining products such as coal, borax, chrome, lead) above all, oil. At the end of the century a beginning was made with the use of oil as fuel, which was soon to result in a boom such as no other natural product had probably ever experienced. The underground oil-stream of enormous volume which flows in this part of the world from the shores of the Mediterreanean to the Persian Gulf and beyond to the shores of the Caspian Sea, has determined more than any other fact the economic and political fate of the area. In many of the oil-possessing countries such as Iran and Iraq, the capital invested in its exploitation is many times in excess of all other industrial investments. But the possibilities of agrarian cultivation such as cotton-growing, tobacco, silkworm breeding, also attracted enterprise and capital into these countries.

Lastly, the existence of an exceptionally cheap source of labour was bound to prove a temptation to foreign initiative. The Oriental labourer was predominantly an extremely frugal element, satisfied with small wages and able also to provide for his primitive needs. The Oriental worker certainly had also considerable shortcomings; his pre-rationalistic attitude to work, his habit of leaving his job as soon as he had earned a few pounds, his lack of endurance and deficient technical skill—all these detracted from his usefulness for modern industrial production, but were not sufficient to jeopardize the big chance of profit presented by his cheap wages.

Sociological Conditions

From what has been said in the preceding chapters it is evident how great, indeed how vital, was the importance attaching to the existence of an entrepreneur class for the establishment of a modern industrial system in the Orient.

Shrewd observers of later developments in the East many years ago expressed their doubts whether the Oriental population would be in a position independently to tackle and solve the tasks with which, in view of the progressive industrialisation of the world, they too would be faced. This applies both to the Turks and even to a people so receptive of Western ideas as the Lebanese and Syrians.[59]

Very shortly before the collapse of the Ottoman Empire a writer of repute sums up his impressions in the following verdict:

> "The typical Turk is, under ordinary circumstances, an honest, truthful, self-respecting man. But I am not sure whether these causes will account for his want of energy or his occasional outbursts of fanaticism. In the normal condition of an average Turkish peasant, a long period of laziness is alternated by short, spasmodic periods of industry. He is neither industrious nor persistent about anything."[60]

There is no need to quote similar statements by other contemporary authors to confirm the picture that we have already earlier drawn in this connection. Despite all the valuable qualities which enabled the Turk to endure a national fate fraught with trials, he lacked the most characteristic qualification of the citizen of the capitalist society in Europe—the modern spirit of initiative.

As regards the Arab-Syrian population settled in the coastal strips of the Eastern Mediterranean, this verdict as to their lack of enterprise needs some qualifying in that we here find elements with pronounced commercial instincts occupying a prominent position. But this enterprising spirit did not develop into that rationalised industrial initiative operating on a broad basis and so characteristic of the European and American business world. The following quotation from the report by M. Huvelin, *Que vaut la Syrie?*, illustrates this point very aptly:

> "The Syrians are indeed pure Mediterraneans, i.e. individualists with all the qualifications and shortcomings this implies. Spontaneous, impulsive, endowed with a good memory and a wonderful capacity of assimilation, versatile and knowing how to display their treasure of initiative and perseverance, they lack, on the other hand, that sense of solidarity and discipline which is necessary for carrying through organisation. If there exists no industry in Syria, this is, partly at least, due to the fact that the Syrians have not the vocation for it. To check the truth of this, it is enough to compare the European spinning mills of the Lebanon with their indigenous competitors. I also do not believe that, even abroad, *capitaines d'industrie* originating from Syria will be found."[61]

The fact that Middle Eastern society has up to the present day extremely few native entrepreneur personalities to its credit, and that local capital formation, however insignificant, has been allowed to flow into quite other channels (real estate, gold, jewellery, luxury expenditure abroad) is alone sufficient to explain the dominant rôle of the foreign entrepreneur and of foreign capital. The foreign capitalists and experts were a necessity, they filled a vacuum, even if they got well paid for their rôle.

In the European provinces and in the Turkish coastal areas of Asia Minor, industry and transport, in addition to commerce, were predominantly in the hands of Greeks. Their century-long tested knowledge and experience of economic life in the Levant made them versatile and efficient entrepreneurs. Jewish elements also played a conspicuous part in the early period of Turkish industrialisation. The enterprises run by the Allatini group in Salonica, for instance, who even in the sixties constructed a steam-mill, and in the following decades changed over from the export of agricultural products to the machine-production of tiles, methylated spirit, textile goods and other commodities, were known beyond the borders of this economic area.

In Asiatic Turkey the smaller industrial concerns in the towns were mostly in Greek or Armenian ownership. In Smyrna and some other coastal towns and in Egypt it was predominantly English, Belgian, German and French firms that were actively interested in industrial branches.

The possibility by pooling a large number of smaller sums of obtaining the requisite capital and placing it in a joint-stock company, did not appeal to the mentality of the Oriental, who always preferred the individual form of investment. His mistrust of such "anonymous" forms of capital management which left the claim of the investor on the strength of his share abstracted from every personal relationship, tended, so far as he was concerned, to rule out this form of enterprise.

That religious factors acted as a damper on industrial development in the case of Moslem promoters as against the position of foreign establishments which were not so encumbered need not be emphasised. It was not merely a matter of the Mohammedan ban on interest.[62] Foreign industrial credits could be granted only by recognised banks and to clients in whose case no objections were to be anticipated on account of the infringement of religious precepts.

The ban on electricity issued by the Sultan Abdul Hamid II in order to avoid coming into conflict with religious traditions and rescinded only at a later period, did not apply to foreign concerns. They could exploit in their sphere all the advantages accruing from the use of electric power. Likewise, for a long time, orthodox Mohammedans were forbidden to take advantage of any insurance system, inasmuch as this was considered an interference with the divine order of things.

The mentality of the Oriental worker adapted itself well to

the employment offered by foreign factories. The bulk of these workers constituted a non-political element uninterested in the important political issues raised by the expansion of European capital in the Orient. The revolutionary ideologies which were rife about that period and found acceptance among the workers in the West, forming the starting-point for social movements of far-reaching consequence, could make no headway or even become a factor of any appreciable significance. The essential idea of the harmony of social interests as formulated and accepted in the Moslem world was demonstrated in the aversion on the part of the Mohammedan workers to taking an active rôle and forming a united front against the entrepreneur-employer class.

The old Oriental guilds which might have become nuclei of a social movement in the course of the nineteenth century fell more and more into decay. The abolition of their privileges—1860 in Turkey and 1890 in Egypt—but marked the end of their ultimately wretched existence.

CHAPTER XXIII

DEVELOPMENT OF INDUSTRIAL PRODUCTION DURING THE PERIOD 1850–1914

Although during the second half of the nineteenth century the population of most Middle Eastern countries showed a steady rise, with an increase in purchasing power of certain strata, the period up to the beginning of the First World War saw no revolutionary change in the structure of industrial goods production. The large sums of capital which flowed into these countries were directed to a considerable extent into goods production, where they brought about new forms of production without effecting any fundamental shift in the predominance of the agrarian economy of the time. Even at the outbreak of the First World War the bulk of the population was engaged in agriculture, and native production of non-agricultural goods was carried on predominantly in the artisan's workshop. It was only in cases where natural conditions offered an incentive, as in mining, or where uniform mass-demand rendered machine-manufacture worth while, as in the case of primary foodstuffs, simple woven fabrics and public utility services, that the machine gained a footing. In all other branches of production, the methods of work, and even the local conditions of production in the town bazaars remained unchanged. Any active industrial policy on the part of the Government which might have helped to further the development of the indigenous sector, was lacking; in fact, industrial progress was often handicapped by the action of the Government itself (e.g. the ban on the use of electricity). The long period during which raw materials and manufactured goods were treated on the same basis in respect of import duty, the absence of reduction in the rates of duty paid on imported machinery, kept local industry on the whole in the unfavourable position into which it had fallen as far back as 1838 after the signing of the agreement between the Porte and Ponsonby.

A report made by the commercial adviser to the German Consulate at Bucarest (1912) contains the following illuminative description of conditions of industrial production in Turkey in Europe before the First World War: "In such circumstances the development of the Turkish factory system of industry did not progress on the whole beyond the first initial stages. These also help to explain the unique phenomenon that even for the preparation of the foodstuffs obtainable in the country itself and produced, if irregularly, for export, no adequate measures are taken. Bulgaria, Serbia, Rumania, *inter alia*, must be drawn upon, for instance, in order to cover the flour requirements of Turkey in Europe: a valuable sidelight when comparing the economic development of Turkey on the one hand and the Christian Balkan States on the other. The little that has been achieved is a creation of the new century, or rather of the last decades, if not to a large extent of quite recent years. Great has been the number of projects cropping up every year for the establishment of the most varied industrial concerns on a larger and smaller scale, but the number and, as a rule, the extent of those which actually materialise is small. Comparatively important, moreover, is the number of factories which are closing down, amongst these being isolated cases where, despite their completion, the work of the factory was never even started."

These often promising beginnings were undertaken almost exclusively by foreigners (non-Turks and non-Arabs), the capital invested was mostly of foreign origin, the engineers and foremen were brought from abroad. Among the industrial entrepreneurs the Turkish element was almost entirely absent. Where it existed, it was generally because, without its co-operation, difficulties on the part of the authorities were to have been expected.

"The last years of the Constitution were very favourable to its participation, the Turks never went beyond the rôle of figure-heads or nominal associates, the sole exception being the tobacco trade which in the strict sense of the word cannot be classed as an industry". (*ibid.*) Despite their small number, as compared with that of the other concerns, the foreign enterprises were a weighty factor from the point of view of capital investment.

Geographically the factories were located in such a way that the harbour towns of Constantinople, Şmyrna, Beirut (formerly Salonica also) and their environment were the principal centres of the existing enterprises. In the provinces of Asiatic Turkey, apart from flour-mills, some rice-polishing factories and tanneries, there were only small establishments using motor power. At the same time the old traditional forms of handicraft and home industry still carried on, struggling hard to hold their own against competing machine-made produce of local and foreign origin. According to the industrial statistics of Turkey for the year 1913, there were at that time 269 undertakings which had already attained certain minimum proportions according to the following criteria:[63]

(*a*) A minimum value of £T1,000
(*b*) Payment of at least 750 days' wages during one year.
(*d*) Use of motor power of not less than 5 H.P.

These statistics show, in addition, that in the concerns enumerated the production value per worker varied to an extraordinary extent. The highest figures obtained in the chemical and paper industry, the lowest in the textile industry. The explanation is to be found in the large proportion of female labour and the temporary nature of the work in the latter industry. A further noteworthy feature is the difference in the degree to which the needs of the home market were met; this was most favourable in the case of foodstuffs, and most unsatisfactory in the case of cotton goods, silk goods and oils.

Branch of Industry	Number of Undertakings	Employees	State-owned	Limited Co.'s.	Private Enterprises
I. Agriculture	76	4,281	1	8	67
II. Ceramics	20	980	1	5	14
III. Leather and Hides	12	1,688	1	1	10
IV. Timber	19	705	—	—	19
V. Textiles	75	7,775	18	10	47
VI. Paper and Printing	55	1,897	1	—	54
VII. Chemicals	12	417	—	4	8
	269	17,743	22	28	219

In Egypt, owing to the concentration of foreign influence in the few larger towns and the accessibility of the population to contact with the outside world, conditions for local handicrafts were less favourable than in Turkey. Apart from the fact that the European population with its ample purchasing power preferred the more expensive foreign-made article, native consumption in the towns succumbed to the influence of the cheap but often attractively turned-out factory goods, and thus helped still further to undermine the local industry. The new law enforcing the sale of agricultural produce by weight instead of by measure of capacity reacted prejudicially on the makers of measures, which trade became superfluous. Arminjou gives us an eloquent description of the effects of this and similar innovations on native industry:

At the end of the eighties the riddle-makers formed a special quarter in Cairo. The development of milling destroyed this branch of small industry. The establishment of a main water supply bringing water direct to the houses caused the trade of water-carrier and waterskin-maker to disappear. As a result of the change-over to the use of European kitchen and table utensils the makers of the beautiful Oriental copper pots and other domestic articles were thrown out of employment, while the Oriental ebony workers and cabinet makers were deprived of their livelihood through the introduction of modern furniture. Every new step taken by the authorities by way of modernising commercial life and encouraging the various branches of industry brought in its train grave repercussions for the workers affected by such changes. Witness the replacement of measures of capacity by weights, of animal means of transport by trams and railways, of water scoop-wheels by pumps, of the old locally-dyed fabrics by cheap imported textile goods, and similar cases *ad lib.* Even where the effects were not immediately in evidence, because the introduction of new processes often proceeded at a slow pace, the whole picture is so clear-cut that it cannot be mistaken.[64] To what extent, incidentally, even in the new industrial concerns animal power was still used to drive the machinery, may be seen from the following table quoted by Arminjou:

	Under consideration		Refused		Authorized	
	driven by		Driven by		Driven by	
	Steam	Animal	Steam	Animal	Steam	Animal
Flour mills . .	38	218	8	2	1,120	939
Oil presses .	6	17	2	16	14	299
Sugar factories (incl. molasses)	—	41	1	72	39	568

On the other hand, foreign capital in Egypt began to realise its plans for certain forms of industrial investment in the country itself relatively early—after the institution of the Mixed Courts in 1874 and the establishment of the legal security necessary for its activities. Thus cotton, sugar and cigarette factories came into existence in Egypt on a larger scale, equipped on modern lines. With the extension of the cotton plantations, plants were established for ginning the seed as well as for the manufacture of coarse fabrics for the local market. The old manufacturing establishments had already been replaced in the nineteenth century by modern factories which with the progress of the manufacturing process in the latest decades were continually being perfected. Sugar factories linking up with an old tradition in sugar production likewise developed in the twentieth century into large-scale establishments.[65] The factories owned by the Société des Sucreries et Raffineries d'Égypte alone employed in 1911 more than 15,000 native workmen. In the Egyptian sugar-factories the basic raw material used is the sugar cane, which is cultivated over large areas in Upper Egypt (Kom-Ombo and Armant) and near Cairo (Hawamdiyya). These factories represent one of the largest industrial concerns in modern Egypt.

In a class by themselves are the large Egyptian cigarette factories which, as may be inferred from the names of their founders, Gianaclis, Kyriazi, Aghatos, Matossian, Sanossian, Simon Arzt, are in the domain of Greek, Armenian and other non-Egyptian elements.

On the whole, the progress and direction of industrial development proper during this period was determined in the case of Egypt also by the three principal categories of consumer goods: foodstuffs, clothing and, at a relatively later date, housing. Comparatively unimportant were those branches of production for which the raw materials had to be obtained from abroad. There existed only a few plants which required the services of a large number of trained experts, devoted to the production of machinery and transport requirements. However, the handicrafts are not entirely ousted by the new large-scale producers. A number of such small industries continue as before to dominate in certain branches; others, although feeling the pinch, manage, thanks to their extraordinarily modest pretensions in the way of capital, skill and income, to hold their own yet for some time to come. Thus we get a remarkable picture in which age-old tradition in production and marketing methods blends with large-scale and rationalised machine-production, and featuring a worker-class divorced from its village home and accustomed way of life.

The problem of labour likewise now begins to assume greater importance. The worker in the modern sense, emerging as a product of and factor in the urban industrial development of the Occident, is at this period still a completely unknown element. Production was organised on a family basis and centred on the employment of women, juveniles and children, and contracting work, in various forms. The workers were mostly from the villages; they would, often father and sons together, come to the town for the season, living according to their old code and their ties to religion, family and provider of work. As the factories grew in number, the worker question manifested itself first in the form of a marked shortage of labour inasmuch as the young generation from the villages was not willing or suited to undertake industrial work. In certain areas (Egypt, irrigated districts in Iraq, Anatolia) what with the simultaneous intensification of agriculture, all additional labour supplies were quickly absorbed. In some provinces of the Turkish Empire conflicts as regards nationality and the introduction of compulsory military service for Christians also caused members of the juvenile age-groups to emigrate; especially did the minorities in the Balkans and the Lebanon lose thousands of young people every year. In all reports of that period, the danger threatening the economic development of the country as a result of emigration is particularly emphasised. Agriculture in particular was gravely affected by the growing shortage of hands, which could not be made good because the emigrants did not return.

Industrial labour conditions, according to the report for the year 1912 already quoted, appear to have been more favourable. The very modest industry of that period could as a rule cover its need for unskilled labour. Yet even a slight disturbance, i.e. shiftings in the demand for labour, sufficed to bring difficulties to light. The sudden boom in the tobacco trade, for instance, which required a considerable number of workers and was in a position to pay them well, coupled with the extensive emigration of the young Christian male population, created a real shortage of labour which made itself felt in every industrial concern with a need for mass-labour.

"The principal cause of this crisis in industrial labour conditions is to be found in the vast development of tobacco-growing and manufacture during the last ten years, and the extremely sharp competition caused thereby on the labour market. In 1902, Régie-controlled tobacco production in Turkey in Europe totalled 13 million kg., in 1910 it exceeded 31 million kg. Production had thus more than doubled, whilst the demand for labour, as a result of the shorter working hours, more specialised work, etc. increased in a still higher measure."

During the period under review, modern ideas of organisation among the workers made their appearance only sporadically, presumably first in the larger towns of Egypt and in Salonica. Thus in Alexandria, in 1903, although there had so far been no actual organisation of the workers, a strike broke out among the cigarette workers, whilst among the tobacco workers in Salonica the beginnings of an organisation already existed in the first decades of the century. The conditions of labour in Salonica, although more favourable than in other towns in the Orient, were unsatisfactory. Thus we find the rates of payment in that town were for juvenile workers (male) 8–10, for female workers 7–8 Turkish piastres per day. In the provincial towns of Turkey, in Syria and Egypt wages were much lower, and in some cases scarcely higher than the rates paid to agricultural workers, although during the decade before the First World War all Oriental countries tended to show a rise in wages.[66] On the whole, no appreciable change took place in labour organisation. The Oriental artisan companies and guilds (*Sinf*) retained their external structure up to the last decades of the nineteenth century and, in a number of cases, even later. As a result of the institution of native courts in 1883 which made the jurisdiction of the guilds' Sheikhs superfluous, and the introduction in 1890 of freedom in the exercise of trade, practically all restrictions in this sphere, and with them the last reason for the retention of the guilds, disappeared.[67] Actually there had been no formal abolition of the guilds as from a fixed date; in practice, the life of these remarkable organisations had expired.

Conclusions as to the Period 1850–1914

The picture of industrial production up to the time of the First World War as described in the foregoing pages, reveals the following outlines, which apply to a large extent to almost all countries in the Middle East.

In these countries agriculture forms the basis of economic life; the population continues to live, as it has always done, on its agricultural activities. The increase in the density of the population which began in the nineteenth century in a number of urban areas and some coastal strips, is maintained by the intensification of commercial activity which set in with the development of the means of communication and the increase in the exchange of goods. Native handicraft had no part in it worth mentioning. In fact, its relative importance visibly declined as compared with that of the newly inaugurated machine production. The growing cleavage between these two forms of production becomes year by year more acute. On the one hand native handicraft, with the bazaars as its centre, tried to hold its own against the double onslaught of foreign goods and the new native industrial production, and to function now as in the past on the old traditional lines; at the same time the new factory system introduced by the foreigners was seeking outlets for expansion, and at the end of the period had already won in many branches a dominating position.

Methods of work and technical processes of handicraft production follow in most cases the primitive forms practised in the trade for generations. The relations between employer and worker are on a patriarchal master-man footing. A large part of the work is wage work. Contractors undertake the execution of certain jobs on the entrepreneur's account, and frequently on the latter's premises, whereafter they change their place of work in order to do the same work elsewhere. Payment is made partly in kind, partly in cash, usually according to the quantity of materials used.

The young factory production which developed alongside of and independently from this as a *transferred* form of production, has a number of tentative beginnings to its credit, not a few of which ended in failure. On the whole, the industrialisation trend follows a spasmodic and unequal course in contrast to the development of machine production in Europe which established itself on a broad basis, creating with irresistible force the foundations for new society. The progress of industrial development in the Middle East suffered not only from the lack of any helpful production policy and the aversion of the big landed interests to the emergence of an influential class in the towns; at times it was even confronted by grave handicaps as, for instance, the Turkish ban on the use of electricity, and the general mistrust of technical innovations.

The *direction* taken by industrial development in the Orient is prescribed by two factors: first, foreign capital aimed at a field of operation as free from risk as possible such as was offered, above all, by public utilities (gas, electricity, telephone, railway and other means of communication) with their relatively big chances of a regular yield of interest on capital and their often monopolist form of constitution. Also the concessionary and therefore mostly competition-free mining undertakings were invariably a domain for foreign interests. In respect of their dimensions, these mining undertakings occupied a special place in that they towered far above the country's customary standards, their production being destined not for the local, but for the world market. The larger the scale of these concerns, the more " inorganic " in comparison to the economy as a whole was the structure of these industries.

One cannot do justice to the picture of this period without dealing with a sociological and political feature peculiar to Oriental society, viz. its heterogeneous character.

The Occidental State, in accordance with the underlying idea of the modern national State, aims at a maximum of homogeneity within the community itself. The differences between the possessing and the non-possessing class are certainly of great importance, but in principle as within the same nationality they are surmountable in spite of the varied interests of the individual classes. The truth of this is always seen in decisive moments as, for instance, during the First World War in the unanimous political will of the people in national States. How different is the position in the Oriental countries! Here we find also, besides the " horizontal " differentiation by income or possessions, a vertical splitting-up of society into a multiplicity of national groups, religious communities, foreign spheres of interest separated from each other by political, ethnical, linguistic, religious and other criteria. In contrast to the achieved or aimed-at homogeneity in the Western State, the population in the Middle East, although loosely held together by a framework formed by political boundaries, is in practice subdivided into numerous ethnic and national constituents, most of them minority elements. This division on the national and political plane corresponds to an almost similar divergence in the economic sphere, so that, in contrast to the largely uniform population of the modern national State which is uniform also in its economic structure, Oriental society is plurally constituted and represents, in effect, a multiplicity of economic systems and structures within the framework of the State.

Middle Eastern Governments managed for some time to ward off the disintegration of society by prohibiting the purchase of land by foreigners, and the claims deriving therefrom. Thus, agrarian society, the foundation of Oriental countries, was for a long period preserved in its homogeneity. It was only the abolition of the ban on land purchase under the influence of the liberal ideas of the second half of the nineteenth century that made a breach through which foreign capital quickly infiltrated. As a rule, the process did not go beyond the business of investment. The foreigners remained investors, but did not become peasants.

On the other hand, in the spheres of industrial goods production, goods circulation and communications we find a very widespread infiltration of plural interests. Existing side by side, and in some cases overlapping, were the following economic sectors:

The Indigenous Turkish group
„ „ Arab „
„ Oriental Non-Moslem group (Armenians, Greeks, Jews)
„ Foreign Western group.

Thus we have a variety of groups differing from each other in their diverse habits both as regards way of life, personal needs, earnings, and in their claims on the services of State or public bodies. In the war of competition between the various sectors for the support of the State, the stronger groups ousted the others. Thus, the norms of these groups came to be determinative for the economic policy of the State, for the trend of goods production, the development of communications and the organisation of trade. Consequently the State was unable to fulfil its functions as supreme authority and lay down guiding principles for the community as a whole. Thus no understanding between the national groups could be obtained; a solution on the lines of a compromise such as was arrived at in European countries on the basis of federative constitutions would have been prevented by the predominance of the foreign interests. These were not willing to forego any of their privileges; in fact, they endeavoured, by joining forces with local special interests, and opposing the formation of truly democratic institutions, to consolidate their position still further. These economic interests became, therefore, more and more powerful, whilst the authority of the Oriental State, which found itself paralysed in its chief function, was steadily on the wane.

Only a revolution or the aftermath of a war could have rescued the Middle Eastern State from the tutelage of the foreigner at that time. The same applies to any inner organisation of the State and its functions. The transition from an Oriental feudal State of the Middle Ages—with the large landowners as the dominating class and few economic ties with the outside world—to a modern civilised State with highly developed forces of production and ramified interests both in respect of trade and communications presupposes a complete change of forms and relationship. For this the existing State apparatus was neither suited nor prepared. A native citizen class able to take over the rôle of the European industrial pioneers was absent; the capital formation necessary to supply the means and the experts required as instructors to initiate and to exploit the experiences gained, could not be conjured out of the earth. But if a start was to be made at all, if the big tasks of reform were to be successfully tackled, everything pointed to the modern State as the supreme and powerful authority; it alone, as the ultimate arbiter of the interests of the community as a whole, could tackle the social reorganisation problems, keep in check the exploiters of the existing régime, inaugurate the legal and political reforms, support the new economic and industrial undertakings or even be instrumental in their creation. Whatever tasks might arise in connection with such a large-scale process of transformation, they called for a new régime fearless of radical intervention, a new conception in which the State consciously assumed full responsibility for the direction of the renewal.

The Ottoman régime was powerless to exercise these functions, even in those cases where its representatives clearly understood the nature of the tasks before them. Undermined from without, it did not possess the strength to withstand the continued threat to its political and economic existence. Inwardly incapable of carrying out the necessary social and political measures for its recovery, it was in no position to pave the way for the self-industrialisation of its economy.

SECTION II

THE INDUSTRIALISATION OF THE MIDDLE EAST BETWEEN THE TWO WORLD WARS

CHAPTER XXIV

THE NEW POLITICAL AND SOCIAL CONDITIONS

1. The Political Background

The World War of 1914–1918 brought about fundamental changes in the whole political, economic and social framework of most Middle Eastern countries. In some these changes were very rapid; in others the war merely served to inaugurate them, and the process of transformation was delayed by retarding forces.

Far-reaching and diverse as these changes were, none equals in fundamental importance that which resulted in the reorganisation of the Middle Eastern State. The forces here at work, more powerful and permanent than those in other fields, succeeded in preparing the ground for a reform of Oriental society from head to foot.

In the case of the Ottoman Empire, the most powerful territorial unit of the Middle East, this result was not achieved before that Empire had sunk to the depths of its existence as an independent State. The downfall of the old Ottoman Empire was sealed by the Treaty of Sèvres in August 1920. But even at that period the scene was being set for the coming regeneration of the Turkish State. The Turkish nationalists led by Kemal Atatürk refused to recognise the Treaty as a valid document. The dismemberment of Anatolia, the very heart of Turkey, and its division into spheres of influence, was put an end to by the war of liberation; the subsequent Treaty of Lausanne, in July 1923, provided the basis for the reconstruction of the State. The drastic political lessons of the war of liberation were applied to the economic sphere with momentous results for the future economic development of Turkey.

The Treaty of Lausanne re-established, for the first time for centuries, a full and unrestricted Turkish State sovereignty. Herein, no less than in the territorial changes effected, lies its importance for the contemporary history of the Orient. These sovereign rights had been deeply undermined by the privileges conceded from time to time by the Turkish rulers; hence the most important clause in the Treaty is contained in Article 28, which reads as follows:

"Each of the High Contracting Parties hereby accepts, in so far as it is concerned, the complete abolition of the Capitulations in Turkey in every respect."

The immediate significance of this clause can hardly be overrated. The Capitulations represented a vital limitation of the sovereignty of the State in its economic policy, its jurisdiction, and indirectly also in the political sphere. With their abolition the following privileges—key positions for industrial development hitherto enjoyed by foreign enterprises—were no longer valid:

(1) The fiscal privileges according to which foreigners were exempt from paying taxes of any description, with the exception of the land taxes.
(2) the privileges of jurisdiction which placed the foreigner *ultra vires* as far as the native courts were concerned, and guaranteed him either the protection of his own consular court or that of the Mixed Courts.
(3) the privileges which gave foreigners the right, insofar as the establishment of industrial and commercial enterprises in Turkey was concerned, to recognise only such Ottoman laws as had been previously accepted by the foreign Powers.
(4) the right of intervention on the part of foreign Powers in regard to the establishment of such Turkish enterprises as might enter into competition with concerns run by their own nationals.

With the cancellation of these privileges the new State gained full economic freedom of action; and thus the chief prerequisite for the launching of the Turkish industrial reconstruction was secured. But apart from this, the territorial changes also formed an important incentive for the co-ordination of Turkey's future economic policy. The focal point of the new production policy was the uniform population with uniform habits and standards of consumption; they made its implementation a far easier matter than for the population of the old Empire composed of elements differing so widely in needs, customs and political claims.

II. Economic and Sociological Factors

The First World War brought European troops for the first time in large numbers into contact with the indigenous population. This contact left a marked impression on native habits of consumption, besides bringing home to them new possibilities as regards the satisfaction of their needs. This new trend was also supported by the undermining of certain ideas and ties hitherto upheld by religion, or by tradition based thereon, in the daily life of the Oriental masses. The rescinding of the ban on the use of electricity, the easing of the interest question, the modernising of the mode of dress for men and women, the breaking-up of the seclusion of the Moslem home, and the participation of Mohammedan women in every-day political and economic affairs—all this meant for the new industrial goods production a substantial extension of scope.

As another very essential factor in the industrial development must be counted the opening-up of Oriental countries as a result of the extension of the communications system by land, by water and by air.[68] In the isolated territories of the Middle East cheap transport facilities, especially for raw materials and articles of mass consumption, were indispensable if the machine-made product was to gain a foothold and the natural resources to be utilized.

The development of communications in the Oriental countries after the war was taken in hand, apart from strategical considerations, principally in the interest of industrialisation.

A factor of far-reaching sociological and political importance for Turkey was the ousting of the former powerful ruling clique as a result of the emergence of a new class which became the holders of power in the new State. The former régime of landed proprietors, court favourites and clerical dignitaries was replaced by one of republican officials. It is true that members of the former ruling classes also joined the new bureaucracy, but only in so far as they were willing to co-operate loyally in the new tasks of the State. The more important administrative posts were occupied mostly by prominent personalities of the revolution and the war of liberation. In addition, the place of foreigners, who once occupied a dominant position in commerce, banking, industry, and the professions, was taken by a Turkish middle class gradually growing in influence and well-being. The State itself, in contrast to the situation in former times, was now interested in having adherents in the towns who could exercise the function of industrial initiators, so vital for the State's new policy.

Thus the changes in the political scene, both domestic and foreign, acted also as important incentives for the reshaping of the social and economic structure of the new Turkey. Industrialisation, which in the years before the World War had repeatedly been attempted, but could never be achieved, was now made possible by the political revolution.

III. Population Trends as Factors in the Industrialisation Process

The growth and movement of the population provided further important incentives to industrialisation. The censuses undertaken in the Middle East during the period dividing the two World Wars disclosed an amazing increase in the number of inhabitants in the various districts. Whereas in the nineteenth century the increase in population evidently centred in the rural districts, the trend of development in recent decades shows a marked rise in the urban population also. Thus we find urbanisation, which is one of the principal concomitants of modern industrial development, increasingly in evidence in these countries.

To what extent the trend of population growth has changed is illustrated, for instance, by a statement made by a reputable medical specialist on health conditions in Turkey at the beginning of this century. He predicted that unless radical measures were taken to check the widespread diseases with which he had to deal, the Turkish population would be extinct in two generations.[69] The data on population increase in Turkey have now demonstrated that those fears were completely unfounded. The growth of the Middle East population of the present day proceeds at a considerably quicker rate than that in the countries of Central and Western Europe.[70] Hand in hand with this general upward trend in population growth goes the urbanisation movement which invariably forms a particularly effective lever in the industrialisation process. The urban population is an incomparably larger consumer of industrial products than the rural. With the increasing number of inhabitants in the towns, the demand for industrial products far exceeds the additional demand caused by the mere population increase as such.

Urbanisation itself is fostered by the fundamental fact that in the production of foodstuffs and raw materials human labour plays a steadily diminishing part. The provision of the world's needs in the way of foodstuffs today requires an incomparably smaller percentage of man-power than formerly. In the U.S.A. the percentage of agricultural workers dropped during the period from 1820 to 1930 from 72 to 22 despite the fact that during this same period the area under cultivation had enormously increased.[71] The same applies to many other countries whenever an appreciable decrease in the agricultural population has coincided with an increase in the area under cultivation. The Oriental countries, with the introduction of modern methods of production in agriculture, came also to be involved in this general trend of social and economic development.

In Palestine, where before 1914 there was no town of over 100,000 inhabitants, the percentage of the inhabitants of large towns to the total population amounted in 1942 to over 25 per cent. In Egypt it rose from 9·2 per cent. in 1910 to 13·2 per cent. in 1937, in Iraq from 7·9 per cent. in 1910 to 9·1 per cent. in 1933. It is only in Turkey that owing to the decrease in the number of inhabitants in the two large towns of Istanbul and Smyrna, both of which were particularly affected by the political changes, this figure shows no inconsiderable drop. True, the growth of the new capital of Ankara was rapid; but industrialisation in Turkey did not allow for large-scale urbanisation, i.e. the growth of big cities, inasmuch as the establishment of industrial enterprises was confined to small and medium-sized towns. On the whole, however, the increase in the population in the larger and medium-sized towns of the Orient continues, and in conjunction with the intrusion of new habits of consumption in the country districts, forms an important factor for the progress of industrialisation. Agriculture can absorb the surplus population but relatively slowly, especially when the areas suitable for irrigation—where the demand for labour is high—are restricted. Actually it was only due to industrial development that the surplus population in European countries during the nineteenth century was absorbed with relative lack of friction. This side of industrialisation, coupled with its other aspects, is one of the main reasons for the resolute pursuit of these plans in Oriental countries also.

CHAPTER XXV

THE NEW STATE POLICY OF INDUSTRIALISATION

TURKEY

The obstacles to a sovereign economic policy having been removed, the main problem for the leaders of the new State consisted in discovering the most suitable ways and means of implementing their new industrialisation policy. Of the necessity for industrialisation there was no longer any doubt. The outcome of the World War and of the Turkish war of liberation had demonstrated that a full measure of national independence was based on independence as regards those goods which are indispensable for the country's military security. To realise this, the development of certain branches of industry became a political axiom, before which economic objections had to stand aside.

On the question who should bear the responsibility for industrialisation, there was less unanimity. It has been repeatedly pointed out in these pages that the particular class which in other countries had assumed the initiative in modern industrial developments was lacking in Turkey. In so far as any industrial enterprises deserving of the name were to be found, they owed their existence to foreign elements. Added to this was the fact that the economic structure of Oriental countries was predominantly agrarian, and that therefore any forced industrialisation must immediately result in the emergence of complicated questions regarding the provision of labour, the margin of prices for the new locally produced industrial articles, selling policy, and so forth.

One institution alone was in a position to perform tasks of such vital, indeed of such revolutionary character. This institution was the State. That is the root from which has sprung the Middle-Eastern *étatism*, that ideology which for years has coloured and influenced the economic and especially the industrial policy of the sovereign Middle Eastern countries. The word *étatism* may be interpreted in various ways. This elasticity is but natural; for the interpretation of étatistic lines of thought must vary a great deal from country to country in view of the difference in the relations between the people and the Government, in the traditions of administration and general education. Étatism was adopted in principle as the basis of reconstruction in the new States; in the Turkish constitution this principle is expressly embodied as a vital characteristic of the new Turkish State, but even here, where the ideas of State-controlled economy have made most headway, a very free interpretation is practised. Étatism begins where private initiative stops. Its task is to unite the interests of the individual and those of the State in order to obtain the maximum favourable results for the nation as a whole. "Turkish étatism is no rigorous conception. It is neither anti-capitalistic nor xenophobe, nor tied dogmatically to any particular doctrine. The activity of the State consists just as much in its exercising a constructive and effective policy itself as in encouraging private enterprises and in controlling and regulating their execution."[72]

This elasticity in economic conception or in economic policy, which to the outside world must certainly appear inconsequent, was, however, nothing but an adaptation to past experience in the development of industrial economy. It is worth while studying the course of Turkish industrialisation in order to gain a clearer picture of the main lines of this noteworthy development. Certain trends towards State encouragement of industry had already crystallised in the form of a law issued as a *provisorium* on December 1, 1913, granting privileges to certain enterprises. These privileges consisted in the cost-free allocation of land, exemption from taxes as well as from payment of duty on raw materials, machinery and fuel. Owing to the outbreak of the First World War which followed shortly after its enactment, the law did not come into full effect; in any case it would scarcely have been equal to the task which the new leaders of Turkey had set themselves, viz. the industrialisation of important branches of production in the shortest possible time. In the first years after the war it appeared as if the vast political task deriving from the victorious issue of the war of liberation would force the execution of large-scale economic programmes into the background. A trade agreement, which as part of the Treaty of Lausanne was signed on the same day by Great Britain, France, Italy, Japan, Greece, Rumania, and Jugoslavia on the one hand, and Turkey on the other, represented a certain set-back inasmuch as for the products of the contracting parties Turkey was obliged to concede the Ottoman customs tariff of September 1st, 1916. This concession did away for the time being with the possibility of a forced policy of protective duties; it was not until 1929, when the period of validity of this convention had expired, that Turkey could implement a new industrial customs tariff. This inauguration of a new protective tariff policy was preceded by an important act of legislation, the prelude to that encouragement of industrial development which Turkey was to undertake after the World War. This was the Law for the Encouragement of Industry enacted in 1927, whose last modification was undertaken in 1933. The law covers all branches of industry using machine power and attaining a certain minimum number of work-days per annum. Certain branches, such as textile factories and carpet-weaving, enjoy the privileges provided by the law irrespective of the size of the factory or the use of machinery. These privileges go much further than those granted in the law of 1913 and make it obligatory, in particular for the State authorities, to give preference to the home product even when the difference in price between the local and the foreign product is as much as 10 per cent. Moreover, the enterprises can claim bonuses or price reductions on the goods to be supplied to them by the State establishments. The law provides further that in the factories entitled to the stipulated privileges all functionaries and specialists—with the exception of the directors and managers—must be of Turkish nationality. The remaining privileges refer to the cost-free allocation of sites for factories up to 10 hectares, exemption from all land taxes payable on factory sites or in connection with factory management, exemption from the payment of duty on all building materials, raw materials and machinery required for the erection and installation of the factories and freight reductions on the State transport undertakings amounting to 30 per cent.

The comprehensive nature of these concessions clearly evidences two distinct tendencies. The first aims at giving the entrepreneur some incentive through the advantages offered to engage in industrial activities, the risk involved being limited from the start by lowering the costs of investment and ensuring marketing prospects. The second seeks in the shortest time possible to render the new concerns independent of the foreign management hitherto considered indispensable for the development of industrial undertakings. The concessions made by the fiscal authorities are by no means inconsiderable in view of the extensive import of machinery and raw materials recorded during this early period of industrial promotion. Over and above this, the bonuses scheduled were claimed to such an extent that two years after the passing of the law the Government decided to rescind it in view of the many abuses to which it led—factories were not infrequently opened merely for the sake of the bonus offered.[73]

During the period of industrial development from 1927 to 1934, the aim of the official policy of industrialisation was to stimulate private industrial initiative by means of bonuses, guaranteed markets and reduction of overheads. The results of this policy were not unfavourable, but did not fulfil the expectations of the Turkish régime, which had anticipated a quicker tempo of industrialisation. This, coupled with the experiences of the international price crisis, led to the adoption of a new conception in the form of the first Five Year Plan of industrialisation, 1933–1938. This Five Year Plan, which incidentally was first announced in 1934, represented a reversal of the State's industrial policy. The State as such now became the principal agent of industrial development.

There were various reasons for this reversal of policy. On the one hand, industrial activity as directed hitherto had left out of account one sector which from the standpoint of the country's defence requirements was clearly of particular importance, viz. the winning of ores and their by-products. The establishment of heavy industrial undertakings necessitating large-scale capital investment was dependent on the obtaining of large sums which at that time were not available, at least not for that purpose. Added to this were the misgivings arising from the heavy restrictions on imports in view of their effect on the maintenance of the standard of living. These restrictions became imperative owing to the fact that during the first six years of the Republic's existence every year registered a large deficit in foreign trade balance which could only be made up by capital export. Indeed, the protective duties introduced in 1929 immediately helped to reduce this deficit; moreover, they caused such a marked drop in the consumption of imported goods that the demand to remedy the shortage by home-production became more and more irresistible. Finally there can be no doubt that this strengthening of étatism was also prompted by the desire to oust the minorities from their as yet fairly strong positions in industry and commerce. In any case in the new plan to be introduced now, the Government itself was to act as the prime driving force and to play the leading executive rôle.

The aim of the Five Year Plan consisted in developing with the active assistance of the State a number of branches of industry which were given priority status. This applied to:

(1) those branches utilising raw materials which were produced in the country itself (cotton, hemp, wool).
(2) those connected with the extraction of minerals and other raw materials, i.e. iron, coal, coke, copper, sulphur, etc.
(3) those producing articles largely consumed in Turkey even

if the raw materials concerned were produced there only in part (paper, cardboard, artificial silk, bottles, porcelain and ceramic articles), and lastly

(4) a number of predominantly chemical branches, producing chemical semi-manufactured goods from derivatives and by-products of primary productions.

According to the figures of Conker, the value of imported goods in the aforesaid categories during the years 1927–1932 amounted to 43 per cent. of Turkey's total imports. Thus, even partial replacement of these imports by locally produced goods would effect an appreciable improvement in Turkey's trade balance.

In the foreground of such a far-reaching plan we must necessarily expect to find the problem of financing. None of the methods hitherto relied upon to foster industrial production could be considered for the new industrial development scheme. There was no place for the small moneylender and usurer, nor for the middlemen and raw material suppliers who had either advanced money on the finished goods or supplied raw materials on credit to the industrial producers. Now other aims were in view, both as regards the magnitude and the principle of financing. For this reason a new course was decided on: the establishment of State industrial Banks.

The execution of the Five Year Plan was entrusted by the State to the Suemer Bank founded by the State in 1933. This Bank, whose shares were taken up by the State, originated out of the fusion of two State institutions: the State Industrial Bureau and the Industrial Credit Bank. Although the Suemer Bank could deal with all classes of banking business, its principal task for the time being was the implementing of the Five Year Plan, and comprised first the management of the industrial concerns which it took over from the State Industrial Bureau, the carrying out of research work and industrial projects to be financed by State capital. Only such factories as had been founded by virtue of special legal authorisation were excluded. Lastly, the Bank was empowered, within the limits of the capital at its disposal, also to assist those industries whose development was considered as being in the interest of the national economy.

The financing of this important sphere of activities was safeguarded by the State placing every year from 1934 the sums necessary for the fulfilment of its functions at the Suemer Bank's disposal. The Bank was to receive for the duration of the Five Year

Plan asum of £T6 millions yearly, apart from its reserve capital which was supplied gratuitously by the State; this amounted originally to £T20 millions, and was raised by degrees to £T150 millions in 1943, of which £T65 millions were paid up. The Bank's programme shows an impressive list of industrial undertakings which in part have a fairly sound capital basis.

In order to raise sums of this magnitude for the purpose of industrialisation, the Turkish State was obliged to make use of every available source of finance; yet in view of the experiences in the past it applied certain safeguards in the case of foreign creditors. The direct allocation of State funds for the financing of industry via the Suemer Bank has already been referred to. In addition to this direct State subvention, private capital was also mobilised when the Ish Bankasi Bank was founded in 1924. That this private capital was forthcoming despite the aversion which this form of investment generally meets with in Oriental countries was due to the fact that this Bank was financed through the most eager co-operation of leading personalities and probably also not without pressure.[74] The organisation and management of the Bank came at first under the supervision of the Ministry of Economy, but the Bank being a private undertaking was not bound by the regulations which the Suemer Bank had to observe in respect of its transactions. As can be seen from the balance sheet, the Ish Bank was able to execute its task of collecting local Turkish funds for the purpose of industrial development in a satisfactory manner. At the end of 1925, the amount of deposits and savings accounts totalled £T88·2 millions; at the end of 1937 £T67 millions, the total participations in other concerns £T43 millions. A further State banking enterprise founded in 1935 is the Eti Bank; its nominal paid-up capital of £T20 millions is in the hands of the State. Its function is the financing of the steel and iron industry as well as the safeguarding of the State mining interests. The Eti Bank took over the Karabuk Iron and Steel Works as well as the management and control of a number of mining concerns, including the coal mines at Zonguldak, the copper mines at Erjani, the iron and manganese exploitation at Divrik.

For the protection of Turkish State interests in the sphere of shipping, a State concern known as the Deniz Bank was founded whose shares were likewise owned by the State. This enterprise, however, was not a success, and in 1938 its liquidation was decided on.

Eventually foreign capital also found its way into the industrial development schemes. In this connection the American Turkish Investment Corporation extended in 1930, i.e. prior to the inauguration of the Five Year Plan, a loan of 10 million gold dollars against the granting of the match and lighter monopoly. The company, which received the concession for a period of 25 years, undertook to establish in the province of Istanbul a match factory capable of meeting the country's home consumption. Apart from the loan, the company was further obliged to pay the Turkish Government substantial concession fees. The match monopoly has since been repurchased by the Turkish Government and the loan repaid.

Agreements for the financing of industrialisation were also concluded with the U.S.S.R. in 1934 in respect of a sum of 8 million gold dollars. In this case, the equivalent of this sum was to be supplied in the form of machinery and equipment required for industrial development. Russia's assistance towards the industrial upbuilding was not, however, confined to the loan; a number of Russian technicians were sent to Turkey in order to take in hand the assembling of the machinery and the initiation of the local workmen and masters in the handling of the plant. In the later stages of the plan also British capital played an important part, especially in the development of the heavy industry. On the strength of an agreement concluded in June 1936, the British industrial concern Brassert in conjunction with the British Export Credit Guarantee Department undertook to advance the Suemer Bank in the form of a loan the capital necessary for the development of the heavy industry in Karabuk. The scheme envisaged was on an ambitious scale and comprised the construction of many separate plants, including a coke factory, two blast furnaces, assembly plant, foundry, iron pipe factory, steelworks and electricity plant. The pig-iron production and the pipe foundry plant were, together with the steelworks, to have a capacity of 200,000 tons per annum; this, however, has meanwhile been increased. The reasons for the implementing of these ambitious plans derived, apart from the ever-present motive of autarky, from the possibility of exploiting the co-existence of iron ore and coal for the development of an iron and steel industry. Unfortunately it was only after the completion of the works that the existence of rich and valuable iron ores was discovered at Divrik, over 650 km. distant; while the quality of the Karabuk ores proved rather low.

In 1936 an extension of the Five Year Plan was decided upon, by which the following projects were added:

1. Construction of electricity works.
2. Manufacture of foodstuffs.
3. Establishment of machine factories.
4. Exploitation of sea products.

In 1938, after the Five Year Plan had already been modified, a new Four Year Plan was proclaimed. The aim of this new plan was the establishment of 18 industrial enterprises, including the development of modern harbours on the Black Sea coast, especially in the neighbourhood of Karabuk, the establishment of a jute industry in the district of Antalya, a factory for agricultural implements in Ankara, meat and canning factories in Trabzon and Bursa, the erection of three new sugar factories, besides a spinning mill and an establishment for the production of synthetic fuel from coal.[75]

In order to ensure more effective State control in the State enterprises, where certain shortcomings had meanwhile come to light, legislation was enacted by which the Ministry of Commerce was given most extensive powers in matters of price-fixing, factory supervision and control of the home and export markets.

The Turkish Government, in the practical execution of its industrial development plans, did not adhere strictly to details. Those points in the programme which were not carried into execution by the stipulated time, were carried out later or introduced in the newly proclaimed plans.

The success of the first Five Year Plan, whose implementation must be dated as from May 1934, and of the Four Year Plan inaugurated in 1938 was satisfactory so far as the technical results were concerned. The major part of the enterprises envisaged in the plans were completed or under construction within the stipulated period.

The outbreak of war prevented the execution of a number of projects. The solution of other problems such as the supply of raw material, financing, purchase of machinery, was also rendered considerably more difficult by the war. The country's geographical and strategic position helped it, however, to gain its ends as regards a number of important demands for the continuance of technical and financial supplies.

To sum up: The industrial projects of the Turkish Government were conceived and carried out in the clear realisation of (*a*) the limitations of private initiative and (*b*) the importance of the industrial sector for the development of the new State. The methods of promotion and financing represented a bold departure from hitherto established practice. They were based on a form of planned industrial development fully subventioned by the State at the expense of the tax-paying population. The guiding principles for the industrialisation as such were mainly determined by extra-economic considerations and therefore called for an excessively high price-structure which established itself beyond the price movement on the world market. The new production centres were not founded on account of the favourable chances for economic success, but in answer to the dictate of the national interest even if the new production machinery owing to local factors—location of factories, climate, insufficient markets and lack of qualified experts and administrators—could turn out only very dear products. Thus, for instance, we find the new factories established not in coastal areas, but wherever possible in the interior of the country. For some plants this necessitated delivery of raw materials and the despatch of the manufactured goods over distances of many hundreds of kilometres, thus causing additional costs which must make themselves felt in the finished product.

Even the introduction of high protective tariffs which these circumstances rendered essential, did not succeed in compensating for the lack of power of competition evidenced by some branches. The most outstanding example is seen in the sugar industry which is one of the first Turkish State industries.[76] The Government, owing to the ill-considered planning of the factories—one was erected on a site where there was a scarcity of water!—and the low yield of the beet fields, was obliged to resort to a costly process of reorganisation and to the closing down of some plants. There were periods when it paid to import sugar from abroad at the price of 11 piastres per kg. rather than to produce it at home where, even after the greatest possible reduction in production costs, it could not be marketed at less than 25 piastres.

Despite these and other shortcomings it would be a mistake to regard the results so far achieved by Turkey's policy of industrialisation as inadequate. It is true that they remind us both as regards the underlying ideological idea and the several failures recorded of the industrialisation plans of Mohammed Ali. In both cases we find a powerful personality acting as the original driving force behind the revolutionary programme; nor was there any lack of opposition to the execution of the plans on the part of the foreign powers, who for economic and political reasons wished to prevent the growth of industrial activities in these countries.

The difference between the two cases—and the reasons of the success of the one—are to be found firstly in the response which the new plans evoked among the people and the leading classes, and secondly in the sovereign position of the Turkish State which could protect its young industrial production by high tariffs—a right which Mohammed Ali was unable to assert. No doubt other factors, too, favoured the industrialisation process in Turkey, but they are far overshadowed in their significance by those mentioned.

The industrialisation of a country with a predominantly agrarian structure, in part excessively forced as in this case it was, could not be carried out entirely without friction. Also the carrying out of the industrial programme itself reveals an abundance of gaps and weak points. Important, inded vital, functions for the success of such a complicated process of reconstruction had to be entrusted to persons who had had no opportunity of acquiring sufficient experience and did not possess the qualities necessary for tackling such tasks. A remarkable law passed in 1938 established a new basis for the management and control of enterprises whose capital was in the exclusive possession of the State. The law was obviously framed in the realisation that the bureaucratic structure of such enterprises did not constitute a sufficient guarantee for a suitable management; it provided, therefore, for the conversion of certain enterprises into another form of commercial company. Thus, above all, the concerns run by the Suemer Bank and also those of the Eti and Deniz Banks were to be withdrawn from the competence of the banks and given a new company form. This form, according to Article 28 of the new law, may be that of a joint-stock company on condition that the shareholders are Turkish nationals and the shares themselves registered in their names. Furthermore, the law for the first time allows private initiative once more freedom of activity in those sectors which have already reached, through State assistance, a certain stage of successful development. The State is prepared, in such cases, to confine its responsibility to sponsoring the enterprises only until they are able to stand alone. A similar line is followed by the adaptation of the control of State industrial enterprises, according to the degree in which the administration is carried out on a rational and economic basis and conforms to commercial and industrial standards. The law provides that the State enterprises which in the management of their business affairs had hitherto enjoyed considerable latitude, were now to be much more critically examined as to their economic right to existence. Consequently, the problems of State industrial development within the framework of a world market dominated by capitalist industries could be more easily tackled.

We have devoted particular attention to the industrial development of the new Turkey inasmuch as, in the experience of the countries of the East, it represents the most definite case of industrialisation as part of a State policy. The progress of industrialisation in this country in which no restrictions on sovereignty interfere with its economic policy and its results will be a valuable source of instruction for the industrial development in other Oriental countries.

The issue as a whole has special significance in view of the attitude of scepticism frequently assumed of late towards the idea of development "from above". The case of Turkey clearly illustrates this form of development and its pros and cons. Where conditions of education are very backward, there is, however, no alternative but to tackle the various tasks firmly "from above", i.e. through the Government or other agencies, while simultaneously seeing to it that the policy of raising the cultural level of the masses to a more mature state is energetically pursued.

The State and Industrialisation In Other Oriental Countries

Apart from Turkey, Iran is the only Oriental country that has accepted the ideology of étatist industrial development and built up a State industrial sector. In Egypt, the Levant States, Palestine, and Iraq, no particular interest on the part of the State authorities in the development of industrial production was shown until the end of the twenties. But in no case did the industrialisation process bear the character of systematic or large-scale planning; in fact, in the mandated territories there was among foreign observers and in government circles a decidedly negative attitude towards the tendencies to industrialisation. Characteristic of these views are such statements as the following, made by the Director of the Department of Excise and Trade in Palestine: "in fact, it would seem probable that it will be a matter of many years before Palestine is likely to be able to claim to be an industrial as well as an agricultural country".[77]

On the prospects in Syria the French Mandate administration, in its report to the League of Nations for 1929, expresses its views as follows: "The prospects of industry must not be exaggerated.

Even though cheap labour is available, still the land does not provide any prospects of large industrial development . . .".[78]

The Western Powers could not reconcile themselves to the emergence of national, i.e. independent industries which would tend to restrict the market for their own export products. Likewise the native owners of vested interests, predominantly landowners and merchants, felt themselves threatened by the prospects of industrialisation which might affect labour conditions to their disadvantage (wages, labour market, etc.). It was only under the influence of the continued drop in prices of agricultural products which caused great suffering amongst the agricultural population that the policy of the official bodies began to relax. When industrialisation was regarded as inevitable by the representatives of the Western Powers, they endeavoured to participate in the development at least as suppliers of the production goods (machinery, semi-manufactured articles). Also the native circles which had previously opposed industrialisation were in view of its capacity of absorbing the surplus population eventually obliged to give it their approval and began in an increasing degree to take an active share in its promotion.

EGYPT

Of all Arab countries the sovereign State of Egypt has devoted most attention to industrial development. The First World War already gave a powerful incentive to local initiative in the industrial sphere. The fact that the country was cut off from its former trade connections during the four years of the war, coupled with the presence of a consumer-body of exceptional purchasing power, the British army, even at that period gave rise to the growth of industrial production. It is true that the Egyptian Government, which during the years of political dispute with England centred its energies on other questions, took for the time being little part in this process. The large and important industries already in existence remained, therefore, up to recent years the province of foreign capital. At this period, however, a State-subsidised financial concern emerged having the development of national Egyptian industries as its principal task. This is the Misr Bank, founded in 1926 with a capital of £80,000; in the course of years, thanks to the personal connections of its founders with Government circles, it came into ever closer contact with the State, which started to use the Bank as an instrument for the promotion of industry. The capital of the Bank increased during the war to over 3 millions sterling and is invested in a number of affiliated companies. The largest enterprise connected with the Misr concern is the company for cotton spinning and weaving whose main factories are situtated at al-Mahalla al-Kubra. From 12,000 spindles and 480 looms in 1927 its equipment had increased at the beginning of the war to 110,000 spindles and 2,500 looms. Since then the plant has again been considerably extended. The following summary comprises the principal Misr companies:

	Year of Foundation
Filature et Tissage du Coton	1927
Egrénage du Coton (Ginning)	1924
Exportation du Coton	1934
Transport et Navigation Fluviale	1925
Transport et Navigation Maritime	1925
Tissage de la Soie	1927
Fil Lin	1927
Theatre et Cinéma	1925
Pêcheries	1927
Assurance Generale	1934
Imprimerie Misr	1922
Misr Airworks	1932
Misr Shipping	1934
Misr S. A. pour l'Industrie du Papier	1934
Banque Misr-France	1926
Banque Misr-Syrie-Liban	1929

The management of the factories founded or supported by the Misr Bank in the years before the war often met with severe criticism, and in all probability many of these enterprises, measured by rigid economic criteria, could hardly be called profitable at that time. The war prosperity period relieved most of the Misr concerns of their financial difficulties. But it appears that even after the war the argument that these companies occupy a position of national standing independent of foreign capital and foreign influence, will help to tide the Misr enterprises over possible periods of crisis.

The trend towards consolidation and expansion of industrial economy has undoubtedly been further strengthened by the Second World War. The establishment of the Egyptian army made possible since the agreement with England has already led to the founding of a number of factories for the supply of military requirements in which the State has a major interest. The rise in the standard of living to be expected as regards the civil population and the enormous amout of liquid capital must tend to swell the wave of industrialisation in the post-War period. With the abolition of the Capitulations in 1937 which reinstated the sovereignty of Egypt's economic policy the last political obstacles to industrialisation were removed.

IRAQ

In Iraq the trend towards industrial development started relatively late. The law for the promotion of industry passed in 1929 offered prospective entrepreneurs a number of privileges on the usual lines (free factory sites, exemption from payment of import duties and taxes). The results of this law, however, are regarded as doubtful; it is only since the establishment of the Industrial and Agricultural Bank in 1935 that any marked initiative in the desired direction is noticeable. The Iraqi Government believed that it could not afford to forego the impetus to the revival of the native national economy anticipated from the announcement of a Four Year Plan. The plan provides for a number of promotion measures in diverse economic fields, but cannot be compared either in conception or manner of execution with similar plans in Turkey or even in Iran. The political and sociological prerequisites for the industrialisation of Iraq will probably be lacking for some long time to come. Amongst the existing factories the textile weaving and spinning establishment at Kazimein near Baghdad far surpasses all others in extent. A number of smaller concerns with machine plant likewise produce textile goods, such as stockings, fabrics, shawls. An important branch of industry is the cigarette trade, which has even been able to oust part of the foreign import from the market. Furthermore, in Baghdad and in the other larger towns there are smaller enterprises for the manufacture of shoes, tiles, perfumes, oxygen, furniture and leather goods. The Industrial and Agricultural Bank operating on behalf of the Four Year Plan has devoted its activities to the preparation of a cement factory, a cotton ginning plant, a cotton goods establishment and other industrial projects. Industrial development in Iraq has so far been scarcely able to change the social and occupational composition of the population.

Iraq's petroleum industry, in view of its capital basis and conditions of ownership, its technical equipment and its scale, occupies a special position in the country's industrial economy. The whole oil industry is in the hands of British companies. The main oil-bearing sites which are now being developed are the fields of Baba Gurgur near Kirkuk, which form part of the concession sphere of the Iraq Petroleum Company. From there the crude oil is carried by a pipeline (which later forks) to the Mediterranean ports of Haifa and Tripoli. The oilfields lying south of Khaniqin are worked by the Khaniqin Oil Company, a subsidiary of the Anglo-

Iranian Company. The oilfields near Mosul come within the concession territory of Mosul Oilfield Ltd.; the oil deposits near Basra belong to that of the Basra Oil Company.

The newly-formed State of Iraq, despite the material advantages it could expect, was not enthusiastic over the plans of the foreign oil concerns and the vast expansion of their activity.

The monopoly status of the Turkish Petroleum Company, the predecessor of the present holders, aroused fears lest the conditions attached to the grant and working of the concession under pressure from the powerful partner would prove unfavourable for Iraq and, as in other petroleum areas under imperialist control, lead to the country's permanent political dependence and exploitation. The company's negotiations with the government of Iraq were, therefore, exceedingly protracted and no settlement was reached until 1925, although the proposals of the Turkish Petroleum Company were submitted as early as 1923. One of the principal conditions on the part of the Iraqi Government was concerned with its participation in the capital of the company, this possibility being mentioned in the agreement of San Remo. Eventually this idea was abandoned, and instead a system of royalties (a fixed annual sum of £400,000 in gold and a mining fee per ton to be paid to the Iraq Government) was substituted.[79]

No less serious objections came from another quarter which in the first years had taken no part in the negotiations, viz. the United States of America. These were directed at the political and juridical aspect of the Mesopotamian oil interests as reflected in the post-war trend of development. In the first place the United States contested the very validity of the concession. The Turkish Government, it maintained, had granted no legal concession but merely given a vague promise to grant a concession at some later period. The second objection on the part of the United States was based on the principle of the Open Door, which through the unilateral method of handling the Mesopotamian oil question on the part of Great Britain had been infringed. Mesopotamia, it argued, was mandated territory in which all States had equal economic rights. Particular exception was taken to the clause in the San Remo agreement by which every petroleum company interested in the development of the Mesopotamian oilfields must come under permanent British control.

It is not possible to deal here with the complicated negotiations and disputes leading to appeals by the United States to the League of Nations. The conflict in this case also ended with the complainant, that is, the American interests, being squared in such a way that the Standard Oil Company, like the French, received 25 per cent. of the shares provided by the Anglo-Iranian Oil Company. The 5 per cent. share promised at the time of the company's establisment to the Armenian C. S. Gulbenkian for his valuable services as agent was borne equally by all partners, so that the various groups participated in the Iraq Petroleum Company as follows:

Standard Oil Company . . .	23¾%
Anglo-Iranian Oil Company . .	23¾%
Royal Dutch Shell Concern . .	23¾%
Compagnie Française des Pétroles .	23¾%
Participation and Investment Co. (Gulbenkian) .	5%

The revenue which the Iraqi Government receives from the oil companies amounts to several million pounds per annum and represents one of the principal items of the State budget.

PALESTINE

In Palestine industrial development has probably reached the greatest intensity, even if, compared to the newly industrialised larger countries and certainly to the older industrial countries, it can produce no imposing figures. But what at this stage of economic development in the Orient is of such fundamental importance is the manner in which industrialisation in Palestine shapes its course. Whereas in Turkey and Iran (and occasionally in Egypt) industry is the focal point of State economic policy—in the two first-named countries the larger undertakings are concerns run by the State or the State banks—industrial plans in Palestine have materialised without State encouragement, moderate Government protection being obtained only with difficulty. The aid which the State usually proffers to young industrial enterprises was provided by the self-organised Jewish population often only to an inadequate degree, even though the credit institutes and research centres were able to render valuable service. It is open to question whether the new national industries in those countries, reared so to speak in hothouse conditions, will be able to hold their own under the régime of free competition to which the young Palestinian industry has been obliged to adjust itself. But it is not only in this point that the industrial economy of Palestine differs from that in other countries. The whole structure of the Jewish industrial sector which combines the bulk of the industrial concerns and the industrial operatives rests on the employment of highly paid workers with wages calculated on a European scale; it must therefore meet the competition from the cheap native labour. In comparison with Egypt or Syria the amount of capital domiciled abroad and invested in the young industry is very low. With the exception of the foreign-owned oil refineries and a few concession undertakings, the capital of the majority of industrial enterprises, probably more than 80 per cent., is in the hands of Palestinian residents. The results are characteristic enough. In Palestine alone do we find a comprehensive labour organisation which comprises the majority of the workers, under whose influence modern labour relations on the basis of the free working contract are emerging; thus, more rapidly than in the neighbouring countries, conditions here are approaching those in industrial countries where the worker is not regarded as fair game for exploitation, but as an important factor in the production process. Over and above this, we meet in Palestine with new social forms of industrial organisation in which co-operative ideas occupy a conspicuous place; the germs of a new alignment in the relations between labour and capital as here in evidence may be of great importance for the solution of burning problems of our industrial age.

Palestine can claim a special position in the industrialisation process of the Middle East, not by reason of the already substantial extent of its production, but on account of the co-existence in that country of several factors which are not to be found in other Oriental countries. This refers to the presence of a body of trained specialists and skilled workers and an investment-minded class of industrialists, a fact due in both cases to political conditions in Europe, which caused these elements, rather unusual in Oriental countries, to come together in Palestine. The establishment of local institutions for advanced technical training coupled with the unremitting influx of capital has provided favourable conditions for the continuance of this industrialisation process up to recent times.

Syria and Lebanon

The amount of State activity evidenced in Syria and the Lebanon is insignificant. In view of the dilatory attitude of the mandatory authorities the development to be seen in Lebanese-Syrian industry is a creditable achievement on the part of the entrepreneurs, though these, it must be admitted, enjoyed several advantages: a certain versatility inherent in the native population, local handicraft tradition, and the relatively rich sources of capital provided by Syrian emigrants abroad. French private capital also participated in certain industrial activities. After a decline during the third decade of the present century the thirties saw a considerable expansion of the industrial sector in the Lebanese-Syrian economy. This may be due to the raising of the general tariff rate in 1926 and the subsequent introduction of certain protective duties. But despite their favourable effect on industrial development in the mandated territories these measures remained isolated steps. They were partly the outcome of fiscal considerations and could not, therefore, bring about a genuine and comprehensive industrialisation.

CHAPTER XXVI

THE ECONOMIC EFFECTS OF INDUSTRIALISATION IN FIGURES

The economic effects of industrialisation can best be numerically demonstrated by a comparison of figures in the spheres of production and foreign trade undertaken from the following aspects:—

(1) Expansion of the Industrial Sector (Number of industrial establishments, number of employed, volume of output, and wages paid);
(2) Increased Imports of Capital Goods, such as machinery, engines and fuel;
(3) Decrease in the Import of Goods now produced within the Country;
(4) Increase in the Export of Locally Produced Industrial Goods.

Statistics in the majority of Middle East countries have not reached a stage that would permit all these comparisons to be made. But a partial analysis may be sufficient to give some idea of the direction and scope of the new industrial development.

(1) The pattern and pace of industrialisation are not everywhere the same. They are determined, apart from political factors, by the specific conditions obtaining in each country, such as natural resources, transport facilities, vocational skill, and the consumption level of the population. Changes such as those brought about in wartime by the disruption of the normal supply channels of a country are bound to exert a profound influence on its production, and may set the pace for many years to come. During the War of 1914–1918, the cutting off of Egypt and Turkey from many of their former supplier countries and the requirements of the large armies stationed in the Orient led to a considerable growth of local industrial production. In the course of the four years of World War I, £84 millions were spent by the military authorities in Egypt alone. The sums expended during the same period by the British military authorities in Mesopotamia, Syria and Iraq exceeded the total capital investments within the Ottoman Empire up to 1914.

A similar development might be observed during World War II. This again has stimulated industrialisation—notably in Palestine, but also in Egypt. Army expenditure in the Middle East up to 1945 has been estimated at more than £700 millions, of which nearly £300 millions were expended in Egypt alone. In view of the vital importance of capital supply for industrial development, the significance of a capital influx on such a scale as this is obvious.

The following is an outline of developments in the various Middle Eastern countries, which are treated here in the order given above.

EGYPT

Unfortunately, statistics of occupational distribution in this country are not up to date; nor are they kept on uniform lines, which precludes a scrutiny of the various industrial branches from this particular angle. The population censuses of 1907, 1917, 1927 and 1937 admit only of limited comparisons.

NUMBER OF EARNERS IN INDUSTRY
(excluding Construction and Building)

1907	281,000
1917	366,000
1927	483,000
1937	478,000*

*As against this figure, which is contained in the Population Census of 1937, the Industrial Census of the same year gives the total number of employees in Egyptian industry as 273,000. Although probably not including the owners of the various establishments, this latter figure indicates that the number of those occupied in industry proper was less than 478,000. According to the *Statistics of Wages and Working Hours in Egypt* of July, 1943, the total number of wage-earners in Egyptian industry is 284,584.

These figures point to an appreciable increase in the number of industrial earners, but are not reliable enough to admit of more than general conclusions. The margin of error would, however, be somewhat reduced if we limited our comparison to the towns of Cairo and Alexandria, which, incidentally, are the principal scenes of industrial activity.

As may be seen from the table on p. 294, certain branches such as wood working, textiles, clothing, the chemical industry, show a considerable rise in the number of persons employed. Even more significant, however, than the particulars set out in this table, which should be used with caution, are the changes that have occurred in the structure of foreign trade.

NUMBER OCCUPIED IN THE MAIN BRANCHES OF INDUSTRY, HANDICRAFTS AND TRANSPORT IN CAIRO AND ALEXANDRIA*

Branch of Industry	1907	1927	1937
Mining, Quarrying and Salines	1,386	2,755	2,151
Textile Industries	6,094	10,366	11,076
Of which:			
Cotton Industry	21	4,065	3,136
Silk Industry (fabrics, spinning and weaving)	3,100	2,427	2,127
Dyeing of Fabrics	898	1,068	656
Tanning	552	1,485	1,762
Making of Leather Articles (excluding footwear)	38	1,512	1,450
Wood working, cane working, etc.	3,281	23,234	21,014
Of which:			
Furniture	1,164	7,584	8,789
Metallurgy and Manufacture of Metal Articles	14,023†	20,886	18,892
Of which:			
Metal Bedsteads	Unspecified	350	1,001
Chemical Industries and Oils and Fats	233	1,749	2,417
Food, vegetable and animal, with Tobacco and Cigarettes	14,043	24,893	20,977
Clothing	16,634	31,610	33,570
Of which:			
Men's Tailoring	6,087	12,225	14,108
Women's Dressmaking	2,867	5,929	4,995
Footwear	7,171	11,342	12,105
Building Industries	32,127	49,150	46,198
Vehicle Construction	1,841	6,665	10,716
Transport and Communications	40,132	53,724	56,141

* In view of the differing classifications of industries in the various censuses any comparison with the figures for 1907 is bound to be inaccurate; the figures for 1927 and 1937 are more reliable.

† The figure 14,023 does not include bedsteads.

IMPORTS INTO EGYPT IN 1913 AND IN 1938[80]

	Unit.	1913	1938	1938 as against 1913 in %
Machinery and Raw Materials:				
Benzine	tons	1,884	33,250	1,765
Printing ink	kg.	42,092	231,437	550
Bars, iron or steel	tons	42,764	74,709	175
Oils, mineral and lubricating	tons	9,039	126,833	1,403
Vegetable oils for industry	tons	3,368	17,371	516
Precision tools and scientific instruments	£E.	56,034	352,681	629
Motors and special machinery for various industries	£E.	741,796	2,324,890	313
Mazout	tons	8,302	229,113	2,760
Wool yarn	kg.	162,868	292,634	180
Silk and artificial silk yarn	kg.	200,094	2,024,202	1,012
Industrial Consumption Goods:				
Matches	£E.	81,368	32,141	40
Beer	tons	7,878	6,021	76
Leather shoes	pairs	792,006	47,178	6
Cement	tons	193,987*	47,414	24
Confectionery and jams	£E.	100,207	38,506	38
Cotton blankets and coverlets	£E.	112,212	7,145	6
Tanned leather	£E.	142,996	31,543	22
Flour of wheat, spelt and meslin	tons	203,547	3,633	2
Cotton yarn	kg.	2,693,885	772,541	29
Bedsteads, metal	£E.	81,614	1,209	2
Furniture, wood	£E.	291,112*	31,987	11
Alimentary pastes	tons	806	109	14
Soap, common	tons	7,303	3,710	51
Carpets	metres	346,719	40,254	12
Tarbushes	dozens	56,565	7,133	13
Cotton piece goods	kg.	29,696,437	16,956,357	58
Glass and glassware	£E.	557,290*	251,346	45

*Average of 1924–8.

IMPORTS INTO EGYPT PER CAPITA IN 1913, 1938 OF CERTAIN IMPORTANT ARTICLES

Article	Unit of measure	1913	1938
Benzine	kg.	0·2	2
Bars, iron or steel	kg.	3·5	4·6
Oil, mineral and lubricating	kg.	0·7	7·8
Motors and special machinery	£E.	0·06	0·14
Mazout	kg.	0·7	14·1
Cement	kg.	13·7	2·9
Cotton yarn	kg.	0·2	0·05
Cotton piece goods	kg.	2·4	1·0
Beer	kg.	0·6	0.4

These figures reveal a sharp increase in the import of industrial capital goods and a simultaneous decline in the import of finished consumer goods—both clear indications of the expansion of local production, particularly as they coincide with a growth in population. Attention should be drawn, in this connection, to the rise in the import of fuel, machinery, wool and silk yarns, and printing ink. A remarkable example of local industrial expansion is offered by the cement and cotton industries.

DEVELOPMENT OF THE CEMENT AND COTTON INDUSTRIES

	Cement (in 1,000 tons)			Cotton piece goods (in 1,000 square metres)		
Year	Production	Consumption	Import	Production *	Consumption	Import
1930	188	380	192	6,000	186,000	180,000
1931	241	406	165	14,500	161,500	147,000
1932	239	442	203	25,000	199,000	174,500
1933	288	374	86	30,000	227,000	197,000
1934	297	382	85	37,500	219,500	182,000
1935	379	441	62	34,500	228,000	193,500
1936	372	407	35	54,500	224,100	169,600
1937	322	364	42	64,000	233,500	169,500
1938	284	331	47	110,000	247,400	137,400
1939	372	408	36	159,000	241,500	82,500
1940	357	362	—	185,000†	251,500	66,000
1941	420	390	—	200,000	267,000	67,000
1942	—	—	—	220,000	—	—

* Excluding hand woven material. † Figures for wartime production of cotton differ widely.

No less instructive is the degree to which the country was able to satisfy its own requirements at the outbreak of war in 1939.

Commodity	Percentage of local demand met by local production
Sugar	100
Alcohol	100
Cigarettes	100
Cereal milling	99
Lamp glass	99
Boots and shoes	90
Cement	90
Soap	90
Furniture	90
Matches	80
Beer	65
Vegetable oils	60
Cotton cloth	40

Further proof of industrial progress is furnished by the growing export of goods manufactured in Egypt. The table below reflects the strides made in this respect.

EXPORT OF IMPORTANT MANUFACTURED ARTICLES

Articles	Unit of Measurement	Quantities			Value in £E.		
		1922	1928	1938	1922	1928	1938
Asphalt	ton	62	42,571	127,873	248	212,863	261,739
Molasses	,,	20	2,574	23,860	386	8,014	52,470
Phosphates	,,	18,084	168,792	402,756	41,806	148,372	307,183
Salt	,,	186,826	167,701	284,948	36,092	25,329	103,471
Sugar, refined	,,	13,126	225	17,461	332,456	5,440	148,652
Tobacco, manufactured	kg.	—	4,045	47,640	—	5,048	10,337
Cotton seed cake	ton	121,128	157,762	256,163	707,968	528,047	914,002

Because of change of nomenclature of foreign trade in 1930 figures are not always strictly comparable.

Finally, with regard to the effect of industrialisation on the social structure of the Egyptian population, it is true that with a preponderance of agricultural occupations, such as exists in Egyptian economy, an increase in the number of industrial earners by ten thousand cannot materially alter the original ratio of rural to urban workers or the essentially rural character of the population.

The number of those employed in industry proper does not so far exceed 10 per cent. of the total working population. Yet there can be no doubt that even a slow rise in this percentage, which will doubtless occur in accordance with the general trend in the countries concerned, is apt profoundly to affect the whole background, economic as well as political, of the Egyptian scene.

POPULATION FIGURES

Census Year	Population in 1,000	Increase %	Number of Earners in Agriculture: in 1,000	Increase %	As % of Total Working Population	Number of Earners in Industry*: in 1,000	Increase %	As % of Total Working Population
1907	11,287	100	2,440	100	—	281	100	—
1917	12,751	113	2,627	108	55·7	366	130	7·6
1927	14,218	126	3,526	145†	60·3	483	172†	8·2
1937	15,933	141	4,308	177	58	478	170	6·4

* Excluding construction and building.
† This sudden increase may be due to an adjustment of occupational statistics for 1917 when preparing the census results for 1927.

PAID-UP CAPITAL AND DEBENTURES OF COMPANIES WITH FOREIGN CAPITAL

	1907	%	1914	%	1933	%
Total in £E millions .	76·9	100	92·0	100	81·4	100
Of which: in Industry and Commerce . .	11·9	15·3	13·4	14·6	20·8	25·5

TURKEY

The statistics available for Turkey confirm the general picture of an industrialisation inaugurated and maintained by the Government, as it has been depicted in the preceding chapters. Again no exact comparison of the results of the various industrial censuses is possible, but from the existing data conclusions may be reached regarding the expansion achieved within the major branches of production.

The extension of the industrial sector is reflected first of all in the rising imports of capital goods and the high share therein of engines and motors.

IMPORT OF CERTAIN CATEGORIES OF MACHINES INTO TURKEY
(VALUE IN £T 1,000)

	1935	1936	1937	1938
Total import of machines, apparatus, and electrical material	9,243	12,202	15,058	23,013
Including:				
Steam engines	230	494	356	572
Locomotives	136	118	89	154
Tractors	—	4	6	4
Motors, generators, electrical transformers	1,041	1,024	1,541	2,534
Accumulators	235	223	337	376
Machinery for the paper industry	761	2	163	438
Machinery for the textile industry	433	1,306	2,168	2,367
Machinery for the glass, cement, wood, stone, and metal industries	369	1,321	767	967
Agricultural machinery	389	826	1,788	1,536
Pumps	177	246	258	546
Machinery for the foodstuffs industry	1,624	1,856	1,877	3,789

OUTPUT OF CERTAIN INDUSTRIES AND MINES DURING THE PERIOD 1939–44[81]

	Unit	1939	1940	1941	1942	1943	1944
Mines							
Coal	1,000 tons	2,696	3,019	3,020	2,510	3,166	3,560
Lignite	1,000 ,,	102	149	179	268	409	531
Chrome ore*	tons	191,644	182,327	150,129	144,704	—	—
Iron ore	,,	239,040	130,344	59,184	19,044	90,432	—
Copper Ingots	,,	6,732	8,736	10,500	8,256	9,732	10,968
Manganese ore*	,,	519	460	1,360	3,313	—	—
Sulphur*	,,	2,606	1,397	3,408	2,081	—	—
Heavy Industry†							
Coke	,,	—	164,635	—	178,127	182,975	208,000
Benzole for Motors	,,	—	—	—	1,758	1,963	—
Toluol	,,	—	—	—	141	99	—
Cast Iron	,,	—	81,248	—	67,350	57,332	69,000
Steel	,,	—	37,408	—	50,107	42,748	60,780
Pipes	,,	—	3,048	—	4,900	9,188	—
Rolling Mill Products	,,	—	—	—	55,821	71,150	—
Naphthalene, raw	,,	—	—	—	666	306	—
Consumer Goods:							
Cotton Yarn:‡							
Govt. Industries	,,	8,160	9,504	9,024	8,880	9,060	9,608
Private Industries	,,	14,664	18,314	17,376	15,756	16,308	—
Wool Yarn:§							
Govt. Industries	,,	3,144	3,684	3,672	3,504	3,468	3,800
Private Industries	,,	3,384	4,740	4,680	4,248	4,284	—
Paper	,,	8,436	9,540	8,916	8,952	10,308	12,583
Cement	,,	283,620	266,640	276,468	177,528	176,280	—
Sugar	,,	94,508	88,669	87,023	57,309	96,418	89,802
Leather	,,	—	—	1,518	1,814	1,815	—
Leather‖	1,000 sq. decimetres	—	—	1,984	2,280	4,058	—
Boots	1,000 pairs	—	—	847	1,026	1,089	911

* Figures refer to sales.
† Figures refer to the Karabuk Works which started production at the end of 1939.
‡ Includes 16 factories only.
§ Includes 14 factories only.
‖ Enterprises of the Suemer Bank.

The second table on p. 299 gives details of the development of production during the recent war period.

It would prove difficult, however, to demonstrate the progress in local production by an analysis of the import and export figures from the viewpoint of the elimination of foreign imports. Turkish State policy in the sphere of foreign trade has been directed towards the throttling of the import of consumer goods. Hence, a decline in imports does not signify the replacement, total or partial, of foreign goods by local production.

Syria and the Lebanon

An investigation by the former Mandatory Government into the degree of employment in Syria and the Lebanon in the years 1913 and 1937 reveals a development at first sight somewhat startling. According to this study, the number of artisans and workers in 203 trades was 203,927 in 1937, as against 309,525 in 1913. The table below contains particulars of the number of artisans and labourers employed in old and new industries, the distribution by sex, age and religion, the type of work, and form of remuneration.[82]

	Total number of labourers and artisans	Distribution according to sex and age			Place of work		Kind of wages		Religious distribution		
		men	women	children	in factory	at home	daily wages	Payment per piece	Moslems	Christians	Jews
1913:	309,525	142,934	131,651	34,940	101,605	207,920	62,294	247,231	132.397	175,053	2,075
1937: (1). Old industries	170,778	90,065	58,413	22,300	89,063	81,715	54,739	116,039	87,061	82,315	1,402
(2). New industries	33,149	24,007	6,379	2,763	33,149	—	17,710	15,439	15,118	17,448	583
Total 1937	203,927	114,072	64,792	25,063	122,212	81,715	72,449	131,478	102,179	99,763	1,985

A cursory examination of this table, which shows a notable falling-off in the number of the gainfully employed, is apt to lead to wrong conclusions. But upon a scrutiny of the various details it becomes clear that the decline must be put down first and foremost to the deterioration of the older trades and crafts, i.e. the shrinkage of the so-called domestic industries, which comprised the manufacture of silks and textiles, spinning and silkworm breeding. The latter branch counted 179,600 occupied persons in 1913, as compared with 65,800 in 1937. The total figure for 1913 in respect of home workers was 207,920, as against only 81,715 in 1937. The majority of those engaged in homework were women who, with the help of other members of their families, could afford such occupation (spare-time work). Hence, the decline of silk-breeding did not mean for them the loss of a full-time job. They could replace it, at least in part, by other domestic industries or, in coastal towns, by trying to find employment in the modern trades which sprang up there at that juncture. The official authority quoted above indeed points out that the loss of the former source of income caused no distress, because the earnings had been used almost exclusively to provide clothing for the women and children.

The decay of silk-breeding, which received a fatal blow through the invention of artificial silk, coincided with important changes in other textile sectors in Syria and the Lebanon. The introduction of modern machinery and methods of production has greatly enlarged the productive capacity of these as well as of other industries. The figures reproduced in the following tables show a

PRODUCTION OF CERTAIN INDUSTRIAL ARTICLES IN SYRIA AND THE LEBANON

	Unit	1933	1935	1937	1938	1942	1943
Cement	tons	64,500	133,450	249,000	251,000	214,744	151,905
Soap	”	431	3,610	2,999	2,903	4,600	7,800
Biscuits	”	64	100	265	400	40	100
Bread	”	480	821	1,205	1,650	—	—
Flour	”	53,200	141,500	167,000	138,000	245,400	288,000
Tanned hides	pieces	106,553	194,900	379,880	297,705	525,000	995,000
Socks and stockings	doz.	118,000	230,000	286,700	367,700	676,000	524,000

IMPORTS OF FUEL INTO SYRIA, 1925–1938

Year	Coal, Coke and Briquettes (in tons)	Crude oil (in tons)
1925	49,282	1,990
1930	80,106	8,521
1935	98,881	23,640
1936	110,721	21,907
1937	139,393	17,396
1938	141,519	19,626

IMPORTS OF CERTAIN INDUSTRIAL MACHINERY INTO SYRIA AND THE LEBANON

In tons

Kind of Machinery and apparatus	1934	1935	1936	1937	1938
Total import of Machinery apparatus and electrical material .	2094·4	3830·7	4205·6	5023·4	4747
Including:					
Boilers* . . .	64·7	26·9	40·1	42·3	199·9
Textile and parts† .	123·4	285·5	599·8	1208·4	785·2
Pumps‡ . . .	22·4	42·2	49·0	79·8	66·4
Generators and transformers . .	57·5	121	150·3	189·9	169·3
Motors . . .	100·4	270·8	190·8	209·5	229·9

* Figures for the years 1936, 1937, 1938 include also superheaters and steam accumulators.
† Figures compiled from all items pertaining to textile machinery and their parts.
‡ Excluding agricultural pumps.

steady rise up to the Second World War in the imports of machinery and fuel as well as in the production of important industrial commodities. The political situation of Syria and the Lebanon during the Second World War prevented the further expansion of industrial production witnessed in Egypt and Palestine.

PALESTINE

Conditions of industrial production in Palestine during the inter-war period are characterised by rapid mechanisation, the formation of a modern worker class, the influx of entrepreneurs, trained specialists and experts, and the industrial processing of imported raw materials. Two trends can be distinguished during this period. Whereas the pace of industrialisation was fairly moderate up to 1933, it has been greatly accelerated since that year. The industrial plants have grown, as regards both equipment and size. This development has been made possible by the emergence of a large local demand of hitherto unknown proportions.

An analysis of the modern economic development of Palestine cannot be made without an adequate appraisal of the fundamental features of this economy, viz. Jewish immigration and the impetus derived therefrom, in industry particularly, but also in agriculture. Nowhere in the Orient has there been so large an influx of Western elements animated by the desire to invest their new country with the superior forms and modes of economic and social existence. Despite the achievements of the "return to the land" movement, prompted by reasons of national regeneration, the industrial callings have remained the chief domain of Jewish activity. It is true that, compared even with young industrial countries overseas, the total figure of those gainfully employed in industry is not imposing, its recent expansion during the war notwithstanding. But the pace of this industrial development is probably unique, as is borne out by the table below.

GROWTH OF JEWISH INDUSTRY[83]
(Excluding Handicrafts)

	1925	1926	1930	1933	1937	1943
Establishments .	536	583	617	970	1,556	2,120
Personnel (owners and workers) .	4,894	5,711	6,777	14,419	21,964	45,049
Annual output £P	—	—	1,653,733	4,630,000	7,891,940	36,287,000
Capital . .	54,000	94,968	1,221,395	5,097,000	11,063,970	20,523,000
Horsepower .	261	613	3,042	49,821	104,866	—

The number of establishments and of those employed therein has multiplied many times, as has the annual output. All this testifies to unusual powers of adjustment and reconstruction both as regards the human material and as far as general economic factors are concerned. This development is the more remarkable if it is remembered that Jewish industry in Palestine had to forego the protection usually accorded to youthful industries and was partly exposed to the disadvantages involved in the Open Door Clause embodied in Article 18 of the Mandate. A remarkable illustration is to be found in the import and export statistics for the peak years 1934 and 1935 reproduced on p. 304. The countries listed in the following table exploited this situation to the utmost, to the detriment of Palestine's industry.

It therefore seems justifiable to expect that with the establishment of a competitive basis the industrial sector of Jewish economy, which revealed its great power of adaptability during the Second World War, will be able to hold its own.

Country	1934		1935	
	Imports to Palestine	Exports from Palestine	Imports to Palestine	Exports from Palestine
	£P.	£P.	£P.	£P.
Rumania . .	953,343	60,485	1,208,204	92,219
Yugoslavia . .	174,440	2,186	201,285	12,241
Hungary . .	115,410	920	202,825	2,107
Bulgaria . .	148,818	4,063	206,382	6,271
Austria . .	348,157	6,532	356,098	10,426
Japan . .	593,552	—	645,695	10,707

Arab industry in Palestine has likewise made remarkable strides, as can be seen from the following table.

ARAB ESTABLISHMENTS REGISTERED BY THE DEPARTMENT OF HEALTH

	1921	1935	1939
Bakeries	151	205	295
Flour and corn mills . .	45	107	141
Aerated water factories .	7	13	17
Ice factories	4	11	19
Oil mills and stores . .	62	133	91
Establishments employing power-driven machinery .	7	313	541
Soap factories . . .	41	14	30

Approximately 4,000 Arabs were employed in Arab factories and workshops in 1939. A census of industry taken in 1943 showed that 8,838 Arabs were so employed, of whom more than fifty per cent. were of the category of "competent tradesmen requiring very little supervision", or higher categories.

The output of Arab and other non-Jewish enterprises (other than concessions) enumerated in the census of industry amounted to £P1,545,000 *gross* in 1939 and to £P5,658,000 *gross* in 1942. The corresponding *net* output figures were £P313,000 in 1939 and £P1,725,000 in 1942.

CHAPTER XXVII

PRESENT-DAY PROBLEMS OF INDUSTRIALISATION IN THE MIDDLE EAST

Industrialisation and National Income

It is no wonder that such a far-reaching transformation as that involved in the industrialisation of an agrarian country, affecting as it does all classes of the population and all phases of the production process, should cause from time to time serious doubts and reflections. Why this expansion of productive capacity, this investment of vast sums of capital in plant and machinery, at a time when, given a sensible adjustment of the world's economic relations, it would seem a simple matter to meet essential needs at cheap prices by imports from abroad? Does the industrial development in the new States of Europe after 1918 not preach the utmost precaution in the creation of new economic interests which may multiply the conflicting issues?

To answer this question we shall leave out of account arguments based on strategical and defensive issues in which economic considerations usually give way before questions of national interests. Yet there remain a number of reasons which clamour for industrialisation as a means for the solution of the problems connected with population growth and standard of living in Oriental countries. The absorption of the rapidly increasing surplus population in these countries can—failing the execution of agrarian development schemes—be effected in the requisite measure and space of time solely by the creation of new employment in industry and related occupations. The same holds good for the rise in the standard of living. A high national income *per capita* of the population always coincides with an occupational structure in which a large percentage of the working population is engaged in manufacturing and intermediary services—the so-called secondary and tertiary callings. On the other hand, in countries where the overwhelming majority of the population is engaged in agriculture, i.e. "primary industries", the average national income *per capita* is very low.

The absorptive capacity of agriculture is thus subject to different laws from that of industry. One of the main reasons is the relatively small opportunity for increasing the production of energy-giving agricultural food items. The present consumption of the Oriental masses, low as it is, satisfies their needs as regards cereals and pulses. An increase in the output of such staple products would lead to no appreciable rise in the standard of nutrition; on the other hand, the scope for improvement in the standard of living in respect of housing, habits of dress, care of health and education, and so forth is extraordinarily large, and consequently offers practically unlimited possibilities for industrial development. Take the case of beds, which in Oriental villages are practically non-existent, as the peasant sleeps on reed mats on the floor. The equipment of the peasants' homes with beds would create employment for numerous bedstead factories for many years to come, involving as it would the production of many millions of bedsteads. The same applies to tables, chairs and other household goods, to glass windows, many installation accessories, etc., which are even today lacking in most of the dwellings of the fellahin. A systematic spread of instruction and establishment of educational institutions would call for the production of paper and writing utensils, the printing of school books, and the construction of school buildings with their equipment. An analogous case is to be seen in the introduction of health services, medicines and hospitals. In short, given even a modest rise in the standard of living of the peasant population in the direction of an approach to European conditions, there would be room for an increase in industrial production in Oriental countries running into hundreds of millions of pounds.[84] A clue to these possibilities is provided by a study of the import figures. Whereas the figure of imports per head of the population in Oriental countries in the course of the last century has been multiplied, it still amounts but to a fraction of the import figure in agrarian countries in Europe, where the development of economic resources has reached a higher stage. Lands like Hungary and Italy, but also countries with a semi-capitalistic structure like Algeria and Palestine, can boast a much larger import volume per head of the population. The same relation is revealed by a comparison of the average figures for the national income of the population (before the Second World War) where we find the large Asiatic and our Middle Eastern countries occupying the lowest place: about £4 per head per annum in India, £12 in Egypt, £20 in Turkey, £26 in Palestine (average for the whole population) as against £80–120 in Western industrial countries. Industrialisation, which represents the fullest exploitation of the forces of nature by the ingenuity of man for the purpose of goods production, is at the same time the principal instrument for the raising of the real income of backward peoples.

IMPORTS PER HEAD OF THE POPULATION

(1) Egypt	£
1800	0·1
1836	0·7
1884	0·1
1907	2·3
1928	3·5
1938	2·2

Per Capita IMPORTS IN 1928 AND 1936 (IN POUNDS STERLING).

	1928	1936
(1) Predominantly Agrarian Countries		
Hungary	5·2	1·8
Italy	5·9	2·0
Latvia	6·6	3·6
Algeria	6·7	5·2
Palestine	8·5	9·6
(2) Industrial countries		
Great Britain and Northern Ireland	24·1	16·6
Belgium (including Luxemburg)	22·7	16·5
Switzerland	26·7	18·2
Sweden	15·7	13·3
Netherlands	29·5	15·4

Still more enlightening is a study of consumption of some manufactured goods per head of the population. It is found that countries with developed industrial consumption and production show a substantial national income per head many times in excess of that for countries with a limited industrial sector.[85]

CONSUMPTION OF INDUSTRIAL GOODS AND NATIONAL INCOME (PRE-WAR FIGURES, MOSTLY 1937.)

Consumption of various Industrial goods	Western Europe	Czecho-Slovakia	Poland	Egypt	Turkey	Palestine
Cotton goods kg	8	4·2	2·3	2	—	3·3
Paper kg	30	13·9	5·1	5·3	2	14·5
Soap kg	6	2·5	1·5	2·7	—	7·6
Sugar kg	32	21	12·5	9·6	5·3	18·3
Wireless sets (number of licences per 1,000 persons)	120	69	25	4·3	2	21·6
National Income* *per capita* (£)	80–120	30	18	12	19	26†

* Differences of purchasing power have not been allowed for.

† Jews, 44.

The raising of national prosperity in the world of the Middle East and the elimination of social distress is possible only by increasing goods production and particularly that of industrial commodities provided all classes share in the proceeds of this development.

The Machine and Oriental Society

Among the sociological aspects of industrialisation in Oriental countries there is one that needs to be specially stressed, namely, the effect which the introduction of machinery has had on the old-established social interrelationships. The introduction of the machine was like the grafting of a new strain on the Oriental stock. Obviously the machine brought to light an entirely new range of economic possibilities and revolutionised the material and technical character of production; but its influence on the social fabric was of no less importance.

In a society for which the phrase was coined: "Hurry is the Devil's work" the appearance of a means of production whose very nature is speed and movement can only be regarded as something alien and disintegrating. It is true that in Europe also the machine caused violent upheavals both in the structure of society and in the production process; but on the whole—thanks to the fact that the new production methods were evolved gradually and owing to the presence of a producer-class who worked at their continued improvement on the spot—its introduction there constituted almost one continuous process. In the Orient, on the other hand, the machine was ushered in without warning, without any such transitional or probationary period; hence it remained for the mass of society a foreign element which was sustained by the native economic mentality only after much reluctance.

The introduction of machinery compels the Oriental to adapt himself to a new, a dynamic way of life which he, like all members of a primitive society, must at first find strange and difficult. The ceaseless activity of this means of production, the persistence of its automatic action which knows no natural pauses such as are dictated by day and night, by fatigue in human beings, and the danger involved in any rash or careless handling of this mysterious apparatus for the exploitation of the tamed forces of nature, all this upsets his measure of time, his contemplativeness, and burdens him with an enforced alertness and presence of mind completely out of harmony with his previous specific mentality. A process of adaptation and transformation is set in motion on the psychic plane which tends to upset the common code of social reaction based largely on the indigenous sense of time, and the Oriental life rhythm. Once we come to calculate, for instance, the expenditure of time in respect of machine production we shall no longer be inclined to disregard the value of the hours spent in the traditional pre-machine production process, as is commonly done in the Orient. Whoever can earn his livelihood by working eight hours a day thanks to the increased productivity of machine work will finally turn aside from an employment which keeps him occupied for ten or twelve hours.

To what a far-reaching extent modern rationalisation of labour methods came to interfere with established practice can be seen, for instance, from the following: Up to the end of the last World War the working day in Arab countries was measured by the rising and setting of the sun. Consequently it was very much longer in summer than in winter, though the daily wage was the same. The Arab clock then in use was based on the periodical motion of the sun. Not until the sun sank below the horizon was the worker entitled to leave his post. The introduction of the mechanical clock and other modern devices into the management of work has here also eliminated the traditional ties between the human working process and the forces of nature.

Thus, apart from appreciating the economic effects of machine production already described above—the cheapening of living through mass production and far-reaching changes in the social and economic structure—we must also not underestimate the reactions produced in the mental outlook of the individual.

Social and Political Effects of Industrialisation

After the First World War the traditional indifference as regards length of working day and general working conditions gradually gave place to a changed attitude. New social and political ideas combined with the influence of trade union tendencies brought about a slow improvement in the position of the workers, the most important among these being the reduction in the working day.

These social movements, however, did not succeed in making headway in the usual European sense; there were no leaders independent of the Government and the entrepreneur class, which were often both represented by the same spokesmen. Moreover, the possibilities of any organisational consolidation of left or revolutionary currents remained very limited. In Turkey the formation of trade unions was prohibited by law. In Syria and the Lebanon the authorities have shown themselves strongly opposed to labour organisation either by dissolving already existing unions on the least provocation or by refusing to authorise the establishment of new ones.[86] In Egypt legal recognition of the workers' right to form trade unions was first granted in July, 1942. But these unions are scarcely more than a fiction. Apart from Palestine the general picture is that workers' movements were simply connived at and any move towards a more aggressive attitude was frowned upon. During the period between the two World Wars the weak class-feeling of the native worker was given little incentive to develop; the Governments endeavoured to protect the wage earners from the crudest form of exploitation by elementary socio-political measures such as regulations against child-labour, employment of pregnant women, compensation for injuries in certain industries. In many cases, however, such measures remained a dead letter.

In view of the wretched position of the fellah the acceptance of employment in the new industrial concerns represented, as a rule, a rise in economic status; there was none of that urge which in Europe, during the Industrial Revolution and later, goaded the uprooted proletariat into the radical camp. Moreover, the native governments, learning from the course of developments in Europe, besides the measures of preventive legislation already mentioned, tended to carry out others of a more positive nature also. Thus, in a number of countries we find arrangements for the welfare of the workers made either by the Government or the industrial undertakings themselves (factory settlements, educational and health facilities) such as can be sought for in vain in the early period of industrialisation in the West. The real test of the stability of the social structure in the century of industrialisation in the Middle East will come, however, only when the number of industrial workers, now only 5 to 10 per cent. of the total working population, shall have risen to several times this proportion.

Thus, our study of the transformation of industrial production ends by leading us once more to a consideration of the rôle of the State in this process. The preponderance of the State and State initiative in the economic and social reconstruction of the Middle East of today was established under a constellation of factors such as no other period had experienced. Witness the coincidence of the following circumstances:

(a) The course of economic activity tends in modern society to veer more and more away from the classical laws of the free market and to be influenced to an increasing extent by intervention on the part of the State and the dominating social groups. The idea of an economic planning process, which would have appeared absurd to most economic thinkers of the eighteenth and nineteenth centuries, today has come into its own both in theory and practice. The execution of such plans, however, everywhere needs the support of a powerful State authority.

(*b*) The rapid development of modern technique and its utilisation for the perfecting of the means of production and transport confers on those who possess these means such vast power in and over society that the State is compelled, if only for reasons of self-preservation, to place this province of perfected technique to a large extent under its own rule. The development of communications in particular made possible by the use of modern power appliances considerably enhanced the omnipotence of the State in Middle Eastern countries, where important travel and transport services have become regular State functions.

(*c*) An alliance between State authority and the bourgeoisie, such as played so decisive a rôle in the development of modern industrial capitalism in the West, was not possible in Oriental society, which lacked every precondition for it. The identity of interests on the part of the captains of the State and the feudal classes in the Orient brought about a sterilisation of industrial activity in the towns; these classes showed indifference, if not actual hostility, to any expansion of industrial production. Thus, in the Oriental territories the necessity arose for the State to take over the functions of industrialisation, if it did not wish to leave the initiative in the hands of foreign capitalist groups and to bear the brunt of the resultant political consequences. The case of Palestine, where the new industry was established without the aid or intervention either of the State or of foreign interests, is unique; here the industrial sector is transplanted from without, through the new immigrants who became permanent residents in their new homeland.

(*d*) The political constitution of Oriental society before the collapse of the Ottoman Empire was based on the "vertical" stratification of the population into religious and national communities. This structure was in the past of great importance for the economic framework of the Oriental State and largely responsible for its deficiencies. The new State could safeguard the development of a new economy only by the elimination of the various conflicting interests or their subjection to the will of the State. The persistent emphasis laid on the priority of national over individual and group interests such as is revealed in every official appeal to the masses aims at the same time at the further strengthening of State authority.

It is doubtful, however, whether the effect of the Second World War will not be to cause a setback in these trends. Protracted wars with their vast output of emergency legislation are not favourable to State authority, particularly in Oriental regions. The final judgment on the stability of the newly-gained position of the State must, therefore, be postponed until the transition period is over.

TURKISH RAILWAYS BEFORE WORLD WAR I

CHAPTER XXVIII

CHANGES IN THE SYSTEM OF COMMUNICATIONS

Among the changes in the Oriental world which affect the existing structure of economy and society in the most radical fashion are those brought about by the development of the communication system. Far quicker than any other changes, they open up new aspects of political and social life and inaugurate a new period in the social history of the Middle East, the distinctive feature of which is the shrinkage of distances. Nothing can better serve to illustrate this contraction of the Oriental space than a few examples. Only fifty years ago the expenditure of time and effort needed to cover even relatively small distances was disproportionately great. The journey from Baghdad to the Mediterranean coast had to be made by camel, and took a fortnight; today it is covered in a comfortable Pullman car in 15 to 18 hours. Even the short journey by coach from the harbour town of Jaffa to Jerusalem took an entire day; the opening of the railway reduced this to 3–4 hours; whilst it is now possible by car to cover this distance in an hour. The position is similar as regards most of the principal travel routes in the Orient. Even without taking air-travel into account, the towns in Oriental countries are today distant from one another by as many hours as formerly they were by days.

Wherein lies the economic importance of the changes in communications? First of all in the immediate repercussions of the acceleration of transport and the opening-up of new areas formerly closed. These repercussions, some of which we have already mentioned when dealing with the changes in the agrarian sphere and industrialisation, consist first of all in the extension of the market, i.e. of the possibilities of sale and purchase as they affect all those goods rendered marketable or districts opened up by the new means of communication. The importance of these new marketing opportunities can scarcely be overrated as far as the individual producer is concerned. The peasant who had hitherto made but a bare existence out of his farm, which he cultivated in order to serve his own domestic needs, finds himself provided with a new basis for his work as a result of the possibilities of marketing his surplus crop and, what is more, of growing new commercial crops and staple products; he handles ready money which allows him to extend his farm, intensify his methods and thus raise his standard of living. At the same time he comes into closer contact with town life, and his whole outlook and style of living are influenced and changed by personal impressions and stimuli.

Side by side with these influences, chiefly noticeable in the rural sphere of production and consumption, we can observe similar tendencies in the towns. Modern mass production is closely bound up with favourable transport facilities, whether it is a question of the mass production of consumer goods or of the conveyance or exploitation of the country's natural resources (mineral ores and oils) whose costs must not be adversely affected by high transport rates. Likewise another prerequisite, the delivery of larger machine-units, boilers, etc., could be realised only with the appearance of means of conveyance with ample cargo space.

But with these effects the significance of the introduction of modern means of communication is by no means exhausted. Over and above the immediate economic results these new facilities have completely regrouped the Middle East both politically and physically, giving it new centres of gravity and all the advantages deriving from easy access. Territories under provincial or local rule existing side by side, with loose contacts or even none at all, become welded together by the construction of modern road and railway systems. Regions hostile in the past to all ideas of progress become part of the modern world, particularly those backward areas where, owing to their isolation from the outside world, obsolete political, social, and economic forms and conditions had survived up to quite recent times.

Traditional Means of Communication in the Middle East and Their Technical Peculiarities

The peculiar form taken by the traditional means of communication in the Middle East is largely due to the nature of the local conditions, which determined both the choice of beasts of burden and the form of the vehicles in use.

The main routes which were travelled over in the wide spaces of the Orient were usually deficient in water, and often for long distances quite waterless. The only animal able to cover such stretches and at the same time carry a full load of heavy goods was the camel, which can do without water for days on end. Other animals such as the mule and the horse could be used only for short journeys, and then only where watering facilities were available at frequent intervals. The superiority of the camel over all other means of transport prevented the development (on the few routes which traverse these countries) of any vehicular traffic worth mentioning. For centuries past inland transport has been the monopoly of the camel caravans.[87]

Traffic on the waterways, which was not handicapped by the obstacles met with on the land routes, was likewise remarkable for the degree to which the means of transport were adapted to the natural conditions. Thus, in addition to the primitive skiffs, ferry-boats and wooden boxes, would be noticed certain specific water craft such as *kelek*, *guffa*, and *muhele*, particularly on the rivers of Mesopotamia. Some brief details of these may be of interest. The *kelek* is a raft or float constructed of inflated goat-skins laid next to each other beneath a framework of wooden poles. This floating bed is covered with bundles of reeds or wooden planks which make a platform for the conveyance of goods or passengers. At one end of the skin-float paddles are fixed for steering. The larger rafts, for which 200 to 300 skins are used, can bear a platform of 50 square metres, accommodating 10 to 15 persons and corresponding loads of merchandise. The bulk of the goods traffic from northern Mesopotamia to Baghdad and the Gulf was conveyed in these *keleks*.

The *guffa* is a vessel in the shape of a flattened bird's nest or basket, made from the stripped leaves of the date palm or of reeds and smeared with pitch. The diameter of a *guffa* is often as much as 3½ metres and the load carried may reach 12 tons.

Special types of sailing boats are likewise in use, particularly on the rivers of Mesopotamia, for the transport of grain. The chief of these is a boat known as *muhele*, up to 18 metres in length, with a carrying capacity that may reach 120 tons. The sailing vessels on the Nile called *dahabiye* have also a considerable cargo capacity; they are fitted with a collapsible mast in view of the many bridges which cross the canals.

How firmly these means of transport have become established in Oriental countries is proved by the fact that they are functioning to a large extent even today, though meanwhile, in some cases for several decades, modern more efficient means of transport have come to take their place or share the goods traffic with them. It must not be overlooked, however, that the volume of mecrhandise carried in former times amounted to but a fraction of the quantities transported on the principal routes today.

The slow progress of modern means of communication in the

East, at least up to the end of the nineteenth century, was not due to technical difficulties alone. The mental attitude of the Oriental States and their rulers, perhaps not without reason, did not incline them to any rapid opening-up of their territories by means of European methods of communication, which more than anything else might be instrumental in causing breaches through which not only technical innovations, but also new ideas and norms in respect of the State and political life, might intrude. Only in one case did this unwelcoming attitude on the part of Government give way in favour of a modern communication project, viz. that of the Hejaz railway.

One of the biggest tasks in the way of transport in these lands was the annual conveyance of pilgrims to the Holy Places of Arabia. It was only natural, therefore, that for the better performance of this task, which with the constant increase in the army of pilgrims became increasingly difficult, recourse should be had to the new methods. It is probable that military considerations contributed to bring about a decision in favour of this ambitious enterprise. But from the very first, when the construction of this railway which was to solve these problems was still under way, the maintenance of religious tradition was strictly insisted upon, as was manifest not only in the ban on the employment of non-Moslem workers on the last section of the line, but also in the form in which the work was financed. The decision to construct the railway was taken in 1897, the costs being defrayed for the most part by the Moslem world, to which an appeal was made emphasising the religious importance of the railway. To what an extent the idea of the line's religious character had taken root is shown by the fact that even after the First World War, despite the vast changes in the political map of the Middle East, the Great Powers in repeated declarations and negotiations recognised the consequences arising from the railway's religious purpose. In the Bompard Declaration of January 27, 1923, the representatives of the French and British Governments, as mandatory Powers for Syria, Palestine and Transjordan, put on record their desire to recognise the religious character of the Hejaz Railway, and the establishment of an advisory council of Moslem members.[88] In 1927 Ibn Saud as representative of the Moslem community as a whole appealed to Great Britain and France for the complete reconstruction of the line and an appropriate subsidy for the repair of the Hejaz stretch.

At the Moslem Congress in Jerusalem in 1931, the matter of the Hejaz Railway was again raised. The resolutions adopted at the Congress reaffirm the Moslem claims regarding the property rights of the Moslem community in the railway as a whole. A similar note was struck by the manifesto of the Syrian Committee for the Defence of the Hejaz Railway, issued on October 21st, 1931. The plan for the railway, which was to link up the desert country of Arabia with the Syrian and Anatolian border districts, was both in motive and method of financing a commercial undertaking, though only to a qualified extent. But it shared this character with a number of other important traffic routes in Oriental lands. It is no exaggeration to say that the majority of the railway lines in Asiatic Turkey were originally laid from motives not purely economic. Their construction was undertaken because the builders were desirous of obtaining by this means—irrespective of the guarantees regarding revenue given by the Ottoman State—concessions for the exploitation of mineral resources or agricultural development, and as compared with these the yield from the railways themselves was of lesser importance. With all their value as communication factors, the railways were also means to other ends: they served the desire for expansion and power on the part of their promoters. Not only does the history of their conception testify to the discrepancy of interests between the country they were intended to serve and the Powers who initiated their construction, but also the actual management of the railways was and usually remained a domain of foreign influence, tending at times to undermine the sovereign rights of the State. Even decisions affecting the directions of the track were to a large extent out of the hands of the Ottoman State. That State's meagre capital resources enabled the foreign Powers for a long time to have a controlling hand over the extension of the railway system of the Empire, thus preventing any adjustment of its national and economic interests.

As a result, up the outbreak of the First World War we find in the Middle East but slight traces of the new achievements in the field of communications or of the density of traffic already attained at that period in Western countries. Modern railways and good roads were very few. The political régime eyed with little sympathy the foreign travellers who wished to become acquainted with these regions. Nor did the nature of the countryside in these parts tend to attract any large travelling public. Inhospitable tracts of steppe and desert, wild, trackless mountains, on the one hand, lack of security and of modern travelling amenities (hotel accommodation, comfortable and rapid means of conveyance), particularly indispensable in the case of protracted journeys on the other, have with few exceptions practically ruled out these districts from the list of tourist countries.

The Opening up of the Orient after the First World War

The collapse of the Ottoman Empire and its division into a number of independent countries interested to see their possessions opened up to international traffic created the political and administrative prerequisites for a regional development of communications in the modern East. In most of these countries the principal branches of the communications system, particularly the railway concession companies, were taken over by the new Governments. Moreover, the progress made in the technique of transport after the First World War resulted in the rapid introduction into the Orient of modern means of passenger and goods transport, such as the motor-car and the aeroplane, and in the construction of a widespread net of roads and railways.

Hand in hand with these innovations came also a growing demand for them on the part of the populations, and consequently an enormous increase in the frequency of travel between non-Oriental countries and the East. Foreign visitors now had for the first time the opportunity to visit Oriental countries in relative comfort and without danger. Lastly, the growth of population and the general rise in the standard of living led to a vast increase and intensification in the movement of merchandise to and from the Middle East countries.

In the use made of the various means of communication by these young countries there are considerable differences. As regards railways the most outstanding developments have occurred principally in one country, Turkey, where with great energy and within a short space of time an extensive building programme has been carried out. The Turkish railway system has been enlarged by 2,630 km., now covering 7000 km. The great international rail connection between Europe and the Persian Gulf, whose last link, known as the Baghdad Railway, played so important a rôle in international Eastern policy before the War, has now materialised, though in a different form from that envisaged by its initiators. Instead of a German-controlled railway line joining Constantinople through western Anatolia via Mosul with Baghdad and Koweit on the Persian Gulf, a railway project was carried out with the new capital of Turkey, Ankara, as its centre. The line cuts straight through Anatolia and links up with the original track in the Taurus, which it follows across the Turkish border to Syria and Iraq.

Since the completion of the connection in Northern Iraq in 1940 the whole stretch from Western Europe to the Persian Gulf can be covered by rail.

Of the new Turkish railways this line running from Ankara to the south is for the time being the only one serving international traffic. The other branches of the newly-constructed system, which today traverse Anatolia in all directions, were built in the first instance to serve Turkey's own inland traffic requirements, so that the various parts of the country hitherto isolated from each other could be closely linked up in accordance with strategic and economic considerations. The chief progress in the construction of the new Turkish railway system occurred in the mid-thirties. Two important railway lines, the so-called "Coal Way" and "Copper Way", were completed during these years. The "Coal Way", as the stretch from Irmak on the Ankara–Sivas line to Filyos in the neighbourhood of the great coal basin of Zonguldak on the Black Sea is called, makes it possible to transport Turkish coal from the country's production area to the interior of Anatolia. The "Copper Way", which enables the copper deposits at Maden–Ergana to be developed on an economic basis, links the towns of Malatya and Diyarbekir in the south-east. With the opening of this line Turkey can proceed to exploit her rich mineral resources, and probably also in the near future begin exporting copper. The development of the Anatolian railway network is being carried on systematically in accordance with the country's economic and strategic needs. The underlying idea is first to link up the towns in the interior by means of a circular track and then to extend this inner ring by branch lines to the Black Sea and the Sea of Marmora in the north, to the Aegean in the West, to the Mediterranean and the Iraqi railway system on the south, and to the eastern provinces and the Iranian junction lines on the east.

In nearly all Middle Eastern countries railway traffic has assumed great importance since the First World War. In Palestine the railway from Kantara on the Suez Canal to Haifa, constructed during the war, coupled with the new network of roads, converted localities hitherto isolated from traffic and market possibilities into a uniform economic region. In Iran the construction of the great North-South railway connecting the Caspian Sea with the Persian Gulf is of the greatest value for the economic and political reconstruction of this country, which has suffered more than all other parts of the Middle East from the inaccessibility of its territory, traversed as it is in all directions by high mountain ranges and other obstacles to traffic. In Iraq the railway (built as in Palestine during the First World War) connecting the centre with Basra in the south was later continued northwards and in recent years has been linked up with the Syrian and Turkish railway systems. In the Lebanon the missing section on the coastal route Tripolis–Beirut–Acre was built during the Second World War.

Still more far-reaching in view of its effect on the personal living conditions of the Oriental population was the introduction of the motor-car. Two results of this are specially conspicuous: first, the extraordinary acceleration of transport seen in local traffic between town and town and between village and town, and secondly the opening-up of the desert and steppe country. For the inhabitants of the steppe and desert zones the inaccessibility and impassableness of their world was equivalent to their independence and sovereignty over these areas. On the day when the motor-car began to conquer the desert the ancient rights of these social groups were doomed. Today the motor-car with the aeroplane is the chief key to the rule of the desert, to the control and partition of this practically boundless area which for the Beduin was the very element of life.

Apart from this inner political function the motor-car plays an important economic rôle in the development of the Orient by creating regular overland connections between the coastal countries and the States situated beyond the desert and steppe. The most important of these inter-State routes are: Damascus–Baghdad–Teheran, Aleppo–Der Ez Zor, Mosul–Rowanduz–Tabriz, Jerusalem (Haifa)–Amman–Baghdad, Caspian Sea–Teheran–Bushire (Persian Gulf). Mention must also be made of the lines Cairo–Suez (Sinai)–Jerusalem and the famous old trade route Trabzon (Black Sea)–Erzurum–Tabriz–Teheran, now enjoying a fresh lease of life. The growth of motor traffic may be seen from the table showing the number of cars in relation to the population. As the summary clearly indicates, the use made of the motor-car as a means of communication is gradually approaching that in European countries.

Lastly, attention must be drawn to the development of the latest means of communication with which modern scientific research has provided us for conveying passengers, goods and news, the aeroplane. The central geographical position of the countries situated on the Eastern Mediterranean and their political ties with European Powers have made them also important junctions in inter-continental air-traffic between Europe, India, Eastern Asia and Australia. With the development of long-distance traffic the number of airlines with termini in Egypt, Palestine, Syria and Iraq (countries which in their turn have been brought within the orbit of international air traffic) has considerably increased. In addition to British, Dutch and French lines plying on these routes there were also up to before the outbreak of the Second World War inter-continental Polish and Italian lines. At the same time we find in these countries noteworthy beginnings of inland air-traffic. All these tendencies point to a marked expansion of air-traffic crossing the Orient in the post-war period.

The traffic policy of the young Oriental countries, whether it concerns the development of railways, roads, or air services, reveals the changed attitude on the part of the State to this important instrument of home and foreign policy. The State, in marked contrast to its practice before the First World War, has either itself taken in hand the execution of new traffic plans or, by constructing networks of roads, airports, etc., given invaluable encouragement to the development of communications. In co-operation with foreign Powers large-scale traffic enterprises are continually being launched, whose importance for the future economic and political fate of these countries can scarcely be foreseen today.

TURKISH RAILWAYS TODAY

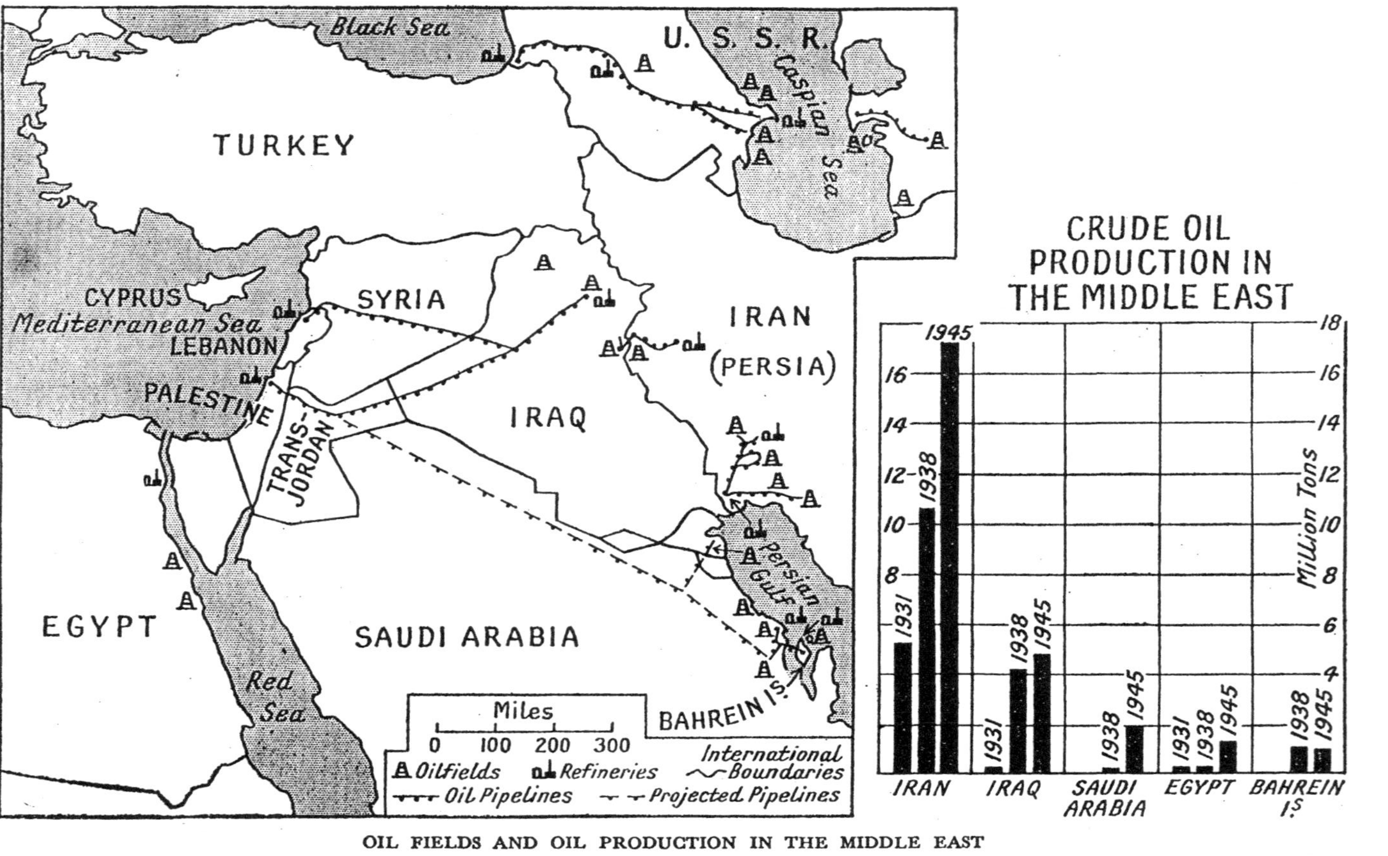

OIL FIELDS AND OIL PRODUCTION IN THE MIDDLE EAST

PART FOUR

PROBLEMS AND ASPECTS OF A CHANGING SOCIETY

CHAPTER XXIX

THE ISLAMIC SOCIETY

In the first three parts of this book we have endeavoured to show how under the influence of modern ideas and events the Oriental State, the stationary agrarian economy and the method of production of goods in Oriental lands are being transformed. The sociological aspects of the changing Middle East, although frequently touched upon in these chapters, have not been given a central place. Some of these aspects, however, are so significant in themselves as to deserve a separate appraisal. Among these are such questions as the special nature of Moslem society, its attitude towards foreigners, slavery, the structure of the Oriental town, the influence of religious tradition on the economic qualifications of the society, the standard of living in Oriental lands, and the position of the Nomad in the modern East. The chapters which follow are devoted to these subjects.

Historical Aspects

A study of the foundations of Islamic society cannot ignore the various meanings of the term "Islam", which may equally well signify a religion, a community, a State idea or an entire congeries of peoples. We use the word here to represent not only a system of religious elements or religious and political doctrines but, above all, that civilisation which, starting from Hither Asia, has created in the countries within its sphere a common culture and philosophy of life based on a uniform creed and a framework of ideas, political, social and State, derived therefrom. Hence the word "Islam" is to be understood in these pages as signifying a general conformity of individual feeling engendered by the all-embracing religious routine of living and enhanced by other features such as the Arabic script and in many countries the Arabic language also. All these elements taken collectively and in their vast spatial extent and spiritual power, elements non-existent in the first centuries of the spread of Islam, constitute today the substance of the great Islamic society. The existence of such a society stretching over lands and seas and based on a tradition embracing all spheres of life, religious, legal and political, forms the starting-point of the present investigation.

In the first centuries of Islam its teachings did not influence the state of society in the countries brought within its fold. The population of Arabia, apart from the urban settlements, was made up of a number of warlike tribes and groups held together by loose ties. These tribes were indifferent to religious ideas. Their social structure was determined by the clan as a unit. The patriarchal way of living among the Beduin tribes revolved, as in all primitive communities, round the family or clan. The individual is conscious of himself as a member of a certain family or clan, behind which background his separate ego and its claims and feelings completely recede.

The spiritual world of the clan member was conditioned by the concepts and forms which, by virtue of old tradition, regulated the life of the tribal society and its relations with the outside world. The individual was hemmed in both in his mental and emotional world; his world of ideas was that of his group. The collective ideas of the clan are accepted by the individual member unquestioningly as his own; his views are the views of the clan to which he belongs, and vice versa. The sinologist R. Wilhelm, in his work on the economic psychology of the Chinese,[1] quotes an anecdote which is characteristic of similar conditions in the Chinese agrarian society. Asked how long he had lived in the neighbourhood, a peasant replied: "Three hundred years; then we arrived in this district from the south".

The mental reaction produced in the peasant mind by such a question is not confined to Chinese conditions alone; it may be found wherever, as in primitive societies, the individual claims no status as such, but regards himself merely as a member of the family, the clan or the tribe. In contrast to the anarchic, loose society of the modern Occident based on voluntary association, the Arab *societas* as preserved intact in the old tribal groupings is a natural development in which the individual is automatically incorporated and is allowed to function solely as a part of such society. Herein lies the deep-rooted reason for the severe persecution of those who dared to interfere with this order from without and to attack and destroy the individual who was under the legal protection of his tribe. It is not the individual's crime that is avenged by the punishment of the individual culprit, but the revenge applies collectively. The joint intervention of the tribe on behalf of its attacked member, whether by blood revenge or its communally financed redemption by the payment of blood money, was the logical consequence of this social conception. It alone, under the conditions of life in the desert and steppe, and especially in view of the absence of the legal apparatus of more developed civilised societies, could guarantee the security of the social organisation. It was with the forces of this integration and identification of the individual with the tribe and its self-imposed system of values that the new teachings of Islam had to contend.

The Idea of Equality

The postulate of equality contained in the Islamic doctrine from the time of its original preaching at first found no acceptance in the Islamic society. Nobility of descent was a valuable asset in the social life of the Arab tribes. The cult of their ancestry, pride in a long chain of noble forbears, was firmly ingrained in their consciousness, and as late as the fourteenth century Ibn Khaldun emphasised the fact that wherever a true "esprit de corps" still prevailed among the tribes no one could become head of a tribe who could not boast of a long and noble descent. For this reason the efforts of Mohammed, himself neither of high parentage nor a member of a particularly distinguished profession, were first directed to the establishment of a new society of equals. Rank in this new society was to be determined not by aristocratic descent but by faith. The antagonism of the old tribal nobility to Mohammed's proclamations was due in no small measure to the revolutionary break they entailed with Beduin social tradition, with its fund of time-honoured notions on the status of the individual and the family and the importance of descent for society. The dispute over this essential postulate of Moslem social teaching was not settled even in the centuries after Mohammed, although in the newly-forming society of Islam the Prophet's doctrine of equality and with it the community of believers founded thereon asserted itself more and more as time passed. The statements of Moslem expositors of the Law and interpreters of tradition indicate that this problem was one which occupied Moslem minds again and again. Baidawi comments in characteristic fashion on the verse of the Koran (xlix, 13) where Mohammed in reply to attempts to stress the value of noble descent says that the most devout of the believers is the most worthy in the sight of God, and that therefore it is not birth but religious zeal alone that determines a man's dignity; he takes this passage and uses it expressly to refute the claims of those who boast of their ancient lineage. All beings are created by God, begotten by father and mother, and are thus equal.[2]

Up to the present day the demand for equality and the suppression of the old tradition of the glorification of descent has not been realised in the sense desired in spite of its emphatic advocacy by the Prophet and many authoritative sources; but the principle was nevertheless recognised and exercised a profound influence. Levy rightly stresses the fact that Mohammed's success consisted in no small measure in his having created a new object of reverence and distinction among social groups in which the instinct to honour the quality acquired by noble birth was particularly strong. Kinship with the Prophet, in fact even the slight degree of relationship deriving from the accident of belonging to his tribe, came to be regarded as the touchstone of true nobility, as a high distinction. Even the new members of this tribe adopted by the Quraish shared in this distinction and possessed higher rank than members of ancient Sheikh families. Thus, whereas the revolutionary abolition of the old ideology of nobility of birth, although accepted in principle, found little practical response in the Moslem world, the idea of a community of all true believers—thanks to a certain shifting of emphasis—everywhere gained a firm hold. The Islamic doctrine, like the ideology of every religious mission, envisages the liberation of the individual from his isolated position and his union with his fellow-believers in one great community where he is offered the deep satisfaction of equal status by virtue of belief alone, and not through "external" values such as descent, material possessions, and so forth. All followers of Islam possess equal rights and duties in this community to which one may be admitted regardless of sex, class, office or possessions; they feel themselves to be a great brotherhood of believers. Even the Khalif himself, Mohammed's representative, was but *primus inter pares*, occupying his high position of authority over whole countries and continents solely by virtue of his faith and the confidence of his followers.

The "Foreigners" and Islam

The process which led to the establishment of a community of believers in Islam was not completed without violent conflicts with opposing movements nor within a short period. One of the problems which aspiring Islam had to solve was the position of the foreigners, both those who represented a purely external, racial, foreign element, and those who, coming from other religious spheres, accepted the new doctrine. Here the new teaching conflicted seriously with pre-Islamic conceptions and the old Beduin instinct of reserve towards the stranger within the tribe, as shown by the fact that the newly-converted were not at once regarded as fully-fledged members of the community of believers. This was the case in spite of the fact that the Koran definitely insists that all Mohammedans, including the Negro and other elements usually regarded in Arabia as inferior, must be treated as perfect equals irrespective of race or language. Furthermore, the attitude of those who as inhabitants of countries converted to Islam persisted in their former religious convictions represented a problem for the new religious community, a community which justified the defamation of dissenters on principle.

The spreading doctrine, therefore, had first to deal with those elements which as yet had not accepted Islam. To these must be added those who probably would not become converts inasmuch as they were strongly attached to other communities. As far as the not very numerous body of foreigners who stood and intended to remain outside Islamic society were concerned, the principle of inviolability was accepted as a necessary prerequisite for the maintenance of commerce. Without freedom of movement and trade on the part of the foreigner, international trade relations are not possible, and it was only in consequence of this view that the rights and privileges of foreigners as they had already existed in the Arab countries before the conquest were taken over and allowed to continue in their old form and style. True, the right of ownership was granted to the foreigner only in respect of his personal belongings and such merchandise as he brought with him or purchased in Islamic countries. The right to own immovable property is reserved, as a rule, to Muslim citizens or to the *Dhimmis* (protected non-Muslim citizens). Under certain conditions, however, even a foreigner could acquire immovable property and thus qualify for the rank of *Dhimmi*.

Apart from the foreigners who remained outside Islamic society, the main problem in the implementation of the Koranic ideology of equality was how to treat newly-converted members of non-Arabic descent. Even in the pre-Islamic period among the Beduin the idea of *Mawali* or clients, the admittance to the tribe of a stranger, who after a certain probationary period was accepted as a full member, was not unknown. After the spread of Islam throughout the conquered countries the number of such *Mawali* of non-Arab extraction increased to a remarkable extent and, as was only natural, they endeavoured to profit as soon as possible by the rights due to them in virtue of their status as protected members. From a material point of view the principal difference in the position of the *Mawali* consisted in his being obliged to pay, instead of the insignificant *Zakat* tax, the far heavier *Kharaj* contribution which was additional to the poll-tax and amounted to about one-fifth of his agricultural returns. This higher taxation did not immediately confer on the converts to Islam after the conquest of their country the full equality they desired. Rather did the fact of their subjection make itself felt in various ways for some time to come, by their being either socially slighted or organised entirely separately. It is understandable that in course of time this gave rise to a counter-movement chiefly inspired by the highly cultivated Persian *Mawali* and based on the declarations of the Prophet and the early commentators as to the equality and brotherhood of all Mohammedans irrespective of race. Opinions differ as to the results of this movement in those days, and any real improvement is ascribed to the growing political influence of the non-Arabic elements and not to the doctrine of equality as such.[3]

The Slaves

A further element which came to possess great social importance in Islamic society were the slaves. In the time of Mohammed slavery flourished throughout the whole of Arabia, both in the towns and among the Beduin tribes. The importance of the slaves for the Arab society of that period was so great that Mohammed, despite its express condemnation on the part of Jewish and Christian tradition, did not demand the abolition of slavery. The slave trade was an extremely remunerative branch of commerce, and remained so right up to the nineteenth century. The social structure of Oriental countries, particularly the management of the household, was extensively based on slave labour. It is remarkable that though the abolition of slavery became, as much as a hundred years ago, the watchword of the European powers, the custom has continued to flourish in the Arab and African countries practically up to the present day. Even in the mandated territories placed under the administration of European countries after the First World War certain forms of slavery, more or less disguised, are still to be found. This applies, for instance, to Transjordan, a country closely connected with Palestine historically, geographically and politically, and it is openly discussed in the reports issued by the Mandatory Power.[4] In the families of the Beduin sheikhs slaves are kept in considerable numbers as personal servants and bodyguard. Many of them are born into this status of servitude. Although the government of Transjordan has joined the international convention on the slave trade, it apparently does not count on the fulfilment of its provisions inasmuch as attempts to alter the position of slaves kept by the tribes meet with little sympathy from the slaves themselves.

What has been said of conditions in Transjordan applies to a far greater extent to a number of predominantly Moslem countries, where the institution of slavery leads a by no means illegitimate existence even today. The position of these slaves is not so degrading as it might appear to the European observer. Apart from the fact that the Koran itself ordains that slaves be treated humanely, their acceptance of Islam in a society in which the brotherhood of all believers should play a central part likewise guaranteed them a more dignified position, although the actual fact of servitude, the legal status of slave, was not abolished.[5]

Nevertheless, the inner sense of equality, the underlining of their claim to religious brotherhood, sufficed to provide the Muslim slaves in many cases with opportunities to rise in the social scale, and brought them to the very highest positions in the State; indeed, a large number of slaves during the period when Islam was spreading became the progenitors of ruling dynasties, among which are the royal house of Delhi and the dynasty of the Mamelukes. This very position of the slave, his lack of relations and isolation from influences rendered him particularly fit for the execution of the plans of his master. This fact often resulted in the more talented of the slaves acquiring a position of intimacy with the rulers and finally themselves attaining to important positions in the State.

Notwithstanding this, the legal status of the slaves has, according to Islamic theory, always been extremely limited. Islam took over the pre-Islamic practice of declaring property in the form of slaves to be acquirable by purchase, donation, inheritance or capture. In early Islamic times the possibility of acquiring slaves by capture applied only in respect of unbelievers, while it was likewise contrary to the law to sell believers for one reason or another into slavery. Nevertheless, this practice has survived down to the present time, and even in countries in such close contact with European civilisation as Palestine the Government has been obliged to intervene in the matter of the hiring out of children on long terms of service amounting in practice to a form of slavery. Estimates as to the extent of the slave trade at the present time arrive at a figure of approximately 5,000 men, women and children who are shipped every year in Arab dhows across the Red Sea to Arabia and sold into slavery. Mr. Eldon Rutter gives the following interesting account of the scenes witnessed by him at an Arab slave market:

"Against the houses there are stone benches, resembling the display counters of shops. And so indeed they are, for these houses are the shops of dealers in human beings. The slaves are sitting on the benches—some silent, some even joking and laughing. The crowd moves slowly past, coolly scanning the unfortunate slaves and discussing their needs with the benighted slave dealers. Few Europeans, I imagine, could walk the length of that street without a feeling of burning embarrassment. The most desirable of the slave-girls are not exposed to view on the benches. They are kept inside the houses where prospective buyers are taken in to view them."[6]

As already mentioned, the patriarchal structure of Arab society led in practice to the complete admittance of the slave into the household or family community, just as the repeatedly advocated humane treatment of slaves was general. The law is on the whole stricter in this respect than the practice, which may have contributed in no small measure to the fact that the institution has survived down to the present day. According to the law slaves are expressly treated as "movable goods" and—with certain exceptions in the case of female slaves who have borne children to their masters—may be freely bought and sold, exchanged, given in security or hired out. As regards their physical needs they possess the same rights as domestic animals, i.e. the right to board and lodging, an appropriate measure of work and, in particular, an interval of rest during the summer days. Slaves may not own property. Everything they acquire reverts to their master. A slave, therefore, may not engage in any independent trade, but only act as his master's representative. Marriage is allowed only with the consent of his owner.

As regards their origin, the slaves in the Arab countries of Western Asia come mostly from Central and East Africa. Abyssinia and the Negro territories from the East coast far into the hinterland account for the largest contingent. In consequence of the complete separation of the slaves from their home associations and their conversion to Islam—for them a matter of course—connubium between free Arabs and female Negro slaves became quite usual. According to most travellers' accounts such mixed marriages occurred in many districts to a wide extent. The practice was particularly rife in the two holy cities of Mecca and Medina, where female Negro slaves of certain origin (above all from Abyssinia) were at times much sought-after marriage candidates. The children of such marriages generally inherited the slave status of their mother, although in the course of time a more lenient attitude obtained, and this, coupled with the frequent manumission of slaves, leads us to regard such a condition of slavery as by no means final.

The sociological importance of the slaves is seen first in their function as bodyguards to the great Emirs, and their suitability as high ranking State officials, and secondly in their emergence as independent tribes.[7] There can be no doubt that the fate of Emir and Sheikh families was often entirely dependent on the existence and intervention of the slave bodyguard. Their suitability for this calling arose from the fact that they were in practice uninterested in the family disputes of the tribes and were an absolutely reliable and efficient tool in the hands of their master. Moreover the rise of individuals as strong personalities from the ranks of the slaves is, as already mentioned, to be attributed to the fact that they were readily entrusted with important functions which it was not desired to hand over to directly interested freemen. The freeing of former slaves and their formation into tribes with their own chiefs, herds and land is likewise an important feature in the general picture, since by this the otherwise strictly preserved somatic uniformity of the Beduin population was disrupted. It is true that in the early period the new tribes of freed slaves were not given rights of complete equality; in all external political questions they followed those tribes and families with whom they had served as slaves. The former Sheikh also decided how many fighting men they must place at the disposal of the ruling tribe in the case of war. But it may be safely assumed that with the increasing pacification and accessibility of the desert and the Beduin territories these relics of an inferior position will one day be abolished or fall into desuetude.

Mention must also be made of the economic function devolving on the slaves. We must not overlook the fact that, apart from the said motives deriving from political factors, the specific social and economic conditions of the Arabian Peninsula played a significant part in the maintenance of slavery. Similarly in the West, notwithstanding the doctrine of equality so definitely developed in Christianity, slavery and slave-dealing had held their own as extremely profitable branches of trade, in which up to the middle of the nineteenth century the most advanced Powers competed. It is thus not surprising that economic interests in the Arab countries, dependent as they were on slave labour and slave-dealing, were able to overcome the easily surmountable religious scruples arising out of the teachings of Islam. Moreover, the old social structure of the Arab tribes rendered it expedient to employ for menial work in the home, workshop and field, workers who were free from the mentality of their Arab masters. The true tribal Arab's aversion to obeying a master, to being tied to a place of work, distinctly favoured the institution of slavery, although nowadays its extent and prevalence as compared with former centuries is considerably reduced, and it is practically confined to remote parts of the Arab world and Africa.

After absorbing the social doctrines of Islam, Arab society, up to the present, has shown a spiritual mentality widely uniform in its essential features and in its scale of social values. The main line of demarcation, which splits the population into two large groups, is drawn by the form of settlement—town dwellers, artisans, peasants on the one hand, and the free sons of the desert on the other. As a result of the increasing pacification after the first centuries of the spread of the Arab tribes, a considerable part of them became permanently settled. Military camps such as Kufa and Basra which had to keep the surrounding country and its inhabitants in subjection had grown into large cities by the end of the Umayyad period; during the same period older towns such as Damascus, al-Hira, Anbar, Bukhara and Samarkand had increased enormously in population and importance.[8] This movement, which took place between the eighth and the tenth century A.D., caused the first large-scale urbanisation process of the Arab peoples and brought in consequence important developments in their social structure and cultural life. It is remarkable, however, that this growth of urban life did not lead to the class antagonism which made itself felt so early in medieval Western society; despite the wide divergences between "sown" and "desert", between wealth and poverty, clearly recognisable throughout the ages in Oriental lands, the sharp class division of Western society remained foreign to the Eastern mind. Even in such striking instances of inequality as the institution of slavery, Islamic society exhibits reconciling features which fit in well with the general trend towards social harmony embodied in the doctrine of Islam. But before we turn to present-day Islamic society, let us first examine the constitution of the Oriental city as a representative sector of that society.

CHAPTER XXX

STRUCTURE AND CONSTITUTION OF THE ORIENTAL CITY

The Oriental city does not, strictly speaking, fall within the framework of an exclusively Islamic society; believers in other creeds are to be found within its walls. But on the whole, urban structure in Middle East countries up to the nineteenth century shows fairly uniform traits, though any attempt at describing the specific character of the Oriental town as compared with its Western counterpart must of necessity involve some schematisation.

Apart from the large centres, most Middle Eastern cities—particularly in the Arab countries—are still amorphous bodies, little more than urbanized villages. The proportion of their inhabitants who earn their living either directly or indirectly by agriculture, is very considerable. Outwardly, the difference between town and village is often only a matter of degree. The town hall, or its equivalent, and the mosque form the centre around which cluster the bazaars; immediately adjoining are the living quarters which, especially on the outskirts, are often indistinguishable from peasants' huts. Rarely can any trace be seen of the stone-preserved heritage of the past that renders the medieval Western city so attractive. The fact that Oriental cities are frequently built on sites of ancient or early medieval centres of Oriental civilization does not alter the sad and neglected impression conveyed by their general appearance. Nor do the relics of a mighty past incline the observer to condone their slipshod growth; he cannot help regarding them as magnified villages where many rural traits have been retained. This judgment is supported by the fact that not a few Eastern cities which today count their inhabitants by tens of thousands were barely more than hamlets a century or so ago, as may be seen in the case of Lower Egypt from the maps of Napoleon's expedition.

In the older Arab cities with mixed populations the separate quarters for families, clans, nationalities, and religious communities serve as a useful guide through the labyrinth of streets and houses. The peculiar relationship—or rather lack of relationship—between these quarters, their segregation from one another, and the lack of community feeling between them are characteristic indications of the Oriental conception of a city, which is in complete contrast to European ideas. Until very recently each quarter had its own civic head (the *Mukhtar*) and its own religious leader. The night-watch engaged by each quarter was responsible for the security of that particular quarter and no other.[9] Strife and conflict between sections of a city are occurrences not unknown in other parts of the world; but rarely do we find instances where some parts of a city are spared while in others the people are massacred wholesale, as often occurred in the Orient. This cleavage of the cities into disparate sections is not due to differences of nationality or religion alone, though these factors must not be minimized. In many cities feuds are still kept up between kindreds, clans and families, each being backed by its own followers. The united citizenry which is so conspicuous in the Western world does not exist even among the homogeneous Moslem-Arab population, where the clan system is an effective bar to any fusion between the various family groups. The Christian doctrines of equality and brotherhood contributed largely to the progress of Western cities by giving them a democratic basis for their constitution. But Islam was in different case, since it could not persuade the powerful associations of autonomous clans and tribes, to whose backing it owed its own success, to practise the equality which likewise forms part of its teaching. Hence these associations long continued to exist and to influence the conditions of local government and the social grouping of the urban populations.

In this we have the reason why no citizenry, that is to say, no corporation or association of free individuals, was ever constituted in the Orient. In Western cities, as Max Weber and others have pointed out, the individual held his citizenship in his personal capacity, and in that capacity took the oath of civic allegiance: it followed, therefore, that by personal membership in the local corporation he assured himself of his legal rights as a citizen. In Moslem cities, however, the status of the individual depended upon his connection with a clan or family organization. If, for any reason whatsoever, he severed that connection, he thereby forfeited his legal status and with it all claims to protection or help. The sheikh (or the successor to the functions of the sheikh), as the representative of a powerful old family, determined the social rank of each man in his locality, since society was so constituted that the individual, whatever his personal merits, had no standing outside its confines. This explains why a phenomenon common in the history of European cities had no counterpart in the Orient: here the town did not emancipate.[10] The peasant who fell out with his clan and came to the city as an individual (i.e. without the backing of his family group) could not, as a rule, work his way into a position from which he could later rise in the world. At best he would have to make shift with those humble employments which he, as an outsider, had any right to expect.

Even a cursory comparison of urban development in the West and the East must take into account not only the predominance in the East of the clan and the integration of the individual within the clan, but also the artisans' corporations which played so important a part in moulding the character of the European cities. There the independent artisans, organized in guilds and frequently patricians themselves, became a political factor of considerable importance. Neither the feudal aristocracy in the country nor the other classes in the cities could undermine their power; in fact these classes were not seldom obliged to yield to the demands of the guilds and to renounce many of their own privileges. At times the independent artisans obtained complete control of the European municipalities and exerted a decided influence upon the central government itself.

There is indeed a striking contrast between the European guilds, which had the proud status of public corporations and enjoyed privileges confirmed by their municipalities, and the Oriental guilds, which were merely associations of weak and oppressed elements whose open or veiled distrust of the municipal and central authorities was a common feature. Here we have one of the reasons why the artisans of the lower middle classes in Europe have always been loyal and submissive supporters of the State, turning a deaf ear to revolutionary appeals, while in the East it is just the artisans who are most responsive to Socialist and Communist propaganda.

Even without drawing detailed comparisons between the inner structure of Occidental and Oriental guilds, it is obvious that the key position in civic affairs occupied by the powerful European artisan-patricians (who were all employers) necessarily enabled them to exercise a very great influence on the social and economic development of their cities, while the barely tolerated unions of Moslem artisans (composed of both employers and wage-earners) could gain them no such privileges.

The factors that shaped the evolution of the Eastern cities after the Middle Ages are in part identical with those that were at work in the East as a whole. The particular conditions that prevailed in them were due, in the main, to the fact that most of the feudal families took up their residence there and that their activities were not such as contributed to the benefit of the population in general. In the Western countries, Italy excepted, the feudal lords usually kept to their castles in the rural areas and were thus unable to affect the internal affairs of the cities to any great extent. The consequences of this choice of domicile on the part of the feudal families can still be traced in the spirit and the methods of municipal administration. Even in recent decades this has been tantamount to a struggle for power between aristocratic old families whose authority has always rested and still rests on rents derived from real property, both urban and rural. When paid offices were instituted in the municipalities, the dominant families seized additional power by possessing themselves of these posts as sinecures for their own members. In many Syrian and Palestinian (Arab) cities it is still regarded as quite natural that numerous officials of the same name (i.e. belonging to the same family) should serve in a single municipality. Similar conditions prevail in regard to ecclesiastical affairs, in the management of mosque property and *Waqf* endowments and in any other connection where there are chances of profitable benefices and perquisites, and it was by these methods that the influential families enhanced their wealth and prestige. Such was the situation which continued with little change until shortly after the First World War. As a rule the Turkish governors refrained from interfering in the local affairs of the Arab districts; and when they did, it was not to abolish abuses. Amusing passages in the minutes of the *Majlises* (local or municipal councils) reveal how personal ambitions were promoted or defended with the utmost frankness. Where leaders and members of municipal councils displayed so little capacity for collective action for public ends, a civic spirit could not possibly develop as it did in the medieval corporations and particularly in the modern cities of the West. There was no impulse to the development of an active citizenry interested in the fostering of public institutions and services, such as schools, museums, hospitals and art.

The various economic types of town prevalent in the West are, as a rule, also to be found in the East. They are: the mercantile town, the artisan town, the capital town living on the administrative services established there. But the Orient produced, in addition, a type of city not elsewhere to be found so commonly and in so clear-cut a form, namely the "holy" city. This type of city, where saints or holy places are worshipped, where some sanctuary forms the centre of a cult around which a whole ring of ecclesiastical institutions is maintained, is a typical consumers' town. The life of such a centre depends on the periodic assemblage of pilgrims who spend a certain period at the holy places, where they usually live on a more generous scale than at home. The illuminating account of his stay in Mecca given by Snouck Hurgronje portrays a town where religious attachment constitutes an economic asset of the first order. But it is not only the two Arab towns of the Prophet that belong to this category; places like Najef, Kerbela, Meshhed and even Jerusalem, Nazareth and Bethlehem drew and partly still draw an essential part of their means of subsistence from pilgrims. Detailed accounts are available which throw a light on the far-reaching extent to which these holy cities have been or are still dependent on the pilgrim traffic.[11] They have, indeed, few economic resources of their own, their whole economic structure being oriented towards the reception of the army of pilgrims and the provision of its needs. The capital movements caused by this traffic often reach large dimensions and represent a source of considerable income for the permanent inhabitants of these towns, whose social mentality is characterised by the somewhat unrestrained manner in which they exploit the opportunities arising from the satisfaction of the pilgrims' religious and material requirements.

CHAPTER XXXI

MOSLEM SOCIETY IN TRANSITION

Moslem society, which in its early beginnings was so markedly influenced by the style of living practised by the Beduin tribes, did not discard these influences even with the passage of the centuries. However seriously its structure was undermined, it continued to bear their imprint even when many of them had ceased to exist. The fundamentals of early Moslem society may be summarised as follows:—

1. The family or the clan, as the case may be, is the nucleus of Moslem society as established on a patriarchal basis.
2. All members of Moslem society are co-equal.
3. The management of the social groups and the community is governed by the democratic principle of chieftainship, which comes to embrace also the principle of monarchy. The idea of a ruling class is discountenanced.
4. Women have equal rights (with the exception of certain legal disadvantages in respect of property and inheritance).
5. Slavery is tolerated in practice, and though emphasis is laid on the equality of the slaves as human beings, the institution as such is recognised as legitimate.

How is this society actually constituted today? To what extent do the old formative principles still appear as active elements and forces? At first glance it seems difficult to discover in the heterogeneous pattern of the present any signs of uniformity or any degree of prominence of those social features and institutions which are regarded as peculiar to Moslem society. A complex structure has taken possession of this old society; new classifications of social groups, new associations and divisions based on property, occupation and economic interests formerly quite unknown appear in the foreground, whilst the old social contours deriving from the tribal and clan communities slowly fade out. The process of modern State formation and its concomitant, the modern trend towards urbanisation, act as the twin engines of social disintegration.

But in view of the inherent power of resistance of the Moslem world, this process of transformation, ramified and in its total effect all-embracing as it is, can replace or modify the old forms and structures but gradually and step by step. It has been shown how that heritage of the pre-Islamic period least in accordance with the modern spirit, slavery, continues even today. Similarly there still exists within the tribes a democratic-patriarchal organisation for the management of the tribal community. Now as in former times in the same social circle the avenging of a crime against the community is carried out collectively. These forms of legal protection for the members of the Beduin tribes have survived till now even in countries where the process of modernisation made its greatest strides in the twentieth century.

Society in the Moslem East still offers in many sectors an ideal example of the constitution of a community in the sense in which that word is used in modern sociology to define an organic *societas*, such as the family or the clan unit, as distinct from the "association", our loosely-knit modern organisations of society. Over and above this, it offers us the possibility of studying even in these days both the original stages of this old social unit and its more advanced phases right up to its disintegration; at the same time it enables us to observe the descendants of the same tribe both as representatives of the oldest form of social organisation and as the adherents of progress in its latest manifestations.

The most significant shift in the structure of Muslim society came about through the rapidly growing inequality in the distribution of private property—due on the one hand to the accumulation of landed property, ground rents and trade profits, and to the growing urbanisation on the other. We know from the Koran how sharply condemned is the excessive formation of capital. It is a characteristic of the true believer "to recognise the right of the beggar and the indigent to a part of their own possessions" (Kor. lxx, 24–25). Other passages in the Koran have a similar ring, such as for instance Sura iii, 86, where the alienation of part of one's property is demanded as a precondition of true piety and justice. These, however, remained isolated exhortations even in religious literature. Actually the particularly favourable geographical position of most Oriental countries up to the discovery of the sea-route to India resulted in the development in many favourably situated centres of a lively exchange of goods which became the source of large fortunes. The possessors of this wealth were far from following the maxims of the Koran, but took advantage of the increasing urbanisation continually to increase their wealth through urban and rural ground rents.

The Oriental Town in Transition

Let us now consider the recent changes in the urban sphere. The alterations in the political and social status of the Orient since the First World War did not remain without repercussions in the political and constitutional organization of the Oriental city. The augmented powers of the central authorities and their desire to promote public education and health, led to a stricter supervision of municipal activities and, at the same time, to improvement in the municipal services and functions and the introduction of administrative reforms.

With the adoption of modern means of transport, making new forms of urban development possible, the appearance of the larger cities has undergone a rapid change and has come to resemble that of the Western city: suburbs have been built at considerable distances from the centres; wide new streets have been cut through ancient quarters (often necessitating the demolition of old market-places and their replacement by new ones in other neighbourhoods); new municipal bodies have been formed which provide water supply, electricity, abattoirs, sanitary services, educational institutions, and the like.

The modern commercial centres which have sprung up are much preferred to the old bazaars, with the result that the business life of the towns has been transferred to the new quarters; and the bazaars, like other obsolescent features of the Oriental cities, are being superseded by modern edifices on the latest European pattern, and are slowly sinking into desuetude as romantic relics of an outworn economic age.

Lastly, we have the process of industrialisation which, though still in its beginnings, has already wrought certain definitive changes in the social grouping of the urban populations, inasmuch as it has brought about a redistribution of wealth and income. Slowly but surely the position of the once dominant classes, whose claims to authority were based on the old social and economic constitution of the Oriental cities, is being sapped, though as yet the contours of the new order can barely be discerned and powerful forces are trying to stem its advance. But the process as a whole cannot be checked. Its main impetus is derived from the city, the centre of the transformation movement, and this impetus, extending far beyond its actual radius, tends to set in motion the process of transformation in agrarian society also. Here the effects on the social relationship up to this day are considerably slower. One of the main reasons for this relative stability was and is the strong position of the big landed proprietor who, as has been shown above, is still able by abusing the new legislative measures in the field of land reform, taxation and production policy to increase his hold over his tenants and dependants.

CHAPTER XXXII

ECONOMIC ETHICS OF MOSLEM SOCIETY

In our introductory remarks we have anticipated the fact that, in addition to the natural factors of a geographical nature and the changes precipitated by external political causes, the religious conceptions of Islam also have had a marked effect on the economic activity and development of the peoples of the Middle East. Notwithstanding the generalisation which the assumption of such influences on living conditions in the Orient implies, any attempt to interpret the interplay of these forces through the medium of a rigid formula should be avoided. Moreover, other religions besides Islam have held their own as powers of no mean order up to the present day. The fact remains, however, that in most Oriental countries and for the vast majority of their inhabitants Islam has become the religion of the *State*. Likewise it is clearly manifest that the ethics of Islam are particularly concerned with man's social behaviour. The adherents of those religious systems which deviate in certain fundamentals from the teaching of Islam, do, in fact, reveal a different mentality in regard to economic issues or even economic activity in general.

The appreciation of this side of Oriental social life, apart from a survey of its general structure, is, therefore, highly relevant, especially at a period when its distinctive features appear to be definitely merging into the general stream of European-American cultural development.

We have hitherto refrained from dealing with the motives and effects of the religious system of Islam—one of the most important sources for the understanding of the social transformation now proceeding in the Orient—an omission which will probably not have escaped the reader's notice. Such an analysis is, however, a specific task of the specialist, quite apart from the fact that illuminating studies of the social and religious aspects of Islam in modern times are already available in a number of recent treatises, above all in the works of H. A. R. Gibb.[12]

Nevertheless, we do not feel justified in altogether ignoring a life-force whose influence on the social and economic habits of thought and action of the people under its sway is so direct and powerful. For the limitations just mentioned, however, the following considerations aim, above all, at elaborating those points which, in the light of the studies of the relationship between other religions and the economic life of their adherents, also throw light on the relations between the religious thought of Islam and the socio-economic fabric of Islamic society.

Although we may assume, in principle, that prospective trends exist in the Orient also which, given similar conditions, will follow laws similar to those of the West, there remain nevertheless striking divergences, both in fundamentals and in individual stages of development, which call for closer study. Our conclusions will in the first place be based on literary evidence, which we shall then attempt to substantiate by references to conditions in actual practice.

The old question may be raised here to what extent the sociologist is permitted to rely on theory and doctrine to interpret or explain social development and interrelationship. R. H. Tawney, in his reflections on a similar issue, has already given a fitting answer in saying that "because doctrine and conduct diverge it does not follow that to examine the former is to hunt abstractions. That men should have thought as they did is sometimes as significant as that they should have acted as they did, and not least significant when thought and practice are at variance."[13] The social analyst who explores our problem against the background of contemporary Islamic social history, has over and above this an important advantage in learning from close observation how far his findings are still valid.

Even a cursory study of the writings of Moslem men of letters and educators suffices to convince us that a definite connection exists between the authoritative precepts and views of Islamic teachers and the aforesaid attitude of its followers. In particular, it may be said of Islamic society that the mentality of the individual and the attitude of the group come under the heading of religious claims. It is our thesis that the social and economic life of the Moslem peoples was deeply influenced by such teachings with lasting consequences for the social and economic development of the Orient. Even without the renowned researches of Max Weber on the influence of religious thought and religion-inspired labour ethics on the shaping and growth of capitalism, the many unique properties of Moslem social ethics as affecting economic life in the theory and practice of Oriental daily life would have forced themselves upon us even today. Almost incontestable, however, are the conclusions derived from a comparison of the evidence of Puritan social and labour ethics elaborated by Max Weber as characteristic of the source of the capitalistic spirit with the evidences of Moslem moral philosophy and social ethics which are no less characteristic for their world. Can we find greater contrasts than those revealed by the following quotations when we compare them with evidences quoted by authoritative interpreters of Islamic teaching as representative precepts of Moslem social ethics?

"If we refer to Baxter's *The Saints' Everlasting Rest* and his *Christian Directory* or kindred works by others we are immediately struck by the emphasis laid on the Ebionite elements of the Gospel when the question of wealth and its acquisition is dealt with: wealth as such is a grave danger, its temptations are incessant, its pursuit not only futile as compared with the surpassing importance of the Kingdom of God, but also morally questionable. Here we find condemnation going much further than that of Calvin, who seeing in the wealth of the clergy no obstacle to their efficiency, but rather a most desirable addition to their standing, allowed them to invest their fortunes profitably, but with the avoidance of vexation; here, asceticism is directed unreservedly against any striving for the acquisition of temporal goods. Numerous examples of this condemnation of the pursuit of money and possessions can be quoted from Puritan works and contrasted with the ethical literature of the late Middle Ages, which is much less prejudiced in this respect. And such scruples are expressed in all seriousness—it behoves us, however, to look into them in order to perceive their decisive ethical meaning and relationship. What is really morally condemnable is the resting on one's possessions, the enjoyment of riches with its consequence of idleness and carnal desire, and, above all, diversion from the striving after "holy" living. And solely because possessions harbour the danger of such reposing is their acquisition questionable. For the 'Everlasting Rest of the Saints' is in the Beyond, on earth man must, to be sure of his predestination, 'fulfil the works of Him who has sent him while it is still day'.

"It is not idleness and enjoyment, but action alone that according to the unequivocally revealed will of God serves to increase His glory.[14] To waste one's time is, therefore, the foremost and fundamentally gravest of all sins. The period of our life is infinitely short and costly in order to establish one's own vocation. Loss of time through conviviality, 'idle talk', luxury, even through indulgence in more sleep than is necessary for health—six to at most eight hours—is morally absolutely condemnable. This has not the meaning of Franklin's *Time is Money*, but these words apply in a spiritual sense: time is infinitely valuable inasmuch as every lost hour is an hour withdrawn from the service of the glory of God.[15] Valueless and possibly directly condemnable is, therefore, inactive contemplation, at least when occurring at the expense of the time necessary for one's calling. For it is less pleasing to God than the active obedience to His will in the execution of a calling. Besides, for that there is Sunday, and according to Baxter it is invariably those who are idle in their calling who have also no time for God when the hour for devotion arrives.

"Accordingly, through Baxter's principal work runs a sermon ever repeated, at times almost passionate, advocating hard, constant physical and mental work. Two motives are operating here jointly. To begin with, work is the old, tried ascetic remedy so highly valued as such by the Church in the West, in sharp contrast not only to the East, but also to almost all monastic precepts throughout the entire world. For it is the specific preventive against all those temptations which constitute what Puritanism terms 'unclean life'—and its function is no slight one. Sexual asceticism in Puritanism differs from monastic only in a matter of degree, not in respect of the underlying principle, and, in view of the fact that it embraces also conjugal life, is more sweeping in its scope than the latter. For sexual intercourse is permissible in marriage only as the means ordained by God for the increase of His glory in accordance with the commandment: 'Be fruitful and multiply'. The same prescription that is used against religious doubts and scrupulous self-torment is applied also against sexual temptation, viz. in addition to a frugal diet, vegetarian food and cold baths: 'Work hard in your calling'.

"But over and above that, work is first and foremost the one and only divine purpose of life. The Pauline words: 'He who will not work shall not eat' apply to one and all unconditionally. Disinclination to work is a symptom of a fall from divine grace."

Other protagonists of such ascetic labour ethics express themselves very similarly: Thus Richard Steele, a Puritan divine, writes in *The Tradesman's Calling, etc.:*

"God doth call every man and woman . . . to serve him in some peculiar employment in this world, both for their own and the common good . . . The Great Governor of the world hath appointed to every man his proper post and province and . . . he will be at a great loss if he do not keep his own vineyard and mind his own business".

Bunyan in *The Pilgrim's Progress* stresses:

"At the day of Doom men shall be judged according to their fruits. It will not be said then Did you believe? but Were you doers, or talkers only?"[16]

To quote Max Weber again:

"Here the divergence from the medieval attitude can be clearly discerned. Thomas Aquinas had also interpreted that passage from Paul. But in his view work is only necessary *naturali ratione* for the maintenance of life of the individual and the community in general. Where this purpose no longer exists, the validity of the precept also lapses. It applies only to the species, not to the individual. Such as can live from their possessions without working, it does not concern, correspondingly contemplation as a spiritual form of activity in the Kingdom of God is naturally outside the scope of this commandment in its literal interpretation."

The essential points of Protestant and Calvinistic ethics centre thus in the value placed on work and vocation, on wealth and its enjoyment, on the other physical pleasures of life, of sexual life in particular, and the value of time. The validity of the questions raised in this context is not affected in principle by the fact that no rigid uniformity can be traced in the Protestant religious systems.

Let us now turn to Moslem social ethics, which also do not show complete uniformity. Nevertheless, two main lines can be clearly traced in Islamic religious thought which have influenced the mode of life of the Believers to a very profound extent. In addition to the various doctrines of Islam which, as we shall see, were instrumental in preventing the formation of a "capitalistic" mentality, we must appreciate, above all, the central position accorded to faith in the whole structure of Moslem thought. According to the Koran the first duty of the believer is that of implicit belief. His actual mode of life is of secondary importance. The Muslim does not cease to be a true believer if he fails to fulfil the so-called duties of a secondary order. It is only when he denies the Unity of Allah and the truth of the Prophet's message that he commits a cardinal sin.[17] The very fact of his mode of living being so comprehensively regulated even down to the minutest details of daily life resulted in practice in the tolerance of slackness in the fulfilment of these precepts as a whole and actually placed a premium on the perfunctory execution of the secondary duties as compared with the easily followed primary commandment in respect of the confession of faith. In comparison with the social ethics of Calvinism and Protestantism and similarly also of late Judaism, with the high demands they made at all times on the conduct of their followers, Islam was a non-committal, un-pretentious, easy-going form of religion. The continual examination of one's own self and general conduct and the importance placed on the results of this examination for the satisfaction of one's religious conscience, as demanded by the first-named religious doctrines, was not conducive to the emergence of a pensive and contemplative life-philosophy. The Moslem had, in comparison, an easy way to complacency so far as his conduct was concerned. "No Moslem has need to offer the Scotch Minister's prayer: 'Gie us a good conceit of ourselves'. He has it already". Thus writes an observer who was able closely to study Turco-Islamic conditions and habits for many years.[18]

This throws a significant sidelight on the value and importance attached to the traditionalist conduct of life in Oriental society. Most illuminating as regards the part played by tradition in the social ethics of Islam is the attitude of Mohammed towards pre-Islamic moral concepts. Nomadic society, as represented by the Arab tribes of the pre-Islamic period, had a highly characteristic way of defining the terms "good" and "evil". "Good" was what the tribes regarded as known and familiar; what they found strange and foreign was for them "Evil".

These definitions of good and evil, whose roots lie in the primitive feelings, in the instinctive reactions of the tribal society, were taken over by Mohammed. When, as often in the Koran, he wishes to describe in a single expression the religious conceptions and conduct of life of the tribes as *good*, he refers to these by the comprehensive term "the known" (*almaruf*) and, similarly, what he disapproves of, what he regards as *bad* behaviour and impiety is termed *almunkar*, literally unknown or foreign.[19] The trend of thought fostered by this tribal heritage is thus an ultra-conservatism, an unlimited respect for tradition; it leads to the recognition of the authorities and the principle of authority as the chief arbiters in the preparation and orientation of the conduct of life. In this milieu the innovator who ventures to come forward with his own original thoughts is turned down and even reviled. Progress is tabooed as prejudicial to the welfare of this society and is combated with religious arguments.

Thus owing to the contradiction between the often extremely rigorous theory and the indolent and tolerant practice, coupled with the veneration of tradition, a trend of mind was fostered which either forestalls every activity on the part of the individual or the State or quickly nips it in the bud. What with the universal use of the Koran as the principal educative instrument for the rising generation of Islam and the other factors aforesaid, the result was an over-emphasis on contemplation. The forces which strive for outward activity were diverted inwards in the direction of an inward contemplation which, among the higher classes, found its expression in a spiritualisation of the lack of the desire to work—a trait so very alien to the Western mind—among the lower in a deadening of the sense for active doing and in a dull content to continue life at the same old primitive standard even when just a little exertion on their part would open the way to an improvement in their conditions of existence.

We now come to the second line of thought in Islamic religious teaching, viz.: the attitude of Islam to riches and their use for the enjoyment of life.

The ascetic tinge found in the early sayings of Mohammed and distinguishable also on later occasions comes on the whole to be overwhelmed and displaced by a more worldly matter-of-fact conception wherein earthly joys begin to figure. In particular the succession of conquests and the accumulation of war booty fostered an increasing regard for wealth and possessions hardly compatible with the original other-worldly ideas enunciated by Mohammed in Mecca. The Mohammedan author Ibn Sa'ad describes with undisguised admiration the extraordinary treasures and riches possessed by the contemporaries of the Prophet. The campaigns of conquest and plunder during the period of first expansion gained for the participants extraordinarily high profits per head which were relinquished by those entitled to them only in the rarest cases. The prime motives for this quest of gain, as recent research into the early history of Islam has shown, were material distress and avarice, coupled with the desire of a pauperised population to quit their impoverished native countries in order on the welcome excuse of spreading a new faith to acquire wealth elsewhere practically without any effort. The contemporaries of the Prophet—although certainly not in the habit of analysing the motives underlying the various expeditions—clearly realised that these were undertaken not only by the warriors inspired by the religious idea but also by a multitude of elements who went to war solely from very material incentives.

"Thus, owing to the favourable external turn taken by the cause of Islam at so early a stage of its history, the ascetic idea which predominated at its inception was forced into the background. For a zealous participation in the spread of the religion of Mohammed offered, among other things, opportunities for the satisfaction of extremely worldly considerations and earthly desires. It was already proclaimed by the moralists in the period after Mohammed that 'now every pious deed must be counted twice in that the Beyond no longer causes us concern, but the *Dunja*, the worldly interest, forms the centre of attraction' ".

This worldly atmosphere, which distinctly favoured the acquisition of wealth as a means to the enjoyment of life, eventually predominated and froze all expression of divergent opinion on the part of the religious teachers. Even the official Koran and *Hadith* interpretation of the recognised Moslem Schools is influenced by this trend of thought and teaches that exaggerated asceticism is evil and cannot be regarded as a deserving religious work whereas, on the other hand, worldly goods and the pleasures of man were instituted for the purpose of being properly used.

Of all occupations trade enjoys the relative favour of tradition. The influence of the caravan and trading centres where Islamic tradition was formed is unmistakable here and, despite occasional discrediting of this occupation on account of the temptations offered to those engaged in it, we are told:

"The trustworthy, just and pious merchant stands on the Day of Resurrection among the martyrs. He enters Paradise."[20]

Naturally there is no lack of exhortations to behave towards clients in an honest, brotherly and obliging manner and not to neglect the soul's welfare for the sake of business. Ghazali, in particular, stresses the dangers of commercial profit-seeking and recommends that certain groups of people, such as the pious, the mystics, the scholars and the functionaries should refrain from any form of business activity.[21] Other precepts are directed against exorbitant prices and above all against speculation and all "risky" transactions in which chance can play a part. But all this cannot hide the decisive fact that trade and the pleasure in making profits and the greater enjoyment of life thereby afforded has found an important, if not all-important, place in the central schools of Islamic tradition.

Islam, like all great religious systems, was—it can hardly be stressed too much— not a homogeneous world of ideas, but always—and sometimes simultaneously—found room for several divergent schools of thought. In addition to the aforesaid mundane and joyful trend we meet with an opposite tendency—fostered in part by Iranian and Eastern Asiatic influences and probably also as a reaction to the worldliness of the former. This opposite movement attracted most of the mystic and ascetic elements and in the course of time developed its own religious domain. This community did not attempt to deny or discard the teachings of the Koran but endeavoured solely to check what it considered harmful exaggerations of Koranic social ethics and philosophy.

Although clashing in many respects with the more materialistic maxims of the official Moslem community, their teachings were on similar lines. Thanks to the glorification of religious contemplation, the contemplative world of ideas and social ethics of Sufism expounded by this group, a part of the Moslem communities of that period were converted into completely submissive believers. This reduction of the idea of Divine Providence to its extreme killed all personal initiative, all understanding of the necessity of an active life, all motive to be up and doing or to make one's way in the world. The followers of this community surrendered themselves to Providence and Fate. " Their will is extinguished and their destiny in God's hand just as the dead body is in the hand of him who lays it out."[22] The consequence of their attitude goes so far that they refuse every activity and effort to procure a regular livelihood. Their particular qualification, which is represented as a virtue, consists in their not counting the morrow in the succession of days. The future and all concern for its needs is completely excluded from their mental horizon. There is nothing which stands in such glaring contrast to the social ethics of the Protestants with their glorification of professional devotion as this conception on the part of Moslem quietism.

Most closely connected therewith is, lastly, the contrast between the significance of the time factor in Islam and its rôle at the beginning of modern development in the West. Not only is every provision for the future, the calculation and inclusion of the morrow in the today discountenanced, but contemplation as such is extolled. On no account must there be any acceleration of the natural slow course of events. "Hurry is the Devil's work" is a classical saying commonly quoted by the Moslem moralists.

It must be well understood that between Sufism and the official concepts of Sunni Islam there were considerable dogmatic differences; but for the point in question these are of an internal nature. In fact Sufism became rooted in the theological literature of Islam at an early date. Notwithstanding its quiet, unobtrusive activity it exercised a remarkable influence on the religious thought of Islam and the mentality of Muslim society.

But let us not rely on literary evidence alone in order to prove our deductions. The practice of Moslem life itself supplies ample material in support of our theses. The lack of initiative, the absence of creative ideas among many native merchants and entrepreneurs is a phenomenon soon apparent to all who have lived for any length of time in Oriental countries. It is referred to again and again by numerous observers who, when seeking to explain it, attribute its cause only in part to the religious teachings of Islam.[23] The fact is, however, that the introduction of insurance, both active and passive, as well as the spread of modern credit dealings, the growth of banking and the Stock Exchange, those prerequisites of modern capitalist development, encountered formidable opposition chiefly in the form of Moslem religious bans. The signing of insurance agreements was regarded by Moslem jurists as forbidden in view of their character of risk (*maisir*). A *fetwa* of the supreme religious council of lawyers (*Mashyakha Islamiyya*) in Constantinople, who were asked for a finding on the admissibility of a life insurance, declared the acceptance of the insurance money as permissible only in view of the fact that the insurance company was located in foreign parts and the policy was issued abroad. In normal circumstances insurance business as well as regular banking and Stock

Exchange business based on the payment of interest on borrowed capital would be inadmissible. The ban on interest (*riba*) plays an important part in the Moslem legal system; even the bill of exchange (*Suftaja*) is discountenanced or actually forbidden by some schools of law, whilst it was not until 1903 that in Egypt, the country in which particularly large sums of capital are invested, a *fetwa* issued by the great reformer Muhammad Abduh started the practice of depositing larger sums of capital with the banks and Post Office savings banks, although up to the present day pious Moslem depositors refuse to accept bank interest.

Naturally, in practice and chiefly as a result of the requirements of trade, ways and means were found of circumventing these prohibitions. Fictitious contracts of purchase of all kinds, double contracts, participation in profits, are devices serving the trade which could otherwise not be carried on without borrowed money. Their importance at the present time is, however, steadily declining, as modern trade practices are gaining ground. In conformity with this development, local insurance companies came into being in important Moslem countries and naturally cater in the first instance for the local public. Nevertheless it goes without saying that the prohibitions and restrictions arising out of religious tradition have been a great handicap on the development of modern capitalist forms of enterprise in the Orient. It is difficult to establish the influence of each individual factor; but in conjunction with other influences deriving from Moslem tradition they were sufficient to weaken the success and position of the Moslem merchant entrepreneur in relation to European and even non-European competitors (Jews, Armenians, Greeks, Copts) to an appreciable extent. A remarkable testimony to this state of affairs is to be found in an outspoken article on this problem by the former Egyptian Prime Minister Ismail Sidky Pasha.[24] Here the question is raised why so many wealthy Egyptian firms tend to fail after a very short time, whereas their European competitors manage to establish themselves and make good. The reason for this is to be found, according to this authority, in a number of shortcomings in the psychology and business methods of the Egyptian merchant: backwardness, rudimentary methods of calculation, fatalism, lack of flexibility and business acumen, lack of inquisitiveness and honesty. Sidky Pasha then goes on to say:

"The Egyptian trader often confuses cash receipts and profits. When he sees the money flowing into his coffers, he deems himself so much richer, and spends without counting, scarcely thinking that these receipts like these expenses represent at times his very capital. Moreover, the fact that he has made a little money is often sufficient for the merchant to devote himself to the pleasures of repose, and leave to others the duty of managing his business, forgetting that one is never so well served as by oneself.

"It often happens that the Egyptian trader, misinterpreting the precepts of the Moslem religion, allows himself to lapse into a fatalism which constitutes the very reverse of the commercial spirit. It is God who dispenses good and evil, he says, and relying on this principle, he scarcely takes the trouble to manage his clients or to attract others. Hence the arrogance, the lack of civility, the stubborn obstinacy which can be noted among a number of our business men, whilst the European business man will go as far as to sacrifice his self-esteem in order to content his clients.

"The Egyptian merchant is hardly interested in being up to date, in innovating, in exploring and in seeking for ways and means which will permit him to forestall and overcome competition. For instance, he is totally uninterested in commercial statistics, whereas I myself was able to note the primordial interest which foreign traders devote to these."

It would be difficult to find a more striking description of the pre-rationalistic entrepreneur, the complete reverse of our Puritan business man, than that thus recorded by a writer of such authority and with such knowledge of the subject. A noteworthy point in this interesting picture is the emphasis laid on the complete indolence in respect of figures, the statistical formulation of facts which must be of great value to the merchant. Here we clearly have a repetition of the negative relation to any interpretation of reality in the form of figures, a relic of old magical conceptions whose effect is felt also in other connections. The famous reply given by the Kadi of Mosul to a friend of Layard comes within the same category. The traveller on enquiring as to the size of the town, the number of its inhabitants, its commerce and historical traditions, received the following answer:

"My illustrious Friend, and Joy of my Liver! The thing you ask of me is both difficult and useless. Although I have passed all my days in this place, I have neither counted the houses nor have I inquired into the number of the inhabitants; and as to what one person loads on his mules and the other stows away in the bottom of his ship, that is no business of mine. But, above all, as to the previous history of this city, God only knows the amount of dirt and confusion that the infidels may have eaten before the coming of the sword of Islam. It were unprofitable for us to inquire into it."[25]

Judging from the foregoing it would seem justifiable to assume that a society thus constituted, endowed with the specific mentality we have described, was not qualified to reach that technical and organisational level of achievement which during the same period was under way in the West. Certain isolated exceptions have scarcely been able to alter the general picture. In order to justify the stagnation in the Orient one is wont to compare the contemplative mental attitude of the Oriental, so befitting the dignity of man, and his religious culture with the soul-destroying activity and machine civilisation of the European. In point of fact, this boasted contemplativeness and inwardness, the professed religious background serves frequently only to camouflage an indolence almost beyond measure, a lack of original force and initiative compared with which the activity of the modern industrialist and engineer, organised, constructive and planned, appears a truly creative achievement.

Nothing, however, would be more erroneous than to regard this phase of Moslem society as permanent. A variety of changes in social and cultural life here accelerated, there retarded, now pronounced, now hidden and groping, punctuate the new scene. In this context the following facts may be mentioned by way of example: in most of the Moslem States Government departments of economics and statistics, originally set up by foreigners, are now run by their own native staffs. Everywhere the establishment of modern credit banks, insurance companies, large industrial plants, etc., is proceeding apace. All and every means of communication are being used in order to open up the countries of Islam. These developments would not have been possible without a marked weakening of the doctrines of Moslem social ethics as affecting economic practice, without the gradual displacement of Islam as the ultimate arbiter of social life. Here, indeed, we can see the same process of adaptation to existent economic conditions, as has occurred also in the case of other religions.

In the new Turkey this process of secularisation took place in a revolutionary fashion. We have described its most conspicuous features in the section dealing with the transformation of the Turkish State. In the more remote Arab territories the process goes on rather slowly, but in the Arab countries bordering on the Mediterranean the movement towards Westernization is in full swing. Marked differences exist, however, between the attitude of the leading classes and that of the masses. Westerners, when asking younger Moslems in leading business positions about the present-day importance of certain Islamic doctrines as affecting economic practice, are not seldom perplexed at the rather deprecatory manner in which the subject is treated. Despite the obvious shallowness of argumentation the observant mind senses that a genuine and far-reaching change is under way, at least as far as the urbanized and more wealthy sections of the Moslem population are concerned. For them the goal is simply to acquire a Western outlook and a Western mode of living. But also among the less articulate classes important shifts can be noted tending towards the acceptance of Western social concepts, superficial as many of these developments may appear to the outsider. The acceleration given to these processes in recent years, under the impact of the Second World War, render the views of Prof. Gibb as expressed in *Whither Islam?* in 1932 even more valid today than heretofore:

"Until recently, the ordinary Moslem citizen and cultivator had no political interests or functions, had no literature of easy access except religious literature, had no festivals and no communal life except in connexion with religion, saw little or nothing of the outside world except through religious glasses. To him, in consequence, religion meant everything. Now, however, in all the more advanced countries, his interests have expanded and his activities are no longer bounded by religion. He has political questions thrust on his notice; he reads or has read to him a mass of articles on subjects of all kinds which have nothing to do with religion, and in which the religious point of view may not be discussed at all and the verdict held to lie with some quite different principle; he finds that in many of his difficulties and disputes it is useless for him to apply to the religious courts, but that he is bound by a civil code which derives its validity from he may not know where, but certainly not from the Koran and Tradition. The old religious interests have ceased to furnish his sole, or even his main social link with his fellows; other and secular interests claim his attention. The authority of Islam is thus loosened in his social life, and it is relegated little by little to a narrower range of activities. Much of this has taken place quite unconsciously; only amongst a small percentage of educated men has it been conscious, and amongst a still smaller proportion consciously pursued. Nevertheless the process has gone on inexorably, and where it has already gone far enough it is irrevocable."[26]

CHAPTER XXXIII

THE STANDARD OF LIVING

Nowhere is the great antithesis of Orient and Occident which colours so many aspects of the social and economic problems under review so tangibly revealed as in the form in which the bulk of the population in Oriental countries satisfy their requirements of life. This applies to their needs in respect of consumption goods in general. It is true that a low standard of living is a phenomenon which is by no means peculiar to the Orient, for it is one shared by many undeveloped countries of today; what accentuates the problem in this case is the fact that the Oriental countries in antiquity were the seat of a very high culture and possessed wealth to a degree almost unknown in other latitudes.

Even if there had not been a lowering of the standard of living as the result of historical factors, the difference between the demand for consumer goods in these parts and in Northern countries would still be far-reaching. Nature, that created here a specific type of man, endowed him also with specific needs. The heaven an everlasting dome of blue, a climate which knows no rain for seven or eight months in the year, these are factors which have had a marked effect on the general nature of habitation, its forms and customs. This is reflected in the limited rôle occupied by housing as compared to conditions in other latitudes where it forms a central branch of commodity production. The extent to which housing for the rural and urban masses in the Orient is relegated to a most inferior place is evidenced, on the one hand, by the unsightly appearance of their houses themselves and, on the other, by the almost complete absence of internal domestic amenities. This contentment has had two extremely important consequences. First the low standard of housing left no scope for the development of many of the domestic arts and crafts which are so prominent a feature of Northern countries, while secondly, the building of a house does not represent the important economic event in the life of the Oriental that it does for the citizen of the Occident.

Anyone visiting for the first time the villages of the fellahin in countries of old Oriental culture, such as Egypt or Mesopotamia, countries proverbial for their wealth, will be extremely disappointed by his outward impressions. However much the inexhaustible fertility of the river valleys may astound and perhaps overawe him, he will be chiefly impressed not by this, but by the strange frugality of the fellah. However much the passage of millennia has affected the fellah economy in other respects, yet as regards this peculiar trait it has apparently not changed much up to the present day,

True, there are differences to be discerned in the actual forms of habitation in the various countries. In the irrigated plains of the riverine countries the dwellings in the villages are built today, as in former times, principally of dried clay bricks; the internal arrangements are primitive beyond words, furniture is not customary, save for straw mats and dried reed or palm branches which serve as beds. In most of the hill districts a crude stone hut containing a single room suffices for the accommodation of the fellah or shepherd, who often enough with the changing season changes also his place of habitation and moves into the valley, where he lives in a tent or in a clay hut. A still simpler form of dwelling is seen in the vast lowlands of Mesopotamia, the so-called *sarifa*, a hut made out of reed matting and built in the form of a tent or half a barrel. For a large part of the population of the Arabian Peninsula, of Iraq, of the Egyptian desert country and even of the countries bordering on the Eastern Mediterranean, the ancient primitive Beduin tent remains as it has been for thousands of years the roving nomad's sole and everlasting form of habitation.

These features are common to all these forms of dwelling: they neither demand from their occupiers any special effort for their construction, maintenance and replacement, nor do they provide those urges and incentives to the development of domestic culture which have become characteristic of settlement in European countries. The paltriness of the tasks afforded by this type of housing with its almost total lack of articles calling for the hand of the artisan and craftsman has been a decisive factor in shaping the cultural history of the Orient.

Natural conditions which for many of the Oriental countries—with the exception of the river oases in Egypt and Babylon—have created particularly poor conditions of production, have also influenced the norm of nutrition. The daily ration of the bulk of the Oriental agrarian population consists even today of a moderate quantity of bread (made of wheat or durrah) with vegetables or rice, supplemented at times by home-made cheese or sour milk. Fat requirements are satisfied chiefly by the olive or olive oil. Meat consumption is small. As a rule sheep or poultry are killed only for special reasons. The use of modern foods makes but very slow headway in the villages, although, of course, coffee and tea have long been popular. But only in the rarest cases does the value of the daily ration of an adult fellah exceed 3–5 piastres (the equivalent of eightpence or a shilling), whilst he will often spend only half that amount in obtaining the minimum of food necessary for his sustenance (pre-war values).

In the matter of clothing, too, it is obvious that climatic conditions in Eastern countries permit of a lower expenditure. In many districts new garments are scarcely bought for the children. Nevertheless, despite very primitive requirements in this respect, we have here one significant deviation. Owing to the fact that Islam is averse to any exposure of the body, especially in women, the consumption of textile goods in Oriental countries has always been quantitatively high, leading even quite early to the establishment of an indigenous textile industry. Yet the economic consequences of this religious injunction, tending above all to increased luxury in dress, were felt more in the town than the village. The peasant could not afford any larger expenditure on his clothing and would, therefore, nurse his one and only garment with the utmost care in order to enjoy its possession for as many years as possible.

This frugal form of living represents one of the principal reasons for the static condition of the entire Oriental social economy at a period when in Europe the foundations of society were being shaken by the new claims and needs of the masses. One of the major social problems of the Middle East today is, therefore, the question how to raise the standard of living, how to effect, above all, an expansion of consumption in the fellah's economy and infuse a new economic and social mentality. In the domain of this tied economy isolated from foreign influences and dominated by a traditionalism which has moulded the economic thought of the fellah until today, this unparalleled frugality of living, this resignation on the fellah's part to the fate of a pariah, was the secret of his passive continuance in this mode of existence. No matter whether his annual income had a money value of £15 or £25, no matter whether a third or a half of his gross receipts went in interest and taxes, or whether the raising of the sum necessary to exempt his son from conscription delivered him completely into the hands of the usurer, the fellah would manage eventually, even if it meant the sacrifice of all progress, of every enjoyment of life beyond the bare necessities, of his children's education, of all opportunities for the development and satisfaction of his cultural needs.

The First World War proved the successful sponsor of new standards in a number of Oriental countries. For the first time nations with European standards came into close daily contact with the native population. The example of the troops and immigrants who poured into the Middle East gave a powerful impetus to local habits of consumption. Articles of food formerly unknown, new modes of dress and habitation, articles of entertainment such as the gramophone, cinema, wireless, means of communication such as the railway, motor-car and bicycle, became popular even in the country districts in a surprisingly short time and helped to form the new Oriental no less than the impact of modern political and social ideas. The mode of life among wide urban circles approximated largely to that in European towns. Expenditure on luxuries, amusements, etc., represents an item in the budget of the modern town-dweller which must not be under-estimated. Most conspicuous is the rise in the standard of housing after the war. European customs even among the native population are superseding more and more the primitive habits of the past. Hot and cold water installations, bathrooms, etc., are no longer the monopoly of a few Europeans, but indispensable adjuncts to new houses. Electric light takes the place of petroleum lighting in the towns. The increased demand for larger and better houses leads to an exodus from the centre of the towns and to the establishment of many pleasant residential and villa quarters on the peripheries. The local traffic problem has been solved by the construction of excellent connecting roads between the centre and the residential quarters. The new villa quarters in the suburbs of Baghdad and Cairo, the modern Government buildings and hospitals in Ankara and Jerusalem compare favourably with those in European towns.[27] Thus the social requirements of the population in these parts outgrow the narrow framework of traditional production, and demand an expansion of their economic activities which, however, is again made possible only by the removal of the legal and traditional barriers described above.

However much this process may differ in tempo at times—there are indeed great differences between town and country—the fact remains that it is under way, and during the short period of its intensification has produced a rise in the social product in which industry, agriculture and other branches of economy have an equal share.

CHAPTER XXXIV

THE NOMADS

As opposed to conditions in the old civilised West, a line of demarcation still runs through the Oriental world, dividing the settled population from the nomads. Settled, semi-nomadic and wholly nomadic modes of life determine the character and mentality of the people in these groups. The differentiation also continues within the nomad population itself. Particular stress is laid by the Beduin tribes on distinctions deriving from descent. Not all nomads are Beduin, nor all Beduin inevitably fully nomad. The Beduin themselves recognise as full Beduin only a certain number of tribes whose ancient and distinguished descent is vouched for by traditions going far back into past centuries. These traditions do not always stand a meticulous examination as to their genealogical details and—as is at times admitted by the Beduin themselves—often include elements of phantasy. This alters nothing, however, as regards the social standing of the tribes and clans recognised as noble, just as the tribes whose equality of birth is disputed seldom manage to get accepted among the aristocracy. Such recognition is not always dependent on a nomadic existence. A number of nomad tribes whose mode of life differs in no respect from that of the aristocratic Beduin attain at best to the rank of protected tribes, i.e. tribes who enjoy the patronage of a noble Beduin tribe.

Social Structure of the Tribes

How are the tribes constituted within themselves? Numerous investigators have studied their social and family organisation, thus enabling us to define certain typical structures of Arab tribes.[28]

As a rule the structure of a tribe, starting from the family or tent community, comprises a number of larger and more comprehensive units based on degree of kinship.

The first unit is the family or *ahl* (tent community); next come the closely related family groups, or generations (*ejal*). The family groups form branch tribes called *ashire* when it is desired to stress the political element, and *hamula* when the emphasis is on the kinship element of their relationship. The actual tribal group which embraces all sections and branches of the tribe, the tribal unit within which the member of the tribe but not the foreigner (at least not immediately) enjoys legal protection, is the *qabila*. Above this tribal organisation there is the blood association, a much looser grouping known as *hamse*, which comprises all a man's blood-relations down to the fifth degree. All the blood-relations of a man within this circle of kinship are in the event of his murder subject to the law of blood feud. The social structure of the Beduin, however, is not always built along these lines, and in many cases we find only the larger trinity of family (*aila*), family groups (*ashire* or *hamula*), and tribes (*qabila*). The head of the tribe is invariably the *sheikh*. The sheikh is generally chosen by the elders as *primus inter pares*, the choice normally falling on the eldest son of the father, so that in a sense it might even be called an hereditary office; but should the eldest son be unfitted for the rank, another son or distant relative of the deceased is elected sheikh. If several subordinate tribes are incorporated in a larger tribal group, it is customary to elect also, over the sheikh, a "Chief Sheikh" who exercises mainly a representative function. The internal affairs of the various sections within the tribe are regulated by the respective competent authorities as represented by the tribal chiefs. The Chief Sheikh represents the tribal group as a whole in relation to the outside world; he negotiates with the Government, is responsible for any lack or default in the payment of tribute, and in such cases is imprisoned by the Government as surety.

The functions devolving on the chief of the tribe are remarkably diverse. This is due to the completely unbureaucratic manner in which tribal affairs are managed. The sheikh, therefore, becomes very soon the real, patriarchal leader of his flock. He knows the legal uses and the traditions of his tribe as well as those of the neighbouring tribes; he knows their genealogy; he must exercise the functions of representative of his sometimes politically fairly influential group; he must ensure peace within the tribe by firmness and equity, whilst being always well-informed as to outside conditions relative to the security of the camp, the quality of the wells, the state of the roads, etc. He decides when to strike the tents and where to pitch. Last but not least, his representative functions also include acts of liberality and hospitality on a generous scale. The accommodation and entertainment of strangers is his privilege. He meets these and other obligations arising from his position out of his private fortune, so that he must normally have larger means at his disposal. The office of sheikh is, therefore, contingent on a certain amount of wealth, which, in practice, results in its being confined to the well-to-do families among the tribes. A matter of particular importance for the position of the sheikh, especially in Beduin communities which have gone in for agriculture, has been the trend of development in respect of conditions of land tenure. The lands under cultivation were originally allotted to the individual members of the tribes as collective tribal property. The rights of the sheikh in this connection were principally of a representative and arbitrary nature; thus, he possessed the right of redistributing the land among the members of the tribe and of settling disputes in respect of rights of ownership. The idea of the unity of the tribe's communal property was symbolised in his person as patron and leader of the community. In order to defray the special expenses incurred as overlord, certain revenues, in addition to the profits from his own share of the land, accrued to him by way of contributions from the others.

Under the influence of later developments the position of the sheikh very considerably changed. He became a large landed proprietor. He is no longer *primus inter pares* and charismatic leader, but becomes the overlord of his followers, who lose their independence and their claims to the land within the community.

Nomad Mode of Living

Among the present-day nomads in the Middle East the Arab Beduin tribes surpass in influence and socio-political importance all other nomadic groups. What follows, therefore, refers mainly to conditions of life among the Beduins.

According to their mode of living and their principal place of domicile the Beduin may be divided into three groups: desert Beduin, steppe Beduin and semi-Beduin. The last-named occupy a position halfway between Beduin and Fellahin, and though still at times living in tents, turn as a rule to the construction of permanent clay huts or houses and engage in agriculture. In the districts bordering on the desert certain of these semi-Beduin groups are wont in the spring to seek out the adjacent steppe country where they graze their cattle. But the bulk of these semi-Beduin must definitely be regarded as settled. The desert Beduin are genuine nomads who rove the vast areas lying between the Syrian desert in the north and the centre of the Arabian Peninsula. In view of the fact that they keep camels exclusively, their mobility is extraordinarily great in contrast to that of the steppe Beduin who, in addition, keep cows, sheep and goats in large numbers and are famous also for their horse-breeding, though its extent is usually exaggerated. The steppe Beduin inhabit not only the districts lying between the desert and the cultivated zones, but are to be found everywhere in the vicinity of the settled population; their internal organisation manifests all the characteristics of a tribal constitution; also they usually place themselves under the rule of one of the noble tribes.

The origin of the nomadic form of life and its basis of existence is directly connected with the nature of the country forming the nomad's place of habitation. The marked difference between winter and summer temperatures and the rainfall causes the inhabitants of the desert, with the approach of the hot season, which in the desert makes itself felt with particular intensity, to seek the cooler areas in the north or more highly situated districts. The same applies, *mutatis mutandis*, to the winter period when the low temperatures in the Northern Oriental countries or in the hills make tent life a hardship, and accentuate the need for a warmer dwelling. A further reason is that even where natural conditions would permit, no effort is made to cultivate the land, so that the need to keep the cattle supplied with water and their sparse fill of grass calls for continual migration between the various grazing grounds. With every day that the Beduin hosts remain at their grazing grounds, the "bite" becomes less plentiful, so that the quest for new camping and grazing grounds is an ever-recurrent necessity. These migrations in quest of pasture do not take place at random, but according to a definite order determined by the water conditions within the grazing areas. In the spring the camel herds trek to the more arid zones, as at this period, owing to the preceding rains, there is everywhere a green carpet of vegetation. As the season advances they draw closer to districts in the vicinity of which well water is available. In the autumn and winter their camps are pitched close to the wells in order to secure a minimum of well water if the rains fail.

In this context it seems appropriate to mention the significant theory of the secular movements of nomads, which in respect of Asia was first put forward by Ellsworth Huntington (in *The Pulse of Asia*) and, about the same time, evolved for Arabia by Caetani. It has recently been elaborated by A. J. Toynbee, in the third volume of *A Study of History*.

In addition to the wanderings of the nomads in an annual orbit covering different grounds at different times of year, there are the huge migrations throughout the ages conditioned by climatic changes on a vast scale.

"Recent meteorological research indicates that there is a rhythmic alternation, possibly of world-wide incidence, between periods of relative desiccation and humidity, which causes alternate intrusions of peasants and nomads into one another's spheres. When desiccation reaches a degree at which the steppe can no longer provide pasture for the quantity of cattle with which the nomads have stocked it, the herdsmen swerve from their beaten track of annual migration and invade the surrounding cultivated countries in search of food for their animals and themselves. On the other hand, when the climatic pendulum swings back and the next phase of humidity attains a point at which the steppe becomes capable of bearing cultivated roots and cereals, the peasant makes his counter-offensive upon the pastures of the nomad. Their respective methods of aggression are very dissimilar. The nomad's outbreak is as sudden as a cavalry charge, and shatters sedentary societies like the bursting of some high explosive. The peasant's is an infantry advance. At each step he digs himself in with mattock or steam plough, and secures his communications by building roads or railways. The most striking recorded examples of nomad explosion are the intrusions of the Turks and Mongols, which occurred in what was probably the last dry period but one. An imposing instance of peasant encroachment is the subsequent eastward expansion of Russia. Both types of movement are abnormal, and each is extremely unpleasant for the party at whose expense it is made. But they are alike in being due to a single uncontrollable physical cause."[29]

Even if we allow for the existence of secular movements on so large a scale and their causes, this does not mean that every sector of the Middle Eastern zone has been under the impact of this phenomenon. Mention was made in Part II of certain climatic criteria that point to practically unchanged climatic conditions as far as Palestine and the neighbouring regions are concerned. However that may be, the chances that a phase of excessive desiccation would in our times lead to a nomad explosion, sweeping over entire continents, are fairly small. A radical change has taken place in the balance of power as between the nomad and the settled population. The progress of civilisation has been primarily a process of settling down, whereby the sedentary population secured an increasing superiority over the nomad in both the military and the economic spheres.

Material Conditions of Life

The opportunities at the nomad's disposal for the satisfaction of his daily needs are of the poorest. His sole capital is his herd, which in the case of the desert Beduin consists mainly of camels, in other cases of sheep and goats also. In former times the true Beduin, who was a cattle breeder, knew no other sources of income than that provided by the sale of the animals he reared and of their products. The hiring out of camels as working animals is not a regular business among the Beduin, but is mostly done by semi-Beduin or fellahin living in or near the towns. Likewise the Beduin themselves do not accompany or escort the caravans.

The figures given for the annual expenditure of a Beduin family are far below those familiar to us from the budgets of Oriental peasant families. A sum of £10–15 (pre-war) is sufficient to cover the needs of a poor Beduin family. This revenue is obtained under normal circumstances from the sale of two or three camels per year which are replaced by the natural increase of the herd. In addition, the Beduin is wont on his rare visits to the town to sell some wool, a few sheep, a certain quantity of butter, and to buy from the proceeds rice, flour, sugar, coffee and dates. If he is somewhat better off he will treat himself and his wife to a new smock, a saddle or a new carpet.

Actually the Beduin is content with his daily meals of rice and the flat loaves of native bread, with a few onions or other vegetables. Besides this he is fond of tea and coffee and his home-made sheep's cheese.

Insignificant as are the Beduin's daily needs and expenses, and ready as he is in bad times to reduce his requirements still further, he tends on the other hand to a display of extravagance far in excess of his means when entertaining guests or celebrating family events. In order to celebrate these occasions fittingly he, like the fellah, is capable of running himself deep into debt for many years to come. Despite these consequences he never ceases to boast of these traits as of a particular virtue.

The terms and concepts applicable to the economic activity of the settled population cannot be employed in respect of the activity devoted by the Beduin to securing his daily needs. His "economy" is no economy in the accepted sense of the word; it lacks the features common to other economic stages and systems, features which constitute the essence of economic conduct. It is directed neither solely at a peaceful mode of earning a livelihood, nor can it be described as a continuous, regular form of activity. As a matter of fact, the livelihood problem is not recognised as one which can be solved by any systematic deliberate effort. The term "Beduin economy" is a contradiction in itself, combining elements which cannot be coupled. The fickleness and instability of external conditions has invested the efforts of the Beduin to gain sustenance for himself and his animals with an unstable, haphazard character.

The Beduin knows nothing of the morrow, of forethought and systematic preparation for what is to come; his world-order is one in which, according to age-long experience, God will ever and again provide him with the essentials of life; it has no room for the ideas of duty and achievement. Undoubtedly his unsurpassable frugality is one of its primary conditions; but in such an atmosphere nothing of any permanency can be produced, no work calling for patient, conscious creative endeavour.

The social mentality of the Beduin is a special problem. What for modern society is the very foundation of life, the well-ordered, demarcated, State-protected settlement, strikes him as a despicable mode of existence, devoid of all value. True, the transformation of our forms of existence tends to affect his approach to life also; but up to a few decades ago this contrast was as acute as ever; in fact, in large parts of the Orient it exists even today. For the common Beduin the desert is his own social province, well-nigh unassailable, boundless in the full literal sense of the word, his very life-element. He has known no State organisation to which he has submitted and whose laws and regulations he has recognised; nor did he attempt on his own account, through an alliance of Beduin tribes, to enter into any kind of super-territorial State relationship. Everything connected with the function of the State in the Orient, such as recognition of the administrative central authority and its organs in the provinces, obligations to pay taxes, to obey laws, he seeks whenever possible to ignore. The term "State" means nothing to him, or at most something negative; he regards State authority even when it represents no direct interference in his domain as a deliberate restriction of his freedom. He recognises no obligation on his part towards a central authority; only occasionally will he enter its service for some warlike activity. The Beduin will place himself at the disposal of one of the desert rulers in return for the prospect of booty, much as the lansquenet of the Middle Ages entered the service of his lord. Just as promptly as he undertook such service will he leave it and betray his former master or ally if a new one promises him more. The same aversion towards every binding connection evidenced in his relations to his overlord, characterises his attitude to every endeavour which is made to organise his social life on a uniform basis, to enlarge the tribal society into an organised State which might then also contain non-Beduin elements. The Beduin is by nature (except in his close tribal circle) an asocial being: within the tribal group equal rights for all; those outside are outlaws whose rights need not be respected.

The Beduin, and even the settled Arab who feels himself as a descendant and preserver of Beduin tradition, resorts easily to self-help, at least wherever the State sees no cause to interfere. He will often revenge the violation of the honour of his family in a drastic manner, in this connection sacrificing without compunction the lives of several people; any appeal on the part of State authority to his sense of duty to the community leaves him insensible and indifferent, no matter whether it is a question of alleviating distress or assistance against threats from outside. His sense of justice reacts in the first instance to offences against the individual. State authority has still no ethical value in his eyes, and can therefore not be violated. There is no deeper contrast than that between this ethical conception and the all-embracing claims of the modern Occidental State which would rather show leniency where the infringement or violation of the rights of the individual are concerned, than leave unavenged any violation of the honour and rights of the State.

The fact that the greater part of the population of the Arabian Peninsula and the adjoining border-zones follow the Beduin mode of life has had a retarding effect on the whole social and economic development of the Middle East. For generations the population there has been inconspicuous either as consumers or producers. There was no room here for any of those stimuli towards a more cultivated mode of life usually associated with settlement and an extensive exchange of goods.

On the contrary: the conceptions and conduct of life of the predominating element in the population have kept that great economic and cultural vacuum intact, a fact which, owing not only to the nature of the country but also to the social and psychic make-up of the inhabitants, has had such a decisive effect on the course of historical events in the East. The nearer we get to the steppe, the less secure is the life of the settled population, and with the absence of security civilisation likewise disappears; the pressure and power of the nomad grows, becoming a threat to everything which favours order, permanency and form. This state of affairs is most conspicuous in the relations existing between the peasant or the inhabitant of the small provincial town and the nomad. An age-old feud exists between these and the true Beduin, who has ever been "out" to ravage the villages of the fellahin, to steal their cattle and graze their fields. The peasant, his inferior in strength and mobility, has always feared and hated him.

In most regions of Ottoman Turkey the Beduin problem—as a problem of the relations between the settled and the nomad population—has continued in all its acuteness up to the beginning of this century, even if occasionally the power of the tribes has been broken for shorter or longer periods. Again and again, up to the most recent decades, we read of raids by the Beduin on the agricultural villages and the extortions then exacted. Where tolerable conditions have emerged, these were based on the *Huwe*, a tributary payment to the Beduin made by the fellahin with the tacit consent of the distant central authorities.[30]

In other districts where the Beduin had no reason for showing consideration, the depopulation of the countryside became an unavoidable fact, and it is surprising to find how far this process has developed in the course of recent centuries. According to Edrisi in 1180 there were still about 600 villages in the old Phœnician region of Sidon alone. At the beginning of the nineteenth century their number had fallen to a few dozen. In the former Pashalik of Aleppo the number of villages is said, according to a source quoted by Lammens, to have dropped in the middle of the nineteenth century from 3,200 to 400, the population from 2–300,000 to 70,000. The same applies to the Hauran area, the districts round the Judean desert and Transjordan. Granted that invasions and the welter of war, clashes between the local rulers and continuous spoliation on the part of the Government and the overlords were also to a certain extent responsible for the decline, the repeatedly recurring expulsion of the settled population by the nomad tribes, Kurds and Turkmans north of the Syrian desert and the Arab Beduin in the south was the underlying if not the sole cause.

The latent threat to the exposed border villages led eventually to a change in their character. The link with the soil is weakened, the peasants in self-defence so to speak no longer incur the risk of investing in orchards and buildings lest their villages may have to be surrendered. Thus the treeless fellah settlement in the borderland between the cultivated zone and the steppe represents a typical transitional form between the two social groups.

With the consolidation of the power of the State and the encroachment of modern means of communication, the Beduin problem, which appeared insoluble so long as anarchical conditions obtained in the provinces, has become one of the central administrative problems of the young Oriental countries of today. The new attempts at solution hinge on strengthening the relation of the Beduin to the soil, in the endeavour to induce him to settle.

Tribal settlement is one of the most interesting and complicated tasks of social reconstruction in Oriental lands. In view of their special geographical nature and the importance of the Beduin element in their population, Syria and Iraq are two States in which this task has acquired particular significance. Its importance from a purely quantitative standpoint is in no other country in the Middle East, apart from the Peninsula itself, so great as in Iraq. Here the problem is twofold. It is a question of

(*a*) how to safeguard the settled population from the traditional Beduin marauding expeditions;

(*b*) how to transform and consolidate the economic and social life of the Beduin themselves.

So long as the easy accessibility of the populated settlement areas provides a temptation for the free Son of the Desert to balance the deficit in his food budget and that of his herd by a raid on the border villages, so long as the controlling authority of the State is not regularly seen and felt, any repopulation of the now deserted border zones is a most doubtful possibility.

For the inhabitants of the villages and provincial towns situated in the border zones the settlement of the Beduin means a marked alleviation in their conditions of existence. But for the Beduin themselves it represents in every respect a fundamental transformation of their mode of life. Formerly independent of any ruling authority and its domain, they are now confined to a certain area. The ancient freedom of the denizens of the desert was doomed, indeed, from the day that the motor-car began to conquer the desert. This means of communication is, apart from the aeroplane, the principal key to that conquest, and the liquidation of that almost unassailable and boundless realm which for the Beduin was his life-element. Added to this is the successive application of control by the State with its instruments of Government such as efficient administration, education, police, legislation, and last but not least, perhaps also conscription. It need not be emphasised that this process of incorporating an "asocial" element into the most highly developed organisation of human society, the modern State, cannot be effected without serious conflicts and disturbances. The Arab saying "To settle means to forfeit one's glory" no doubt expresses a genuine feeling. Despite the known improvement in the material conditions of the Beduin it is not unusual for groups that have already been "settled" to revert to their old nomadic life. In many cases the attempts are unsuccessful from the start, and the place selected for settlement is not even occupied. In other respects also the results of settlement and contact with civilisation are often not encouraging, particularly in their early stages. Thus we read in the British Ten Year Year Report on Iraq of the results, for instance, of the education of the sons of the Beduin sheikhs in the towns as follows:

> "The result of the education of the few who go to school is not entirely happy. They return to the tribe, if they return at all (and often enough they stay idly in the towns), to criticize their fathers and despise their womenkind, they lose the old patriarchal manners and virtues and lack the knowledge to rule their tribes, in short they return unfitted for tribal life. No steps at all are taken for the education of the girls, even among the settled tribes, and it is perhaps best so. The tribal girl marries early; she must have several crafts at her finger-ends."[31]

But notwithstanding all these initial setbacks the settlement process of the Beduin, once started, cannot be altogether halted. Indeed, certain tendencies such as the declining importance of the camel as a means of transport and the superiority of modern means of communication for the conquest of the desert will in any case compel him to base his life on some other source of livelihood than camel breeding. Besides, the modern State itself has the greatest interest in the assimilation of this social group with its anachronistic style of living. Traditions and customs dating back thousands of years cannot, it is true, be abolished within a short space of time. However, given a lead by a powerful State authority, the process of social adjustment and settlement among the nomads will go on irresistibly, in line with the general transformation of society in our day. Thus the oldest human community, a community where the ties between man and nature are closest, will eventually succumb to the dual forces of urbanisation and mechanisation.

CHAPTER XXXV

SUMMARY

Having endeavoured in the preceding chapters to establish the decisive facts connected with the changing structure of State and Economics in the Middle East and its various aspects, this concluding chapter is devoted to a brief recapitulation of these findings.

I. The State

How has this transformation made itself felt in the province of the State? During the past hundred years the Oriental State, whose particular nature was determined by certain specific criteria, has undergone a fundamental change. As a result of the increasing contact of the Oriental world with the West the seeds of modern nationalism and the modern conception of the "State" were planted and took root in the Oriental countries. The adaptation of Western ideas ultimately gave birth to new State forms and political institutions which, however, have yet to prove their powers of vitality. The revolutionary technical changes, which were introduced above all in the system of communications, undermined the structure of domination in the sprawling Oriental State where administration was based on the almost unrestricted independence of the provincial potentates. Thus the way was paved for the introduction of a ramified system of administration controlled by a central authority. The rationalisation of administrative methods reduced the influence hitherto exerted by favourites and cliques and made room for a civil service largely composed of officials specially trained for their duties, whilst the tendency towards secularisation, gathering strength from Western sources, weakened the dominant status of religious institutions and ideologies whose position in the course of decades was either rendered ineffective or totally destroyed.

What tangible results of this forceful movement—apart from the various often mutually contradictory transitional phenomena—appear to be of a permanent character?

1. The new conception of the "State" in the Orient begins by questioning the idea of the indivisibility of religious and secular authority. Out of the struggle for the maintenance of this alliance the secularised State emerged largely victorious. Thus, the Turkish republic rests on a manifestly secular basis; religious life has been

relegated to the private sphere, and what was symbolic of the Islamic State down to recent times, the personal union of the Khalif as religious head of the Moslem community and secular ruler, has been abolished. In other countries of the Middle East the tempo of secularisation is considerably slower, but the process continues to make steady headway.

2. The general importance of the "State idea" for the establishment of modern society and the transformation of the former unpolitical masses into conscious citizens was fully recognised first in Turkey, but later also in other Oriental countries, even if in principle only. Far-reaching measures to shape a new State conscience and spread education in this sense have been resolutely taken by the leaders of the new Turkey.

3. The principle of nationality made itself felt not only in the accentuation of the "national" in all State and public spheres; it led also, in the case of the greatest Oriental State, Turkey, to the creation of a truly homogeneous national State. To achieve this end, this State did not flinch before radical interference in the structure of the population. Since the Greco-Turkish resettlement the population within the area of the Turkish State consists for the greater part of elements which, by virtue of language or national feeling and in part of descent, consider themselves as Turks. In other Oriental countries where several nationalities live within one State entity, the national rights accorded to them on the basis of the former plural constitution have been to a wide extent curtailed.

4. This fundamental change in the form of the State also resulted in a radical encroachment on the province of sovereign rights. The despotic régime is superseded by forms of government wherein the rights of the population are constitutionally safeguarded. In certain cases the young Succession States are denied self-government until certain criteria of State maturity are fulfilled, the possibility of the arbitrary conduct of political affairs being curtailed by the introduction of supra-State organs of control.

5. The economic and legal sovereignty of the Oriental countries was restored to them on the abolition of the "Capitulations." The power of resistance of these countries to economic pressure and superior force has, contrary to opposite prognoses, so far proved remarkably strong.

6. In the legal sphere the modernisation of the civil and the

criminal law already inaugurated before the First World War has been extended and perfected by the introduction of new legal codes. Substantial parts of the former legal traditions have, however, been retained, so that law and jurisprudence in the Oriental countries are in a definite state of transition. Capitalist economic interests have managed to assert themselves, and the modern legal institutions indispensable for the effective functioning of a capitalist economy, such as the right of free disposal of landed and other property, modern banking and credit transactions and the mobilisation of capital, particularly the capital of joint stock companies and Stock Exchange business, have found their way into the Middle Eastern countries. Side by side with the religious laws limited to matters of personal status and succession, a system of secular legislation has been evolved, framed on the legal practice of progressive countries and tending to cover ever wider sections of economic and social life.

7. In the sphere of finance, the abolition of the dualistic system of taxation, according to which foreign powers possessed extensive rights of intervention, restored the full sovereignty of the Oriental State, thus creating the conditions for an autonomous financial and taxation policy. Fundamental changes have also occurred in the distribution of the burden of taxation. Hitherto the system of taxation imposed by the Oriental State had guaranteed the rule of the big landowners over the population, which suffered grievously under the biassed load of taxation. The inauguration of financial reforms, which started as early as the middle of the nineteenth century, led to a remodelling of the taxation structure, culminating in recent years in the introduction of an income tax in almost all Oriental countries, as a result of which modern ideas of taxation have for the first time found a recognised place in their financial systems.

II. Agrarian Society

The measure in which the shackles on independent thought and the cramping effects of tradition-bound action have retained their grip on Oriental society is far stronger in the agrarian sphere than in other sectors of the Arab world. The causes of this stagnation we have found to be attributable, apart from natural factors, to politico-social conditions, particularly to the heritage of Oriental feudalism and conditions of land tenure. So far as the individual farmstead is concerned, its stationary character was caused, on the one hand, largely by the condition of the soil, the primitiveness of the farm implements and equipment, the inferior quality of livestock, and the bad means of communication; on the other by the absence of a healthy sense of acquisitiveness in the make-up of the Oriental peasant. The extremely low productivity of Oriental peasant economy resulted from the combined effect of these various factors.

For agriculture in general the chances of development were likewise limited. What was lacking above all was the stimulation of production derived, as during the reshaping of agrarian conditions in Europe, from the enormous (absolute) increase in the urban population. In addition, political and social conditions in the Orient were all conducive to the accumulation of large estates in the hands of one individual. The lien on the individual rights of disposal imposed by specific legal institutions, above all *Waqf* and *Mushaa*, tended to hinder all initiative on the part of the individual cultivator. Oriental feudalism lacked the personal relationship (*homagium*) which united the feudal lord and his liegeman; absent, too, were other criteria of a landed feudal aristocracy. The relation of the landowner to his property was from the very beginning a mercenary one, his property being nothing more than a source of rental.

The Moslem land law, which classified the land according to certain legal categories and thereby prejudiced its mobility, aimed in the first instance at coping with the financial problems of the Moslem community, but by so doing neglected the questions of land development, tenancy and collective ownership, all matters of the utmost importance for the welfare of agriculture.

The forces at work in the gradual opening-up of the agrarian sphere derive, first, from the weakening of the hold exercised by the tradition of Moslem land law in the religious world of thought; secondly, from the decomposition of feudal rights in the nineteenth century; and thirdly, though these were relatively late in making themselves felt, from the technical innovations in the field of irrigation, cultivation and communications. What, now, was the course taken by this structural transformation?

1. Here, too, one of the principal prerequisites for the politico-social inroads made in this sphere resulted from the new political and modernist ideas relative to the State and its function; this growing State-mindedness, coupled with the secularisation of the law, discounted successively the old principles of social order,

although its actual effects were felt only slowly. Thus today in almost all Oriental countries conditions of land tenure are seen to be in a state of transition inasmuch as the State is steadily removing the religious and legal restrictions on land tenure (Dead Hand—*Waqf*—collective ownership) whilst, on the other hand, it is releasing State lands for sale to the tenants besides intervening more actively than heretofore on behalf of the rights of the individual tenant in relation to the large landowner.

2. The legal abolition of the feudal system in the Ottoman Empire in the first half of the nineteenth century came from above, as a rational measure of State policy and legislation. The peasants had no part in it. Yet the dominant social position held and developed by the landed proprietor for centuries in relation to the peasantry and, up to not so very long ago, to the townsfolk also has consequently remained intact. The opportunities created by the new tax and land legislation for the forming of new estates were quickly seized by the large landowners themselves—contrary to the real intentions of the legislator. The exploitation of the peasants as a result of rent extortion and tax farming and their unworthy treatment by landlord and State up to the most recent times kept the rural population in a state of extreme indifference towards the State and State institutions.

3. Whereas in dry farming only slight changes are recorded, inasmuch as the conditions prevailing in this sphere were not conducive to reforms, conditions in irrigated farming—thanks to the splendid achievements of modern irrigation technique—prove more amenable in this connection. The increased population in the village found a safety-valve in the enormous demand for labour peculiar to the economy of irrigation where, in accordance with this very labour factor, the unit of farming is but a fraction of the area customary in dry farming.

At the same time the individual farm was affected only slowly by the changes occurring in the sphere of land legislation and agricultural technique. On the fellah farm the traditional implements and devices, methods of cultivation, etc., continue to be employed. Most significant, on the other hand, are the changes seen in agriculture as a branch of national economy, in the weight of its production within the sphere of production as a whole, in the irrigation plants serving the whole country, in productivity and conditions of land tenure.

Thus in all Oriental countries the extent of the so-called monocultures has been considerably reduced by the introduction of new crops and the variation of existing branches; credit and marketing conditions have been steadily improved and the organisation of agricultural interests effectively promoted. Imposing schemes of development and ambitious irrigation projects have dominated the agrarian policy of most Oriental countries in recent decades, whilst at the same time efforts are being made to effect an improvement in the agricultural yields per unit of area as well as in the quality of the products themselves.

The upshot of these changes in all spheres can be seen in the agricultural revival in this part of the world, in its emergence and integration as a producer in modern world economy, where the countries of the Middle East, endowed by nature with such exceptional gifts, can once again assume the rôle they occupied in ancient times. Nowhere in the Old World is such an accumulation of unexploited agrarian possibilities to be found as in the vast plains and irrigation zones of the Orient, which are settled today to but a fraction of their agricultural absorptive capacity. Nowhere is such a grand chance offered for the solution of complicated settlement questions as here. The remarkable spadework done by the Jewish settlers in Palestine indicates that millions of people in these parts of the globe might find work and bread at a decent standard of living and bring to the rest of the world also the fruits of these richly-blessed lands.

III. Industrial Goods Production

The industrial goods production of the Orient seemed at the turn of the nineteenth century doomed to inevitable decay. Consumption requirements offered no incentive to the development of industrial production on up-to-date lines, let alone industrial mass production. In so far as any such demand existed, it was easily met by the increasing import of European goods, so that native handicrafts, native methods and initiative and the local trade guilds were paralysed. Attempts on the part of far-seeing and energetic Oriental rulers like Mohammed Ali in Egypt and Mahmud II in Turkey to impose an industrial revolution on the Oriental countries by the introduction of novel methods along mercantilist lines were premature and failed. These efforts, as well as all subsequent endeavours on the part of native statesmen, were no match for the much superior forces of reality in view of

(*a*) foreign interests and their overwhelming predominance over those of local economy and the State;

(*b*) the absence of a citizen class able and willing to tackle the process of modern industrialisation;

(*c*) the general lack of understanding so far as State measures for the fostering of industrial development are concerned.

It was only later, when the great reshuffle after the First World War enabled the Oriental countries to obtain a certain status of autonomy and freedom of action, that European-inspired industrial planning—under the ægis of the State—came to be favoured both in theory and practice.

The independent Governments of the Oriental countries in resorting to industrialisation as a deliberately chosen political and economic instrument in the new State-sponsored national development aimed, on the one hand, at reducing their political and military-economic dependence on the advanced producer-countries and, on the other, at raising the standard of living of their hitherto predominantly agrarian populations.

Considering the short preparatory spell during which such modern industrial projects have been at work, the results are not unsatisfactory:

(*a*) The degree of self-sufficiency in the matter of important industrial products shows a marked rise. A large variety of essential industrial goods is now produced locally, and plans for their export are under way. Likewise the national income has increased to a remarkable extent both as a whole and *per capita* of the working population, although the problem of the high cost of many new industrial products has not yet, despite low wages, been satisfactorily solved.

(*b*) The question of the responsibility for the direction of the industrialisation process likewise awaits solution. The assumption by the State of the specific functions of the entrepreneur has only in part been able to compensate for this lack. So far no complete equivalent has been found for the absence of those qualities which in the West brought about the greatest transformation of human society since it came into being. This accounts for the defects and contradictions seen in many of the new industrial projects, and the inability on the part of the youthful industries to reconcile the question of profitability with the *raison d'état*, the dictates of State policy.

(*c*) The most important technical result is the replacement of handicraft work by machine production. The prolongation of the production process caused by the splitting-up of production into many phases, as compared to the work of the artisan which covers the whole process, is balanced to a considerable extent by the speeding-up of the tempo of production. With the introduction of the machine the time-factor is awakened in the consciousness of the Oriental, giving rise to deep-going psychological changes.

Hand in hand with this noteworthy progress is being made in the training of indigenous skilled workers for modern mechanical production.

(*d*) There is a distinct rise in the standard of living as a result of industrialisation, especially the satisfaction of new, formerly non-existent needs; but this is gained at the cost of a certain sacrifice. The worker who exchanges the primitive seclusion of his life on the land for the freer atmosphere of an industrial worker in the town, exchanges in so doing the security of a rural existence, however meagre, for the crisis-beset livelihood of a factory worker. He risks today, however, considerably less than did the villagers who drifted to the towns in the period of the Industrial Revolution in Europe, the social conscience of the State being more fully alive to the interests of the worker whose conditions it controls.

(*e*) So far as the State is concerned industrialisation in the Orient was bound to enhance its power. In the West the State authorities had the urban middle class as partner in the execution of this process; hence the great power of this stratum in State and Society. In the East this class was absent. Thus in those cases where the State takes the initiative in industrialisation, it compensates itself by using the industrial economy largely as a political means of furthering its own ends. The reorganisation of the system of communications by the State sprang from the same motives. By making these newly extended services available first for national and political tasks, the State has considerably strengthened its own position. The purely economic functions fulfilled by the State-controlled communication services in most Oriental countries is in comparison quite overshadowed.

IV. Changes in the Structure of Society

The concluding chapters of this work started with a survey of the primitive societal groupings typical of the Middle Eastern countries; family, clan and tribe represent the fundamental forms and collective responsibility, collective consciousness and collective reaction are characteristic elements of society. The power of persistence of these primitive features and social traditions was so strong that such significant institutions as slavery and polygamy, despite disapproval on the part of the steadily rising power of Islam, have survived up to the present day. In the course of centuries the social structure of Moslem society has begun to loosen, but, in general, it has remained intact up to recent times. It is only now that the old forms show signs of disintegration at a tempo hitherto unknown. This is attributable to several causes:—

(1) The forces which conduce to this process are sustained in the first instance by the changes which during the same period made their influence felt in all other spheres of life. We refer particularly to modern economic interests. The primitive groups with their tribal organisation are still less able to resist the lure of better living conditions than are the inhabitants of the villages and towns. The severity of the living conditions to which the tribes are exposed in the inhospitable steppe and desert country of the Middle East must—in view of the progressive improvement in the standard of living which the town and the urban zone offer—inevitably threaten the integrity of their organisation.

(2) In the same way, the new developments in traffic and communications and the introduction of modern means of transport have helped to expedite the social disintegration of tribal society. The desert, which represents for the Beduin an inviolate domain of infinite space, has been conquered by the motor-car, the aeroplane and the radio. The strength of the tribes, which lay in their rulership and their elastic strategy of evasion alike, was thus broken. In the times when the central power could not assert itself in the provinces the Beduin problem, above all a question of political authority, was regarded as from every point of view insoluble. As a result of the strengthening of State authority and the introduction of modern means of transport for commercial and military purposes it has been reduced to an administrative problem. The solution of this and allied questions is being sought in settling the Beduin on the soil. This promises to be a long-drawn-out process likely to

occupy the countries concerned for years to come. Once effected, however, the settlement of the Beduin will relieve the already settled population of the ever-present anxiety for the security of hearth and home which the existence of marauding tribes was wont to cause. Their eventual subordination through the instruments of State authority, such as efficient administration, education, police and jurisdiction, should lead within a reasonable space of time to the incorporation of these groups with their peculiar social forms into the ranks of settled society.

(3) The effects of the growth of urbanisation on Oriental society went very deep, although frequent changes occurred in the urban scene. The earliest towns, especially in the Arab lands, were closely bound up with the movement of trade and caravan traffic which favoured the growth of commercial centres without interfering with the tribal structure of the local population. As Islam spread, holy cities came into existence—partly deriving from former "holy" sites—whose power of attraction was by no means negligible. Their emergence arose almost exclusively from the fact that the site in question was the periodic meeting place of a stream of pilgrims for whose subsistence, accommodation, etc., the local population had to provide. In modern times the trend towards industrialisation and the resultant architectural changes in the pattern of the town, coupled with the shift in the earlier social structure, have all combined to mould the face of the new Oriental towns. The formation of towns or town quarters with a predominantly industrial population is in the air. The elements which have hitherto been dominant in the town and whose claims to power in accordance with the old social and economic structure of Oriental society are based on their property are finding their economical and political influence gradually reduced. This process of social re-orientation is one which cannot be kept in check, despite the forces of counteraction. Its dynamic centre is the town, from which it draws its main impetus, and thus, extending far beyond its actual radius, it serves to accelerate the process of disintegration in the social body even in agrarian society and among the Beduin groups.

(4) The emergence of a worker class is a further significant symptom of the transformation of Oriental society; though this process is considerably slower than in the West. The workers themselves still remain, as a rule, closely associated with their place of origin, mostly in the villages. On the other hand, analogously with

the trend of development in the West, the number of persons engaged in so-called secondary and tertiary occupations, i.e. the share of the working population in industrial production, in trade and commerce and in public services of every description shows a steady increase, thus assimilating the occupational structure of the Oriental countries slowly but irresistibly to that of the West.

(5) One of the chief spiritual processes marking the end of the Middle Ages in Europe was the elimination of the power of the Church in thought and deed. This process reached the Orient also, and led to a rationalisation of the various spheres of life. This is manifest in the ridding of economic life of the many retarding factors of irrational origin no less than in the open and hidden campaign against the claims of religious tradition in science, the State and even within the religious sphere itself. At the same time it has become evident that contemplativeness and traditionalism, values particularly extolled in the religious system of Islam, have in the course of centuries produced a dominating influence on the attitude of its followers towards worldly problems. The tolerant and compromising philosophy of life advocated by such teachings, together with the definitely hampering influences of religious tradition, are in no slight measure responsible for the economic and technical inactivity of the Moslem world. This, too, explains to a considerable extent the discrepancy between the record of achievement of Oriental civilisation and that of Europe since the Middle Ages.

What, now, is the lesson to be learnt from our journey through the social history of the various countries under review? Are we to regard at least in broad outline this all-embracing transformation process as a grand coordinated movement, as the karmic unfolding of Europeanisation, as the incorporation of the pre-capitalistic irrational world of the Orient into the "disenchanted" rationalistic civilisation of the West? The temptation to search for and to recognise in the recent development of Oriental society the trends and features deduced from the history of Western capitalism is by no means slight. Phenomena familiar to us from the modern economic and social history of Europe, if with differences due to time and place, are frequent enough in the development of the modern East. It is our considered opinion, however, that a large number of analogies appear to be counterbalanced by an equally important number of divergences in respect of typical processes, and further that the course of events in the Orient was dictated largely by a law of its own for which no universal applicability can be claimed. True, many phenomena known to us through the trend of development in the West are recognised here also: rupture of the close tie between producers and means of production; industrialisation as a step towards the attainment of economic autonomy and the raising of the standard of life; rising opposition to the social and economic disenfranchisement of the peasantry; spread of technical progress, often at a feverish tempo; assimilation to the Western style of life, especially in the towns; suppression or sacrifice of religious, civil and economic tradition; rationalisation of legislation; nationalisation of the State and growing assumption of economic and social functions by the governments. Apart from these parallel features, however, momentous divergences between the two spheres are to be seen: in the inner structure, in the social and political standing of the towns within society as a whole, in the nature and activities of the feudal aristocracy; in the progress of art and science and their relation to other spheres of life; in the development of new State and social forms; in short, in all that we recognise and define as the cultural productivity of a civilisation. Reference has already been made in this work to the unique phenomenon of the flourishing Western town; even after its decline it was able to muster sufficient creative powers to inaugurate the Industrial Revolution and produce the technical leaders and the initiators and pioneers of the new globe-encircling enterprises and plans which eventually drew the Orient also within their orbit. In the East the native population was not capable of producing personalities who understood how to inaugurate and develop industrialisation, nay, the new organisation of economy as a process embracing economic life as a whole. When as a result of the technical and economic revolutions Europe experienced far-reaching social changes, new social classes, especially after the beginning of the present century, fought for and obtained a growing share in political affairs. After having for several decades exercised the strongest influence on the nature of the contract of employment, i.e. on conditions of employment and wage rates, the workers of these countries were able to appropriate a substantial share of political power. In a number of cases they were able even to assume control of the State as a whole. In Oriental countries, beyond a few weak feelers in this direction, no definite action was taken. Despite assistance from abroad and the examples set by the aforesaid countries the people in this sphere lacked determined leadership to champion the interests of the socially and economically disenfranchised. All this is no accident, just as the difference in the scientific achievements of the two civilisations is no accident. Nor is it an accident that such a discrepancy exists between the standard of political and State institutions in the West—often attained at the cost of heavy sacrifice—and that resulting from the primitive policy of taking over existing forms and adapting them to the needs of the Oriental States. The wealth and variety of such forms culminated in the West in the subtle organisation of British constitutional life with its emphasis on the maximum of personal freedom and the rights of the individual citizen coupled with the fullest loyalty to this self-imposed order. Even the corporative State of Europe, despite everything that can be said against it, testifies to the ingeniousness and originality of Western thought. The paltriness and poverty of the Oriental State system, leaving out of account external ceremonial, is very obvious in comparison. Notwithstanding the fact that nowadays it is by no means deficient in power, nor in great State traditions dating from the days of its pristine glory, it lacks the scars of those great historical battles for spiritual and constitutional freedom of which even today every Western State institution bears the imprint.

Thus it is not surprising that the constitutions of the young Oriental countries, despite their technical perfection, have not yet won firm and loyal support on the part of the population or even of the governing classes; that even grave infringements of the constitution do not call for the convening of the High Court of Justice, to say nothing of minor offences and actions prejudicial to the interests of the State or its statutes. What we find here is, according to our deep conviction, no mere difference due to reasons of time; it is a difference which, transcending time and place, stirs far deeper strata. In one respect, to be sure, we are ready to concede a parallelism in the course of events and its conformity to similar laws. This applies to the social patterns and processes encountered on that plane of life termed "civilisation" in the narrower sense of the word as understood by, among others, Alfred Weber. He uses this term in relation to those elements of human culture which are transferable from people to people thanks to the use of technical, practical and applied arts and methods. Where, however, deeper-lying strata are involved, where it is a question of the "interplay of cultural values and agents which create no cosmos of universally valid and necessary things" but operate in the form of manifestations and creations occurring but once and unrepeatable in character, there, indeed, the whole contrast between Oriental and Occidental civilisation is clearly discernible. As far as the striving towards the "cosmic", towards a higher rationalisation of thought and the coordination of economy, technique and State is concerned, there, truly, the all-embracing force of modern civilisation comes into its own; but not in the underlying principles as embodied in religion, philosophy, art, or rational scientific theory. Here the borderline is reached, and a limit set to the transformation of Oriental society on the Western model, albeit the reasons for this appear to be withheld from man's power of perception.

POSTSCRIPT

THE MIDDLE EAST AT THE END OF THE SECOND WORLD WAR

A world catastrophe so great as the Second World War was bound to leave a deep impression on the Middle East, one of the vital areas of world strategy. Although many of the trends described in this book have remained unaffected by the war and its aftermath, a number of facts and problems have assumed a new significance, and there has been a continuous shift in loyalties and bonds. The political structure erected in the years following the First World War has been exposed to a heavy strain, which has proved too much for some of the new State formations and conventions.

During the war the chief considerations in this sphere were, of course, strategic, the more so as military events soon proved the immense value of this region as a bridge between the continents. The immediate effects, though less apparent at the beginning, were an intensification of the interest taken by the various Powers in the Middle East. Wherever there was a tender or weak spot, attempts were made by them to fill a possible vacuum. Soon after the entry of Russia and America into the War, signs of a new world-wide contest became visible around the Middle Eastern meeting ground, a vista which since then has overshadowed future world politics.

Not that the outstanding geographical and military importance of this region was unappreciated before 1939 or even before 1914. Even in the nineteenth century the rivalry between England and Russia, then already great Powers, dominated world politics. It was clear even then that whoever should be the heir to the decadent Ottoman Empire would hold the key to the domination of the Eastern Mediterranean, Arabia and India. The cautious support given by England to the Porte guarded the Dardanelles up to the First World War against Russian intrusion. After the Russian revolution and the abandonment of the expansionist ambitions of the Tsarist régime it seemed as though Russia had permanently renounced her territorial and other claims in the Middle East. Russia's obvious encouragement of the Oriental national movements pointed in the same direction. France seemed to follow the old methods of power politics more than any other nation. But this did not prevent her from losing her position in the Levant in the course of the Second World War. She finally had to accede to the complete independence of the Levant States over which she had previously exercised a Mandate. England, in accordance with her traditional pro-Moslem attitude, supported the Arab countries in their striving for independence. She hoped to reap the fruits of this policy in the post-war period, expecting then to be recognised as the leading patron of "independent" satellites. Such an alliance with the independent Succession States was to lead to a consolidation of her strategic and imperial interests in the Middle East.

However, post-war developments took a somewhat different course, for which three factors are mainly responsible. They are:

(*a*) the growing certainty that the Middle East represents one of the richest petroleum reservoirs of the world;
(*b*) the reappearance of Russia on the Middle Eastern scene;
(*c*) the political and social unrest within the Middle East.

The Second World War, far more than the First, has served to demonstrate the decisive significance of oil both for the conduct of war on sea, land and in the air and for modern industry and transport. The successful borings in the various Arab oil zones, which were continued throughout the war, have introduced these lands and the goodwill of their rulers into world politics. From that time onwards, the safeguarding of the rights of oil exploitation and of the transport of this precious commodity through friendly territories has occupied a prominent place not merely in English Oriental politics but in those of America as well. The interest of the United States in this sphere became more marked when it succeeded in acquiring valuable oil concessions within what had been originally an English-controlled zone. According to the Preliminary Report of the Technical Oil Mission to the Middle East, the recent oil discoveries in Arab countries have shifted the centre of gravity of world oil production from the Gulf-of-Mexico—Caribbean Area to the Persian Gulf Area. The Report continues as follows:—

"When one considers the great oil discoveries which have resulted from the meagre exploration thus far accomplished in the Middle East, the substantial number of known prospects not yet drilled, and the great areas still practically unexplored, the conclusion is inescapable that reserves of great magnitude remain to be discovered. The proved and indicated reserves of this area are comparable with those of the United States, yet all of the Middle East reserves have been discovered by the drilling of less than a total of 150 wildcat wells. In the United States we drill more than twenty times this number of wildcat wells each year.

"8. It is the opinion of this mission that, given reasonable time and a very moderate amount of oilfield material, any single one of these four groups (holding oilfields and oil concessions) can develop and maintain within its own properties sufficient production to supply world requirements from the Middle East area for many years to come. For the next ten to fifteen years at least, the Middle East area is likely to develop and maintain productive capacity of as much as four times its probable market outlet."
(Cp. *Bulletin of the American Association of Petroleum Geologists*, Vol. 28, July, 1944, p.921.)

In the light of these facts it is quite understandable that oil should have become a primary consideration in all decisions affecting the future political destiny of the Middle Eastern areas.

The second factor mentioned is the reappearance of Russia on the Middle Eastern scene. Her victories in Europe have not merely carried her armies beyond the physical boundaries of the Russian Empire. The impetus provided by these military successes has led to a revival of her old expansionist aspirations, activating also her Oriental policy. Since the termination of hostilities, Middle Eastern history has been largely characterised by the contest between English and, in part, American interests, and Russian expansionism. Compared with the position in the time of the Tsarist régime, there is, however, some difference. The new Russian advance has the character of a kind of mission, and political claims are frequently coupled or even identified with an economic and social ideology. Similarly it would be a misleading simplification to label the 1946 *question d'Orient* by the name "Moscow-Baghdad"—an analogy with the slogan "Berlin-Baghdad", which was so disturbing a factor of world peace at the beginning of the century. It is not only the geographical difference that invalidates the analogy. Thus the Russian provinces in South-Western and Central Asia have much more in common with their neighbours beyond the frontier than Imperial Germany ever had with her south-eastern satellites. The distinction to be made is that between a policy aiming at fundamental changes in the internal condition of newly-won territory and a mere extension of influence whereby all internal matters remain untouched and unchanged once the territorial objects have been secured. Yet one thing is obvious, the new Russia is bound to represent a potential centre of attraction of the first magnitude in a region characterised by mass poverty, backward social conditions and methods of production, and an indifference towards State forms. The animosity of the present ruling classes towards Russia may, it is true, slow down the tempo of

Russian penetration. However, so long as Oriental Governments and their Western sponsors are unable to counter the Russian ideas by advancing more effective ones, Russian propaganda will fall on fertile ground so far as the Oriental masses are concerned.

The new Russian policy in the Middle East has resumed another traditional political line. Russia is attempting to regain her former position as protector of Orthodox Christianity in Oriental lands. If she succeeds, she will obtain a hold on a not uninfluential section of the Arab population.

Under the impact of all these influences Oriental nationalism has assumed various, and frequently opposed, forms.

In Western countries the urge towards national independence was, as a rule, frowned upon and even combated by the feudal classes. Quite a number of the European nationalities, a century ago, looked upon national liberation as being but a part of economic and social liberation, the goal of all great national revolutions. As against this, Oriental national leaders almost to this day have scarcely had such aspirations, a fact which may be explained by their origin and their specific environment and interests. Now the strong point in the Russian ideology consists in its combining the human, i.e. economic and social, aspects with the national. Hence its strong appeal to large sections of the population. The attitude of the latter towards promises and programmes of reform has, in fact, become rather sceptical as a result of wartime experience. This had shown them how little their countries and Governments were in a position, or prepared, to solve the social and economic problems caused by the exigencies of war. Soaring prices, profiteering, unbridled speculation and corruption, reckless accumulation of wealth at the expense of the masses were the direct effects of the changes in the sphere of supply and production.

The wealth which accrued to certain sections of the community as a result of the enormous army orders and other military expenditure in Oriental countries may soon vanish. What will remain in the memory of the living generation is the impression produced upon them by their governments, namely that of egoistic cliques hunting for profit and positions, a band of autocratic rulers who ignored the interests of the common man and despised democratic institutions. It is owing to these features and these groups of people that British observers and politicians—who, by the way, in no small measure share the responsibility for these developments—have of late become so sceptical with regard to the benefits and effects of the transfer of Western institutions. "We have given them self-government for which they are totally unsuited. They veer naturally towards dictatorship. Democratic institutions are promptly twisted into an engine of intrigue;—thus the same bunch crop up, after each coup in a different guise, until disposed of by assassination."[32] Thus, while the war was going on, the Oriental peoples themselves were not greatly concerned about the big world problems for which the battle was fought: the menacing of the freedom-loving world by Fascism and the use of tyrannical and barbarous methods for the solution of national and racial conflicts. The universal conflagration was in their eyes no more than one of the many struggles between various groups for power and possessions, a fight caused solely by a clash of interests.

But since the end of the hostilities a change is being felt. Under the impact of war an acceleration of social processes set in, manifesting itself in a growing internal tension. New social groupings emerged, showing a clear Leftish tendency. Now these radical movements are scarcely less nationalist than the more conservative sections of the population. On the contrary, they frequently outdo them in their hatred of everything foreign; and their influence is steadily rising. There is no strong line of demarcation between the socialist and communist elements, engaged mostly in trade union activities, and those whose chief rallying ground is their dislike of foreigners and the opposition shown to foreign interests and their intrusion into the Middle East. The waning of England's power, which manifests itself in her retreat from former key positions in the Middle East and India, has naturally increased the impetus of these Leftish currents. In Iraq, the country nearest to Soviet influence, communism, supported by a number of communist daily newspapers, has become a movement not to be underrated. The Speech from the Throne delivered in the Iraqi Parliament in December, 1945, was severely criticised by the press and by members of Parliament. The main points of these attacks—in themselves a proof of the roused social consciousness of the public—were the spread of corruption, utter neglect of the fulfilment of the basic functions of Government in the field of health, education and welfare. But criticism alone cannot mend these things.

In the Middle East the progress of social and political life consists largely in an approximation of its structure to that of the Western democracies. It is a long and wearisome process, requiring much patience and devotion on the part of all concerned. For it is easy to imitate Western patterns; but the new forms remain mere façades if they are not fitted into the local setting, becoming a constituent part of the particular social and political framework of the countries concerned. The introduction of the franchise will defeat its purpose if it is immediately turned into a tool of the various factions and cliques already in power who, under the guise of democracy, continue their old autocratic rule. The adherence to the precepts and practices of modern Statehood as practised at present is, therefore, nothing but lip service, and, even worse, is being used to obstruct genuine progress. In these circumstances, the small groups honestly concerned with the welfare of the State are unable to achieve their ends. The belief in a rapid democratisation of the Oriental State is therefore an illusion.

The whole position is reminiscent of the developments that preceded the French Revolution. But whereas the French Revolution, like other European revolutions prior to the Russian example, served to reduce or abolish the privileges of certain ruling classes, it did not essentially alter the old economic order; nor did it affect the position of the middle classes, from which more often than not the leaders of the revolution originated. An overthrow of the established régimes in the Middle East would, however, proceed more along Russian lines, and would lead to a total reversal of the social and economic fabric. The landowners and the wealthier urban citizens would have to bear the brunt of such an upsurge of the destitute masses. Yet neither would foreign interests and concessions be spared. What would be the outcome of such a drastic change? Small as the chances of betterment by peaceful methods may be, this does not mean that a violent overthrow of the existing economic and social system is bound to be an all-round success. Important prerequisite conditions for a successful execution of experiments on the Russian model are absent. The Oriental peasants produce within a family unit and are individualists in their mentality. The socialisation of agriculture would thus meet with great obstacles in Oriental lands. Besides, an extended and comprehensive activity as displayed by the Russian régime would be possible only if it were directed from a centre, combining intellectual with administrative power. For the time being no such central agency is visible. On the other hand, a sudden removal of those now in power would be worth while only if others capable of doing the job were present and willing to take over.

Whereas the immediate outcome of the present process of fermentation is still doubtful, one thing is certain: social issues have now come to the fore, while purely nationalist currents are losing ground. If the First World War has served to release the explosive forces of nationalism in the Middle East, the Second has set free the motive power of social forces. With Russia as a sympathetic onlooker these forces may contribute to speed up the adjustment of these parts of the world, for generations notorious for their backwardness, to the levels attained by the West.

NOTES AND OBSERVATIONS

The following notes are not intended as a complete bibliography, which would fill a small volume. They mention the books used in connection with this study and in addition contain numerous observations, explanatory and otherwise, that for various reasons could not conveniently be inserted in the text. The notes are numbered separately for each Part.

NOTES TO PART I

1. Lord Acton, *History of Freedom and other Essays*, London, 1919, p. 19. In our deduction in the text we disregard the quantitative element of the masses, which is so closely associated with the modern State concept as a criterion for the existence of the contemporary State. A group of several thousands or tens of thousands of people may constitute a social and political unit, but not a modern State. The same holds good as regards another criterion, the control of a sufficiently large territory.

2. Cf. Max Weber, *Wirtschaft und Gesellschaft*, Tübingen, 1922, p. 30.

3. Cf. Harry Luke, *The Making of Modern Turkey. From Byzantium to Angora*, London, 1936, p. 7.

4. While at the establishment of the Ottoman Empire this distribution included only Greek, Armenian and Islamic *millets* (Arabs and Kurds being included in the last-named), there were at the beginning of the twentieth century no less than four Christian *millets* of the Orthodox Churches alone, three *millets* of the Monophysites and five of the Uniate Church communities. In addition there were the Roman Catholics of the Latin rite, and the Jews, while as from 1850 the Protestants also formed a *millet* of their own. The *millet* association kept its members united, gave them a sense of cohesion and a centre and protected such numerically limited communities as the Jacobites and Nestorians from assimilation or dissolution. A *Rayah* who was not a member of a *millet* would have no civic status and in practice would have been, as compared with modern conditions, without nationality; whereas without the *millet* system the small Christian Churches would have vanished. (Cf. Luke, *op. cit.*, p. 101).

5. The Arabic language has no word to express the idea of "State". The words *Hukuma* or *Daula* properly mean "Government", though the word *Daula* has in recent times been used for "State". There is likewise no term precisely synonymous with "citizen" and "citizenship".

6. In the year 1683, when the Ottoman Empire reached its greatest extent, the following countries were included under the rule of the Sublime Porte:
Hungary: 1699, Lost to Austria.
Crimea, South Russia, etc.: 1774, Virtual expulsion of Turks; 1784, annexation by Russia.
Egypt: 1808, Virtual autonomy under Mohammed Ali; 1882, British occupation; 1914, repudiation of Turkish suzerainty; 1922, establishment of "Kingdon of Egypt".
Serbia: 1815, Partial autonomy; 1829, complete autonomy; 1878, independence.
Rumania: 1829, Turkish protectorate becomes nominal; 1878, independence. (Bessarabia non-Turkish since 1812).
Greece: 1829, Independence; 1882, 1913, 1920, additional Turkish lands annexed.
Caucasus Lands: 1829 and 1878, ceded in part to Russia.

Bulgaria: 1878, Weak protectorate; 1885, Eastern Roumelia added; 1908, independence.
Bosnia: 1878, Under Austrian control; 1908, annexed by Austria.
Cyprus: 1878, Ceded to Britain.
Tripoli: 1912, Surrendered to Italy.
Albania: 1913, Cut adrift from Turkey.
Macedonia: 1913, Divided between Serbia, Greece, and Bulgaria.
Thrace: 1913, Lost in part to Bulgaria (later became Greek).
Aegean Islands and Crete: 1913, Lost to Greece.
Arabia: 1918, Seceded as "Kingdom of Arabia".
Palestine: 1918, Occupied by Britain.
Mesopotamia: 1918, Occupied by Britain and Arab insurgents.
Syria: 1920, Occupied by France.

7. Since we are here chiefly concerned with the main lines of development in the mother country, details of the course of events in the dependent territories are not referred to even where they took a course of their own.

8. Their general designation was *Nizam-i-Jedid* = "New Decree", i.e., the New Institutions.

9. The young Stratford Canning, later Lord Stratford de Redcliffe, wrote as follows: "From their high claims to honour and confidence they had sadly declined. They had become the masters of the government, the butchers of their sovereigns, and a source of terror to all but the enemies of their country. Whatever compassion might be felt for individual sufferers, including as they did the innocent with the guilty, it could hardly be said that their punishment as a body was untimely or undeserved." (Cf. S. Lane-Poole, *The Life of the Rt. Hon. Stratford Canning*, London, 1888, Vol. I. p. 419).

10. Harold Temperley, *The Crimea*, London, 1936, pp. 41/42.

11. *Tanzimat* is the plural of the Arabic word *Tanzim*, meaning organisation, arrangements, or in this case: reforms.

12. The main dates are: Code of Commercial Law of July, 1850; Land Law of April, 1858; Penal Code of August, 1858; Maritime Law of August, 1863; Procedure Rules for Commercial Lawsuits (*Handelsprozessordnung*), November, 1861; Law concerning Ottoman Nationality, January 1869.

13. It seems remarkable today that at the time of these reforms the publication of a Constitution should have been expected to save the life of an Empire which, in view of its national composition, its doubtful military strength, and the territorial acquisitiveness of the European Powers, could have scarcely any prospect of maintaining its existence.

The initiators of the Constitution, particularly Midhat Pasha, started on the assumption that "escape from the threatened downfall could be sought only in a renewal and transformation from the ground up. In order to achieve this, the powers that slumbered in the people had to be rendered useful. For this reason all Osmanlis, Moslems and Christians alike, were to be induced to co-operate in the great function of strengthening their common Fatherland through its own powers, and of defending it against its foes". (Cf. G. Jäschke, "Die Entwicklung des osmanischen Verfassungsstaates", in *Die Welt des Islams*, 1917, Vol. V, pp. 18 ff.)

In actual fact, the Constitution strengthened the confidence of Turkish intellectual circles in the future of the Empire, and made it more difficult for the Powers to achieve their ambitions.

14. On December 12th, on the proposal of Great Britain, the representatives of the Great Powers met at Constantinople for a preliminary conference regarding current Balkan questions of international importance. The proposals of

the Powers crystallised in a plan according to which the Sublime Porte would have not only had to agree to far-reaching territorial concessions and the grant of administrative autonomy to Bulgaria, Bosnia and Herzegovina, but also to accept the establishment of an international Commission to supervise the execution of the conditions laid down. The publication of the Constitution led to a rejection of this plan on the part of the Porte.

15. The clerics who took part in the Commission for the Preparation of a Draft Constitution expressed their misgivings on several points regarding the plan of the Government on account of the harm that would be done to the Sharia. The Ulema were quieted only by the approval of the Sheikh al-Islam, their spiritual chief. (G. Jäschke, *op. cit.*, p. 12.)

16. The supporters of the Reform Movement, who afterwards united under the name of "Young Turks", conducted their propaganda, for the recall of Parliament and the restitution of the liberties gained, from abroad and in particular from Paris and Geneva, where the "Committee of Union and Progress" nursed the idea of the Constitution through the medium of literature and journalism.

17. The absence of uniformity in the interpretation of the religious prescriptions can be seen by the plea of Musa Kazim, who later became Sheikh al-Islam, in support of this law which, by providing for a division of powers, left the Sultan and the Khalif with little more than the purely representative position of a parliamentary ruler. Musa Kazim defended the law of 21 August, 1909, with the words that the power belonged to the community of Islam as a whole, and not to any individual. Mohammed had always asked the people for counsel, and the Sultan had been raised to the rank of Khalif only by the will of the people.

18. A detailed account of the history of the Constitution and its legal meaning is given by G. Jäschke in his above-mentioned essay and in another study, entitled "Die rechtliche Bedeutung der in den Jahren 1909–1916 vollzogenen Abänderungen des türkischen Staatsgrundgesetzes" ("The Legal Meaning of the Amendments Effected in the Fundamental Turkish State Law between 1909 and 1916"), which appeared in *Die Welt des Islams*, 1917, Vol. V, No. 3. Repeated references are here made to both of these essays.

19. *Encyclopaedia of Islam*, article on *Khalīfa*. Differences of opinion as to who was actually entitled to hold the office of Khalif led to the development of many conflicting doctrines and sects.

20. When Selim I victoriously entered Cairo in 1517 and made an end of the Abbāsid Khalifate by taking its last representative, al-Mutawakkil, to Constantinople, he had already been accustomed to the association of the title of Khalīf with his own person and that of his forebears by the practice of a century and a half (*ibid.*)

21. With the collapse of the Mogul Empire in the eighteenth century, the Osmanli Sultan became unquestionably the most imposing figure in the Moslem world; but even his power was threatened by his aggressive Northern neighbours. Following the war with Russia (1768–74) he was compelled to withdraw from several territories on the north coast of the Black Sea, and to recognise the independence of Crim Tartary. Catherine II claimed the patronage of Orthodox Christians resident in Osmanli territories. The Osmanli representatives, who drew up the Treaty of Kuchuk Kainarji in 1774, made use of the title of Khalif on their part in order to raise an analogous claim for the Sultan and to introduce a clause into the Treaty which secured the Khalif the religious authority over the Tartars whose secular lord he could no longer be. From this time on Christian Europe began to be under the misapprehension that the Khalif is the spiritual head of all Moslems just as the Pope is the spiritual head

of all Catholics. Spiritual authority was ascribed to him over all his co-religionists, even when they were not his political subjects. There is reason to believe that this widespread misapprehension on the part of the Christian world had its effect on public opinion in Turkey itself. (*ibid.*).

22. G. Jäschke, *Welt des Islams*, 1917, p. 29.

23. C. H. Becker, " Die Türkei im Weltkrieg", in *Islamstudien*, Vol. II, Leipzig 1932, p. 261.

24. Similarly, a special tribal law was established in order to provide for the peculiar legal customs of the Beduin population. Here the judges were the Sheikhs, and they decided cases not in accordance with general legal practice but on the basis of Beduin tribal tradition. How far this difference in the legal sense of the groups mentioned can go against the general legal prerequisites for the existence of the legal system of the modern State current among us can be shown by a reference to the legal point of view in the Beduin territories. The Beduin knows nothing of crime against the State. A criminal action such as murder, which is pursued everywhere primarily by the State, is here not the subject of any action which, if we may make the comparison, corresponds in any way to that undertaken by a State legal prosecutor. Punishment is called for and carried out only by the dependants of the person affected and his social group, the comrades associated with him. Murder or manslaughter can be compensated for internally between the parties concerned by either blood vengeance or blood money. The concept, developed in Western criminal law, of murder as an attack on the foundations of society and the morality of the State is not familiar to the Beduin living in traditional Beduin society.

25. Cf. on these points Joseph Schacht, "Zur soziologischen Betrachtung des islamischen Rechtes", in *Der Islam*, Vol. 22, 1935; also G. Bergstrasser's *Grundzüge des islamischen Rechts*, Berlin, 1935 (ed. J. Schacht).

26. "So long as tribal and other communal divisions remain strong, unrestricted individual freedom to dispose of land would be dangerous to public peace and contentment." Sir Ernest Dowson, *An Inquiry Into Land Tenure and Related Questions*, 1931, p. 35.

27. The Young Turk "Committee of Union and Progress" announced a programme at Easter 1909, the first article of which reads: "The party will endeavour to extend the autonomy of the people and fully to carry out the constitutional system based on the division of powers."

28. Mohammed Ali, one of the outstanding personalities in the early struggle against Oriental mismanagement, was famous for his arbitrary legal decisions. A man who was convicted of theft in an armaments factory was to work for life in irons if he was young; if he had already reached more mature years, he was hung as a warning. Cf. H. Dodwell, *Mohamed Ali, the Founder of Modern Egypt*, Cambridge, 1931, p. 230.

29. J. L. Burckhardt, *Travels in Nubia*, London 1819, p. xxxv f.

30. Nassau Senior, *Journal Kept in Turkey and Greece*, London, 1859, pp. 143/144.

31. H. Dodwell, *op. cit.*, p. 194.

32. *Ibid.*, p. 229.

33. Quoted by Luke, *op. cit.*, pp. 62/63.

34. A. H. Layard, *Autobiography*, ed. Bune, 1903, Vol. II, p. 25.

35. H. Dodwell, *op. cit.*, pp. 165 ff.

36. C. D. Cobham, *The Patriarchs of Constantinople*, Cambridge, 1911, p. 8

37. Cf. chapter xiii on *Waqf* below, and Note 17, Part II.

38. *Report on Palestine's Administration* 1920–1921, London, 1922, p. 110.

39. *Türkische Post*, 27 Dec. 1935; In Iraq the Government has been obliged expressly to forbid officials to accept presents from foreigners. (Cf. *Baghdad Times*, 20 Feb. 1939.)

40. Thus in Syria and Lebanon, for example, the number of officials in State service in 1937 was 15,301 (including 4,199 gendarmes). In Palestine the number amounts to 9,071, including those in the railway administration; but excluding police, whose numerical strength was 4,754. Even thinly populated Transjordan has 927 Government officials, not including the members of the Transjordan Frontier Force.

41. J. Barker, *Syria and Egypt, Under the last Five Sultans of Turkey*, ed. E. B. B. Barker, London 1876, p. 41.

42. H. Temperley, *op. cit.*, p. 9.

43. C. Ritter, *Vergleichende Erdkunde der Sinai-Halbinsel, von Palästina und Syrien*, Berlin, 1852, pp. 828/829.

44. *Ibid.*

45. J. Barker, *op. cit.*, p. 147.

46. H. Dodwell, *op. cit.*, pp. 205/206.

47. J. Barker, *op. cit.*, pp. 147/148. *Mazbatta* here means a petition signed by all members of the *majlis.*

48. Mrs. E. A. Finn, *Palestine Peasantry*, London, 1923, p.11, and *Report* by the Registrar of Co-operative Societies [in Palestine] on developments during the years 1921–1937, Jerusalem 1938, p.11.

49. The administrative classification of the original lands that had already established itself in accordance with the original burden of taxation was, however, retained. Cf. on this Chapter XIII in Part II.

50. Tax-farming and military fief (cf. also Chapter XIII) often in practice merged into one another, or existed side by side. The concept of *iqta*, which characterised both tax-farming and the military fief, was not always used in a single sense. Under the first Khalifs it meant the transfer of land to personal property, and later its leasing out, whereas in the second half of the Middle Ages it meant a military fief, and finally tax-farming once again. According to Ibn Jemaa (as quoted by Tischendorf), the word had the general and comprehensive meaning of "bestowal of State land". According to him there were three main kinds of *iqta;* the first being a grant as actual property, the second for usufruct, and the third for participation in mineral resources and trading income. Within these categories there were again a series of subdivisions. According to this author there could be no question of lands subject to tribute ever being ceded as actual property, since they belonged to the entire Moslem community. The various forms of grant of participation in the exploitation of mines, salt, and other mineral resources as well as of roads, mills, and markets are noteworthy. Here the character of endowment is transformed into an ordinary exploitation of market and trade concessions. (Cf. P. A. Tischendorf, *Das Lehenswesen in den moslemischen Staaten, insbesondere im osmanischen Reich*, Leipzig, 1872, pp. 17 ff.

51. Parallel with these processes in the higher administrative sphere, the transfer of the right of tax-collection for smaller districts to tax-farmers went on in the provinces.

52. Only because it was impossible to control the situation otherwise, was military duty made a condition of occupation of a grant. (Cf. C. H. Becker, *op. cit.*, Vol. I, p. 240.

53. Cf. C. H. Becker, *op. cit.*, p. 239.

54. *Handwörterbuch der Staatswissenschaften*, 4th Edition, Article on "Steuerpacht" (tax-farming), Jena, 1926, p. 1128.

55. Hassan Tahsin Bey, "Der Staatshaushalt und das Finanzsystem der Türkei" in *Handbuch der Finanzwissenschaft*, Vol. III, Tübingen, 1929, p. 292.

56. *Ibid.*, p. 291.

57. A payment peculiar to the early Islamic State was the *Zakat.* This payment did not originally have the character of a rigorous tax, but was a contribution towards the maintenance of the poor. It developed into one of the main Islamic taxes levied on the possession of gold, silver, commercial goods, the produce of the soil, camels and cattle.

58. Arabic countries such as the Yemen, Kuweit, etc., which even before the War were only nominally included within the Ottoman Empire, are not here specified.

59. In Greek Macedonia alone no less than 17 different migration movements took place between the outbreak of the Balkan War in October, 1912, and the end of 1924. The purpose of them all was to achieve a homogeneous resettlement of the national groups which had previously been living together in colourful mixture. Some of these transfers were an immediate result of military operations. Others took place on the basis of express agreements between the participating countries, Bulgaria, Serbia, Greece and Turkey. Each individual case covered the emigration and resettlement of tens or hundreds of thousands of people.

60. "As from May 1st, 1923, there shall take place a compulsory exchange of Turkish nationals of the Greek Orthodox religion established in Turkish territory, and of Greek nationals of the Moslem religion established in Greek territory. These persons shall not return to live in Turkey or Greece respectively without the authorisation of the Turkish Government or of the Greek Government respectively."

61. The sometimes grotesque exaggerations to be found in the same historical description can only be explained with reference to this goal. "Turkish history shows the Turkish nation that since the rise of mankind their race has been the highest and most noble human type in the world and that in the course of centuries it has been the genius and capacities of that race which have opened up on the dark skies of humanity the bright horizons of the successive cultures . . . Turkish history teaches the Turkish nation that every spot in the world that bears the traces of human beings also bears the stamp, never to be erased throughout time, of the dominion and culture of their race; that they have founded hundreds of States the greatest ever known. . . ." (p. 327, German ed.)

62. Mohammed Ali ordered merchants, shopkeepers, scholars and theologians who did not understand the meaning of education and were therefore only "fit to carry loads on their backs like porters and donkeys", to engage in heavy physical labour on certain days by removing the dirt of the streets on their own backs. (Cf. H. Dodwell, *op. cit.*, p. 194.)

63. This contemporary history has been treated in considerable detail in a number of accounts, and does not need to be repeated here. The last and most comprehensive description, which notwithstanding its pro-Arab bias is more informative than all previous works, is *The Arab Awakening* by George Antonius (London, 1938).

64. George Antonius, *op. cit.*, p. 84. The demands included:
"(1) The grant of independence to Syria in union with the Lebanon;
"(2) the recognition of Arabic as an official language in the country;

"(3) the removal of the censorship and other restrictions on freedom of expression and the diffusion of knowledge;

"(4) the employment of locally-recruited units on local military service only."

65. These consisted chiefly of two associations, one established in 1909 in Constantinople as a club for Arab visitors to and residents in the capital, and first tolerated by the Young Turks. The number of members may have run into thousands. The second society was established in 1912 at Cairo with the name "Ottoman Decentralisation Party" and the objective of convincing the Turkish authorities of the necessity for a decentralised administration and of winning over Arab public opinion. Alongside this, several secret societies which worked with openly revolutionary objectives also sprang into being.

66. "In spite of the correspondence and interchange of views between the various sections of the Arab world, in spite of the manifestos and literature issued in the name of the Arab peoples, in spite of the essential unity of the aims and purposes of Arab Nationalism, the Movement tended to break into sectionalism limited by the horizons of immediate locality. The rank and file of the Movement, no less than the sectional leaders, regarded with mistrust any leaders whose ascendancy seemed to overshadow their own interests and to detract from their own importance." (Cf. P. W. Ireland, *Iraq, A Study in Political Development*, London, 1937, p. 237.)

67. The McMahon assurances read as follows:

"The two districts of Mersina and Alexandretta and portions of Syria lying to the west of the districts of Damascus, Homs, Hama and Aleppo, cannot be said to be purely Arab, and should be excluded from the limits demanded.

"With the above modification, and without prejudice to our existing treaties with Arab chiefs, we accept those limits.

"As for those regions lying within those frontiers wherein Great Britain is free to act without detriment to the interests of her ally, France, I am empowered in the name of the Government of Great Britain to give the following assurances, and make the following reply to your letter:—

"(1) Subject to the above modifications, Great Britain is prepared to recognise and support the independence of the Arabs in all the regions within the limits demanded by the Sharif of Mecca.

"(2) Great Britain will guarantee the Holy Places against all external aggression and will recognise their inviolablility."

Cf. *Correspondence between Sir Henry McMahon . . . and the Sharif Hussein of Mecca*, July 1915–March 1916, London 1939 (Cmd. 5957) p. 8.

68. In the agreement of 15 Sept. 1919, Britain declared herself prepared to evacuate until 1 Nov. 1919 all territories to be transferred under the Sykes-Picot Agreement to France or to the Syrian-Arab State, with the exception of Mosul, which should be included in the British sphere of interest. France in turn undertook to occupy only the coastal regions of Syria, but not the hinterland, including the towns of Homs, Damascus, Aleppo and Hama. Palestine and Mesopotamia were to be placed under British mandatory rule, while a national Arab State was to be established between the Syrian coastal strip and the mandatory territory of Mesopotamia. This arrangement was sharply rejected by the Arab National Movement.

69. The peculiar form of the Mandate in Palestine was largely due to the promise given to the Zionists during the war in the form of the Balfour Declaration, to encourage the establishment in Palestine of a Jewish National Home.

70. W. H. Ritsher, *Criteria of Capacity for Independence*, Beirut, 1934.

71. *Minutes of the Permanent Mandates Commission, Twentieth Session*, pp. 123/24.

72. W. H. Ritsher, *op. cit.*, pp. 126, 130 ff.

73. A vivid description of the situation in Iraq shortly before the First World War has been given by the British Resident in Baghdad and was quoted by Gertrude Bell in *Review of the Civil Administration of Mesopotamia*, Cmd. 1061 (1920), p. 1. It reads as follows:
". . . . Iraq is not an integral part of the Ottoman Empire, but a foreign dependency, very much in the rough; and its government by sedentary officials according to minute regulations, framed at Constantinople for Western Turkey, can never be satisfactory. I had no idea before coming to Baghdad of the extent to which Turkey is a country of red tape and blind and dumb officialdom, nor of the degree in which the Turkish position in Iraq is unsupported by physical force."

NOTES TO PART II

1. *Hermes*, Zeitschrift für klassische Philologie, 1884, Vol. XIX, p. 393.

2. M. Rostovtzeff, *Gesellschaft und Wirtschaft im römischen Kaiserreich*, Leipzig, p. 2.

3. "Religious charismata, the rights of conquest and especially the dependence of land rent upon a centralised organisation of land tenure, soon made the chief of the State the supreme landowner." F. Heichelheim, Art. on "Land Tenure (Ancient World)" in *Encycl. of the Social Sciences*, New York 1933, Vol. XI, p. 78.

4. Franz Steinmetzer, *Über den Grundbesitz in Babylonien zur Kassitenzeit*, Leipzig, 1919, p. 7;
Louis Delaporte, *The Babylonian and Assyrian Civilisation*, New York, 1925, p. 101.

5. F. H. Breasted, *History of Egypt*, London 1922, p.229. The rate of taxes in Ancient Egypt in the case of State (King's) land was 20 per cent. of the crops. This figure agrees with that given in Gen. xlvii.

6. H. Kees, *Kulturgeschichte des Alten Orients, I. Ägypten*, München, 1933, pp. 42 ff.

7. A. Gollak, *Leheker Toldoth Hamishpat Ha'ivri b'Tkufath Hatalmud* ("Researches into the History of Hebrew Law in the Period of the Talmud"), (in Hebrew), Jerusalem, 1929, pp. 109 ff.

7*a*. E. Zachariae von Lingenthal, *Geschichte des griechisch-römischen Rechts*, third edition, Berlin, 1892, p. 324.

8. In order to ensure a certain stability of revenue and at the same time to help prevent conversion to the Moslem faith for the sake of evading the taxes, these tax liabilities were regarded as a permanent charge on the land.

9. A. N. Poliak, "Agrarian Problems in the Middle East," *Palestine and Middle East*, Sept., 1938.

10. C. H. Becker, "Islam und Wirtschaft," in *Islamstudien*, Vol. I, Leipzig, 1924, p. 58.

11. "Not less than three-fifths of cultivated and perhaps nine-tenths of ultimately cultivable land in Iraq belongs nominally and legally to the State; that is to say, has not been registered as the private property of any individual." (From *Special Report . . . on the Progress of Iraq during the Period* 1920–1931, London, 1931 (Colonial No. 58), p. 125.

12. Cf. the various textbooks and commentaries on Islamic land law.

13. E. Pröbster, in *Islamica*, Vol. IV/4, p. 419.

14. "Until 1277 of the Mohammedan era, 28 years ago (i.e. in 1863), all the lands outside the cities and their environs and Mount Lebanon were held on the communal principle, and apportioned to the cultivators as above. At that date the Government introduced the *tatwîb*, and has steadily pressed upon the peasants the necessity of dividing the lands and taking out *tâbu* deeds for them in severalty. In the Buqa' and around Damascus and in many other parts of the country there are no more lands held in common and each proprietor holds his own real estate." Rev. G. E. Post in *Quarterly Statement, Palestine Exploration Fund*, 1891, p. 105.)

"The Turkish laws which have been introduced within the last few years in Palestine with reference to land tenure and which are being rigorously enforced, are changing all these ancient laws and customs, *much against the will and the wish of the people*." (Cf. Bergheim, "Land Tenure" in *Quarterly Statement, Palestine Exploration Fund*, 1894, p. 195).

15. In the beginning *Waqf* land also comprised State lands which had been transferred to the Moslem community either by force or agreement, but remained in the possession of the owner on payment of the *Kharaj*.

16. Family endowments are almost as old as those for the public good . . . Such foundations, while being a charitable object in keeping with religion, in the first place secure the descendants an income for all emergencies and in particular protect the property in times of insecurity from unscrupulous rulers, although in practice they did not always have the result desired.

17. Orientalist literature deals in detail with the origin of the *Waqf* institution, a subject which however needs no further elucidation in this connection. According to a tradition of Moslem jurists 'Omar, before becoming Khalif, is said to have acquired valuable land at the division of Kheibar and to have asked the Prophet whether he should give away the property as *sadaka* (charity). The Prophet replied: "Retain the thing itself and devote its fruits to pious purposes." 'Omar followed this advice with the proviso that the land must neither be sold nor bequeathed by will; the profits should belong to the poor, needy relatives, pilgrims, guests, etc. In times of emergency the guardian of *Waqf* property might benefit therefrom to a modest extent. (Cf. Art. *Waqf* in *Encycl. of Islam*.)

18. "Did the Holy Fathers, the lights of the Faith, spend their lives in hoarding up treasure after treasure? No, that they never did; but sure enough those are doing so who profess to be the disciples, followers of these Holy Ones. Daily, even hourly, their thought and aspiration is directed towards the acquisition of immense estates, the erection of magnificent buildings, the purchase of horses, oxen, camels, sheep and goats." (Cf. E. Zachariae von Lingenthal, *Jus Graeco-Romanum* (Leipzig) Novellae Coll. III, Nov. 19, 20 21 (transl.).

19. "The inquirer into the affairs of the Church of Jerusalem learns, at first with incredulity and finally with concern, that it has been the practice for prominent members of the Brotherhood of the Holy Sepulchre during the past two generations to amass considerable fortunes out of the personal offerings of pilgrims; that these fortunes, if not spent or disposed of in the lifetime of those who acquired them, have devolved at their deaths on the Fraternity; that members of the Fraternity have been permitted to invite subscriptions from correspondents among the pious public in other Orthodox countries, notably in Russia, and that the Brothers thus collecting money have been under no proper obligation to account for it." (*Report of the Commission appointed by the Government of Palestine to inquire into the affairs of the Orthodox Patriarchate of Jerusalem, etc.*, Oxford, 1921, p. 234.

20. On the resemblance to the Byzantine *Emphyteusis* cf. for instance C. H. Becker in his essay on "Steuerpacht und Lehenswesen" (reprinted in *Islamstudien*, Vol. I, p. 234.)

21. The investigations of Poliak have done much to clarify the circumstances connected with the origin of Oriental feudalism, and cleared up some misinterpretations of former authors. Poliak appears, however, not to do full justice to Becker, who has certainly made an important contribution to the sociological exploration of the Oriental and Occidental feudal systems and their differences. Poliak's main objection is directed against Becker's thesis that in the Orient the military forced their way only subsequently and improperly into the existing system of benefices, in contrast to the conditions in the Occident where the enfeoffment of the knights with landed property for the purpose of equipping the army was the primary factor. According to Poliak, in the Orient also it was predominantly the military who were invested with fiefs, as a rule in the form of tax-farming estates. Apart from the fact that in his view the feoffees included in their ranks not only military, but also other influential or deserving persons, he himself states in another context that the tribute paid by these feoffees from the profits of their estates was *later* remitted against the obligation to military service. (Cf. Poliak in *Palestine and Middle East*, 1938, p. 379). These details, however, are not decisive inasmuch as Becker was far more concerned with analysing the social repercussions emerging from the absence of the personal feudal tie.

22. A modern analogy to this form of self-equipment on the part of military formations may be seen in the assignment of entire districts to regiments and divisions which occurred in Soviet Russia in 1931. In this case it was not difficulties in the way of financing, but of provisioning, that led to the allotment of extensive agricultural areas to certain bodies of troops. Cf. *Wochenblatt der Frankfurter Zeitung* of April 5, 1936, "Militarismus in der Sowjetunion": "When in 1932/33 the food situation of the country deteriorated to the verge of starvation, the Government not only ensured adequate provisions of all kinds for the army, but saw to it that the various formations received their own agricultural food bases. Regiments and divisions became landowners, and were thus in a position to procure additional food supplies from their own farms."

23. H. Prutz, *Kulturgeschichte der Kreuzzüge*, Berlin, 1883, p. 166.

24. M. Delbès, "Les possibilités économiques de l'État des Alaouites," in *Bulletin de l'Union Économique de Syrie*, 1928, p.193.

25. Kazim Riza, *Die türkische Landwirtschaft und ihre wichtigsten Betriebszweige*, Ankara, 1935, p.11 (German and Turkish);

Kazim Köylü, "The Situation of Agriculture in Turkey and the Prospects of its Evolution," in *Monthly Bulletin of Agricultural Economics and Sociology*, Vol. XXXIV, No. 5, Rome, May, 1943.

26. Cf. Chapter XVII below.

27. The estate to which the above applies comprises an area of 60,000 hectares on which are domiciled 2,000 fellahin families in 40 villages, besides 4,000 semi-settled nomads.

28. Ahmed Fahmi writes in his *Report on Iraq* (Baghdad, 1926):—"The agreement made between the cultivator and merchant when the latter loans money to the former is not transacted on the basis of interest, as interest is prohibited by religion. The agreement mentioned above is therefore concluded in either of the following forms:—

"1. By adding to the sum loaned 50 per cent. of it and preparing the promissory note accordingly. For instance, a cultivator borrowing Rs. 1,000 signs a promissory note stating that he has actually received

Rs. 1,500 and that he binds himself to repay the amount at harvest-time.

"2. The practice of undertaking to give produce instead of the money loaned, after deducting 15 per cent. of the cost of this produce. For instance, if a cultivator wishes to borrow 20 lire at a time when the market price of a toghar (2,000 kilos) of rice is 20 lire, the cultivator actually receives 17 lire only, giving the lender a promissory note for 1 toghar (2,000 kilos) of rice to be delivered at harvest-time.

"3. The debt agreement is of course made at a time when produce has passed out of the hands of the cultivators, who are therefore much in need of funds. The time of settling the debts coincides with the period when all the produce is gathered in the granaries. The period of borrowing and settling is therefore a matter of 5 to 6 months, the interest also being payable for this period only.

"4. The prices at which the produce is estimated at the time when the cultivators borrow, are not, of course, in favour of the borrower, who is in continual need of funds."

29, 30. A. N. Poliak, "La Féodalité Islamique," *Revue des Études Islamiques*, Paris, 1936, p. 262; and, by the same author, *Feudalism in Egypt, Syria, Palestine and the Lebanon*, 1250–1900, London, 1939, p. 64.

31. R. Gradmann, *Die Steppen des Morgenlandes in ihrer Bedeutung für die Geschichte der menschlichen Gesittung*, Stuttgart, 1934, pp. 55 ff.

32. Deuteron. viii, 8.

33. Gradmann, *op. cit.*, p. 58.

34. This index is intended also to give some clue as to the nature of the various soils. Without going into scientific differentiations this may be explained as follows: an area with little rainfall and high average temperature favours the evaporation of the soil moisture and consequently a rapid, dry decomposition of the humus-forming substances; causes, in short, arid conditions of the soil. When the rain factor is below 40, the soil in question, according to Lang, must be classed as arid; if above, i.e. if the amount of rainfall increases in a certain ratio to the temperature, humid soils are formed which, as the rain factor further rises, become increasingly richer in humus content. I am indebted to Dr. I. Rosenau of Jerusalem for help in compiling this table.

35. Cf. *Palestine Blue Book*, 1938, Jerusalem, 1939.

36. Characteristic of this tendency was, for instance, the destruction of the banana plantations in the central Jordan Valley, where the gradual insalination of the soil as a result of artificial irrigation led to the dying-away of the new banana plantations. Similar cases are common among irrigated crops in Egypt. In southern Iraq the author noticed dead groves of palms which were largely conspicuous by the white patches of salt on the ground. On the other hand, permanent flooding of the insalinated soils has lately been used as a means of reducing the salt content. In this case the salts are washed down into the lower soil strata by the surplus water which remains on the surface for a longer period. Attempts to free insalinated soils from their excessive salt content in this manner and to use them as agricultural land have been undertaken, so far with success, in a Zionist settlement north of the Dead Sea.

36*a*. F. Lozach, *Le Delta du Nile*, Cairo, 1935, p. 62.

37. Most commercial crops in Europe were introduced from abroad. As chief examples of such changes in the agricultural system mention may be made of the rapid spread of the newly introduced potato, maize, tobacco, as well as the extension of corn-growing at the expense of the great European forests. Cf. also Karl Sapper, *Allgemeine Wirtschafts- und Verkehrsgeographie*, Leipzig, 1925, pp. 65–67:

"Where in the moderate zone the rainfall is scarce (prairie climate) we find extensive steppe-like fields of grass or herbage, in places changing into scrub, which . . . are now used for cattle-raising, if not brought under the plough, as is the case to a large extent in Hungary, Rumania, South Russia, in the prairies and pampas of America, which have become, in fact, the principal granaries of the world . . .

Where cattle-raising has become the chief occupation, the character of the vegetation has been considerably changed by the cultivation of grasses and clovers, by the spread of thistles and other weeds, in places also by the planting of trees in suitable spots (pampas). . . .

. . . As the density of the population increased, the forests were more and more rooted out, the land being gained for tillage or for cattle-raising which, thanks to the nutritious, juicy grasses, could be carried on for the most part in a settled form (albeit predominantly by the use of stall-feeding). In the more densely populated countries of Central Europe, for instance, the forest has been eradicated wherever the land was suitable for tillage or intensive stock-breeding, whilst sandstone areas and other unfavourable sites were reserved for afforestation."

38. It is remarkable how the truth of this experience is confirmed time and again by history and even by recent events. Lord Cromer, in referring to Egypt and other Oriental countries, made the following striking observation:—

"Agriculture is the principal and, indeed, almost the only resource of most Asiatic States. Neither the devastation caused by war nor the evils resulting from the most gross forms of misgovernment can altogether ruin the agriculture of any country." (Cf. Earl of Cromer, *Modern Egypt*, Vol. I, London 1908, p. 58.)

39. K. Marx, *Das Kapital*, Vol. III, 2, Hamburg, 1921, p. 326. Marx was probably one of the first scholars to give these aspects of Oriental society attention.

40. C. S. Jarvis, *Desert and Delta*, London, 1938, p. 136.

41. B. Thomas, *The Arabs*, London, 1937, p. 266.

42. C. M. Doughty, *Travels in Arabia Deserta*, London, 1928, p. 94.

43. K. Riza, *op. cit.*, p. 25.

44. *Ibid.*, p. 21: "Thus, for the above-mentioned reasons (lack of capital, repair shops, etc.), the ploughs distributed by the Government among the peasants in recent years litter the fields like scrap iron."

45. A. Rühl, *Vom Wirtschaftsgeist im Orient*, Leipzig, 1925, p. 47.

46. Cf. *Mitteilungen der Türkischen Handelskammer für Deutschland*, Berlin, 20th August, 1938.

47. *Ibid.*

48. W. Sombart, *Der moderne Kapitalismus: Die Vorkapitalistische Wirtschaft*, München, 1928, pp. 804 ff.

49. Cf. A. Bonné, *The Economic Development of the Middle East*, London, 1945, p. 47: "An 'International Unit', first used by Colin Clark, is defined as the amount of goods and services that could be purchased for $1 in the U.S.A. over the average of the decade 1925–1934."

50. A. Bonné, *op. cit.*, p. 10.

51. Note, for instance, the stress laid on Marx's view ("Artificial irrigation became the *sine qua non* of agriculture in the East") by the gifted scientist K. A. Wittfogel in "Die natürlichen Ursachen der Wirtschaftsgeschichte," *Archiv für Sozialwissenschaft*, Vol. 67, 1932, pp. 594–600.

52. Cf. Christiansen-Weniger, *Die Grundlagen des türkischen Ackerbaus*, Leipzig, 1934, p. 159.

53. Christiansen-Weniger, *op. cit.*, p. 161.

54. Both the Bible and later the Arab traditions refer regularly to goat's milk and mutton, seldom if ever to beef, as an article of consumption by the masses.

55. K. A. Wittfogel, *Wirtschaft und Gesellschaft Chinas*, Vol. I, Leipzig, 1931, pp. 236 ff.

Richthofen has stressed this connection more emphatically than anyone else as regards China: "The importance of irrigation is based not only on the supply of water; another essential function derives from the fact that the plants are supplied with mineral food in solution. The soil thus receives its organic nourishment . . . mineral substances are introduced mostly in solution and can reduce the consumption of nutritive material from the soil year by year." (Quoted by Wittfogel, *op. cit.*, pp. 226/7).

Writing of India, Sapper, *op. cit.*, p. 136, says: "Noteworthy also is the natural manuring of the river valleys and large river deltas by inundation; in India, where plant food has been returned to the fields in quite inadequate amounts, these play a very important part."

Cf. also P. Vidal de La Blache, *Principles of Human Geography*, London 1926, p. 75: "The largest human settlement must have been located in the section of the lower valley where the overburdened stream succeeded in depositing its load."

56. W. Willcocks, *The Irrigation of Mesopotamia*, London, 1911.

57. F. Charles-Roux, *La production du coton en Égypte*, Paris, 1908, p. 301.

58. W. Willcocks, *op. cit.*

59. Cf. R. Junge, *Das Problem der Europäisierung orientalischer Wirtschaft*, Weimar, 1915, p. 174.

60. Cf. Col. E. Noel, "Qanats", *Journal of the Royal Central Asian Society*, May, 1944, pp. 190 ff.

61. According to Kazim Riza, *op. cit.*, p. 45, the data referred to do not include farm rent and expenditure after the harvest.

62. Cf. S. Mazloum, *L'Afrique*, Paris, 1939, p. 236, and Bonné, *op. cit.*, p. 147.

63. Cf. A. Grohmann, *Südarabien als Wirtschaftsgebiet*, Part II, Prague, 1933, pp. 10/11; likewise W. H. Ingrams, *A Report on the Social, Economic and Political Condition of the Hadhramaut*, London, 1936 (Colonial No. 123) p. 57.

64. C. Rathjens and H. v. Wissmann "Sanaa," *Zeitschrift der Gesellschaft für Erdkunde*, 1929, pp. 333/34.

65. S. Dubrowski, "Über das Wesen des Feudalismus, der Leibeigenschaft und des Handelskapitals," in *Agrarprobleme*, Intern. Agrar-Institut, Moscow, 1929, p. 214.

66. André Latron, *La vie rurale en Syrie et au Liban*, Beirut, 1936, p. 213.

67. A. Bonné, *Palästina, Land und Wirtschaft*, Berlin (3rd Ed.) 1935, pp. 152/3.

68. "Now it is generally accepted that the intention of the Ottoman legislator, when promulgating the Land Code, was to establish the actual cultivator on the land; and when that cultivator has remained on the same land and effected improvements of a capital nature by his labour, his claim is clear. But the claim of the larger man instanced, who will almost invariably have co-operated in some indispensable way . . ., cannot be equitably or advisedly disregarded." (Dowson, *op. cit.*, p. 24); cf. also S. Longrigg, *Four Centuries of Modern Iraq*, Oxford, 1925, pp. 306 ff.

69. The following modern surveys of Mohammed Ali's reforms have been used here: H. Dodwell, *op. cit.*; A. E. Crouchley, *The Economic Development of Modern Egypt*, London, 1938; M. Sabry, *L'Empire Égyptien sous Mohamed Ali et la Question d'Orient*, Paris, 1930. They vary in their appraisal of the foreign influences but, notwithstanding some discrepancies in single data, contain fairly similar accounts of his economic and administrative activities. As regards information on the more recent growth of population, ownership and distribution of land, etc., see the *Annuaires Statistiques* issued regularly by the Egyptian Statistical Authorities.

70. Lord Cromer relates in *Modern Egypt* (Vol. I, p. 38) that during the great financial crisis prevailing in Egypt at the time of the Berlin Congress two of the most iron-fisted pashas were sent to the provinces in order to collect the taxes. They were accompanied by a staff of money-lenders who were ready to purchase the harvests of the farmers in advance, i.e. in practice, naturally at ridiculous prices, particularly in view of the scarcity of the crops. In some cases the corn was sold to the merchants at 50 piastres per ardeb and delivered a month later when it had reached the value of 120 piastres.

71. For a detailed account of recent developments of *Waqf* property see Art. "Waqf" in *Encyclopaedia of Islam.*

72. A. N. Poliak, *Feudalism*, etc., London, 1939, p. 77.

73. Cf. *L'Informateur Financier et Commerciel* of 12th December, 1941. For broader arguments, both pro and contra, see for instance the controversy in *L'Égypte Contemporaine, Revue de la Société Royale d'Economie politique de Statistique et de Legislation*, Vol. 1927, between Mohamed Aly Pasha and Sheik Mohamed Békhit.

74. Comprehensive measures for the improvement of the individual water supply system were also introduced. Mohammed Ali claimed that he had increased the number of *sakiehs* in use by 38,000, or over 50 per cent. (Cf. Dodwell, *op. cit.*, p. 211.)

75. The main canals in question are the Ibrahimiye, Ismailia and Behera Canals. The number of dams which have been constructed in Egypt is six. Apart from the reconstructed Mohammed Ali Barrage, there are the Assuan, Esneh, Assiut, Nas Hamadih, and Ziffa dams.

76. Figures taken from Crouchley, *op. cit.*, p. 259. According to Crouchley the figures given for the cultivated area refer for the period 1813 to 1892 rather to the cultivable than the cultivated area. In the absence of agricultural primary statistics the tax figures showing the area subject to taxation are usually quoted as "cultivated" areas though they have been very probably below the actual area cultivated.

77. According to the *Iraq Times* of 22nd July, 1939.

78. *The Survey of Palestine*, 1946, Vol. I, p. 399, gives a total of 2,550 wells and boreholes for 1935; since then the number of modern wells has considerably risen.

79. A. Bonné, *The Economic Development of the Middle East*, London, 1945, p. 47.

80. E. Nassif, "L'Égypte, est-elle surpeuplée?" in *L'Égypte contemporaine*, Cairo, 1943, p. 765.

NOTES TO PART III

1. Karl Marx, *Das Kapital*, Vol. I, Stuttgart, 1919, p. 320.

2. E. Lipson, "The Invention of Machinery, its Economic and Social Results," in *Great Events in History*, London, 1934, p. 532.

3. The following are illustrative examples of industrial agglomeration during the past hundred years: (Number of inhabitants in thousands):

	1850	1900	1930
Nottingham	57	240	269
Birmingham	233	759	969
Sheffield	135	411	518
Lodz	34*	315	605
Essen	7·2**	119	649
Dortmund	7·6	143	535
Gelsenkirchen	14·6***	37	333
Lille	76	210	202
Lyon	177	459	580
Detroit	116	286	1,564
Pittsburg	156	452	670
Chicago	30	1,699	3,376

*—1870 **—1843 ***—1880

(Source of the figures: W. Sombart, *Das Wirtschaftsleben im Zeitalter des Hochkapitalismus*, München, 1928, pp. 405 ff. and *Statistisches Handbuch für das Deutsche Reich*).

4. E. Wagemann, *Struktur und Rythmus der Weltwirtschaft*, Ch. 3, Berlin, 1932.

5. In view of the great importance of State intervention, particularly within the most highly developed sectors of production, its presence and extent should be recorded in any such classification of economic systems. *Étatisme* or State control still being in a state of flux, there is the difficulty of reducing its varying forms and degrees to a concise formula.

6. A. E. Crouchley, *The Economic Development of Modern Egypt*, 1938, p. 256.

7. W. Sombart, *op. cit.*, p. 388. Part of the figures in the table are computations from data quoted by Sombart, part from *Stat. Handb. f.d. R.*

8. E. W. Lane, *The Manners and Customs of the Modern Egyptians*, London, 1936 (Everyman's Library), p. 581.

9. H. Guys, *Statistique du Pachalik d'Alep*, Marseille, 1853, pp. 58/59.

10. A. Ruppin, *Syrien als Wirtschaftsgebiet*, 2nd ed., 1920, p. 453.

11. Lane, *op. cit.*, p. 134.

12. The extent to which this state of affairs persisted almost up to our own day is illustrated by the following quotation from E. G. Mears, *Modern Turkey*, New York, 1924, p. 330: "The typical Anatolian peasant does not handle the equivalent of fifty dollars in cash during the whole year. The purchase of a foreign-made commodity is a great event in his life."

13. The most outspoken among these writers is Lane, who expresses himself as follows: "An essentially inartistic Semitic nation, they overran countries abounding in the remains of decaying styles, and used the craftsmen of those countries to build their mosques and palaces; at first adopting the old art, and afterwards engrafting many of its features into a new style of their own. The earliest Arab buildings were predominantly Byzantine, and that style always continued to exercise a strong influence; but soon one more markedly Oriental was added to it, and to the half-formed Arabian art then springing up . . . They have never excelled in handicrafts. Their workmen were commonly Copts, Greeks, and Persians; and though they must have learnt from these peoples, they appear never to have been able to dispense altogether with their services." (*op. cit.*, pp. 602/603.)

14. Ibn Khaldun, *Prolegomènes Historiques*, Vol. II (ed. par l'Institut Impérial de France, Tome XX), Paris, 1865, p. 365.

15. Lane, *op. cit.*, pp. 302/303.

15*a*. C. F. Volney, *Œuvres complètes*, Paris, 1868, p. 156.

15*b*. According to M. Clerget, *Le Caire, Étude de Géographie Urbaine et d'Histoire Économique*, Le Caire, 1934, p. 229.

16. Guys, *op. cit.*, p. 72: Other causes of the town's decline, according to Guys, are the disturbances which occurred there, earthquakes, and, finally, the new sea routes across the Black Sea as well as direct from the Persian Gulf to Italy and England.

17. *Ibid.*, p. 102.

18. Georges Douin, *La Mission du Baron de Boislecomte*, Le Caire, 1927, p. 268.

19. M. Sabry, *L'Empire Égyptien sous Mohamed Ali*, Paris, 1939, pp. 359/360.

20. Guys, *op. cit.*, p. 68.

21. A. v. Kremer, *Reise in Mittelsyrien und Damaskus*, Wien, 1853, p. 253.

22. D. Urquhart, *La Turquie*, Vol. II, 1876, p. 57.

23. C. Texier, *L'Asie Mineure*, Vol. II, Paris, 1908, p. 447.

24. H. Vambery, *Der Islam im XIX. Jahrhundert*, Leipzig, 1875, p. 209.

25. The case where consumer goods such as clothing and shoes, kitchen and domestic utensils are made at home by the consumer for his own use—even when paid labour is temporarily employed for this purpose—represents a category by itself. Home work, when of a permanent character and intended for sale, naturally comes under industrial production proper.

One of the principal requirements met by home labour is the construction of the dwelling house; the Oriental peasant is in the habit of building his house himself, for which he will use either clay reinforced with straw, fieldstones or roughly quarried stone or, as in southern Iraq, reeds also; for houses of a somewhat better class a village artisan will be engaged who has specialised in this work. The construction of the houses depends to a large extent on the nature of the raw materials locally available. Clay and stone are therefore the building materials almost exclusively used. Wood is employed only in villages where trees grow in the vicinity, pinewood in the Lebanon, palmwood in Egypt and in southern Iraq.

26. M. Clerget, *op. cit.*, Vol. II, p. 236; R. Junge, *Das Problem der Europäisierung orientalischer Wirtschaft*, Weimar, 1915, pp. 209, 211; H. Schurtz, "Das Basarwesen als Wirtschaftsform", *Zeitschrift für Sozialwirtschaft*, Vol. IV, Berlin, 1901, pp. 150 ff.

27. According to Guys, the following important industries were to be found in Aleppo in 1844:

Number of factories*	337
Trades (métiers)	1,691
Workers	4,481
	Frs.
Gross value of production	4,477,065
Value of raw materials	2,851,244
Manufacturing costs (wages)	1,165,341
Total costs of production	4,016,585
Balance	460,480
Value of production sold on the home market	1,119,257
Value of production exported abroad	3,367,808

* Including 186 silk weaving mills, 20 cotton mills, 12 soap factories, 66 tanneries.

28. ". . . . stalls (*hanuts*) and warehouses respectively constitute the bulk of the immovable *waqf* property . . .; retailing is invariably carried on in rented stalls. Their construction thus devolves on the rich, who invest their capital therein. Hence it is not the small shopkeeper who builds his own stall, but the large-scale entrepreneur, who erects these premises in large numbers. The manufacturing trades, too, usually work in rented premises or factories. (Cf. C. H. Becker, "Zur Kulturgeschichte Nordsyriens im Zeitalter der Mamelucken," in *Islamstudien*, Leipzig 1924, Vol. I, p. 270.)

29. Cf. Art. "Sinf" in *Encyclopaedia of Islam.*

30. This office was often exercised with particular cruelty. *Vide* Lane, *op. cit.*, p. 126.

31. C. Snouck Hurgronje, *Mekka*, Vol. II, Den Haag, 1889, pp. 35/36.

32. Lane, writing on conditions in the thirties of the nineteenth century, gives a detailed account of the initiation ceremony of the apprentices in certain guilds in Cairo (known also as *Shadd el Wallad*), and the religious rites in which it abounds.

33. H. Thorning, *Beiträge zur Kenntnis des islamischen Vereinswesen auf Grund von "Basṭ Madad et Taufiq"* (Türk. Bibliothek XVI, Berlin, 1913, pp. 123 ff.)

34. Cf. Art. "Futūwa", in *Encyclopaedia of Islam.*

35. Cf. Art. "Sinf", *ibid.*

36. A special feature indicating the weakness of the Oriental guild system was introduced into it by the admittance of soldiers. These elements came to lord it over the craftsmen, posing as their protectors but being more often than not their co-partners and extortioners. When in 1709 the magistrate summoned the leaders of the guilds in Cairo before him and pointed out that it was not permissible for them or their members to belong to a military organisation, they refused to obey, claiming that the guilds were composed of soldiers and soldiers' sons. The attitude of the guilds as then constituted was very antagonistic towards the European merchants. (Clerget, *op. cit.*, Vol. II, p. 136, according to Jabarti); their subservience to the Janissaries increased more and more until these were removed.

37. M. Sabry, *op. cit.*, p. 21.

38. In 1812, on the instigation of Mohammed Ali, 500 workers came from Constantinople to Cairo; in 1816 he had a further 200 Armenian skilled workers sent there.

39. Although the steam engine was represented in Egypt by some specimens, the machinery in most of the new factories was driven by animal power (buffalo, donkey or camel). In the textile industry oxen were the favourite form of

motive power. Despite certain advantages (mobility, ample supply) these animals entailed considerable disadvantages: they required proper feeding and attention; at times heavy losses were suffered owing to epidemics; in the running of the machinery itself the jerky pull of the animals led to frequent breakages of machine parts.

40. The plans for the foundry are ascribed to the chief engineer to the Pasha, a Mr. Galloway, who designed them on the lines of a large London foundry owned by his father. (Cf. Crouchley, *op. cit.*, p. 70.)

41. M. Sabry, *op. cit.*, p. 357.

42. H. Dodwell, *The Founder of Modern Egypt, A Study of Mohammed Ali*, Cambridge, 1931, p. 253.

43. Crouchley, *op. cit.*, pp. 73 and 88.

44. Bowring to Campbell, December 17, 1837; quoted by Dodwell, *op. cit.*, p. 219.

45. *Ibid.*, p. 220.

46. Crouchley, *op. cit.*, p. 73.

47. H. Temperley, *England and the Near East, The Crimea*, London, 1936, pp. 32/33.

48. Dodwell, *op. cit.*, p. 218.

49. The setback in industrial production and the abolition of the monopolies did not result in any immediate financial loss for the Pasha. The fellah, who was no longer obliged to sell to the agent of the government monopoly at the low government prices, received from the merchant the higher market price and proceeded to expand the cultivation of staple crops; his tax capacity was thus strengthened.

50. The slackening of England's interest in the Anatolian Railway plans is said to be accounted for by the prospect of tension in Russo-German relations, a development which for England would not have been unwelcome. This view is taken mainly by German authors.

51. Cf. also on this point Chapter 28: Changes in the System of Communications.

52. *Statistique des Sociétés Anonymes par Actions travaillant principalement en Egypte*, Département de la Statistique Générale, Le Caire, 1933, p. 293.

53. Cf. E. G. Mears, *Modern Turkey* (ed.) New York, 1924, p. 357.

54. The figures given in the table represent the total paid-up capital and debentures of companies in which some or all of the share or debenture capital (or both) was subscribed abroad. (Cf. A. E. Crouchley, *The Investment of Foreign Capital in Egyptian Companies and Public Debt*, Technical Paper No. 12 issued by the Ministry of Finance, Egypt, Cairo, 1936, footnote on page 106.)

55. The general political background of this epoch has been described at length in Part I of this book.

56. See also Chapter II above.

57. The scientific and political discussions on the Capitulations at that time turned chiefly on points of international law and were in the main devoted to questions of the sovereignty of jurisdiction.

58. Nevertheless it would be a mistake always to consider the economic advantages as being in the first instance the immediate motive of imperialist expansion. To prove such a nexus has become increasingly difficult since the general drive of the big Powers for colonies which started towards the end of the last century. Ever since the first discussions on imperialism, a

number of authors have indeed turned against this simplification of the issue. F. Schumpeter, in a noteworthy essay "Zur Soziologie der Imperialismen" (*Archiv für Sozialwissenschaft und Sozialpolitik*, 1919, Vol. 46, p. 296) writes *inter alia:*

"The concrete objects that happen to be in question are often of quite secondary importance. Owing to the competition—the kind of competition that has little in common with the normal—the profit to be anticipated therefrom is in most cases fairly low. The main point is, first, to grab something, no matter what it may be, and then to exploit this something as a base or bridgehead for the conquest of new markets and in the fight for their exclusive possession. This costs all concerned fairly dear—often more than it yields or can reasonably be expected to do in the future. All concerned become furious about it and take good care that their co-nationals share these feelings. All concerned are driven to employ means which each would regard in the other as proof of an almost unrelieved moral depravity . . ."

59. Seventy years ago, Karl Marx with his penetrating mind stressed the differences in the qualifications of the various nations for the modern economic system ("Some nations, like the Turks, have neither the temperament nor the disposition for capitalist production"), a fact from which he draws far-reaching conclusions as regards the development of primitive societies. The problem has already been treated here in Chapters XV and XX.

60. Pears, E. *Turkey and its People*, Methuen, London, 1912, p. 38.

61. P. Huvelin, *Que vaut la Syrie?* Paris-Marseille, 1919, p. 30.

62. The rigorousness of the Mohammedan ban on interest was such that any recognised form of borrowing through the banks was out of the question. At the inauguration of an Egyptian Post Office Savings Bank in 1901 it was necessary to obtain a declaration of tolerance by the religious authorities headed by the Sheikh Mohamed Abdu, confirming that deposits in this bank would not conflict with the Law. In view of the fact that participation in profits was recognised by the Koran in the case of changing trading profits, the purchase of shares in commercial undertakings was declared permissible as being a form of "participation". The application form issued by the Post Office Savings Bank contains a special clause for the Mohammedan depositor, the signing of which authorises the Postmaster General to use the money in a manner that will not clash with religious injunction. Part of the investments in the Post Office Savings Bank consist, therefore, of shares in companies operating in Egypt, i.e., stocks showing changing profits in contrast to debentures or loans at a fixed interest rate. Incidentally, there are at the Post Office Savings Bank as well as in other banks in Egypt even now no inconsiderable sums on which no interest is paid.

63. Cf. Rohan Conker and Emile Witmeur, *Redressement économique et Industrialisation de la Nouvelle Turquie*, Paris, 1937, pp. 56 ff. It appears that the list of industrial undertakings is not complete as far as the factories in Ottoman Syria are concerned.

64. P. Arminjon, *La Situation économique et financière de l'Égypte*, Paris, 1911 pp. 179 ff.

65. According to the Arab writer Ibn Dukmak, there existed, as far back as the time of the Mameluke Sultans, 58 private sugar-producing plants which, however, were not always kept running simultaneously. In addition to these, there were also other important factories belonging to the Sultans.

66. Some interesting data on the beginnings of trade union movements in Palestine are given in the Bulletins issued by the Department of Labour of the Palestine Government. The first strike in Palestine occurred in 1902.

67. In 1877 MacCoan listed more than 40 trades that were organised in guilds. In 32 trades the artisans were members of two guilds. Cf. F. C. MacCoan, *Egypt as it is*, London 1877, p. 298. But less than forty years previously Bowring in his *Report on Egypt and Candia to Lord Palmerston*, 1840, still counted 164 guilds in Cairo alone.

68. Cf. particulars given in Chapter 28 (below) on Communications.

69. E. G. Mears, *op. cit.*, p. 155.

70. Cf. A. Bonné, *The Economic Development of the Middle East*, London, 1945, pp. 9 ff.

71. *U.S.A. Yearbook of Agriculture*, Washington, 1932, p. 907.

72. R. Conker and E. Witmeur, *op. cit.*, p. 70.

73. Further special measures of assistance were granted during the following years for certain branches of industry. Thus the sugar industry in 1934 was encouraged by the special enactment of April 5th, according to which for a period of 8 years no consumption tax was imposed on the sugar produced, and similarly the cultivation of sugar beet was exempt from land tax for a period of ten years.

74. The bank in question was founded by order of Kemal Atatürk, the then President of the Republic.

75. Vide *Report on Economic and Commercial Conditions in Turkey*, No. 729, issued by the Department of Overseas Trade, April, 1939, pp. 17/18.

76. The first two sugar factories were founded in 1926. In the thirties a number of additional factories were opened in quick succession.

77. *Report on Immigration, Land Settlement and Development* by Sir John Hope Simpson, 1930, p. 116.

78. *Rapport à la Société des Nations sur la Situation de la Syrie et du Liban*, Paris, 1921.

79. In regard to the development during the first years of the inter-war period cf. A. Bonné, "The Concessions for the Mosul-Haifa Pipe Line," in *Annals of the American Academy of Political and Social Science*, Philadelphia, Pa., Nov., 1932.

80. M. I. Schatz, "Le Développement Industriel de l'Égypte, vu à travers les statistiques démographiques et douanières". Special Number of *Revue d'Égypte Économique et Financière*, April, 1940.

81. See "Conjuncture" (published by the Turkish Ministry of Commerce), and other official sources; figures for Heavy Industries from *Suemer Bank Report for* 1943. For a general account of Turkish economic problems see also B. Ward, *Turkey*, Oxford, 1942.

82. According to *Rapport à la Société des Nations sur la situation de la Syrie et du Liban pour l'année* 1937, p. 218. As official statistics were, to a large extent, collected jointly for Syria and the Lebanon, there are no separate figures available in respect of each country.

83. Cf. *Statistical Data on Palestine*, 1945, issued by the Department of Statistics of the Jewish Agency for Palestine, Jerusalem, 1945. A useful statistical reference-book is the *Statistical Handbook of Middle Eastern Countries*, Jerusalem, 1945, in respect of the whole Middle East; the problems of industrialisation have been treated in K. Grunwald, *The Industrialisation of the Near East*, Tel Aviv, 1934, and S. Abramovitz and J. Gelfat, *The Arab Economy in Palestine and the Middle East*, 1944 (Hebrew).

84. Cf. A. Bonné, *The Economic Development of the Middle East*, pp. 69 ff.

85. The figures in the tables are partly calculated, partly taken from the Monthly *Planning* (*PEP*), London, 1945, No. 223. For figures of national income cf. *The Economist*, No. 5331, of 27.10.1945.

86. Cf. the Chapter on "Industry" by George Hakim in *Economic Organisation of Syria*, ed. S. B. Himadeh, Beirut, 1936, p. 172.

87. Some idea of the extent of these camel transports is given by the fact that every year some 50,000 laden camels passed through the town of Erzurum. (Cf. E. G. Mears, *op. cit.*, p. 221.)

88. The declaration in question reads as follows: "The Governments of France and Great Britain, acting in the name of Syria, Palestine and Transjordan, in order to give effect to the desire to recognise the religious character of the Hejaz Railway, declare their willingness to agree to the formation of an Advisory Council, of which the function will be to communicate to the managements of the different sections of this Railway in Syria, Palestine and Transjordan, and the Kingdom of the Hejaz, any recommendation of which the object is to assure the maintenance of the line and the improvement of the conditions of transport of pilgrims."

ADDENDUM TO PART III

Household Expenditure in Cairo

(According to Lane, *op. cit.* p. 581).

	Piastres.
Wheat, eight ardebbs, about	400
Grinding do.	50
Baking	40
Meat, from one ratl and a half to two ratls (or one piastre and a half) per diem	550
Vegetables, about half a piastre per diem	185
Rice	100
Semn (or clarified butter), two kantars, about	325
Coffee	185
Tobacco (Gebelee)	200
Sugar, half a kantar, about	100
Water	100
Firewood, seven hamlehs (or donkey-loads)	75
Charcoal	100
Oil (for two or three lamps), a kantar, about	125
Candles (tallow)	100
Soap	90
	2,725

The above sum total is equivalent to £27. 5s. sterling; consequently, the weekly expenses are about 10s. 6d.; and the daily, 1s. 6d., or seven piastres and a half. The tobacco in this account is almost entirely for the use of the master of the family; the women in his house very seldom smoking.

NOTES TO PART IV

1. R. Wilhelm, *Chinesische Wirtschaftspsycholgie*, Leipzig, 1930, p. 34.

2. On this and related subjects cf. in particular R. Levy, *An Introduction to the Sociology of Islam*, 2 vols., London 1931/32. Levy's contribution to the sociological exploration of the early stages of Islamic development is most valuable and has repeatedly been referred to in this Part. Compare, further, the article on "Djahiliya" in *Encyclopaedia of Islam* and the literature mentioned therein. As to the new idea of equality, Levy quotes a story from the *Kitab al Aghani* to illustrate this mental transformation: "The prince Jabala ibn al Azham of Gassan, on the occasion of a pilgrimage to Mecca, had his cloak trodden upon by a common Arab tribesman in the crowd that was thronging to carry out the ceremonies of the hajj. The Prince struck the Beduin a blow in the face and the latter complained to the Caliph Omar. The Caliph after summoning the offender told him he would give his victim leave to retaliate in kind for the blow. 'How can that be possible', asked the astonished prince, 'he being a man of the people and I a prince?' Omar replied: 'Islam made you one with him and you can hold no superiority over him except in piety and good works'. 'I thought that in Islam my status would be even higher than in the days of Barbarism', remarked the prince. 'Rid yourself of that idea . . .', was Omar's reply." (Cf. Levy, *op. cit.*, Vol. I, p. 79.)

3. R. Levy, *op. cit.*, Vol. I, p. 88.

4. *Report on the Administration of Palestine and Transjordan for the Year* 1934, Appendix VII, p. 28 (Colonial No. 17).

5. Oriental travellers of the nineteenth century frequently comment on the relatively tolerable condition of slaves in Arab countries. Doughty, a renowned explorer of Arab lands, depicted their position as follows: "Bred up as poor brothers and sons of the household they are a manner of God's wards of the pious Mohammedan householder. If their lords fear Allah, they send them away with presents after a certain time." (Cf. *Arabia Deserta*, Vol. I, p. 554, Cambridge, 1888). But there are also other, rather caustic voices. A century ago, the growing pressure of public opinion had already led to attempts at the abolition of slavery in India. "Slavery, as far as established by law, was abolished in India by Act V, 1843, but the final blow was dealt on January 1, 1862, when the sections of the Indian Penal Code dealing with the question came into operation." (W. Crooke, *Islam in India*, 1921, p. 112. A remarkable attempt of recent date was Art. 7 of the Treaty of Jedda, signed in May, 1927 between the British Government and Ibn Saud, the ruler of Saudi Arabia, with a view to suppressing the slave trade in Arabia. The actual measure of success attending this Treaty can be gauged from the numerous reports on the continuation of the slave traffic in subsequent years. (See also text.)

6. E. Rutter, "Slavery in Arabia," *Journal of the Royal Central Asian Society*, Vol. XX, July, 1933, p. 321; cf. also *The Times* of March 8, 1929.

7. E. Bräunlich, "Beiträge zur Gesellschaftsordnung der arabischen Beduinenstämme" in *Islamica*, Vol. VI/I, 1933, pp. 82 ff.; cf. also Part I, Chapter V, pp. 46 ff. above.

8. R. Levy, *op. cit.*, Vol. I, p. 92.

9. The tribal structure of the older Arab towns has been pertinently described in Snouck Hurgronje's work on Mecca, Vol. II, Den Haag, 1889. But

even towns outside the orbit of tribal influence are presenting, or did at least until quite recently, very similar features. J. Weulersee, in the *Bulletin d'Études Orientales*, Vol. IV, Cairo, 1935, has given an interesting analysis of Antioch, entitled "Antioche, Essai de Géographie Urbaine". Although the author mentions the gradual disappearance in our own days of certain of the traits peculiar to the Oriental towns of yore (e.g. the watchman appointed for each quarter separately was abolished as late as 1930), he stresses the difficulties experienced in the introduction of reforms, as follows: "Cependant, malgré son affaiblissement, l'ancienne organisation montre encore sa puissance par la difficulté que l'on éprouve à pouvoir le remplacer: le projet de regroupement de la ville en huit grands quartiers plus ou moins conformes aux modèles d'Occident n'a pu encore être appliqué devant les plaintes et l'opposition des habitants. C'est que ces vieilles institutions ont des racines profondes en Orient. Il faut d'abord faire une grande part aux traditions d'autonomie locale que les États musulmans en général et L'Empire Ottoman en particulier ont toujours respectées. Despotiques par à-coup, ils laissaient aux sujets dans le cours normal de la vie une liberté qui confinait à l'indifference." (p. 40).

10. As to the Western town, cf. Max Weber, *Wirtschaft und Gesellschaft*, p. 528.

11. Kerbela, the large burial town of the Shiites in Iraq, is visited by 200,000 pilgrims annually (*Encyclopaedia Britannica*, 11th ed., p. 753). Even supposing that this figure is somewhat exaggerated, yet a traffic of tens of thousands of pilgrims cannot but exercise an enormous influence on the economic life of these fairly small towns.

12. The main contribution is included in H. A. R. Gibb, *Whither Islam?—A Survey of Modern Moslem Movements in the Moslem World*, London, 1932.

13. R. H. Tawney, *Religion and the Rise of Capitalism*, London, 1937 (Pelican Books), p. 28.

14. Baxter's *Christian Directory*, Vol. I, pp. 375/6: "It is for action that God maintaineth us and our activities: work is the moral as well as the natural end of power . . . It is action that God is most served and honoured by . . ." (Quoted, according to Max Weber, "Die protestantische Ethik und der Geist des Kapitalismus", in *Gesammelte Aufsätze zur Religionssoziologie*, Tübingen, 1920, Vol. I, pp. 165 ff.)

15. Baxter, *op. cit.*, p. 79: "Keep up a high esteem of time and be every day more careful that you lose none of your time, than you are that you lose none of your gold and silver. And if vain recreation, dressings, feastings, idle talk, unprofitable company, or sleep, be any of them temptations to rob you of any of your time, accordingly heighten your watchfulness." (Quoted *ibid.*, *op. cit.*, p. 168.)

16. Richard Steele, *The Tradesman's Calling, being a Discourse concerning the Nature, Necessity, Choice, etc., of a Calling in General*, 1684, pp. 1, 4, and Bunyan, *The Pilgrim's Progress*, quoted by R. H. Tawney, *op. cit.*, p. 216.

17. R. Levy, *op. cit.*, Vol. I, p. 68.

18. E. Pears, *Turkey and its People*, London, 1912, p. 37.

19. R. Levy, *op. cit.*, Vol. II, pp. 70/71.

20. Cf. article on "Tidjāra" in *Encyclopaedia of Islam* (according to Ibn Maja).

21. *Ibid.*

22. Qashayri: *Risala*, pp. 89, 1.7 ff.; according to R. Levy, *op. cit.*, Vol. II, p. 97.

23. Alfred Rühl, *Vom Wirtschaftsgeist im Orient*, Leipzig, 1925; C. H. Becker, "Islam und Wirtschaft" in *Islamstudien*, Vol. I; W. Barthold, *Mir Islama* I.W.D.I.I. (1913).

The chapters in this book dealing with the qualifications or aptitude of the Oriental worker and producer dwell at some length on his deficiency in this respect and its consequences.

24. The article was reprinted in the *Journal du Commerce et de la Marine* (Alexandria) of October 4, 1940.

25. A. H. Layard, *Discoveries in the Ruins of Nineveh and Babylon*, New York, 1853, p. 663.

26. H. A. R. Gibb, *Whither Islam?* . . ., London, 1932, pp. 335/36.

27. In Palestine this development has been enhanced by the Jewish immigration from Europe. Capital import and the "mass demonstration" of European habits of life, called out by these large immigration waves, have resulted in a more rapid Europeanisation of the urban scene and of the housing habits of the towns that absorbed the Jewish newcomers. The *Report of the Health Department of the Palestine Government for the year* 1933 contains the following description:

"House construction advanced rapidly and the type of house was of a high standard, well planned and built, adequately ventilated and provided with first-class baths and sanitary installations.

28. Cf. in particular the following works:

A. Jaussen, *Coutumes des Arabes au pays de Moab*, Paris, 1908;

H. St. J. Philby, *Arabia of the Wahabis*, London, 1928;

S. Austin Kermett, *Bedouin Justice, Laws and Customs among the Egyptian Bedouins*, Cambridge, 1925.

29. A. J. Toynbee, *A Study of History*, Oxford-London, 1935, Vol. III, pp. 16/17.

30. A. von Kremer, *Mittelsyrien und Damaskus*, Vienna, 1853, p. 169.

31. *Special Report . . . on the Progress of Iraq during the Period* 1920–31, London, 1931, p. 236 (Col. No. 58).

32. Somerset de Chair, *The Golden Carpet*, London, 1944, p. 106.

INDEX

For Product Safety Concerns and Information please contact our EU representative GPSR@taylorandfrancis.com
Taylor & Francis Verlag GmbH, Kaufingerstraße 24, 80331 München, Germany

www.ingramcontent.com/pod-product-compliance
Lightning Source LLC
LaVergne TN
LVHW020519100826
845148LV00010B/1281

* 9 7 8 0 4 1 5 8 6 3 3 4 6 *